November, 1992

To Alan,
   fellow intellectual and friend,
in solidarity & with warmest
regards.

       Harvey

Politics, Death, and the Devil

Politics, Death, and the Devil

Self and Power in
Max Weber and Thomas Mann

HARVEY GOLDMAN

University of California Press

BERKELEY   LOS ANGELES   OXFORD

University of California Press
Berkeley and Los Angeles, California

University of California Press, Ltd.
Oxford, England

© 1992 by
The Regents of the University of California

Goldman, Harvey, 1946–
    Politics, death, and the devil : self and power in Max Weber
and Thomas Mann / Harvey Goldman.
      p.   cm.
    Includes bibliographical references and index.
    ISBN 0-520-07750-4 (alk. paper)
    1. Weber, Max, 1864–1920—Contributions in political science.
2. Mann, Thomas, 1875–1955—Political and social views. I. Title.
JC263.W42G65   1992
306.2—dc20   91-36815
                                                CIP

Printed in the United States of America
9 8 7 6 5 4 3 2 1

Contents

To Gloria, Ilene, and Paula

Preface and Acknowledgments

In *Max Weber and Thomas Mann: Calling and the Shaping of the Self*,[1] I argued that both personal crisis and the culture of their class led Max Weber and Thomas Mann to focus on the issues of "calling" and "personality" for purposes of self-understanding and the understanding of culture. Weber, believing he had identified the Puritan calling as an essential element of the spirit of capitalism and the origin of Western development, thus analyzed a conception of personality he thought distinctive for the West and showed its dynamism in comparison with ideals of the person in other cultures. And Mann, having dramatized the decline of the calling in a segment of the bourgeois class, revitalized the calling for the bourgeois artist, at the same time showing that the calling could isolate its adherent and make the self a prison. In that book, however, these issues were considered primarily in terms of the problem of finding *personal* meaning through work. I had not yet fully understood the active and worldly dimension of these concepts, particularly the way in which Weber and Mann sought an antidote to personal and cultural weakness through practices for generating strength, mastery, and power. Nor was I able to consider there their social and political thought, properly so called. This book is therefore a sequel to that work, though it concludes with an analysis of Mann's *Doctor Faustus*, the book that started me on this project long ago. Its purpose is to explore the concern with power and mastery that lies behind Weber's and Mann's conceptions of calling and personality, to understand how these issues became a problem for them, and to analyze this discourse in their social and political thought, particularly in their attempts to resolve problems of politics and culture in Germany.

This analysis of Weber's and Mann's concern with the self belongs to the growing body of work—in social and political theory, philosophy, anthropology, and literary theory—concerned with concepts of the person and the problem of what is often called the "constitution of the subject."[2] The problem of the self and subject is now best known through the later works of Foucault.[3] Of course, traditions of shaping the self have a long history, particularly in religion. The idea of self or soul and its relation to society, power, and politics have been concerns of Western culture at least since Plato, and the self as an object of reflection has been worked on to achieve many different purposes: justice, knowledge, and the good (Plato); harmony and self-control (Stoicism); salvation (Augustine); political power (Machiavelli); scientific knowledge (Descartes); authenticity (Rousseau); autonomy (Kant); nobility (Nietzsche); health (Freud). In the Christian tradition, especially during the Reformation, work became a central part of reflections on the self. Before that, it was precisely when one did not work, or among those who were not obliged to work, that the search for meaning, knowledge, power, or self could be pursued.

Weber and Mann seek both meaning and power for the self by drawing on a variety of traditions, especially ascetic ones, as an antidote to the exhaustion of other cultural traditions in Germany whose vitality was fast disappearing. In so doing, they show the significance of linking social and political thought to conceptions of self and active worldly practices, even if their resolutions of the problems they confronted seem inadequate to us. Indeed, even in failure, they point to issues that the contemporary world must confront after Nietzsche's analysis of self and power and his critique of ascetic ideals.

For all of their help, advice, and encouragement, I would like to thank Peter Breiner, Christine von Bülow, Anna DiLellio, Ester Fuchs, Daniella Gobetti, Alan Houston, Norman Jacobson, Gail Kligman, Friedrich Kratochwil, Sabine Kudera, Hartmut Lehmann, Doug McAdam, Gianfranco Poggi, Martin and Brigitte Riesebrodt, Michael Rogin, John Ruggie, Mary Ruggie, Judith Russell, Naomi Schneider, Gershon Shafir, Renate Voris, and Alan Wolfe. My very special thanks go to Tim McDaniel, Alan Milchman, James Miller, Guenther Roth, George Shulman, and Alan Silver.

For their support, I would like to thank the Spencer Foundation, Dean Ward Dennis of Columbia University's School of General Studies, and the Ruth Hettleman Award. For their hospitality, I am grateful to the Thomas Mann Archive, Zurich; and the Institute for Sociology, University of Munich.

Some parts of this book were delivered as talks at Wellesley College; the Center for European Studies at Harvard University; Yale University; the Deutsches Haus, Theory of Literature Seminar, and Society of Fellows in the Humanities, all at Columbia University; CUNY Graduate Center;

the University of Texas at Austin; the University of California at San Diego; the University of Arizona; and the German Historical Institute, Washington, D.C.

One who is disconsolate and lonely could not choose a
better symbol than the knight with death and devil, as Dürer
has drawn him for us, the armored knight with the iron,
hard look, who knows how to pursue his terrible path,
undeterred by his gruesome companions, and yet without
hope, alone with his horse and dog.

Nietzsche, *The Birth of Tragedy*

The Nietzsche who really mattered to me . . . [was] the
one who marked out *one* picture with lasting love among
all plastic art—Dürer's "Knight, Death, and Devil". . . a
symbol for a whole world, *my* world, a Nordic-moralistic-
Protestant, i.e., *German* one.

Mann, *Reflections of an Unpolitical Man*

Everyone who was close to you saw your chivalry and
upright manliness and regarded your incorruptible loyalty to
your convictions as a modern incarnation of Dürer's knight
between death and devil.

Tribute to Max Weber by his friend Hermann Braus,
in Marianne Weber, *Max Weber: A Biography*

1   Self and Power, Self and Nation

What is good?—Everything that heightens the feeling of
power, the will to power, power itself in man.
What is bad?—Everything that stems from weakness.
What is happiness?—The feeling that power *increases*, that a
resistance is overcome.
Not contentment, but more power; *not* peace at all, but war;
not virtue, but proficiency.

Nietzsche, The Antichrist

The discourse of European writers and thinkers in the late nineteenth
and early twentieth centuries—and also of the popular imagination—is
riddled with professed fears of weakness and impotence, of loss of power
as a product of biological decline, decadence, social decay, and disillusion.
Ironically, however, that discourse views loss of power and proficiency
not only as a consequence of decadence, but also as a product of the
great achievements of civilization and rationalization.[1] The symptoms of
weakness seem to appear in deformed social relations and social roles,
in overheated and morbid culture and individual creative life, and in the
apparent helplessness and drift of politics. Indeed, "acquired" social
weakness now seems to push the "inherited" natural weakness of certain
classes and of the self to new extremes.

The onset of this obsession with weakness and powerlessness has many
causes, among them the shaking of stable patterns of values and purposes
through rapid and unwelcome social change; but once the fear takes
hold, it works to prevent the emergence of renewed meaning and purpose, of a renewed significance for work within society as it presently
exists. With Schopenhauer and Nietzsche as its philosophical chroniclers,
one of its symptoms is even an "attack" on life itself and on all remaining
forms of strength and power: a fetish is made of death in response to
death's apparent meaninglessness and insignificance in modern civilization. In Germany, this is not only a turn-of-the-century phenomenon; it
reappears in the longing for escape at the end of World War I and in

the culture of the 1920s. From the lack of strength described in Thomas Mann's *Buddenbrooks* to the willful embrace of illness in *The Magic Mountain*, from the political decadence diagnosed in Max Weber's "National State and Economic Policy" to the chastisements of escapism in "Science as a Vocation," Mann and Weber confront this decadence with calls for regeneration and renewal in an attempt to rescue the nation and the meaning of death and work from increasing powerlessness.

Weber's and Mann's discourse of strength and power is principally concerned with identity and mastery and their basis in ascetic service, but this discourse, as we will see, is also intimately bound up with what seems at first an altogether different problem—their obsession with death and devils. Death is central to Weber as the limiting experience that reveals the genuine helplessness of modern life, but it is also the field on which meaning and power must be conquered. Within Weber's program of recovery, the opposition of God and devil then becomes central, largely from Weber's belief in the enduring need to posit enemy, devilish values as an intimate part of positing one's own godly values, an act that, for him, is the foundation for positing one's self. But Weber also draws on the language of devils from his need to conceptualize the temptation and the danger latent in human ventures that he insists must be conceived in terms of serving "gods." This concern with death and devils is equally strong in Mann, though for him the situation is somewhat different because, as a protodecadent, he deals with death as a self-conscious toying with the negation of bourgeois life, which, ironically, may ultimately allow an opposite affirmation of life to appear. Further, Mann's preoccupation with devils seems more personal than Weber's, for the devil first materializes in Mann as a dark side of the self that must be "sublimated" into art, but it is later "split off," becoming the guiding value, though inverted, for a lost artist.

Concerned with the weakness of the times, Weber's theorizing reveals an implicit concern with what we can call the strengthening and "empowerment" of the self, which informs his interpretations of and programs for the crisis of modern society and politics in Germany. Mann's fictionalizing and political essays after World War I also show a form of empowerment, though of a rather different kind: in his case, aggrandizement and expansion of the self derive from identification with Germany, a view that underlies his interpretations of German culture and society and the new possibilities of art. Despite Weber's and Mann's concern with the self and its power, however, the self is rarely mentioned directly in their work. Instead they deal with "disciplines" of the self like the "calling" and charismatic education, with conceptions of the transformed self like the "personality," and with the different "roles" that empowered selves occupy, whether they are shaped for these roles or by them. In Mann these roles include the artist (as opposed to the decadent), in Weber the entrepreneur, the scientist and politician with a calling, and the charismatic leader. "Practices of the self," to use Foucault's language, play a crucial role in the central metanarratives of their work.

In their concern with the self and the practices that fashion it, Weber and Mann carry forward a century of German cultural traditions. Beginning in the late eighteenth century, formal religious practice and Christian belief lost much of their appeal among the intellectual classes in Germany as sources of ideals and models for the shaping of identity and the guidance of action. This weakening, accentuated by a shifting balance of power between the aristocracy and the bourgeoisic, led to the generation of nonreligious "techniques" and codes for the shaping and legitimating of the self: Kantian conceptions of moral law and personality, the ethos of *Bildung*, or self-cultivation through scholarship, and the ideal of *Kultur*. In Norbert Elias's words, the German middle-class intelligentsia began to legitimize itself to itself through its possession of "*das rein Geistige* (the purely spiritual) . . . the inner enrichment [and] the intellectual formation (*Bildung*) of the individual, primarily through the medium of books, in the personality."[2]

By the late nineteenth century, however, the new techniques and practices that had aided in shaping and equipping bourgeois individuals for lives and roles in nation, culture, and class were seriously weakened and persistently challenged by the pressures of a rapidly developing capitalist society. Complicating matters further, the model of the bourgeois family, the discipline of the traditional bourgeois calling, and the power of bourgeois class loyalty and identification were severely strained as vehicles of support for identity and as sources of practices for shaping the self.[3] Although class practices and cultural ideals had helped hold the increasingly bourgeois social order together and guide individual life choices, these were now threatened by social and cultural changes: rising social mobility and the sharpening of class conflict, the intensification of capitalist competition, the pace of developments in science and technology, the advances of technique and rationalization into every sector of life, the imperatives of specialization in a period of mass education, and the pressures of the market in every form.[4] Nietzsche, who criticized the overuse of history as a model and basis for life; Georg Simmel, who warned about the overwhelming of "subjective spirit" by "objective spirit"; Ernst Troeltsch, who feared society was turning away from impersonal ideals toward personal masters; Mann, who fought to preserve *Kultur* against civilization; and Weber, who strove to master rationalization, all testify to concern with the pressures of rational capitalism and the undermining of these practices and ideals within bourgeois circles.

Weber's and Mann's concern about the advance of rationalization and civilization is sharpened by what they see as the inadequacy of traditional German practices of the self—in particular, the defects and decline of the tradition of *Bildung*. The crisis of *Bildung*, as it developed in the nineteenth century, reflected the inability of German bourgeois culture to sustain a commonly shared, legitimated, or groundable model of self-development and self-shaping. The ideal of *Bildung* upheld a notion of personal value and meaning creation that was rooted simultaneously in the values and products of ancient culture and in the self's development and unfolding through its encounter with them. But *Bildung* had come under attack both from the needs of an advancing rationalistic and specialized culture and from philosophical opponents, including Nietzsche. Further, it had been reduced to little more than another decorative possession of the bourgeoisie, whose motto came to be *Bildung und Besitz*: *Bildung* and property.

Weber became a critic of *Bildung* on behalf of a specialized world whose tasks, he argued, could not be accomplished by *Bildung*, a world that must recognize the unavoidable failure of the effort to grasp culture as a whole. More important, from the point of view of the ascetic, restless ideal that he defended, the ethos of *Bildung* was a practice more suitable for a self-absorbed cultivated class or a passive bureaucratic elite; as a practice, it was unable in the modern situation to strengthen the self sufficiently to resist autocratic patterns, innovate, and lead. *Bildung* helped render the bourgeoisie submissive to the social order, fortifying the passive self-development that Weber thought already typical of the ideals of Pietism so deeply rooted in German culture. He opposed the ideal of an inner pattern that took the person's being and nature as given and positive, full of potential and richness, defending instead a discipline to subject and shape the self for action.

Mann, more attached culturally to the bourgeois class, first defended *Bildung*, though in a subverted way, only to overcome it eventually through his identification with the nation. To Mann, *Bildung* reflected the self-absorption of the bourgeoisie in a time when its ideal was no better than flight from reality. If anything resembling that ideal were to survive, self and nation would have to recognize that self-development must involve confrontation with the political, social, and cultural differences that divide the nation, acknowledging them rather than driving them out. The greatest priority, he argued, was to rescue the ideal of "Humanity"—central to the original ideals of *Bildung* but long submerged by the negative forces at work in German culture—as the new ultimate ideal that everyone, Germans and others, must serve.

Responding to the crisis of bourgeois life in Germany, Weber and Mann began in individual and personal crises of work and identity, which they first experienced in their notions of "calling" but resolved by refounding the calling in their own lives. Each then generalized his personal resolution and practice, prescribing it as the only valid response to the intensified need of the time for direction, strength, and ideals. Weber, having studied a wide range of practices of the self, opted for a revival of older disciplines from the Western religious tradition. Mann, having rescued the artist from the decay of the bourgeois family, opted for a continuation of the practices he himself inherited, but augmented by the shoring up of identity through identification with the nation. For both Weber and Mann, the task of any new practice for empowering the self was to strengthen the self against both inner desires and outer pressures, empowering it to conquer the resistant and discordant materials of life and world.

Weber, viewing the modern crisis more in terms of society and politics than culture, did more than Mann to link forms of self-empowerment to active, practical forms of world mastery. He examined more thoroughly the problem of power and the social roles that sustain or inhibit the capacities to rule, innovate, and master, while Mann focused more narrowly on the "artistic" self, though arguing that it was related to the bourgeois self and his model of the "German self." Thus Weber concentrated more on power to command the world and conquer it for higher purposes, while Mann searched for the strength to carry out the tasks imposed in the calling. Still, self-mastery as a means to world mastery—however metaphorically "world mastery" is understood—was the goal for both.

The conception of self with which Weber and Mann begin derives from Protestantism, as mediated by the history and experience of the German bourgeoisie, and they ground their own practices of the self in a variety of ways. First, they develop interpretations of history: the shaping of self for strength and the submission to a calling for power are based on analyses of sources of strength and power that the West exhibited historically. For Weber, the role of Puritanism in empowering the first entrepreneurs revealed a source of inner strength and power that helped make the Occident uniquely what it was and became the model for his own prescriptions. For Mann, the bourgeoisie, as the class "home" of the impulses of work, calling, and innovation, was the most important historical actor in the drama of the West's development of power and of the justification and legitimation of the modern self. The bourgeoisie's reliance on calling was the model for Mann's establishment of the identity of the artist. Thus Weber's and Mann's practices are based on a renewal of, rather than substantial breaks with, previous practices of the self. As the Puritans and the bourgeoisie had been able to extend world mastery on the basis of practices of self-mastery, so too the newly mastered and strengthened selves of the calling, shorn of their former objects and ideals in religion and economic pursuit, would, they believed, be able to undertake the tasks of value positing, world mastery, and guidance of the nation.

Second, Weber and Mann both cast the modern crisis in a form that calls for their new solutions. Rationalization and the advance of technique as tools of world mastery led to the elimination from the world of traditional sources of meaning, initiative, and self-fulfillment. At the same time, the bourgeoisie, as the "bearer" of society's values, was unable to justify itself in its leading position and remain a source of strength and self-fortification for its sons. Since the forces that warded off weakness have disappeared from society, they argue, new forms of self-mastery and mobilization are required to rescue Germany and the self from disaster.

Third, Weber's and Mann's practices are built on diagnoses of the natural self's weakness, worthlessness, and impotence, deriving from the conviction that the natural self is valueless or unacceptable as given and that the person must therefore be "redeemed" from it: the weak parts of the self must be excluded or dominated, curbed and subjected to the stronger, better self, strengthened by service to an ultimate ideal. Indeed, the self has to prove itself before this ultimate ideal, value, or Other that becomes an internalized "witness" to the self's undertakings.

Interestingly, Weber's and Mann's works drew on textual strategies borrowed from what would normally be considered the domain of the other. Weber constructed a "fictional" or mythic subject of history and social theory, the Occidental personality, rooted in the methodological fictionalism of ideal types. He ascribed to this mythic subject a world-historical role and built on it a philosophy of historical innovation and a theory of character formation that he later deployed to rescue and redeem both a self and a social world in crisis. Mann, in contrast, turned to a "social theory" and a model of Germany to build political allegories of self and nation. He did this to rescue a solipsistic artistic self that he had originally constructed in response to the failure of a weakened class's model of individual life. In the process, though, this theory also fueled the purposes and themes of a fiction on the verge of exhaustion, making possible a new type of novelistic work.

In fact, Weber and Mann find both personal redemption and re-demption of the nation through the use of social theory combined with fictions or models of the subject. The need to identify a renewed means for the constitution and justification of themselves as subjects led them to push their discoveries toward social theories with which they hoped to build bridges between themselves and the world and to rescue both the world and the self from the self-destruction of European culture. Ironically, they both suggest that the self became fragile and the social world rigidified precisely through the worldly influence of older fictions of "self-fashioning."[5] Yet, motivated by World War I, and despite their historical understanding, both Weber and Mann believed that self and world could be put on track again only through the redeployment of these same fictions, revitalized for a secular and postbourgeois world.

THE PROBLEM OF THE SELF

To Foucault, a "subject" is constituted or created out of the "self" through "an ascetical practice . . . not in the sense of abnegation but . . . of an exercise of self upon self by which one tries to work out, to transform one's self and to attain a certain mode of being. I am taking the word 'asceticism' in a wider sense than Max Weber, but it is much along the same line."[6] Shaping the self into a subject is then the outcome of "historically analysable practices," consciously imposed or pursued.[7] It is a relation of the self to itself that makes a subject and by which one constitutes oneself as a subject. Yet, as Foucault notes, "these prac-tices are . . . not something that the individual invents by himself. They are patterns that he finds in his culture and which are proposed, suggested and imposed on him by his culture, his society and his social group."[8] For Weber and Mann—but also for Durkheim, Simmel, and Troeltsch—the key category of self-transformation is not the "subject" but the "personality," a concept with roots in Goethe, Humboldt, Kant, and the neo-Kantians of Weber's and Mann's time, all of whom contributed to the tradition that made the creation of personality the goal of disciplines of the self.[9] In this language, personalities are the true subjects or agents.

As Foucault remarks, "the subject is constituted through practices of subjection."[10] Yet to Weber and Mann, the need for practices of sub-jection or self-fashioning is predicated primarily on the inability of the modern self to constitute or "save" itself by itself. That is, the modern self must be saved from its condition: it requires something outside itself—yet not part of culture or society—to rescue it from meaninglessness. It is unable by itself or in conjunction with secular culture alone to acquire a sense of identity and self-worth, find strength and a meaningful direction for life, and win approval, love, or position. Because the "natural" self appears as a hateful object in the work of Weber and Mann, self-transformation aims, first, to overcome the guilt created by its natural condition; second, to identify a "higher" self; and finally, to defend this "higher" self against the threat of external blame and internal self-hate by curbing or renouncing what are taken to be the self's illicit desires and qualities. The self then derives meaning and purpose through disciplined submission to a goal or object and finds justification through success in a calling. Weber's and Mann's practices, then, aim to produce a self acceptable to an internalized Other that is imagined or created as a witness to the self's action, and whose mode of self-shaping will also be acceptable to external Others, whether the family, bourgeois society, or the nation.

But to Weber and Mann, providing meaning to the newly fashioned self cannot be separated from the generation of strength and power—the power of world control through the power of self-control. The creation of meaning is the basis for empowering the self for mastery and innovation or for achieving liberation from and the overcoming of restraint, inhibition, self-consciousness, and decadence. While Foucault argued that the self is unquestionably shaped *by* relations of power in institutions and social practices, the issue for Weber and Mann is a countervailing one, the generation of selves *with* power, and for Weber in particular, the shaping of selves *for* power.

Power has, of course, been a much-desired object throughout human history and thought. Weber's and Mann's search for a generalized form of power in and for the self is mediated by Nietzsche. Although he criticized the use of knowledge to acquire power over life in *The Birth of Tragedy*, Nietzsche came to believe that "the fundamental instinct of life ... aims at *the expansion of power*."[11] Life is grounded on a will to power, on "a will to overcome, a will to throw down, a will to become master, a thirst for enemies and resistances and triumphs." Indeed, the " 'development' of a thing ... [is] the succession of more or less profound, more or less mutually independent processes of subduing." Thus, "every animal ... instinctively strives for an optimum of favorable conditions under which it can expend all its strength and achieve its maximal feeling of power."[12] It is necessary, says Nietzsche, to recognize the will to power behind even the strivings of the weak and to create a caste of healthy, "sovereign" individuals with power over themselves, their fate, and their world. "Above all something living wants to *discharge* its strength—life itself is *will to power*."[13] In Nietzsche's discourse, strength is stored up in the self as potential, while will to power is a longing and capacity to realize this strength, become master, and subdue. For Nietzsche, this will is natural, innate, and instinctive, especially in the noble type of human beings, as long as convictions that teach weakness do not prevail. For Mann too, initially, such a will was natural, and decline in will reflected declining biological processes. But for Weber the will to power is, in general, not natural; instead it is rooted in specific social and cultural, usually religious, practices. Western culture generally and Calvinism specifically, in his view, generated a will to power among certain groups, while other cultures did not.

Finally, Weber's and Mann's conception of self is not of a self shaped by interaction or socialization; it is, rather, a *counter*socialized self, shaped to resist the effects of relationships and social norms. Weber and Mann defend a conception of the self that one can call "closed," with a single "face," deliberately resistant to the influences of others and to the appearance of other "selves" from "within." They oppose any "open" conception that would see the self's boundaries as fluid and changeable, rather than fixed, or might see the self as something to be discovered, unfolded, and accepted, rather than deciphered and renounced for a higher mode of being. Yet the self is always both open *and* closed, for, though Nietzsche says "our body is but a social structure of many souls," it remains ours and no one else's.[14]

WEBER, SELF, AND POWER

Weber's belief in the need for a contemporary discipline of the self as a source of power derives from his analysis of modern history. Numerous arguments have been made that Weber's fundamental problematic and governing theme is the nature and advance of rationalization and its contribution to the uniqueness of the West.[15] While it is certainly true that Weber analyzes rationality and the West's uniqueness, such a claim is only part of the story; that is, Weber believes not only that the West's uniqueness rests on rationalization, but also that it was shaped historically by its capacity to create what I am calling "empowered" selves—selves with a unique power to master conditions and overcome resistance, permitting fundamental innovation in society and politics.[16] Thus, despite its arguments for the importance of rationalization and the tools created to measure it, Weber's "metanarrative" cannot be construed simply in terms of the progress and difficulties of rationalization, inevitable or otherwise. In fact, his work reveals a dialectic between "practices of the self" and the imperatives of institutions and social order, a conflict of innovation and creation, on the one hand, versus conformity and compliance, on the other, set in objective conditions the self has both created and inherited. His work also contains the story of a search for forms of strength and sources of motivation that would give modern Western selves the power to overcome social and institutional resistance, the resistance of others, and inner obstacles, permitting them to innovate.

Thus Weber has a significant historically grounded microsociological dimension, not just a macrosociological one. The institutionalization of rationalization is for him the newest objective condition, the most contemporary form of social power in the context of which to pose the problem of the person and the situation of actors, the problem of character and social structure. This is not meant to imply that Weber's work is not centrally concerned with structures and institutions as objects of analysis, but in his work the question of institutions often leads to the question of the type of person they make possible as well as to the question of what created them or might have held them back, then sometimes to the question of *who* created them and what inner and outer obstacles they had to overcome, and invariably back to the question of what *enabled* such creators to overcome obstacles and innovate. The ultimate question—posed for the present and the future—is about what it would take to control and master existing institutions and create new ones.

Thus a central concern of Weber's work can be formulated as the relation of self and power: the relation of the self to its own power and the relation of the self to the social power of institutions that shape the self and press their imperatives upon it.[17] Whether one believes that there is an "inherent" logic of rationality in Weber or that his work is a "developmental history," Weber's understanding of rationalization in its modern Western form cannot be adequately analyzed without reflection on his concern for the empowerment of the self.[18] Yet precisely because rationalization is the contemporary form of social power, it is an essential component of Weber's analysis of innovation, since it represents and is the product of new human powers, at the same time setting parameters and limits for innovation and social practice once it is embodied in institutions.

In a 1932 essay entitled "Karl Marx and Max Weber," Karl Löwith, the first major analyst of Weber's conception of rationalization, tried to shed light on the idea by comparing Marx on alienation with Weber on rationalization.[19] But despite its subtlety and insight, Löwith's comparison only obscured the issue, for he juxtaposed a concept in Marx that concerns the undermining of human powers with a concept in Weber meant to grasp a larger systemic, and impersonal, social dynamic. In contrast, it should be clear that if any comparison is to be made with Weber on rationalization, it must be done with Marx on capitalism, not on alienation, and if a comparison is to be made with Marx on alienation, then it must be done with the correlate in Weber to Marx's notion of the estrangement of human powers in commodity society, and this correlate is what I will call the implied problem of "disempowerment." That is, the parallel to alienation in Weber's work must be sought in the ways persons are rendered inwardly powerless by social orders and in the forms of weakness and deprivation imposed specifically by rationalization. Marx gave little attention in his later work to the philosophical analysis of the actor and the problem of how the revolutionary subject of history was to be shaped to develop the will to initiate a break with capitalism. But although Weber shifted his attention from capitalism to rationalization and the West, he retained as an integral object of analysis the forms of self that are generated by different cultures in contrast to the West, and in particular, the nature and social effectiveness of disciplines for the generation of empowered selves.

Practices of the self to generate power, to empower the self for innovation in and mastery of the rationalized world, are needed precisely because, to Weber, rationalization not only dis*enchants* but also dis*empowers*. Indeed, in its form as rational discipline, rationalization "increasingly reduces the significance of charisma and individually differentiated action."[20] Rationality now provides the limits within which social orders, institutions, and individuals may develop, providing new techniques of control and administration but weighing on individual actors and undermining other forces that generated practices of self-shaping in the past—tradition, religion, cultivation, charismatic education, and so on. To regain the vitality it once had, the West, in Weber's view, now requires, first, new means of self-mastery and forms of empowerment to permit it to remaster the institutions it has created. But it also requires, second, a new, individualist "metaphysics," that is, an acceptance of the "polytheism" of the modern world, coupled with the willingness of individuals to posit or recognize their ultimate values as "gods." These gods give the self a "mission," make demands that put the self in tension with the existing order, and provide the basis of an empowering form of service to lead the self to master the world. Although the West must rely on rational means and techniques for self-mastery and world mastery, it also needs such a source of *inner* power to mobilize in confrontation, not with tradition as the Puritans had done, but with embodied rationality and the weight of institutions, and not to overcome them, as the Puritans had overcome tradition, but to control and use them. Weber's language for this confrontation is replete with metaphors of war and the battlefield. Newly fabricated selves must dedicate themselves to war and battle on behalf of their gods in order to create meaning and find a model ethos for a new self.

Rationalization, of course, must not be construed only as an obstacle to the self's power; the Puritans' example alone shows its role first as a product of *their* inner power, and then as a tool of power, an aid to mastery over nature, economy, politics, salvation. But its very nature and its institutionalization make *it* master over the modern world, and Weber argues that society needs those who can use and control it at the same time, rather than be mastered by it. In Weber's view, rationalization threatens to impose itself totally on self and society, depriving them of the capacity to posit anything but their own submission to a rationalized order requiring obedience. Yet Occidental rationalization is partly a creation, however unintended, of the unified, ordered self of Puritanism, whose spirit once provided an ethos that empowered individuals to rationalize the world on behalf of sacred tasks. These creations, however, now control their creators. Rationality promised mastery of the world but has come back to master the self, shaping it to its own demands through the pressure of material needs and social order, no longer "needing" a unique spirit or ethos to support its functioning, undermining and eliminating the original preconditions that allowed innovation and empowerment of the self through self-mastery. Indeed, Weber was convinced that in modern Germany both the will to power and the paradigms of self-shaping and training for rule "carried" by leading classes of the past and potential leading classes of the future could no longer be relied upon to produce autonomous subjects. He thus argued for a discipline to fashion selves empowered to master the institutions by which submissive and obedient selves were fabricated. His practical critique of bureaucracy is thus joined to a cultural critique of a society fabricating a bureaucratic self.

But in Weber's work, it is not only institutionalized rationalization that must be confronted; the type of self shaped by devotion to materialism and excessive submission to rationality must also be overcome, both within oneself and among the defenders of the bureaucratic ethos. In *The Protestant Ethic*, Weber remarks that modern character is shaped exclusively by rational and material institutions and interests, adapting to the modern order without the need for an inspiring ethos of the kind required before capitalism was triumphant.[21] But his late work announces the need in the present for a return of ideal motives and practices of the self to allow a new form of self to arise and become a countervailing force to rationalization.

Weber, of course, analyzes the shaping of subjects *by* power, both in the past—in Western Catholicism, the traditional economy, and other religious cultures—and in the present—in bureaucracies and systems of rationality of other kinds. But he also analyzes the power *of* the self in its relation to the power exercised *over* the self in different rationalized "spheres." This is why the theme of "tension" that emerges in his religious sociology is central to his conception of self and power: Weber searches for practices that put the self in tension with the everyday realms of the world and may serve as levers for change and innovation. In the sociology of religion he analyzes different kinds of inner power, sources of power, centers of power and their relations to social power, revealed in the capacity of some religions to generate the ideal interests, motivations, and ultimate values that create tension and fortify individuals and groups to resist or remake the world. Wolfgang Mommsen puts it this way:

> The probability that such ultimate values will initiate far-reaching societal changes increases with the degree of opposition between ultimate ideals that are given to, and are binding upon, the individual and the everyday reality. Precisely because the individual sees himself confronted with extraordinary challenges, which are in sharp contrast to the traditional conditions and customary ways of life, he is forced to change radically "from within" the way he conducts his own life. In this way there arise accumulations of energies in society that have a capacity to innovate and to break up the established order and to restructure it fundamentally.[22]

Yet the notion of the "power of the self" is not an explicit concept in Weber's work, though in his discussion of concrete examples and types of person innovative power invariably appears as an attribute of the "man of vocation," the "Occidental personality," and the "charismatic leader." Even power as a concept is not given a central role in *Economy and Society*, where it is defined as "the chance within a social relationship to carry out one's own will even against resistance, no matter on what this chance rests." Indeed, because Weber considers the concept of power to be "sociologically amorphous," even in more concrete social relations, he prefers "domination" as a more precise category for describing relations of power, even though it means, more narrowly, "the chance of

a *command* to find obedience." But Weber moves toward a more Nietzschean conception of the self's power when he adds: "All conceivable
qualities of a person and all conceivable constellations can put someone
in the position of carrying out his will in a given situation."[23]

For Weber, the powers of the self are never a question merely of
endurance or persistence, or of the capacity to execute commands. Those
are the strengths he associates with the Lutheran calling in the past and
contemporary German culture. It is the capacities to initiate, overcome
resistance, and attract followers that are the crucial aspects of the self's
power, those that he associates with the Calvinist calling and formerly
Puritan peoples. This type of power links his project on religion and the
spirit of capitalism to his proposals for coping with rationality and mastering modern politics, where the power of the self in relation to social
realities and practices of self-shaping is a central theme. Foucault seems
to recognize the centrality of this problem when he remarks: "Max Weber
posed the question: If one wants to behave rationally and regulate one's
action according to true principles, what part of one's self should one
renounce? What is the ascetic price of reason? To what kind of asceticism
should one submit?"[24] But Foucault formulates Weber's goal incorrectly,
for although Weber did analyze the kind of renunciation that enabled
the Puritans to rationalize the world, and although he did try to specify
the kind of asceticism to which he thought the self should submit for
present-day needs, he did not do so on behalf of submission to reason
or rationality abstractly understood, but rather on behalf of the need
for power, the need to master rationalization itself, submitting to its
requirements but conquering its imperatives for the realization of the
transformed self's ultimate values.

Weber proposed his solution precisely because he believed that in *The
Protestant Ethic* he had discovered not only an element contributing to
the development of a unique spirit of modern capitalism but also a
spiritual discipline of enormous consequence that transformed and fortified the natural self of the Puritan believer into a hardened tool of
divine purpose in a way never before seen in worldly action on such a
scale. Indeed, the explanatory heart of *The Protestant Ethic* has less to
do with the historical linkage of Calvinism and the spirit of capitalism
than with Weber's positing of the existence and action of a unique type
of self newly constituted in the Reformation.[25] In effect, Weber argued
that for capitalism to have developed in the West there was a need not
only for a "regime of truth," as Foucault speaks of it, and for the separation of classes, accumulation, and the circulation and use of money
as capital in pursuit of ever-renewed profit, all of which Marx had already

recognized.[26] There was also a need for a mode of power found not in techniques or rationality *outside* the self as material preconditions, but found and engendered *inside* the self: in Weber's view, a new kind of person must have existed before capitalism was established, whose appearance changed the destiny of the Occident. This power was rooted in ascetic triumph over the natural self and the need to discharge anxiety about salvation through a search for proof of grace in world mastery for God's purposes. Weber's conclusions are based on the crucial role he ascribes to the idea of calling in modern culture and to the extraordinary powers and "taming of the soul" with which, he claimed, the Calvinist calling endowed what I have called "the first great entrepreneurs." Weber calls the Puritan calling "a powerful unconsciously refined arrangement for the breeding of capitalist individuals" that "has existed in no other church or religion."[27] The ways in which other cultures and religions contributed to forming persons, and whether or not they empowered them for innovative action and resistance to an established ethos or institutions, became a central concern of his later work.

Weber uses the history uncovered in *The Protestant Ethic* as the ground of a knowledge he hoped to confirm by comparative study and which he tried to mobilize for contemporary purposes. Hence it is a mistake to imagine that he considered the "new self" of Puritanism as nothing more than a historically situated means to the modern social order. In fact, the new self is an object of investigation *in its own right*, the key to *The Protestant Ethic*, and a central component of Weber's schemas of self and world, in all orders where innovation or mastery and direction of the order are important.

Indeed, Weber's work reveals a theory of historical innovation, in which most innovative social change depends not only on necessary material and political conditions, but also on the emergence and mediation of empowered actors whose strength is rooted in an ascetic character and whose spirit is capable of overcoming resistance and commanding obedience. Other cultures have contained empowered selves, but in Weber's view no culture other than that of the modern West contains widespread practices, whether produced by religious or other ideal motivations, that empower the self *from within* systematically to undertake innovations against the strength and resistance of inner and outer obstacles.[28] There are, of course, many rich and complex practices of the self in premodern Occidental as well as non-Occidental cultures, embodied in systems of education and in religious technologies for creating ethical and moral subjects, and they are a principal concern of his sociology of religion. But according to Weber, these do not create systematic worldly innovators, nor do they rival the substance or the scale of Western practices.[29] Of course, one might add that they also do not create excessively rational systems of domination, control, or production. Still, it is urgent, according to Weber, to restore this capacity for action and power to the West to rescue it from being depleted and overcome by its own creations, and this restoration can only come, he believes, through a secular revival of the calling—of practices created in the Reformation but mobilized for the tasks of the present. Weber's "called" individuals are all patterned on his portrait of Puritan entrepreneurs. The archetypal innovative individual is called "the man of vocation" in *The Protestant Ethic*, the "Occidental personality" in the sociology of world religions, and the "politician and scientist with a vocation" in the late essays.[30] Indeed, the "charismatic" individual in Weber's studies of economy and society is also such a person, and a most important one, because authentic charisma "where it appears constitutes a 'calling' in the emphatic sense of the word: as 'mission' [*Sendung*] or inner 'task.' "[31]

Weber's notion of the empowered self underlies his program for the ascetic regeneration of Germany and the taming of rationalization. Weber fused his conceptions of self and power with conceptions of leadership drawn from the history of political thought to create not only scientists and *Berufsmenschen* generally, but politicians specifically, empowered to master the political institutions fabricating submissive selves. Weber built his notions of political and social order on the ascetic conceptions of self he used to analyze Western culture. On the basis of his historical and social scientific knowledge, he formulated practices of subjectivation and world mastery for the tasks of society and culture, and practices of self-mastery and power-political ethics for the tasks of politics. But this foundation leads him to unworkable and undemocratic, if not actually dangerous, proposals for renewal and to a one-sided analysis of power. He excludes collective solutions to political problems and reduces politics and the control of rationalization to the carrying out of decisions made by ascetic elites serving Godlike ideals on the model of service in war. Further, Weber uses the notion of "ideal interests" in culture too often as if such interests worked generally just as they do in religion. He thus applies the notion too narrowly as a source for the shaping of individual selves, with little regard for cultural meanings and collective and political traditions and practices. This prevents him from developing concepts other than domination and its legitimation as the glue of politics, thus excluding other aspects of political culture and other types of power that play a strong role in the survival and functioning of political order.

Indeed, even in their own terms, Weber's proposals lack what he thought had been essential for the success of Puritan patterns of self-shaping—the *motivation* to ascetic service and the rewards of "practical sanctification." One can always prescribe a practice of self, but what secular motivations are there to induce submission to it? Weber hopes that the desire for power and the need for meaning will be enough to attract capable individuals to take control of a weakly established political power and to inspire them as well to these ascetic practices. But attraction to power is not necessarily accompanied by inclinations to ascetic self-mastery, and Weber is left to hope that nationalism might be an adequate motivation and ideal. The future was to show a very different, and horrifying, use of nationalism for the purposes of self-sacrifice and world mastery.

Further, at the same time that Weber reveals a component of the "regime of truth" needed for capitalism's development, he imposes a new regime of truth on Western development since the Reformation. What he identifies as the strong self or subject of Occidental culture Weber makes into a "universal subject" of historical innovation, not in the sense of "present everywhere" but in the sense of paradigmatic or archetypal, and best embodied in charisma. Weber's work implies that cultures that lack this subject lack the power to break radically with tradition on their own, without the aid of conquest or the importation of institutions from abroad. Weber's perspective remains the search for equivalents of the ascetic empowerment of the Puritan self. Of course, as Thomas Metzger has argued, it is possible to evaluate practices of the self from other points of view—for example, their ability to shape selves that can adapt to and incorporate orders they have not themselves created.[32] But for Weber's project this point of view is not relevant: self-generated mastery of the world is the important standard because of its centrality to the identity of the West.

Weber's excavation of Puritan models for the purpose of finding a new self-empowerment and mastery of the world is embedded in a romance of "strong selves," a narrative allegory based on the paradigm of the Puritans, who unintentionally built an iron cage for themselves and now must recover their old ways in order to break out of that cage again and become its wardens, while leaving the rest of humankind inside. It is a heroic fantasy that imagines that a few specially empowered selves can and must now master the rational orders of the world, whether its heroes are Puritans, prophets, or men with a calling for politics. These views are partly Nietzschean in origin, partly Protestant, and partly the remnant of Weber's liberal individualism, which, despite his disclaimers, is necessarily pessimistic because it longs for impossibilities and defends options doomed to failure, as subsequent history would show.

Along with this romance there is a profound analysis of institutions, powers, and social forces. But at those points where Weber's analysis is embedded in a metanarrative that precludes the entry of other forces into the story, it must be rejected. Other human powers, other concepts of innovation and action, are excluded or overlooked when they do not fit the moral of the story or the demands of the narrative. Unable to conceive of any collective political and social actions endowed with a remnant of power to face the weight of rational orders, and recognizing no other sources than ones like religions to strengthen and shape the self or the body politic for modern needs, Weber did not leave behind a credible analysis of the real possibilities of modern society.[33] With the tools he inherited and those he invented, he was unable to provide a solution to the problems he confronted.

MANN, SELF, AND NATION

While Weber was creating the "fiction" of the new man in *The Protestant Ethic*, Thomas Mann was analyzing the cultural practices of the self within the bourgeoisie. His work begins with a portrayal of weakness, of loss of strength and power, within a segment of the bourgeois class. In Mann's interpretation, the biological decline of strength among the bourgeoisie undermines its proficiency (*Tüchtigkeit*) for world mastery and subverts the visible effects of its strength in the world, namely, power over events, over human beings, and over the self's own destiny. Thomas Buddenbrook, the main character of *Buddenbrooks*, interprets his visible loss of power over the world as loss of inner strength for mastery, which becomes a loss of strength even for living, and is present also in his son. But despite the decline of traditional bourgeois proficiency, in Mann's work the older forms of strength and power are reborn in the bourgeois artist. Mann appropriates modes of self-mastery taught by the practices of the bourgeois calling in order to create, fortify, and legitimate the self of the artist, who can no longer devote himself to traditional bourgeois occupations or social goals and consequently cannot find his place among the traditional upholders of bourgeois values.[34]

The strength the artist finds by adopting the practices of self anchored in the bourgeois calling rescues him from the potential decadence, despair, and weakness produced by the crisis and exhaustion of the bourgeoisie. This adoption empowers him for the conquests of art—both the conquest of his artistic material and, through it, the conquest of society represented by the acclaim of the literary public and the economic success that results. In Mann's artistic world, strength and power are generated by weak bourgeois sons making themselves strong through ascetic practices of the calling, devoted to the practice of art rather than accumulation. Indeed, literary creation itself is a form of practice on the self for Mann. It requires the "dying to life" of the natural self before writing can begin, so the artistic self can emerge and dwell in the coldness and distance required for creation. It demands the repeated chilling of feeling so that balance and form can be created and not overwhelmed by unseemly and uncontrollable ordinary feeling. Of course, early on, Mann laments the effect this practice has on the self. But in fact, he nonetheless creates what he thinks is the only kind of self fitted for art, an artistic self modeled on the bourgeois pattern, equipped for the kind of redemption art can offer, despite art's sacrificial demands. In *Tonio Kröger*, Mann prescribes and universalizes this model and this practice for the whole domain of art.[35]

However, despite Mann's rescue of the artist from decadence and impotence by the creation of an empowered self in the calling, the artist extolled in *Tonio Kröger* obtains a rather limited field of power and strength, as Mann's own fears of sterility and weakness attest, and power and strength begin to fail, as shown in *Death in Venice*, a story about the practices and distortions of the artistic self. Homosexual longing is only one of the forces that break apart the practice of the artist and then the artist himself. In fact, the artistic self of Gustav Aschenbach no longer has the power it once possessed in its earlier self-fortification—neither power over itself, nor power over the materials of art, nor power anywhere in life. The project of generating power through an individualistic bourgeois discipline of the self and self-absorbed artistic practice alone is shown in this story to be exhausted, and the capacity for self-mastery and world mastery based upon it is gone. Thus Mann reveals that the ascetic practices that shape the self have potentially unforeseen, and potentially disastrous, consequences for the self—as Weber argued in a different form in *The Protestant Ethic*. The self that has been shaped through the practices of this discipline is revealed to be *mis*shapen.[36]

Mann's work reveals, often despite his intention, that the artist in a calling, alone and self-absorbed, cannot generate inner power by himself for long; it is no accident that Mann's ideal artist always tries to relate himself to a greater whole, as in *Tonio Kröger*, where he relates himself to the bourgeoisie as its ironic lover and to art as its embodiment. But in establishing the artistic calling within himself and his characters, Mann was unable to identify completely either with the bourgeois class of his origin or the general artistic self-understanding of his time. Ultimately, his "ironic" position "between" them did not allow his self-exploration to refer to anything outside his own self. In *Royal Highness*, he even tried to relate himself to the nobility, as if the artist were the true aristocrat, in order to overcome the inadequacy of his bourgeois identity—to which he had felt superior in any case, despite his apparent love.[37] *Death in Venice*, however, showed the exhaustion of the artist's identifications with a particular class and revealed, further, the inability of the artist to reinvigorate himself by reinterpreting himself as the model of German manliness, the warrior and soldier. Mann's pre–World War I works thus tell a story of the exhaustion of strength that can no longer be squeezed out of the ascetic self alone, making necessary the search for other sources of power.

The exhaustion of the capacity of older practices alone to sustain the artist, to empower him for the demands of creation and world conquest, leaves him in a problematical, if not dangerous, position. Mann himself overcame the constriction of these exhausted practices, reestablishing inner power through the identification of the artistic self with an even higher and more comprehensive entity—Germany (higher yet isomorphic to his artistic self, he thought)—thus virtually fusing the artist's self with the nation. In effect, the artist "borrows" the strength of Germany for his own struggles, underwriting his project with its power and significance, transforming himself and generating a new self-legitimation and identity. This is the "breakthrough" to Germany and to life, to use the language of *Doctor Faustus*. It proclaims the artist's identity and value as a version of the nation writ small—a product of the internalization of the nation and the externalization of the self—masking this proclamation as the "discovery" of the analogous natures of artist and nation. Now Mann's artist and Mann himself have the source of power and self-legitimation they require to inspire art and the artistic self. The self is fortified through identification and appropriation from a new source of power, and Mann defends this source during World War I against the "draining" of its power threatened by the advance of rationalization, or "civilization," represented by the war of the West against Germany.

Germany is not just any source of power and practice, though. The artist, having understood himself as a product of the "disease" that weakens a part of the bourgeoisie, finds that the bourgeois social world is now completely diseased, inadequate to sustain art and, after the defeat of Germany in World War I, even normal life. The traditional modes of shaping the self through *Bildung*, reinforced by the self-satisfaction of bourgeois life in the calling, have failed on a mass scale. The development of the self through the encounter with the traditional materials of culture and the experience of class supremacy can no longer strengthen even the ordinary bourgeois of Germany. *The Magic Mountain* testifies to Mann's view of the inadequacies of the guidance of the times: the new practices of the self must be founded on an education no longer narrowly personal and historical but social and political, as a means to the restoration of health and strength. The self must overcome its obsession with death, turn back to life, while expanding to incorporate the issues and concerns of the nation.

But already in *The Magic Mountain*, a new, higher ideal and source of power and self-legitimation begins to emerge out of the trash heap of Mann's earlier history: Humanity—bitterly attacked in the wartime *Reflections of an Unpolitical Man* and even mocked in the novel in the person of Settembrini. Humanity, as a theme out of the German past of Goethe and Herder and of the heritage of *Bildung*, begins to appear in Mann's essays and political writings as an ideal originally and essentially German but also transnational in its aims. For *The Magic Mountain* does not actually lead to an empowered and active mastery of the disparate and tortured materials of German culture; rather, it leads to an ending in war that is not a resolution. In *The Magic Mountain*, German culture leaves the self in a stalemate from which it cannot rescue itself; once again, Mann's novelistic truth goes far beyond his and Weber's explicit ideals. But Mann does provide a *false* rescue, thus undermining that truth. He shows the self to be lost without the intervention of an external power, the "grace" of war, and from this grace, the narrator of the novel absurdly imagines a new love song of Humanity to arise. But since the actual historical outcome of that war was mass death, revolution, and National Socialism, a new effort at understanding was necessary.

The difficulties of active mastery in conditions of exhaustion and the potential disaster that can result from the identification of self and nation thus become the subject of *Doctor Faustus*. Here, as in *The Magic Mountain*, a "devilish" individual and nation encounter a product of humanistic cultivation; but here too, an artist, crippled socially and inhibited artistically, confronts the weakness and exhaustion of a tradition and culture, an exhaustion that radicalizes his search for the rescue of a self now totally disempowered by the end of tradition and by the lack of certainty and direction in the times. In this condition, the artist—who is also Faust, and Germany, and Nietzsche rolled into one—imagines a new source of direction in a reconciliation of art with the *Volk*. To accomplish this, however, he reaches out for an identification with dark and devilish powers, under whose sign and in whose service he recovers strength and power to carry out his artistic and redemptive project, but at the price of isolation and madness. Here in a more radical form, the limits of identification with the nation come through, but once again Mann undermines the novelistic truth by holding out a problematical ideal at the end: Mann's alternative is the revival of the ideal of Humanity as the only "good" source of meaning and empowerment. It is in the service of this surrogate Christian god that even the devilish artist—and Nietzsche—must find their direction in Mann's narrative.

The empowerment that comes from identification with the nation thus shifts the artist's focus to a new field for artistic conquest and understanding, but this fusion of self and nation creates new problems, for the novelistic realization of Mann's new understanding is undermined on the level of novelistic form. By using concepts like the calling and service, drawn from his class past, to grasp modern problems of self and nation, Mann creates a rhetorical disharmony between the tale told in his stories and their endings, masked by an irony that actually conceals ideological purposes, conscious and unconscious. His new resolution is problematical for the very reason that makes this understanding possible in the first place, namely, the fusion of self and nation in allegory. After World War I, there are henceforth two levels of existence in certain of Mann's work: the self, and the self/nation. These two levels, embodied in the form of political allegories in *The Magic Mountain* and *Doctor Faustus*—the weak self/Germany and the devilish self/Germany—create problems of integration on the level of art. The central formal issue for the study of Mann's late work, therefore, is not irony but allegory—or rather, political allegory, produced by the fusion, analogy, identity, and bond with the national polity.

Allegory first appears in Mann's work well before World War I. He had always treated the artist's life as symbolic, and despite the unsuccessful allegory of the artist as prince in *Royal Highness*, Mann argued that certain of his later novels, *The Magic Mountain* and *Joseph and His Brothers*, were made possible by that earlier allegorical work.[38] In a letter to Hugo von Hofmannsthal, he defended allegory and the novel of "ideas" as "a high form," claiming that "one cannot better elevate the novel than by making it ideal and constructivist," that is, a construction bearing or embodying ideas rather than a purely realistic form.[39] *The Magic Mountain* and *Doctor Faustus* are novels of Germany that are no longer only symbolic but allegorical and political. Although they draw us into the experience of their characters despite the characters' dual natures as emblems or allegorical forms, this emblematic and allegorical function sometimes vitiates the living quality of the characters and forces events into the novel whose only role is to satisfy the need for a strong parallel with events in Europe or Germany. More important, the allegories—and the lessons that Mann insists be drawn from them— lead to demands on the narrative that produce endings that are false to the novels' stories and characters and betray the novels' logic. The characters cannot choose and live out what their nature and circumstances demand, because the allegory demands that choices be made for them based on the needs of a moral tale that subverts itself.

Instead of the logic of a symbol governing a story or an individual character's development, in allegory the logic of the symbol alone is not allowed to develop out of itself.[40] It is governed by, or made to conform to, another level of story, theme, or ideas whose demands take it over. As Northrop Frye observes, "We have allegory when the events of a narrative obviously and continuously refer to another simultaneous structure of events or ideas, whether historical events, moral or philosophical ideas, or natural phenomena."[41] Yet the most successful twentieth-century allegories, like *The Plague* or *The Trial*, develop complete symbolic universes without striving to mirror or directly discuss contemporary events; within these allegories, moreover, characters function without having to participate in the literal debates of the outside world to strengthen their link, and the novel's link, to the times.

Mann's characters, however, are forced to dwell in two realms: they are both realistic *and* elaborately allegorical, very human *and* tools that constantly reflect on contemporary debates in Mann's world, moving quickly from one level to the other. This makes for very rich novelistic work, but the logic of Mann's symbolization is nonetheless forced onto a path dictated by allegorical need. Ultimately, the level requiring allegorical accommodation to Mann's interpretation of Germany undermines the realistic "personal" life of the characters, which explains why the personal lives sometimes make less sense in their own terms and in terms of their logic than in terms of the allegorical purpose. At the same time, the accommodation of the allegorical level to Mann's absolute commitment to the necessity of an individual's service in a calling undermines the realistic analysis of Germany in its own terms. Thus, what empowers the narrative on one level undermines it on another. This raises the question of whether these characters can be adequate symbols of Germany and whether Mann's allegory does not do violence to the interpretation of Germany, exercising a problematical control over interpretations of the events in the novel and over the possible interpretations of the works themselves.

Finally, although Mann shares Weber's conceptions of calling and personality, his fictional works constantly subvert the explicit ideals he and Weber maintain and defend by revealing the dangerous consequences that lurk within them. But Mann's interpretations of German political realities are themselves undermined because of his effort to comprehend Germany allegorically on the model of a self. He thus often mistakes social and political ills for metaphysical or merely internal problems, fails to grasp fully the impossibility of recovering exhausted cultural ideals of calling and personality, and both reflects and contributes to what has become a commonplace understanding of how a nation, and especially Germany, can go wrong.

The following chapters explore Weber's and Mann's understanding of the threat to meaning, strength, and power produced by the advance of rationalization and the crisis of values inherent in the challenge to *Bildung*. They go on to analyze Weber's and Mann's interpretations of the specific German dilemma in culture and politics and their proposals for regeneration. These include Weber's use of a model of service in war as an ideal for the recovery of personal meaning and the mastery of rationalization, and Mann's fusion of the artistic self with the nation. Mann's work shows that even this identification of self and nation does not necessarily lead to active mastery of crisis and the social world. Weber becomes even more concrete and pointed in his proposal for generating an empowered political calling for Germany, motivated by the urgency of the nation's problems—though Mann in turn, and despite himself, shows the desperate solutions the self will adopt when the possibilities for meaning and strength are circumscribed by the language and necessity of service. Finally, we will briefly discuss what would be involved in overcoming the premises of and necessity for their practices for reempowering the self.

2　The Crises of *Bildung* and Science

The "crises" of education and of the sciences that began in Germany in the late nineteenth century were symptoms of a profound shift that was undermining ideals of society and the self which had been defended for a hundred years. The immediate intellectual cause was what Weber called the "disenchantment" of the world through science and rationalization, but the deeper social causes lay in the advance of capitalism, pressures for more technical education, and demographic shifts that ended the purely elite nature of university education and brought students in by the thousands. The combination of social change and the critique of traditional ideals undermined formerly stable and accepted patterns of belief, conceptions of personal development, and ideals of social order—grounded partly in humanist ideals of cultivation and partly in faith in science as the key to the future. As a consequence, the faith in science and in humanist cultivation were cast into serious doubt.[1]

Weber's defense of new disciplines of the self develops against this background, culminating in his bleak portrait of the effects of disenchantment on science and modern intellectual life. Because of the link between *Bildung* and *Wissenschaft* in the older educational ideals, Weber's discussion of science also raises general questions about meaning and work and about the character, ideals, and nature of education that had existed since the period of German idealism, Weimar classicism, and the reforms of Wilhelm von Humboldt. Weber reveals the widespread skepticism of German youth about universities and the possibility of *Bildung*, as well as their longing for rescue from directionlessness and purposelessness. His understanding of the crisis of the sciences and its implications for the shaping of character are thus bound up with a critique of the ideals of German education and their institutionalization.[2]

Mann's confrontation with *Bildung* begins in World War I with his defense of German "inwardness" (*Innerlichkeit*) and its ideals. Germany's defeat and Mann's self-reevaluation led to his critique of *Bildung* and to his attempt to show that self-formation in postwar Germany had to pass through an education in modern society and politics, rather than immersion in literary classics of the past. His wartime attack on "civilization" was followed by acceptance of—indeed, defense of—its forces and the rationalized world they brought, despite the fact that they also brought what he considered the end of German "depth." But in his ultimate defense of Humanity, Mann attempts to revive an ideal cherished in the tradition of *Bildung*.

The origin and nature of *Bildung* reveal a crucial dimension of German preoccupation with the self and its relation to social change. In its origins, *Bildung* was a discipline of the self that was central to the struggle of nonnoble groups for a sense of self-worth, inner strength, and fulfillment in response to personal domination in the absolutist state and by the ideals of the nobility. It was, further, a source of self-development and inner unity in response to threats to the self posed by the increasing division of labor and pressures for specialization. Although *Bildung* was integrated by Humboldt into the German university, the development of the sciences and rationalization in the nineteenth century threatened it and the strength it generated by bringing social fragmentation and specialization into its well-protected university home. *Bildung* as an ideal had already begun to detach itself from the broader ideals and frames of belief that once had sustained it, becoming contemplative and withdrawn, focused on narrow personal fulfillment and tending to degenerate into an empty ideal of the vulgar bourgeoisie. Now the pressures of science and the division of labor threatened to rob it of the last remnant of the inner power it had once promised.

These cultural crises of a society under pressure and in transition form the background for Weber's and Mann's encounters with *Bildung*. They are crises of *Bildung* as a guide to self-formation and crises of the university, but also crises of faith in the situation of knowledge and *Wissenschaft* at the beginning of the twentieth century. Allowing for some factors unique to Germany, Weber and Mann assimilate these crises generally to the advance of rationalization and civilization in all their forms.

BILDUNG AND THE GERMAN UNIVERSITIES

The Origins of Bildung

The significance of the concept of *Bildung* for the development of German culture cannot be overestimated.[3] From Kant and Humboldt through Goethe and the German Romantics, to the later defenders of an ideological version of the ideal, the language of *Bildung* is at the center of German reflection on self and action. One historian claims that the "period between 1831 and 1933 ... can be called the century of

Bildung (in the specific German meaning of the word) and of the *Bildungsbürgertum.*"[4] Gadamer even argues that the "idea of self-formation or cultivation . . . was perhaps the greatest idea of the eighteenth century" and that the intellectual change it induced "still causes us to experience the century of Goethe as contemporary."[5] According to Hans Rosenberg:

> *Bildung* as conceived by the German neo-humanists in the age of Lessing, Herder, Winckelmann, Goethe, Schiller, Kant, Fichte, and Humboldt, meant much more than advanced school training, general and vocational. *Bildung*, no doubt, called for trained minds and for more and better knowledge, but no less for character and personality development. *Bildung* implied supreme emphasis on inwardness and tenderness of the heart. It invited man to seek happiness within himself by orienting his total life toward the harmonious blending of spiritual elevation, emotional refinement, and individualized mental and moral perfection.[6]

Following the Napoleonic wars, Humboldt, the great educational reformer, transformed his ideals of self-development and cultivation (*Bildung*) into a policy of university reform when he became a leading figure in the Prussian reform period.[7] He strove to overcome the limitations and weaknesses of the outdated universities of Prussia with a program requiring both humanistic cultivation of the mind and the challenge of research.[8] For Humboldt, *Bildung* was opposed to the Enlightenment idea of encyclopedic knowledge. At the same time, as Konrad Jarausch observes, in contrast "to the estate system of training, in which each individual received the teaching 'proper' to his calling, the neohumanists aimed at *allgemeine Menschenbildung*, all-around development of the free individual personality."[9] For Humboldt, *Bildung* is "the process of self-becoming [*Selbstwerdung*] of the individual, who embodies in himself a true and ethical world" and for whom fulfillment is based on "improvement of our inner selves." Thus, *Bildung* means "self-formation" rather than "education" in the sense of training or learning.[10] It means "the unfolding of a unique individuality through an integral engagement . . . with a group of venerated sources, chiefly the classics. *Bildung* suggests something like a transfer of grace from the source to the learner."[11]

Kant used the term *Bildung* in a different sense from the one it later took on. He meant it as "cultivation" of an already existing talent or capacity, as "culture of the soul, which one can also certainly call physical." That is, one cultivates the self as one would a precious plant in nature. But cultivation of the self as part of nature contrasts with that process of self-transformation that goes on in the sphere of freedom, for "to give laws to freedom is something completely different from forming [*bilden*] nature," even if it is one's own nature.[12] In other words, to Kant, *Bildung* remained a limited goal, because the shaping of an endowment of nature, even its elevation into something higher, remained part of nature, like the nurturing of a seedling that grows according to its own "natural" law. Indeed, for Kant "personality" could not be created through *Bildung*, but only through the overcoming of the natural and physical self by the imposition of moral "laws" on oneself in "freedom."[13] These laws are derived from pure practical reason, which does not consult the "nature" of the self, but imposes norms derived from reason, external to imperatives of the natural or physically given self. To the extent that we can follow such laws, we "tame" the self, elevate ourselves above nature, and dwell in freedom, where we are then truly "personalities"—but only then.

Humboldt, however, distinguished "culture" in the sense of "cultivating" from *Bildung* in the sense of forming, and further proposed a different attitude toward the "taming" of self: "If in our language we say *Bildung*, we mean something both higher and more inward, namely the attitude of mind which, from the knowledge and the feeling of the total intellectual and moral endeavor, flows harmoniously into sensibility and character."[14] With Humboldt, according to Gadamer:

> *Bildung* no longer means "culture," i.e., the development of capacities or talents. The rise of the word *Bildung* calls rather on the ancient mystical tradition, according to which man carries in his soul the image of God after whom he is fashioned and must cultivate it in himself. . . . It is not accidental that in this the word *Bildung* resembles the Greek word *physis*. Like nature, *Bildung* has no goals outside itself. . . . In this the concept of *Bildung* transcends that of the mere cultivation of given talents, from which concept it is derived. The cultivation of a talent is the development of something that is given, so that the practice and cultivation of it is a mere means to an end. . . . In *Bildung* contrariwise, that by which and through which one is formed becomes completely one's own.[15]

Thus to Humboldt, "All *Bildung* has its origin alone in the interior of the soul," for "the formation of human beings" means "not educating them toward external goals." Indeed, despite his concern for the worldly effects of *Bildung*, he did not wish to orient the human being any more to utility and practicality than did Kant. The goal of the human being is "to form himself in himself," which is never to be seen as a mere "means" toward any other result: the person's ultimate purpose is to strive for "the unity of his whole being, which alone gives the person true value."[16] This unity is provided not by the Kantian command to the natural self that it control desire, inclination, or whatever is native to it and instead obey the laws of reason, but by the imperative to form oneself according to the "law" of one's own self. Even so, despite the differences from Kant's view, *Bildung* did affirm the "unfolding of the personality" as one of its highest goods.[17] To accomplish this unfolding, the self must follow an "inward" pattern and allow it to flourish, rather than be governed by laws prescribed by reason and intended to overcome nature and the flesh. This pattern determines the personality as it develops and harmonizes all of its faculties, making it a "whole" rather than a "servant" of "the higher laws" of practical reason and morality. *Bildung* thus became an "ethical category alongside personality [*Persönlichkeit*]."[18]

In contrast to Kant's moral agenda, then, Humboldt's educational agenda aimed at making *Bildung* the principal goal, defending it as the true ground of action in the world. In fact, to Humboldt, *Bildung* is a source of power: "*Bildung* has to do [not] . . . with knowing and talking but rather with character and action [*Handeln*]."[19] It draws on our strengths, unifying and empowering us to act through our very being. "The true goal of man . . . is the highest and most harmonious formation [*proportionierlichste Bildung*] of his strengths [*Kräfte*] into a whole."[20] For Humboldt, true morality thus consists in the motto: First, "form [*bilde*] yourself," and then "affect [*wirke*] others through that which you are." It is the transformed self, therefore, that acts through its being, example, and personal sway. The effect of such a person is palpable. "The truly great person . . . the man who is truly cultivated in the intellectual and moral sense, exerts by these qualities alone more influence than all others, simply because such a man exists among men, or has existed."[21] Thus for Humboldt, the "idea of the primacy of the will," the self's power to shape things outside and inside, produced by the formation of the self, is the "very essence" of *Bildung*.[22] Yet this capacity of the will is not inherited, nor is it developed through technical training or practical experience, but through the "self-formation" of the self in itself, mediated by immersion in scholarship, which eventuates in forcefulness and influence. Affected, perhaps, by his reading of Adam Smith and Adam Ferguson and by fear of the consequences of division of labor and increasing specialization in society, Humboldt defended individual particularity and spontaneity in his notion of *Bildung*, attempting to combine into an empowered "totality" those mental powers that threatened to be fragmented and weakened in a society that was coming to prize one-sided development of the self and its capacities.[23]

There is another side to *Bildung*: the absorption or internalization of culture derived from immersion in the products of human creativity. Indeed, Humboldt wrote: "He who can say to himself when he dies: 'I have grasped and made into a part of my humanity as much of the world as I could,' that man has reached fulfillment. . . . In the higher sense of the word, he has really lived."[24] Thus, *Bildung* in its original sense was concerned with the generation of strength from within based on all-around development, focusing on "being" and the self's unity and unfolding and including a struggle for the liberation of the self from goals and imperatives set from outside.

Yet Humboldt was not altogether satisfied with the "pursuit of harmonious and fully developed faculties." After a period of inactivity and private cultivation of the self—and possibly under the influence of Goethe and Schiller—he became interested in "concentrating" on the accomplishment of concrete tasks. Humboldt had started out in government service but after a time withdrew in order to focus on self-development and his family. Now, after years of public inactivity, he longed for something new. "A man must give himself up to *one* limited definite objective and lose himself, at least for a time, in its pursuit." He had once believed that a man counts only because of what he is, not what he does, but now he felt it was time for him to produce something.[25] Yet despite his renewed interest in applying himself to a task and his involvement in his career as culture minister of Prussia, Humboldt still maintained that the self could only grow from within, nurtured by learning, rather than from engagement with the powers and forces of the world.[26] Even if one was so engaged, it was necessary to cultivate detachment and be rooted in the wholeness of one's inner self, which must remain disengaged and grow according to its own law. One must "see one's actions as a negligible factor in the world process and only important for one's private view of things and private evaluation of them." Later he wrote, "One must have a world of one's own within, over which the waves of life roll on, while it quietly grows unseen."[27]

The ideals of *Bildung* were not simply the fantasies of utopian theorists. On the contrary, they entered into practical life, for the neohumanist reformers had an enormous direct and immediate influence, especially on the bureaucratic elites. They "ennobled public service and justified the claim of the educated to political leadership."[28] This happened at a time—the latter part of the eighteenth century—when noble status had begun to lose its ancient prestige in Germany, and, in Hans Rosenberg's view, a principal contributing factor was the theory of *Bildung*: "the appearance of a new standard of grading the worth of man and of gauging merit, dignity, and social position. Personal eminence, based on notable intellectual or artistic efforts and creative attainments, challenged the primacy of the centuries-old division of society." Higher education thus became "an attribute of social repute," and *Bildung*, as an ideal, became a weapon in an attack by a new "aristocracy of merit" struggling for social recognition against the claim of the traditional nobility to possess "ingrained human and social superiority." With such an "inner" grounding of worth to fortify their identity, those who struggled to rise were able to resist the temptation to ape the manners and social practices of the aristocracy so as to appear "superior." As Rosenberg argues, "*Bildung* undermined the traditional separation of the classes, but also the ancient practice of equating the aristocracy with the nobility." This new ethos and standard was present above all in the Prussian bureaucracy in the period Rosenberg calls the "twilight regime of 1786–1806," which seemed to accept "the novel standard of excellence and social responsibility engendered by the ascendancy of *Bildung*." Those who became "educated persons" (*Gebildete*) or "inner aristocrats" obtained a greater share of self-esteem as well as a "heightened sense of social worth," relying on standards "independent of, or in opposition to, the traditional valuations of the nobility."[29]

Still, this ethos and standard of social repute was for many merely decorative or else of use in struggling up the social ladder or the ladder of bureacratic promotion. And indeed, the ideal of *Bildung* degenerated in the nineteenth century, especially after the failure of the revolutions of 1848 and again after the achievement of empire in 1871.[30] Yet those sincere in their adherence found not only a new ethos to animate their lives but also a new strength derived from service and devotion to ideals rather than individuals. As Rosenberg observes, "The call for *Bildung* gave focal direction to their lives. Self-disciplined dedication to an idea in the place of subservience to a personal master vitalized their political loyalties and their zeal to render public service." Drawing also on Kantian conceptions of the freedom of the will derived from reason alone, they struggled to escape "tutelage" to their superiors and to become inwardly emancipated from the control and guidance of another person, in particular from their bureaucratic superior or royal master. They relied on an appeal to individual conscience and judgment and to "freedom anchored in self-control," in preference to an automatic compliance with administrative orders. These "new men" formed "an inner attachment to an objectified rational order, to the idea of 'the' sovereign state," which was far preferable to them than their former "submission to an eccentric monocrat." For them, "it was short of unbearable to be called upon by the 'master' to rest content with functioning like cogs in a machine." The formerly "royal servants" now called themselves the "servants of the state" and the "professional officials of the state," identifying with their hierarchical organization and the state itself, rather than with service of a single lord. Thus, the different self-concept and sense of worth that the new men derived from *Bildung* both empowered them for action and allowed them to demand that they be treated as human beings, with decency and respect.

> To those with delicate souls and to men with serious intellectual interests, the neo-humanistic conception of man and the new individualistic philosophy of the freedom of the moral will as the answer to the unqualified demand to duty proved an inexhaustible spring of energy and fortitude in effecting their mental and moral emancipation from the tutelage of royal omniscience. With replenished inner resources, they stood ready to shunt "impossible" demands, not because of spite and obstinacy or for the sake of personal advantage or material class interest, but on ethical and humanitarian grounds.[31]

Thus, *Bildung*, allied with Kantian notions of the independent moral will accessible to all rational creatures, generated inner strength and energy, reorienting the emerging *Gebildete* away from personal service toward impersonal service of an ideal object—in this case the state—and grounding their sense of self in the new standards of knowledge and learning.[32]

Yet the struggle between Kant's notion of taming the self through reason and Humboldt's idea of forming the self from within was not so easy to harmonize, and it persisted into the twentieth century. Even Humboldt's own struggle between self-limitation and specialization, on the one hand, versus wholeness and integration, on the other, was replayed in the conflict between Goethe and the Romantics over *Bildung*, personality, and individuality. As Roy Pascal remarks, despite Goethe's initial enthusiasm for the ideal of wholeness and totality, he recognized "the necessity of 'Einseitigkeit' [one-sidedness] and the definition of 'Bildung' in terms of this necessity." He accepted the inevitability of specialization, seeing it, "if freely chosen, as a necessary means to the fulfillment of the personality." For Goethe, totality was "something to be achieved only by a community as a whole, not by an individual in himself."[33] Bruford observes that, although Goethe seemed attracted to an ideal of "harmonious all-round culture such as Humboldt had envisaged," he believed such a possibility had been attainable only by the ancients. Thus, he abandoned "the modern humanistic ideal of harmonious 'Bildung' " and embraced the belief that "a man of his day could not develop the full harmony of his nature and would do better to aim at being, and to have himself educated as, a fragment, a single part."[34] Nevertheless, Goethe's works reveal an ambivalence, for they also show Goethe's "spontaneous and involuntary resistance to the doctrine he himself is affirming, his protest on behalf of 'Bildung' of the free personality, against the social and practical necessity of one-sidedness."[35]

The Romantics, in contrast, were hostile to self-limitation and renunciation, specialization and selfless work for the well-being of the community.[36] For Schlegel and Schleiermacher, "individuality" formed the kernel of the human being. Indeed, Schlegel defended the "formation [*Bildung*] and development of individuality as the highest calling [*Beruf*]" of the human being, as "godly egoism." The Romantics conceived individuality as a mixture of many elements of self and feeling, refusing to accept reason as the essence of personality.[37] Yet although they displaced reason from its ruling position, the Romantics still sought "the unification of different powers of the spirit and the soul."[38] Their concern with the particular and uniquely characteristic in each person "stood in contrast to the eudaemonism of the Enlightenment as well as to the Kantian ethic of duty." Indeed, "[in] the place of an ethic of obligation [*Sollensethik*]," as Kant had wanted, "they wanted an ethic of being [*Seinsethik*]."[39]

Thus the questions and terms of the debate over self-development were set early on. Toward what end and by what means was the self to be shaped—toward personality built on freedom and rules of morality, or toward personality derived from wholeness and integration from within? By means of laws prescribed to the self, or by means of the self's inner law and nature? Through devotion to a single task, submission to a single person, or cultivation of individuality?[40]

Changes in the Ideal of Bildung

Bildung and its elements performed another function in the social economy of the self, a function that eventually contributed to its decline: they acted as "a substitute for religion."[41] As Schnädelbach observes, the "theological-mystical origin of this concept of *Bildung* has been persuasively demonstrated."[42] Ringer puts it thus:

> Decisive for the idea of *Bildung*, as Bruford makes clear, were the meanings inherited from religious modes of thought and feeling. For Schleiermacher and even for Humboldt, the self that was to be cultivated was a "higher" self; it stood opposed to a merely natural self that was to be controlled and transcended. The object

of *Bildung* was . . . a personal liberation from the needy, time-bound self of everyday utilitarian man, an "inner freedom" from entanglement in the merely "external" . . . a sense of "humanity" as salvation. . . . The Lutheran doctrine of "inner freedom" and the Pietist emphasis on the individual soul's unique path to salvation have long been regarded as important influences on German Idealism and Romanticism. . . . Self-cultivation and "humanity" provided an immediate access to a timeless realm and an only partly secularized version of Christian teleology.[43]

Indeed, Humboldt himself began to see self-cultivation as

a pursuit of "the salvation of the soul." . . . I use this expression intentionally in order not to exclude any means that a man may use for his own spiritual improvement. For he can raise himself to a higher stage of spirituality by a continually fuller and purer development of his ideas, by more and more vigorous efforts to improve his character, or he can reach the same goal by the shorter path of simple piety.[44]

But to Ringer, decline was inherent in the very language and nature of *Bildung*, and danger lay in the eventual disappearance of religious-like conviction in the saving powers of such a path.

Fully secularized, the language of *Bildung* in fact became a rhetoric of privacy . . . a privileged retreat from ordinary life; the "inward" turn of thought, once emptied of religious significance, took on the character of passive and essentially gratuitous contemplation. . . . Gone was the universality of the great Idealist and Romantic teleologies of an unfolding world-spirit or of a self-contemplating humanity. What was left was the purely individual teleology of *Bildung* as personal fulfillment, which could be further reduced to aesthetic refinement in abstention from life.[45]

Thus, "When the religious element weakened as a source of meaning during the course of the nineteenth century, the ideals of self-cultivation and of humanity became increasingly 'formal,' devoid of determinate 'content,' "[46] and potentially usable in radically different ways.

Bildung, with roots in Lutheranism and Pietism, therefore transmitted a mode of character formation and an ideal of life related to the "inward" and emotional religions. Thus, in addition to fortifying the social identity of bourgeois strata, much of the educational and philosophical ideology of the first half of the nineteenth century can be described as a secular substitute for religion among the educated strata of the *Bürgertum*, who confronted the slowly growing fragmentation and disruptions of modern life and their continuing ambiguous status vis-à-vis the traditional nobility. Even the rise of the new, disenchanting ideologies of science may not have been so great a break with the old faith as first appears.

But there was another dimension that disappeared from the tradition of *Bildung* and reappeared in altered form. It is clear how central to the German tradition the attainment of personality has been, whether through the morality of Kant, the all-sided *Bildung* of Humboldt and Schiller, or the specialization and service to a single and unifying task portrayed by Goethe. Indeed, R. Hinton Thomas argues that "the unfolding of innate qualities into the balance and harmony of 'Persönlichkeit' " was always as important as the dimensions of *Bildung* that stressed the building of happiness and strength in and through the self. But, he says, what is too often forgotten is how intimately personality was related to the highest ideal the German classicists defended: Humanity. They drew on this ideal to tame both the egocentric aspirations of the self and, later, the aspirations and overexaltation of the state.

> This concept of "personality" is a central and crucial feature of "Bildung," and no word is more characteristic of the terminology associated with it. "Personality" was a matter of the self in the first instance, but in the tradition of "Bildung" it was also drawn outwards in idealistic directions.... "Personality" ... had a strong ethical force, the goal of which, in the classical period, was "Humanität." ... It is these associations of "personality," art, and "Humanität" that, above all, gave the concept of "Bildung" its noble image and led it to epitomise for so many the most refined characteristics of German culture.[47]

Through the transformation and use of personality in the "new" political discourse of the latter part of the nineteenth century, however, personality became separated from Humanity as its ethical ideal and overarching value. Instead it was applied to the narrower chauvinist ideals of the nation, the state, and ultimately the *Volk*, to defend exclusivity; to exclude the foreign and strange, especially Jews; and to defend the "purity" of the individual personality, the personality of the state, and the *Volk* against those who would corrupt it.

Hinton Thomas argues that by focusing exclusively on self-cultivation we are distracted from the "extent to which features from the tradition of 'Bildung,' especially as far as the decisive notion of 'personality' is concerned, became an active force in the political arena," especially among conservatives.[48] *Bildung* was not confined to "the pursuit of something purely private and personal," as in the early bourgeois era, when it "created an independent sphere of individual possibilities and of individual development." The classical view of personality helped the bourgeoisie by supplying

> the belief in an essence to be preserved and developed, and in a balance and harmony demanding the exclusion of whatever might disturb it. . . . Characteristic of "personality" was the way it was associated with, and directed towards an uplifting set of values, such as might compensate for, and justify, so intense a concentration on the private world of the self. These did not need, however, to be of the kind subsumed under the concept of "Humanität," and there was no reason why in different circumstances the idealism to which "personality" was drawn should not . . . assume other forms—and this is precisely what happened . . . reminiscent of the association, at the beginnings of "Bildung," of an ego-centredness compensated for by service to an idealism directed towards the general interest. Originally it was "Humanität," the "good" and the "beautiful," that had provided the idealism. Increasingly after 1848 the source was an idealism of a different kind, the idealism of the "völkisch" movement.[49]

After 1848, *Bildung* was extended to the self-cultivation of the *Volk* and entered into the "partnership" between nationalism and "the classical idea of 'personality,' " serving as an ideological bulwark of the state and conservative classes and a justification for repression. This was related to "the defection of the German bourgeoisie from its more liberal aspirations before 1848," for personality "became divorced . . . from its connections with 'Humanität.' "[50] In conditions under which industrial society was throwing the problem of self-formation into crisis and threatening to overwhelm individuality, the pace of this change was accelerating.

Weber and Mann both strove to rescue and recover aspects of the original complex: *Bildung*–Personality–Humanity. Weber, while critical of *Bildung*, defended the centrality of personality, though he detached it from service to Humanity in order to free it for ascetic service to other values. Mann focused less on personality than on the reorientation of *Bildung* and the necessity of restoring humanity as its ultimate ideal. Thus Weber, although he opposed the degenerate and *völkisch* appropriation of personality, made the concept more independent than it had been, while Mann tried to revitalize the ideal of Humanity in conditions far removed from its birth and possible social support.

Changes in the Reality of Bildung

The Wilhelmine decades "witnessed that social amalgamation of the triad of birth, wealth, and education into the imperial elite which blended feudal social forms with bourgeois property and academic culture."[51] Central to this development was university education, by which the *Bürgertum* could acquire the status of "notable," forming an "educated stratum" (*Bildungsschicht*) in which social distinction was derived from learning rather than birth or wealth.[52] But along with the problematical transformation of *Bildung*, the German university was undergoing a structural and ideological transformation as well, with expansion in enrollments, increasing significance of the sciences and specialization, and growing dissatisfaction with the capacity of the tradition of *Bildung* to provide a pattern for self-development. As Jarausch points out, the "material" rewards and "intangible" benefits of status that derived from attending the university produced an enormous growth in enrollment, straining the university's capacity to meet the demands of so large a student body, and leading to an "institutional diversification" beyond the traditional model of the university to meet growing needs for education. The tradition of *Bildung*, which viewed higher education as an end in itself and a badge of social merit, strongly inspired these enrollments, even if the "content" of *Bildung* was not, in fact, "functionally related to modernization," or to the needs of the professional class.[53]

But the intensification and expansion of academic specialization, coupled with increasing competition from technical and commercial colleges and the transformation of the student body, threatened to undo "the philosophical synthesis of *Bildung* (cultivation) and *Wissenschaft* (scholarship) by consecrating the latter and adding professional training as central goal for the majority of students." The reduction of the university to "a training center for state officials," as well as "the fragmentation of knowledge, led to the abandonment of the central neohumanist concern of liberal education for all but a small self-motivated minority of students."[54] This was accompanied by the growing effort of the state to harness the university to its practical needs and to nationalist and antisocialist ideology. Thus, "Humboldt's initial concept of *Bildung* as liberation of the individual personality, which implied a degree of social and political emancipation, was no longer a living force in Imperial Germany. . . . The *Bildungsideal* of the liberation of man through cultivation had little effect on the social and political behavior of the majority of the *Gebildete*."[55]

In addition to the social transformation produced by large enrollments in a problematical job market and by the socialization of students through student "corporations" or fraternities,[56] increasing focus on the sciences and the intensification of specialization "heightened the tension between 'general cultivation of the spirit,' practical 'training for future teachers,' and the ultimate aim of scholarship. Increasing specialization of *Wissenschaft* . . . eroded the philosophical unity of liberal education" and transformed the traditional faculties into "a series of discrete subject areas." Although the ideological hold of the Humboldtian tradition remained strong even among scientists, reformers, arguing that classical training did not prepare students for practical life or the tasks of leadership, wanted more specialized scientific education and fought to create independent science faculties. According to Jarausch, this fragmentation of the faculty, as well as the attack on *Bildung* by scientists, led academic philosophy during the Second Empire to abandon what had once been central to it—"its claim 'of teaching a positive *Weltanschauung* '"— though the university continued to cling to "a waning scholarly-bureaucratic ethos." Indeed, by the end of the nineteenth century educational reforms had "largely jettisoned humanistic cultivation in favor of a greater mastery of a particular subject matter." But this evolution was unable to produce a new set of cultural goals to replace the older ones. In its wake was left an ethos of professional training and concern with social position and advancement that did not satisfy desires for "meaning" or aspirations for a comprehensive worldview to inspire and give direction to personal life and professional concerns. "The explosion of empirical science and the rise of positivism ruptured the self-evident unity of scholarship and moral teaching without providing new certainties." The gap was largely filled with the ideologies of nationalism, imperialist expansion, anti-Semitism, and political conformity. After 1870, political cultivation "vacillated between positivist covert and patriotic overt indoctrination," for the " 'sterilization of the idealist-humanist conception of *Bildung*' after 1870 weakened the ethical influence of liberal education on students."[57]

The danger for the tradition of *Bildung*, then, lay both in the pliability of the concept of *Bildung* itself and in the social transformation of the university and the rise of the sciences. But given the tradition of *Bildung durch Wissenschaft*, the changing nature and role of the sciences became central to the reevaluation of *Bildung* and the creation of new ideals.

THE CRISIS OF THE *WISSENSCHAFTEN*

Though the neohumanists believed the models for *Bildung* were to be found principally in antiquity and that *Bildung* could derive only from an education steeped in classical languages and literatures, *Bildung* was believed more generally to be achieved through immersion in systematic scholarship (*Wissenschaft*) broadly conceived. The branch of scholarship that was most prized varied over time, from classical philology to history.

But *Bildung* could not, like mere learning, be brought to the person from outside: it was the product of a special undertaking by the self. Indeed, according to Schnädelbach, "Humboldt's ideal of *Bildung*, to which his concepts of science and the university conform, is the image [*Bild*] of the inquiring human spirit, which brings itself to the highest insight and ethical perfection through self-activity." Ultimately, neohumanist concern with *Wissenschaft* inspired the development of an ethos of research that was eventually considered to be as essential to the university as teaching. Thus, instruction focusing on *Bildung* and fundamental research focusing on the acquisition of new knowledge were to be combined in the same persons and the same faculties.[58]

Yet to the reformers, if science were viewed merely as the accumulation of knowledge, it would be completely lost to *Bildung*. As Humboldt wrote, "Only science that derives from the inner [*das Innere*] and can be planted in the inner also forms [*bildet*] character." The university therefore had to combine "objective science" with "subjective *Bildung*."[59] One of the most important steps in the development of German education was thus achieved by tying *Bildung*—which might otherwise have become a goal striven for in private, in closed literary circles or intellectual salons—to the formal instruction provided in universities, embodied in the motto *Bildung durch Wissenschaft*. But with the advance of specialization, the construction of special research institutes, and the emergence of the ideology of science in the nineteenth century produced by enormous investment of the state and the great advances in the natural sciences, anxiety increased among *Bildung*'s devotees. They feared that teaching oriented toward *Bildung* might become separated from research, that the rise of specialist science might diminish the role and function of science as a contributor to *Bildung*, and that the enterprise of science might become so vast that individual scientific workers would find themselves diminished rather than "elevated" by their involvement in the imposing edifice of the scientific establishment.[60]

The Longing for Weltanschauungen

The consequences for the sciences of the social and ideological changes affecting Germany and the growing disillusion with *Wissenschaft* as a source of *Bildung* and life direction were of increasing concern among German scholars after the turn of the century, including Weber, whose "Science as a Vocation" was directly inspired by these issues. Ernst Troeltsch remarked after the end of World War I that, during most of the nineteenth century, it had seemed possible that "in pure questions of *Bildung*, a freely moving and always personal synthesis of the elements of culture" was attainable. But that "is all gone today: people long for obligation [*Bindung*] and unity, for dogma and law in spiritual life."[61] The older ideal of *Bildung* had permitted quite variable personal syntheses and developments, but emphasis on the perfection of individuality had been undermined by the pursuit of bonds and commitments in a social order that prized unity of the community above individuality. As Hugo von Hofmannsthal said of youth in 1927, "They want to tie themselves down to necessity. . . . For it is not freedom which they seek but obligation [*Bindung*] . . . striving for true constraint [*Zwang*]. . . . Wholeness . . . that soul and mind and the whole spirit should become one, is what is at stake today."[62]

By the time of the unification of Germany in 1871, the ideal of *Bildung durch Wissenschaft* had been seriously challenged by attacks on the importance of the classics and by the defense of more "practical" education and education in the natural sciences. After unification, with the vast expansion of enrollments and the continued prestige accorded those with a university education, *Bildung* became less an ideal than an ideological prop of the classes that could afford it. It was also an object of desire for classes aspiring to the security they hoped would come from the achievement of bureaucratic careers, for which such an education was a prerequisite.[63] In the midst of shifting cultural ideals and powerful social forces of modernization, the "stiffness and specialization of the academic disciplines" led to the conviction that these disciplines no longer offered any ideal of cultivation, compared with the older promises of *Bildung*. Those motivated by the emergent desire and apparently urgent search for *Weltanschauungen* went unsatisfied.[64] As Friedrich Paulsen observed, "*Wissenschaft* does not satisfy the hunger for knowledge; nor does it fulfill the demand for personal cultivation; it requires the staking of one's last strength, and rewards with meager fruits. The feeling of such disappointment is widespread."[65]

In Wilhelmine society—internally contradictory, with unparalleled industrial expansion linked to a neofeudal social and political order, and a concern with culture linked to a driving desire to expand the frontiers of science and apply the results to practical industrial and military problems—there was a pervasive feeling that clear and unequivocal responses to social dilemmas were difficult to develop and meaningful personal ideals hard to find. Though many rejected the Wilhelmine establishment and prevailing social and personal ideals, there was confusion about which alternative and positive policies to pursue or *Weltanschauungen* to follow.[66] Dilthey characterized the period after 1880 as an "anarchy of *Weltanschauungen*," "without foundation" (*bodenlos*), whose old certainties of religion, philosophy, and social ideals had been weakened. Given, on the one hand, the new challenges posed by the sciences and, on the other, the critiques of scientific positivism, conviction about the possibility and value of knowledge was waning. "There has arisen recently a subjective, limitless vortex of emotions. Every day more books appear which promise salvation through a subjective view of the world based upon some kind of introspection or self-immersion of the subject in itself. Everywhere the conviction is growing that objective, methodical knowledge is impossible."[67]

Paulsen, a colleague and friend of Dilthey's, expressed similar sentiments. "Everyone now works harder than ever before, but the inner necessity and rationale of the enterprise is not there; one has the feeling that the result for inner, personal life does not correspond to the expenditure of energy."[68] Disappointment was not confined to the natural and biological sciences, but extended to all branches of *Wissenschaft*, including the most hallowed branch, history. Karl Joel, sounding like the early Thomas Mann, wrote in 1911: "We stand at the present with all this hoary experience and youthful decay, but we do not know what to do. We understand every tendency of thought and are eclectic from sheer abundance of learning. We no longer endure any tendency—we are thoroughly skeptical and critical. But such skepticism threatens to rob us of even the last legacy left by the nineteenth century: the sense of history."[69]

Although it was only around 1919–20 that German academics began to speak explicitly of a "crisis" of the sciences,[70] the last decades of the nineteenth century, with their doubts about the adequacy of *Bildung*, announced the coming of this crisis in every way short of open statement, among both professional academics and their students. This crisis was clearly one of character formation, of *Bildung*, and indeed of culture generally. Simmel provides a particularly pointed language for expressing the crisis. In the development of modern culture, he writes, there is a "preponderance of what one may call the 'objective spirit' over the 'subjective spirit.' " That is, there is a disproportion between the culture embodied in things and cultural artifacts, on the one hand—in what Weber and Rickert call "cultural goods"—and the cultural progress and capacities of the individual, on the other.

> This discrepancy results essentially from the growing division of labor. For the division of labor demands from the individual an ever more one-sided accomplishment, and the greatest advance in a one-sided pursuit only too frequently means dearth to the personality of the individual. In any case, he can cope less and less with the overgrowth of objective culture. . . . The individual has

become a mere cog in an enormous organization of things and powers which tear from his hands all progress, spirituality, and value in order to transform them from their subjective form into the form of a purely objective life.[71]

Thus the individual is overwhelmed by the size and weight of culture or objective spirit, robbed of the power to appropriate its contents for himself. Further, the individual is depleted through the expropriation by society of the individual's formative capacities and achievements, or "subjective spirit," in order to build the externalized edifice of culture, or "objective spirit." The parallels with Marx's theory of alienation and exploitation, imported into the realm of the "creative individual," intellectual, or spiritual worker, are quite clear.

Yet Simmel paradoxically concludes from his analysis that, to deal with the dilemma of the "atrophy of individual culture" brought about "through the hypertrophy of objective culture," the individual must strive for "the utmost in uniqueness and particularization."[72] "The individual's urge toward self-perfection ... may also be an objective ideal whose goal is ... a supra-personal value realized in the personality."[73] This ideal requires going beyond the extremes of both egoism and mere self-absorption, on the one hand, and concern with the welfare of the "Thou" and of society, on the other, to embrace the "third alternative," embodied "most impressively perhaps in the figures of Goethe and Nietzsche": the possibility "that the perfection of the individual as such constitutes an objective value," rather than being only an expression of "subjective" spirit or value, and that it should be valued as such "irrespective of its significance for any other individuals."

> This value, moreover, may exist in utter disregard for the happiness or unhappiness of this individual himself, or may even be in conflict with them. What a person represents in terms of strength, nobility of character, achievement, or harmony of life, is very often quite unrelated to what he or others "get out" of these qualities. All that can be said about them is that the world is enriched by the existence in it of a valuable human being who is perfect in himself.[74]

This is in fact an argument for the renewal of *Bildung*, using Goethe and Nietzsche as models, yet it is an impossible task in the social setting Simmel describes, as he himself seems to realize. First, Goethe and Nietzsche are such rare and superior individuals that it is hard to use them to justify the efforts of normal persons. Second, drawing on a language similar to Weber's, Simmel reverts to saying that this struggle for self-perfection actually requires an absolutist commitment to a "cause." "The acting individual feels himself to be only the object or executor—who at bottom is accidental—of the task his cause puts to him. The passion for this cause is as little concerned with the I, Thou, or society as the value of the state of the world can be measured in terms of the world's pleasure or suffering." Thus, to transcend the pressures of society and find a realm for strength and personal development, one must put aside one's own willing and become the agent of a "higher" power, as Simmel believes Goethe and Nietzsche were. But, says Simmel, society is not interested even in this form of self-perfection, except insofar as it furthers social purposes. It cares more for the socially usable—the specialized, we might say—than for the content of this effort. "Society claims the individual for itself. It wants to make of him a form that it can incorporate into its own structure."[75]

As Ringer points out, in the circumstances and conditions Simmel describes it could only become more and more difficult "to attain the personal, 'subjective' synthesis of 'cultivation.' "[76] This difficulty casts doubt on the viability of the project of "self-completion" through *Bildung* in a culture overwhelmed by "civilization" and its artifacts and by the imposing structure of society and its needs. The advance of civilization and the proliferation of its products—normally identified with progress—have become too differentiated and vast for one to absorb or appreciate fully. Further, the individual's efforts toward self-perfection come up against the wall of social pressure and negative valuation: "the individual's striving for wholeness appears as egoism," even though "the very quest of society is an egoism that does violence to the individual for the benefit and utility of the many."[77] These contradictions, coupled with enforced specialization, put an enormous burden on the individual, especially one accustomed by desire and tradition to seeing *Bildung* and character development, as well as guidance for *Weltanschauungen*, rooted in immersion in scholarship and knowledge. The discrepancy between historically rooted expectations and presently given realities is the problem. Since these new conditions were the product of the advance of rationalization and the sciences in all their forms, the question of the nature and value of science must be posed directly.

The Question of the Sciences

The crisis of the sciences as experienced in the early part of the century was actually a crisis in the relationship of society and the individual *to* the sciences and to their worth and significance, a crisis of faith in the sciences stemming from questions about what would, at a much later time, be called their "relevance." The crisis *of* the sciences, then, must be distinguished from the crisis *in* the sciences, though they are related. The crisis in the sciences—that is, in the methodology, technique, and possibility of scientific knowledge—was becoming an issue at the same time as the crisis of the sciences, though for different reasons. As Heidegger put it in 1925:

> One speaks today in a double sense of a crisis of the sciences: formerly, inasmuch as contemporary man—and above all the young—believes himself to have lost an original relationship to the sciences. If one recalls the discussion that followed the lecture of *Max Weber*, one is indeed doubtful of the sciences and their meaning; one considers the standpoint of *Max Weber* as doubtfulness and helplessness; one wants to give a meaning again to science and to scientific work and attempts it in that one builds a *Weltanschauung* upon it and from there on constructs a mythical conception of science.

Although he respects the importance of this sense of the crisis, Heidegger casts doubt on the possibility of a straightforward resolution and considers the construction of *Weltanschauungen* based on the sciences to be nothing short of the creation of mythical meaning. Seeing hope for deriving "meaning" from the sciences to be fruitless, Heidegger, like Husserl before him, set aside the social crisis and focused on the second sense of the crisis, the philosophical one, as the most important and only authentic one: "The real crisis is the one in the sciences themselves."[78] Later discussions of the sciences in the 1920s—of their weaknesses, limitations, and crisis—also focused on Weber's views as a crucial and much-disputed position on the question.[79] Although Weber claimed that the root of both crises lay in the advance of rationalization, and although he believed he could deal with the crisis *in* the sciences, he held out no more hope than Heidegger for a "traditional" resolution to the problem *of* the sciences.

Around 1890, and continuing well into the Weimar period, German academics began to express the feeling that their intellectual traditions were declining in vitality, losing meaning and relevance both for the life of the nation and for the times, all of which added up to a crisis of culture. Many resented the extension of education to masses of students, who, they thought, lacked idealism and were oriented only to practicality. But many also believed that increasing specialization and the internal evolution of the *Wissenschaften* had led to neglect of the issues essential to genuine education, to a lack of "vital" *Weltanschauungen* among both themselves and their students, and to a loss of "connectedness of learned work with the . . . personal life of the individual." Though initially fascinating in the first half of the nineteenth century, the achievements of specialization had become less and less attractive to many circles as they threatened to replace all other educational and cultural interests and ideals. Agreement regarding any larger purposes of scholarly inquiry had vanished, replaced mainly by questions of technique and method in a university that was seen more and more as a professional training ground for career seekers. What had formerly been "the metaphysical totality of learning" had evolved, or perhaps degenerated, into a "sum of specialized disciplines."[80]

The crisis was accompanied by a public and widespread longing for "synthesis," for the integration of knowledge, as exemplified by the idealist revival around the turn of the century that opposed the empiricism and positivism of the time. This revival took different forms, all the while reflecting what Ringer calls the desire for "a spiritual revival, a reactivation" of the professoriate's "own moral leadership." A number of efforts were made at practical educational reform, often based, as in former times, on a view of education as " 'the intellectual and spiritual formation of the personality toward ethical freedom' " and " 'the cultivation of individuality, an elevation toward personality.' " Such efforts were intended to shape the curriculum to satisfy the historically conditioned and "profound yearning for the restoration of an idealistic *Weltanschauung*." They were also intended to show the interconnectedness of knowledge and to guide students to a "consciousness of values" and an "integral *Weltanschauung*." But at the same time, and consistent with Germany's national and imperial aspirations, they were meant to generate attitudes of civic loyalty.[81] These efforts at reform were prompted by the crisis of *Wissenschaft* and by the blame affixed to scientism and positivism for the defeat both of idealism as an academic philosophy and of neohumanist goals. Reformers strove to overcome these crises through institutional transformation.

The crisis of *Wissenschaft* was often described in terms of science's inability or failure to yield *Weltanschauungen* or spiritual orientations owing to its extreme specialization, or in terms of its failure to produce the "effect" of *Bildung*. That is, science failed to shape the self into the rounded, culture-absorbing personality capable of generating its own *Weltanschauungen* that was so prized by humanists since Humboldt. As Ringer says, the "real difficulty with specialization was taken to be its tendency to separate science and scholarship from a certain kind of integral philosophy. Specialized science lacked precisely the dimension that had connected idealistic *Wissenschaft* with *Bildung* and with *Welt-*

anschauung." To counter this tendency, academics and students put forth "a demand for wisdom, for reflection about ends, for the knowledge of the sage, the prophet, or the harmoniously cultivated man."[82] The theologian Adolf von Harnack suggested, perhaps predictably for a theologian, that "modern science has not emerged as the steward of life in the highest sense and has not given any great inner elevating impulse to life."[83] But theologian or no, he expressed the conviction of many. Paulsen, the great historian of the university, put it this way:

> Scientific research does not seem to accomplish what was promised of it: a comprehensive and completely assured *Weltanschauung* and a life wisdom secured in necessary ideas. Such things were given to earlier generations by religion or theology. In its place there came philosophy as its heir in the eighteenth century. . . . Then a new generation . . . turned toward science: exact research was to assure us the ground under our feet and give us a faithful picture of the world. But science does not achieve this. . . . It does not lead to a worldview that encompasses the whole and satisfies imagination and soul.[84]

It is not surprising that hopes for a replacement for religion and philosophy could not be met by science, at least in this form. Still, academic reformers hoped to find a way back to *Bildung*, but this time by going around science. The pedagogical reformer Alfred Vierkandt was a representative of this approach.

> We are experiencing a new need for unity, a synthetic tendency in all the world of learning—a type of thinking which primarily emphasizes the . . . concepts of value, purpose, and goal, rather than that of causality. . . . [Education] must create conscious ethical convictions, conscious sympathy for duties and values. . . . It must have among its objectives a conscious . . . *Weltanschauung* of an idealistic nature.[85]

Specialized *Wissenschaft* could not meet these needs, but neither could any other potential source of cultural renewal. These needs were finally satisfied, in a destructive form, by political means.

Long before the war, Troeltsch wrote in 1921, "a full revolution took place . . . in the area of the spirit and of *Wissenschaft*," in the midst of the overdevelopment of cultural life and of the "solidification and specialization of the academic sciences, which no longer presented an ideal of *Bildung*." This revolution ultimately meant a turn away from inward and impersonal ideals and toward personal masters, the "submission [*Hingabe*] to strong personalities, . . . the desire for a new personal leadership [*Führertum*] and a new connection of science with life." It meant further "a complete upheaval, growing from within, of scientific thought and of the ideal of *Bildung* itself. Away with naturalism and with the intellectualism that is virtually identical with it, but also away with historicism and with the specialization and relativism of the ossified academic knowledge industry, which is identical with historicism: these are the best-known slogans."[86]

Those clamoring for such a turn were impelled by a "thirst for unity of *Weltanschauung* and for unity of a living law [*Gesetz*]." This impatience with science and the search for a higher unity and direction, Troeltsch observed, was no temporary dissatisfaction with an otherwise trustworthy intellectual inheritance, nor was it a mere concern for the problem of the sciences in themselves. It was a symptom of something greater and more ominous, a major revolt against a whole tradition of Western culture, a revolt that had begun in the nineteenth century and was continuing in the 1920s when Troeltsch wrote. "For the 'revolution of science' is in truth the beginning of the great world reaction against the democratic and socialist enlightenment, against the rational self-mastery of reason that organizes unrestrained existence and the therewith presupposed dogma of the equality and sensibleness of humankind."[87] The contemporary need for "synthesis, system, *Weltanschauung*, organization, and value judgment," he noted, "is extraordinary." And it is "not just a problem of *Wissenschaft*, but a practical problem of life."[88]

While the German professoriate was having its crisis over status, the value and meaning of its teaching, and the role of specialization and the sciences, a parallel development was occurring among German youth. Affected not only by large enrollments and the usual struggle for status and security in German society, the young generation was the real audience for higher education and education's failing traditions and conflicting purposes. It was the young who questioned intensely the significance of *Bildung*, university education generally, the sciences, and all those traditions of meaning and purpose upheld hitherto, and they questioned them even more intensely under the pressure of war. Some efforts at school reform were motivated by, and even aimed directly at, the need and desire of youth to escape from the pursuit of mere "knowledge" in order to "live through" or "experience" (*erleben*) real "values" within the social and cultural world.[89]

The concept of *Erlebnis*, which emerged in the discourse of the youth movement after the turn of the century, denotes the content of an intense "experience." Concern with it was part of youthful protest against the estranging character of modern industrial society, against the dominance of "objective spirit" and the marginalization of "subjective spirit." As a concept it first gained academic currency in the 1870s, derived from the word *Erleben*, which means living through an experience and which, as is clear from its root, is centered on *Leben* or "life" and the desire to be involved in it, to be closer to it, to seek out its essence, to experience it deeply. These yearnings were enunciated in *Lebensphilosophie*, as Gadamer suggests:

> Schleiermacher's appeal to living feeling against the cold rationalism of the enlightenment, Schiller's call for aesthetic freedom against mechanistic society, Hegel's contrasting of life (later, of spirit) with "positivity," were the forerunners of the protest against modern industrial society which at the beginning of our century caused the words *Erlebnis* and *Erleben* to become almost sacred clarion calls. The rebellion of the Jugend Bewegung (Youth Movement) against bourgeois culture and its forms was inspired by these ideas, the influence of Friedrich Nietzsche and Henri Bergson played its part, but also a "spiritual movement" like that around Stefan George and, not least, the seismographical accuracy with which the philosophy of Georg Simmel reacted to these events are all part of the same thing.[90]

For some time, Wilhelm Windelband noted in 1910, "a hunger for *Weltanschauung*" and "the longing of the time for a comprehensive meaning for all of reality" had attracted youth much more than university study had, and it had also begun to attract some academics. This yearning led them to alternatives to the specialized scholarly disciplines, or to earlier philosophers—no longer to Kant, Windelband lamented, but to the "romantic idealists" Fichte, Schelling, and Hegel. Moreover, he remarked, one could observe a significant turning away from interest in reason and the rational toward an interest in the irrational as the "underground" of living. "Once again the irrational is announced as the holy secret of all reality, as the fount of life lying beyond all knowledge."[91]

Profoundly dissatisfied with academic life and the imperatives of Wilhelmine society prior to World War I, students and the young, intellectual and nonintellectual, organized and independent, moved to compensate for what was missing from modern life and their experience of it—into political activity in generally conservative causes, into "back to nature" movements, and into religion and the life of the churches. Progressive university students too, represented by groups like the Freistudentische Bund (Independent Student Union), a left-liberal student group whose Munich branch later organized the lecture series in which Weber delivered "Science as a Vocation," criticized the universities for their narrow specialization and separation from the needs of everyday life. They pressed for a restoration of *Bildung* "in order to shape the character of academic youth" and to turn the universities, through study and other means, into a "school for life."[92] Other students, finding their needs unmet by the organized academic disciplines and confronting increasing bureaucratization in the university, turned to the student life of "corporations"—the drinking and dueling fraternities. They either slid into political apathy or turned to agitation for national and imperialist goals and against progressive university policies. As Jarausch remarks, borrowing the terminology of Fritz Stern, "Corporate character building reinforced those strains of formal instruction and of adult politics that tended toward academic illiberalism."[93]

Some young people, often overlapping with university as well as nonuniversity students, both progressive and unprogressive, became part of the "youth movement," known collectively as the *Wandervogel*. The aspirations of this movement were initially toward simple escape into nature from the confining strictures of urban industrial civilization, but its members soon became concerned with how to become "integrated" human beings, both personally and within society. Yet according to Walter Laqueur, the youth movement was mostly an "unpolitical form of opposition to a civilization that had little to offer the young generation, a protest against its lack of vitality, warmth, emotion, and ideals."[94] The *Wandervogel* was one example of numerous movements of opposition, rejection, or distancing from social and cultural life that appeared in Wilhelmine Germany amid the "disenchantment" of the world through science and rationalism, the stresses of authoritarian, imperialist, and industrializing society, and the loss of stable and accepted patterns of personal development and social order. As Troeltsch observes:

> It is the revulsion against drill and discipline, against the ideology of success and power, against the excess and the superficiality of the knowledge which is stuffed into us by the schools, against intellectualism and literary self-importance, against the big metropolis and the unnatural, against materialism and skepticism, against the rule of money and prestige, against specialization and bossism, against the suffocating mass of tradition and the evolutionary concept of historism.[95]

Protest was everywhere, as much among radical expressionists as within the youth movement, as much in the work of Mann as in that of the more radical heirs of Nietzsche, all obsessed with "life," youth, feeling, "experience," and the desire to escape what they saw as an overly cerebral existence and the inhibiting and disenchanting consequences of intellect and the obsession with learning.[96] As Wolfgang Sauer remarks, the "intellectual movements of the early 1900s, not excepting that of the *völkisch* Right and the youth movement, rose clearly in revolt against Wilhelmine society." Indeed, these movements were at the same time highly diffuse and often unfocused, for in imperial Germany there was "simply no position from which opposition could be at once clear, coherent, and practical. Seen in this perspective, the *Wandervogel* solution of abandoning rational thought and withdrawing into the woods seems a little less puzzling."[97]

Intellectuals, academics, and students were thus beset by the consequences of the transformed social and political conditions of German life. The effect of these conditions on cultural traditions, educational goals, and ideals induced feelings of weakness and helplessness and undermined a sure sense of purpose or collective identity, close identification with the ideals of their class, and a clear path to personal meaning. Whether youth responded with nationalistic and authoritarian sentiments or not, the outbreak of war finally provided the sense of duty and purpose they could find nowhere else, just as the youth of the rest of Europe responded likewise to the drift of their lives.[98]

3 Rationalization, Identity, and Death

Weber suggests that the traditional notion that *Bildung* could be effected through the study of *Wissenschaft* led to the expectation that modern university disciplines should contribute to shaping individuals for a life of meaning, purpose, and action in accordance with ideals. But the evolution of the disciplines toward greater specialization and distance from this task has left a gap between youth and its desires, on the one hand, and science and its capacities, on the other.[1] In any case, *Bildung durch Wissenschaft* was a mode of self-*development* rather than of self-*mastery*, and thus, in Weber's view, even in the best of circumstances it could not be a spur to the form of activity, action, and conquest required for the rationalized world. The question is whether it is possible for specialized education to be combined with education for self-mastery and action, even if in some way other than the educational tradition prescribed.[2]

Weber's critique of *Bildung* is based on his argument for the need for empowerment in the period of rationalization, and he situates the significance of rationalization and specialization for meaning and character building within systems of education generally.[3] According to Weber, there are two opposite types of educational goals: to awaken charisma, in the sense of heroic qualities or magical gifts; and to supply specialist training (*Fachschulung*). The first is typical of charismatic structures of domination, the second of rational and modern bureaucratic ones. Yet one can neither teach nor train for charisma, but only strive to awaken (*wecken*) and prove the existence of "gifts," which, if they are to be awakened, must already be present in exceptional individuals, though latent, in the form of a "purely personal gift of grace." If they are latent, they can be awakened only through what Weber calls a "rebirth of the whole personality." Specialty training (*Facherziehung*), in contrast, strives to train (*abrichten*) the individual for practical usefulness in technical and administrative tasks and is in principle achievable by everyone. Between the poles lie the types of education (*Erziehung*) that aim at "*cultivating* the pupil for a *life conduct* characteristic of a status group."

Cultivation involves the transformation of a person's basic attitudes and personal conduct, and includes the ideal of *Bildung*.[4]

In Weber's view, contemporary debate focuses almost exclusively on only two modes, specialization versus cultivation:

> Behind all the present discussions about the foundations of the educational system [*Bildungswesen*], there is involved in every decisive place the struggle of the type of the "specialist man" against the old "cultured humanity," subject to the incessant spreading of the bureaucratization of all public and private relations of domination and to the steadily increasing significance of specialized knowledge, entering into all the most intimate questions of culture.[5]

Cultivation strives to educate for a "certain inner and outer conduct of life" according to the cultural ideal of a particular stratum. In principle, everyone can be educated in this way, and only the goal differs among different strata. Thus, warrior strata educate individuals to be courtiers or knights, priestly strata to be intellectuals or scribes, and so forth.[6] Cultivation was the educational goal in feudal, theocratic, and patrimonial structures of domination, also in English administration by notables, Chinese patrimonial bureaucracy, and even under the rule of demagogues in Greek democracy. It sometimes aimed at a knightly type, as in feudal Europe, or an ascetic type, as in priestly education, or a literary type, as in China, or a gymnastic-musical type, as in ancient Greece, or the type of the gentleman, as in England. The ideal of the "*cultivated personality*" distinguished the members of a ruling stratum, within a given structure of domination, by their possession of a "cultural quality" rather than specialized knowledge. Since military, theological, and legal expertise was cultivated at the same time, however, specialized knowledge was demanded along with cultivation. Still, the focus of such education was never primarily on its "useful" elements.[7]

In Germany humanist cultivation had been the traditional prerequisite for official careers in the civil or military administration. It had also been the sign that its possessor belonged to a cultured status group, the *Bildungsbürgertum*. Yet in common with the Occident generally, this educational qualification was usually linked to "rational *specialist* training" (*rationale Fachabrichtung*), and such training, in Weber's view, had begun to displace, or at least challenge, qualification in terms of status. Indeed, the German humanist gymnasium, the home of classically oriented education for cultivation, is increasingly defended, Weber says, by stressing its non-character-related significance and the practical value of formal education through the study of antiquity. In such a system increasingly dominated by specialized training (*wesentlich fachmässige Abrichtung*), there are few domains—most notably, military barracks and student corporations—where anything resembling the old ascetic means for awakening and testing charismatic qualities can still find a place.[8] This may account for the increasingly important role of the German student fraternities.

Weber characterizes the two goals of German education as "the moulding of human beings [*Menschen zu prägen*] to propagate political, ethical, artistic, cultural or other conviction [*Gesinnung*]" and "*specialized* schooling developed by qualified *specialists*," what Weber calls specialized *Bildung*. Though he insists that one cannot determine the task of education "scientifically," Weber regularly and strongly advocates the second goal, since specialist education specifically avoids making the "ultimate, highest personal decisions" or creating *Weltanschauungen* for students. It can no longer be assumed, he implies—indeed, it must be forcefully rejected—that the "forming" (*Bildung*) of the character of human beings can be carried out by the specialized discipline of science, nor is it acceptable that teachers exercise undue influence over students' choices or values, preventing the confrontation of the student with his or her own conscience and making it seem that specialized education *can* provide standards for making the "ultimate highest personal life decisions." Specialist education, rather, must try to educate students to "intellectual integrity" while contributing to "general education in thinking," self-discipline, and an "ethical attitude" (*sittliche Einstellung*).[9] It requires self-restraint from teachers and aims to create autonomous students by "serving" them through knowledge, while recognizing the epistemological limits of what science can provide.

The "collapse" of *Bildung* lies behind not only Weber's strictures about the tasks and limits of education, but also his prescriptions for the broad regeneration of German culture and politics. Yet his prescriptions derive as well from his analysis of rationalization. In fact, rationalization in the form of modern science played a principal role in undermining the ideal of *Bildung*. In Weber's view, Occidental rationalization, bound up as it was with the development of science, had created the crises of both Occidental culture in general and German culture in particular.[10] In fact, the Occident's most unique feature, he concluded, was the extent and development of rationalization in every sphere of cultural life.[11] Rationalization was the most fateful force in the destiny and future not just of the Occident but of the whole world, far more fateful than capitalism or class struggle.

Weber analyzed the disempowering effect of rationalization and the possibility for a regeneration of inner power principally in his 1917 lecture "Science as a Vocation."[12] He addressed himself there to the problem of meaning and loss of power that the self faced in rationalized society, arguing, first, for the necessity of the discipline of the calling as a new tool of self-mastery and, second, for a "deification" of values to give the tamed self meaning through a "mission." Confronted with the advance of rationalization and the wish for *Wissenschaft* to reveal ultimate truths, Weber limited the authority of science as a source of truth in the context of a culture whose fundamental ideals could no longer be justified either by religious belief or through widely accepted social and cultural ideals and purposes. Science had to become a *tool* of the self, rather than a means to the self's flowering. Weber advances this proposal against the wishes for direction and belonging, for submersion and immersion of the self that he saw in his contemporaries' search for *Weltanschauungen* as an expression of "true" personality: such impulses could not motivate or equip the self for the actions required in the modern world. For such action, power must come from within, even if that power implies dependence on an impersonal ideal "external" to the self. It is a power that must be exercised first over the self, then over science and every other tool, to be used by the self to gain power over the spheres of the rationalized world. But in making a revised version of the Puritan concept of calling the central practice of the self for rationalized society, Weber went even further.

In *Economy and Society* Weber had defined the modern calling (*Beruf*) as an occupation or profession, as "that specification, specialization, and combination of performances of a person, which for him are the foundation of a continuous opportunity for income or earnings."[13] But in explaining the calling for science, Weber laid out a whole "technology" for the shaping of the self. The consequences of this discipline would be not only the production of income, but also the creation of personal meaning and the generation of enhanced power for the mastery of a self that threatened to be wayward and of a world whose rational orders threatened to overwhelm their creators. Thus Weber recovered the older discipline of the calling from a modern discourse that had separated it from its earlier content and had adjusted it to the demands of a secular industrial work force.

Weber claims that since the true scientist knows that science gives no direct answers to questions about "meaning," he practices science, "if it is to be a 'calling,' 'for its own sake.' "[14] But Weber's arguments imply something more radical, for, in his work, science as a vocation is *not* really done for its own sake, the sake of an impersonal object, but for the sake of the very personal redemption of the self from meaninglessness and powerlessness. In effect, what Weber proposes is that the individual give the goals of science so great an importance that living in its service becomes a way of life no longer obliged to give answers: *it will be an answer* to the question of meaning. With the goals of science made into "gods," the self is now engaged in a "mission," is freed of questions about meaning, and is rescued from mere routine and oriented toward innovation, capable of being empowered to carry out the tasks of its "god."

To Weber the practice of science is a symbol and ideal type of all rational disenchanted life-activity, which requires an ethos that can transform selves into adventurers and risk takers, not mere placeholders. Stripped of the justifying sources of meaning and the older contexts it had in the past, science—and, by implication, all life governed by rationalization—can become meaningful and an arena for empowered selves, in Weber's view, if it is lived in "service" of or "subjection" to a "higher cause," in this case the "high cause" of science within the discipline of the calling. Instead of *leading* to the higher truth, goodness, or a desired object of meaning—no longer possible in the modern situation—*science itself* becomes a sanctified object of mysterious devotion and passionate service, of life in a calling. The calling—and its object, now understood as its "master"—now bears, in an individualistic way, a burden of meaning formerly borne collectively by society and religion. Thus Weber produces a nonsociological account of individual meaning-formation, setting aside tradition and social patterns, practices, and associations as sources, to rely only on religion and its secular substitutes in an individualistic solution to the problem. In the bondage of Weber's call to vocation, all questions of meaninglessness are ended, and the self is empowered through service.

Weber proposes the calling as a solution to the problems of meaning in all spheres of activity and to the problem of mastering rationalization: to Weber, the right understanding and practice of the calling is meaning-giving and empowering for the "spiritual aristocracy," the "virtuosos" capable of bearing its discipline and its demands. But Weber's proposals inevitably lead him to divide the world of values into "gods" and "devils" in Manichaean fashion, and because his conception of service in a calling is based on a model of soldiers in war, he leaves society in a condition of spiritual combat with little capacity for mediation or communities of purpose. His solutions, meant to confront the loss of meaning and power in rationalized life, instead fill the world with gods—each fighting for supremacy through its "agents," the called individuals—and they fortify individuals, but only as soldiers of their faith. Believing that he is challenging the threat to freedom and dynamism that rationalization presents, Weber misses the threat posed to the individual and society by his own solution.

RATIONALIZATION, SOCIAL CRISIS, AND DEATH

Rationalization

Weber conceives the humanly meaningful world as divided into separate "spheres" of human activity more or less delimitable as politics, economics, religion, aesthetics, sexuality, law, science, and so forth. Their "contents," the objects striven after and created within these spheres, Weber calls "cultural goods."[15] Naturally, the spheres change over time, as does our understanding of them. Indeed, this schema—which separates, if it does not isolate, human activities from one another—is itself a product of specifically modern social development and theory, determined by the advance of capitalism, modern science, and the modern state. The ways in which modern experience and self-understanding are radically different from earlier periods is what leads Weber to develop his notion of Occidental rationalization.

Weber suggests that rationalization is responsible for the evolution and development of the spheres into their present form, and in his analysis of the rationalization of these spheres he reveals the tasks to be undertaken to master a resistant world, deprived of its earlier forms of power.[16] We can call "local rationalization" the process, in a particular sphere of human activity, of "theoretical mastery" of the activity through development of "increasingly precise abstract concepts," which in turn affects the contents of the sphere or the relations of persons to it. Of course, this process leads beyond theoretical mastery to practical consequences and effects, indeed, to "technological" power and capability, to "the methodical achievement of a specific given practical goal through more precise calculation of the adequate means."[17] But though local rationalization proceeds at different paces in different spheres, Weber understands it as an aspect of a larger process that includes all local areas, what we can call "global" or "universal rationalization," which denotes the "increasing systematization and rationalization of community relationships and their contents" on a larger scale and throughout society.[18]

In Weber's terms, local rationalization means that the objects or goals of a sphere of activity are made the focus of purposeful, systematic, and increasingly "conscious" pursuit, with knowledge mobilized to make their realization more certain and deliberate. Weber describes this process as "sublimation through knowledge," that is, increasing mastery of activity and refinement of the means proper to it through the conscious mastery of the "logic" of a particular sphere, its nature and processes. Indeed, as a consequence of this pursuit humankind is led to the discovery and systematization of the logic and "laws" Weber presumes each sphere of human activity follows, understood in its purest form, though in practice a specific sphere may not have been "rationalized and sublimated according to its inherent lawfulness" to a very great degree.[19]

To Weber, humankind under the influence of rationalization thus increasingly conceives its activities as potentially and actually "autonomous" and separate. It strips them of religious, ethical, and "material" or "substantive" content and insulates them against substantive imperatives directed at controlling them. Thus questions of "technique" and method become more and more the object of reflection for practitioners within these spheres. For example, politics sheds ethical or welfare purposes as its principal goal and comes to be understood and mastered purely in terms of what Weber calls the "factual pragmatism of 'reason of state,'" whose outcomes are determined by the impersonal "logic of power relationships" alone. Economics is stripped of all regulation by ethical codes and is treated in terms of strict impersonal calculation according to the market. Science, rejecting "in principle" every attempt to ask for a "meaning" for events that happen in the world, turns the world into a "mechanism deprived of god," a "cosmos ruled by impersonal rules." And so on.[20] Weber puts it succinctly, if opaquely, this way:

> The rationalization and conscious sublimation of the relationships of human beings to the various spheres of cultural goods [*Güterbesitze*], external and internal, religious and secular, pushes toward making *conscious: inner inherent lawfulnesses* [*innere Eigengesetzlichkeiten*] of the individual spheres in their consequence. . . . This is a quite general . . . consequence of the development of the (inner- and other-worldly) cultural goods into [objects that are] rationally and consciously striven for, sublimated through *knowledge*.[21]

Rationalization, in Weber's view, thus brings independence of the spheres of activity from one another and from ethical and "material" control. It brings a recognition of their autonomy—their "inner inherent lawfulness" in which, so to speak, they give laws to themselves—but also of their potential conflict with one another and possible irreconcilability. Each activity becomes more "technical" as the "laws" of its domain become the central object of attention and manipulation and as each activity is freed from ethical, religious, or metaphysical values that had once affected or directed it. These spheres come into conflict with religion, for example, as "they" struggle to be independent of ethically oriented forces. But "they" also resist attempts, even from secular powers, to impose an overarching value on their domain, for, by the logic of the sphere as seen from within, such external values would undermine or interfere with the "laws" that govern them in an "ideal typical" sense and that alone, "they" believe, make possible any rationally pursued success.[22] But it is just this resistance to substantive or material imposition of an ethic or higher value that is at the heart of the threat to human power and meaning presented by rationalization.

In the political realm, for example, the "rational rules of the modern order of power" dictate action.[23] Modern politics must be oriented toward impersonal reasons of state, pragmatism, and maintaining or overturning the distribution of power within or outside the state. Ethical questions of who is "right" have nothing to do with success in politics, Weber maintains, for success is determined only by "relations of power."[24] Thus for practical reasons, and because of its "impersonality," politics resists subjection to "substantive ethical standards" (*materiale Ethisierung*).[25] Rationalization has also been a force in the historical evolution of administration, from the personal staff of princes to bureaucracies with division of function, hierarchy, and command. Thus, rationalization is a two-sided process in politics: politics has come to be oriented toward considerations of power only, in the sense of *raison d'état*, and its administration is oriented toward calculation and the execution of commands, functioning through an elaborate bureaucratic machinery. For Weber, the danger to politics comes when the rational apparatus comes to believe itself capable of guiding a state through calculation alone, leading it to supplant, for one reason or another, the creation of independent leadership, which turns out to be of supreme importance even for a politics ruled by *Staatsraison*.

The domain of the economic realm, the market, is governed by "calculable rules" and functions "without regard for person."[26] "Rational economy is objective [*sachlicher*] enterprise. It is oriented to *money* prices, which originate in the interest struggle of men among one another in the *market*." It is not possible to regulate an economy that has become "impersonal" in such a way according to any ethical norms, because that economy, to maximize efficiency, must follow "its own immanent inherent lawfulness."[27] Just as politics aims at success in terms of relations of power, economic action aims at success in terms of maximized efficiency. Yet despite being an apparently formal standard, this has "substantive"—though not "ethical"—implications, because it defines and then excludes regulatory norms as external, extraneous, and intrusive. But, according to Weber, *impersonal* relations cannot be regulated by ethical rules that originated for the purpose of controlling—and are applicable only to—*personal* relations and dealings. The impersonality of the domination of capital, for example, appears so "indirect" that one cannot "seize hold of a real 'master' " of whom to make ethical demands. Though "masterless slavery" may be ethically questionable, Weber here agrees with Marx that it is not possible to criticize ethically the conformity of individuals to its demands, since such demands are set by purely "objective situations" to which all must conform or else go under.[28] Ignoring impersonality "brings economic failure, and in the long run, economic downfall."[29] Thus, "the formal lawfulness of the capitalist economy is oriented strictly towards commodities [*Tauschgüter*] and only to these. . . . The community of the market is the most impersonal practical relation of life into which humans can enter with one another," because it "knows only regard for the thing, no regard for the person." Thus, it is the realm of "absolute *objectification* [*Versachlichung*]." Indeed, "the creation of social relationships [*Vergesellschaftung*] through exchange in the *market*" is the archetype of all rational social action of whatever kind.[30]

Still, the economic realm too needs "leaders," in the form of entrepreneurs who can take appropriate risks, provide vision, and exercise skills of command. As in the political realm, formal administrative considerations alone may come to dominate economic decision making and investment, leaving little room for the vitality, inspiration, and innovation necessary for real economic strength and expansion. Thus something other than purely formal concerns *must* enter into the actions of the entrepreneur in the economic realm and the leader in the political one. Whatever standards of success may apply, they do so only on behalf of goals and objects that do not originate *within* the bureaucratically structured realms themselves.

Even so, for Weber, in both the modern political and economic apparatus calculable rules alone must determine action within bureaucracy, for the economic and political support of modern culture demands calculability, "precise, unambiguous, continuous execution of the business of office," and thus politics and economics both demand more and more the "humanly disinterested, thereby strictly 'objective' [*streng sachlich*] expert." Modern bureaucracy becomes more perfect the more "dehumanized" it becomes, that is, the more it is able to exclude from its concerns personal, irrational, and emotional elements "which escape calculation."[31]

Yet this only applies to the "business of office." The question of what kind of person can provide leadership and directing force by mastering the apparatus, and where such a person will come from, as yet remains unanswered, except in one sense: collective, rather than individual, control and setting of direction is excluded as unviable or impossible. The question of the directing individual is all the more urgent to Weber, the more education and socialization direct talent toward positions of technical expertise and functions within hierarchies of command and the more these apparatuses resist control by forces or principles that are "substantive" and determining.

Meaning, Culture, and Death

It is in intellectual life that the problem of meaning and the burden of disempowerment are experienced most self-consciously and intensely, though it is also through that life that rationalization, in the form of science, has done so much of its work. According to Weber, science has created a "cosmos of natural causality" that rejects "in principle" every attempt to ask for a "meaning" for events. It has driven out God and showed the universe to be governed by impersonal rules. Yet whereas science insists that it is "the only possible form of a thinking reflection on the world,"[32] it cannot prove this, nor can it provide "ultimate values," which must be left to the choices of individuals—though even this conclusion cannot be established scientifically. Only "a hierarchical ordering of values unequivocally prescribed by *ecclesiastical* dogma" could redeem science and the world from this potential lack of value.[33]

Rather than a source of meaning, science has been, and is, a source of power. It teaches technical mastery, but does not ask what is meaningful, nor whether there is meaning.[34] What the technical advances of the sciences mean is that "one can *master* all things—in principle—through *calculation*." This power of mastery through calculation also brings, ironically, a form of "*Entzauberung*," "demagification" or "disenchantment": there are no longer magical powers whose effects and origins cannot be calculated, and unlike "savages" for whom such magical powers exist, we today ignore "magical means"; "technical means and calculation" are all we need for mastery.[35]

The irony is that, though it is a source of power, science is also the source of the loss of meaning: when intellectualism demagifies the world, its processes "lose their magical meaning content, and now 'are' and 'happen,' but do not 'mean' any more."[36] In earlier times, when the world still "meant" something, science had a broader range of "power" to explore, discover, or give access to meaning. But the advance of science has undermined confidence in meaning, in Weber's view, reducing science's own power to the merely technical and disempowering by undermining the earlier justifying convictions that gave science its value in and for society. If science is to have meaning, it must derive it from broader cultural evaluations, for one cannot prove "with the means of science" that "what comes out of scientific work is *important* in the sense of 'worth knowing.' "[37] Thus: "The belief in the value of scientific truth is a product of specific cultures and is not given by nature."[38]

Science is not only unable to prove its own value; it cannot direct humankind toward action of any kind. "It can never be the task of a science of experience to determine binding norms and ideals in order to be able to derive recipes for practice [*Praxis*]." Thus, an empirical science "is capable of teaching no-one what he *should do*."[39] As early as 1904, Weber had written:

> Only positive religions—more precisely expressed: dogmatically bound sects—are capable of lending to the content of *cultural values* the dignity of unqualifiedly valid *ethical commands*. . . . The fate of a culture epoch which has eaten from the tree of knowledge is that it must know that we cannnot read off the *meaning* of world action from the ever so complete result of its analysis, but must be capable of creating it ourselves, that "*Weltanschauungen*" can never be the product of a progressing knowledge of experience.[40]

Indeed, says Weber in neo-Kantian fashion, a "science that has become mature" knows that even its concepts are only constructions and not "empirically valid" in the sense of completely grasping reality.[41]

It is the necessity of specialization and narrowness, under conditions of rationalization, that has undermined the techniques of the self based on the cultivation of wholeness and completeness, as in the tradition of *Bildung*. "Not only externally, no, but inwardly, the matter stands so: that the individual can get the sure consciousness of doing something completely perfect in the field of science only in the case of the strictest specialization."[42] The fact is that in all areas of rationalized life, "the restriction to specialized work, with the renunciation of the faustian universality which it involves, is above all the presupposition of worthwhile action in today's world." Nothing can be accomplished that is not the product of specialization. Thus, " 'deed' and 'renunciation' unavoidably imply one another today." Goethe, in fact, understood already in the eighteenth century that the educational ideal of a full and harmonious humanity was no longer possible.[43]

Specialization is linked to another problem that makes work in rationalized society, especially in science, undermine *Bildung*: namely, science is "yoked to the course of *progress*," which continues without end, despite the effort to accomplish something "that will *endure*."[44] In science, as in rationalized society generally, no achievement is ever truly complete: whatever the scientist has accomplished "is antiquated in 10, 20, 50 years. . . . That is the fate, yes: that is the *meaning* of the work of science. . . . To be overtaken scientifically is . . . not only our common destiny, but our common goal. We cannot work without hoping that others will come further than we."[45] Thus, those who further the cause of rationalization through a "calling" can never experience "completion" but must live toward the future. They must not only submit to and endure progress, but they must also positively affirm it and devote themselves to it as the true meaning of their work. Weber's work therefore implies that faith in progress is essential to those who advance the sway of science and rationalization. Indeed, Weber observes that progress has always been a compensation for the lack of other faiths. "The idea of 'progress' first appears as necessary if the need arises to endow the religiously emptied course of human destiny with a this-sided and yet objective 'meaning.' "[46]

Heinrich Rickert once remarked that progress, "if the word is to have any precise meaning at all, signifies the same thing as *increase in value*, i.e., the enhancement of the value of cultural goods."[47] But Weber not only questions whether progress really brings enhancement of value, but also wonders whether it undermines meaning and "inner" power on behalf of external, technical control. "Has then this process of disenchantment, continuous in Occidental culture for thousands of years, and above all, this 'progress' to which science belongs as the link and motive force, any meaning which surpasses now the purely practical and technical?"[48]

It is important to recognize this as the situation not just of the scientist but of the modern "cultivated person" (*gebildete Mensch*) as well. In fact, though the world of culture does not will itself to be "surpassed" as science does, to Weber it is, ironically, as affected by cultural progress as science is. Weber says that the ultimate value of those who prize culture within the tradition of *Bildung* has been "the pure inner-worldly perfection of self," which, it is imagined, derives from "possessing" as much of culture as possible. Yet "if one evaluates it with its own standards," the possession of culture, the affair of a "spiritual aristocracy," is meaningless, for the process of "perfectibility" and "appropriation" should, in principle, continue without end, just as the production of "cultural goods" or the progress of scientific research does.

> And the more the cultural goods [*Kulturgüter*] and the goals of self-perfection are differentiated and abundant, the more narrow is the segment that the individual, passive as appropriator, active as co-creator, could encompass in the course of a finite life. So much less, therefore, could the harnessing into this external and internal cosmos offer the likelihood: that an individual could assimilate the whole of culture or that he could assimilate what is in any sense "essential" in it, for which, moreover, there was no definitive standard.[49]

To Weber, this means that *Bildung* not only does not empower; if we look to it for our life's meaning, it also renders death meaningless. The life of the man of culture is "situated within 'progress' . . . amidst the ongoing enrichment of civilization with thoughts, knowledge, problems." Such a life seizes only a small part of what the "life of the spirit" brings forth; indeed, everything it grasps is "provisional, never final." Because there is always further development and progress, life must end while there is still far to go. Thus the "cultivated man" dies in mid-course, surpassed by the march of progress he has enthroned, without completeness, exhausted perhaps, " 'tired of life,' but not: 'satisfied by life' " through completion of an "organic cycle" in which the human being is brought all that life can offer, with no more "riddles to solve." These riddles in the modern world call forth ever newer cultural solutions and products to satisfy the need for more knowledge. "Abraham or any farmer of olden times," feudal lords and war heroes, completed a cycle and could die "satisfied," based on the "naive unambiguity of the contents of their lives." But for a modern human being, death is just an end to incompleteness and is "meaningless," because it does not "complete," round out, or fulfill: it simply "ends." The "meaningless 'progressiveness' of life" makes death meaningless. And if death is meaningless, life is meaningless.[50]

For this reason—and anticipating Mann's hero in *Doctor Faustus*—Weber claims that it is meaningless to live a life devoted to the *advance* of rationalization, science, and culture, to the "continuous enrichment of civilization." Using the language of "service," Weber claims that service of cultural goods is totally senseless when it does not remain a mere occupation but "is made into a holy task, a 'calling' " that becomes the servant of "valueless and moreover generally self-contradictory and mutually antagonistic goals." To turn the advance of culture into a calling, to "serve truth" at the cost of meaning, is absurd to Weber—as to

Nietzsche, though for different reasons—especially when the calling is modelled on Puritan service to God.[51]

Rationality, progress, and "cultural development" thus add up to a "stepping out of the organically prescribed cycle of life." Humankind has lost the possibility of setting "natural" goals and "natural" limits to striving. From this apparently natural standpoint, and obviously from the religious standpoint, life under the rule of rationalization is in serious difficulty. Though *Bildung* has been rendered meaningless by the advance of rationalization, it is not as if science, part of that advance, has any more answers than *Bildung* has.

> Tolstoy has given the simplest answer with the words: "It is mean-
> ingless because it gives no answer to the question that is alone im-
> portant for us: 'What should we do? How should we live?' " The
> fact that it does not give this answer is indisputable. The question
> is only, in what "sense" it gives no answer, and whether, despite
> this, it could not still give [an answer] to the one who puts the
> question correctly.[52]

Science as a "Vocation" [53]

A strongly anti-bourgeois essay by Franz Xaver Schwab in 1917, entitled "Vocation [*Beruf*] and Youth," dramatized widespread youthful disappointment with the meager rewards and excessive demands of intellectual callings in rationalized society. Schwab, drawing on the notion of *Beruf* as profession, argues that *Beruf* is the "boundary problem" for youth: "Where there is youth, there is not yet vocation; where there is vocation, there is no longer youth." The issue of calling, he suggests, is at the center of the spiritual situation of society. "The war is today the dominating event, but vocation is the kernel." No-one has yet found the courage to overthrow the idols of vocation, though the times suffer from "bourgeois-vocational feelings of duty." Yet to aesthetes who hope to find a solution by opting out of society while retaining a sense of calling, escaping from bourgeois callings into the calling of "culture," Schwab says there cannot be a true vocation in the service of intellect or spirit. He turns to *Lebensphilosophie* for a solution. "The only thing that can be useful to us is: clear knowledge and living feeling [that come] from the relationship between the simplest basic powers of our being: Life and Spirit." Vocation corrupts spirit and life, which must instead be "ennobled through the service of higher values." In times like these, only a prophet can express the unity of life. Perhaps, Schwab hopes, it will be possible to return to a mode of existence where the higher life can once again look down on the vulgarity of usefulness and practicality, when it will no longer be distinguished to take an interest in vocation. Perhaps success in a vocation will no longer be an honor, but only a success, and sometimes even a shame. The time is coming perhaps when the highest thing a respectable person may say about his vocation is this: that it gives him fun, or better, that he no longer has a vocation.[54]

But youthful disillusion was not a product of the war. Weber had observed earlier that the increasing "rationalization of violence [*Gewalt-samkeit*]" that accompanied "the development of violence away from its personalistic heroic and social character toward the rational 'state' " had already promoted disillusion and "increasing flight into the irrationalities of apolitical feeling."[55] Disenchantment often led to retreat into religion as an ersatz for political frustrations, or into "community" as "a religious, cosmic, or mystical relationship."[56]

> A completely understandable attitude, very popular with youth, has been put into the service of some idols, whose cult we find widely spread out today on all street corners and in all magazines. These idols are: the "personality" and "experience." Both are closely connected: the idea prevails that the latter determines the former and belongs to it. One torments oneself to experience—for that belongs to the life-conduct, in accordance with its rank, of a personality—and if it does not succeed, then one must at least act as if one had these gifts of grace. Formerly one called this "experience" "sensation" in German. And concerning what "personality" is and means, one had then, I believe, a more correct idea.[57]

Pursuit of "experience" reflects a desire for renewal of the self through "life," "redemption from the rationalism and intellectualism of science," expressed by the search "after religious experience" and "experience in general." Since all "experience" is irrational, says Weber, its pursuit reflects "intellectualist romanticism" and the desire to immerse oneself in the irrational and be empowered by it. Science actually contributes to this condition, for not only does it give no guidance to life: it opposes faith, and is "the power specifically foreign to God."[58]

The longing for experience is not the appropriate corrective to an overly rationalized and reified world, but an expression of a desire for flight and a sign of decadence, "the product of a diminishing power to endure inwardly the 'everyday.' " To Weber, lack of inner power is "unmanly." The signs of weakness—loss of power, desire for flight, self-display, "rushing after 'experience,' " and longing for leaders and prophets—reflect an inability "to look into the stern face of the fate of the time" and be "equal" to an everyday life in which Christian absolutes are no longer adequate. Modern society is producing individuals without "courage" or inner strength, who escape into "weak relativization" to avoid the imperative of "intellectual integrity" that requires them to face up to the ultimate values of their lives.[59] The youth movement is thus *not* merely misguided or mistaken, but impotent and cowardly, adding up to loss of manliness.[60] His awareness of decadence, weakness, and loss of inner power moves Weber to try to resolve the problem of meaning, both for itself and as a prerequisite to the regeneration or recovery of power. Manliness must be restored to the rationalized world, and youth must be transformed into men like the soldiers that have gone into battle. Only a self-transformation that makes youth into the "moral" equivalent of soldiers will enable them to overcome their lack of manliness. Thus, in Weber's interpretation, the crisis of science and rationality actually manifests itself not only intellectually and socially but also as a crisis of strength and weakness.[61]

War, Death, and the Calling

Weber revealed his solution to the problem of power and meaning in the discussion of war and death in the "Intermediate Reflection: Theory of the Stages and Directions of Religious Rejection of the World," which his wife says was written before the war and the first version of which was published in November, 1915.[62] Yet the most important passage appears only in the revised version of 1920, revealing the significance of the lengthy war experience on Weber's understanding of death and the calling.[63]

War, says Weber, gives a soldier "the feeling of a meaning for and a consecration of death." The individual can "*believe* that he knows he is dying 'for' something." This unique experience differs from the common experience of death, since death comes to all, and one cannot say "why precisely to him and precisely now." Indeed, with the advance of rationalization and culture, even the situating of death within a "cycle" of life is gone: death has become an "end" where only "a beginning seems . . . meaningful." But this is not a problem for the soldier in war: "why and wherefore he must endure death . . . can be for him so doubtless, that the problem of the 'meaning' of death in its general significance (in which the religions of salvation are induced to grapple with it), finds no presuppositions for its emergence."[64]

This observation is the basis for Weber's proposal. For, apart from the soldier, the only others in the modern world to whom death may be equally unquestioned and hence meaningful, in Weber's view, are those who "perish 'in the calling' [*und ausser ihm nur dem, der 'im Beruf' umkommt*]"![65] This remarkable claim, added in 1920, reveals the significance of death as the limiting fact that governs not just meaning but meaningful action. It also reveals the deeper meaning, value, and purpose of the Weberian concept of calling, which Weber himself only fully discovered through World War I. Weber's real task has become nothing less than to make the individual a soldier on the battlefield of the "impersonal gods" of a calling, who must submit himself to selfless service of, and struggle for, the "cause" or "object" (*Sache*) or value, which empowers him. Through the discipline of the calling, the warrior on this battlefield will no longer have to seek meaning, nor wonder about the meaning of death: his "service" itself, like military service, will *confer* meaning; his mission will give strength; and his death will be as consecrated as the soldier's. This process of converting individuals into spiritual warriors is the heart of the Weberian calling and his solution to the problems of meaning and death, self and power.

For those who live in traditional society, the cycle of nature includes the cycle of their life, and their death, as part of nature's cycle, has its place within it. For those with religious belief, death has its place in a god-created order that guides action and makes suffering and mortality meaningful. But, in Weber's view, for those without religion, especially in "disenchanted" society, the possibility for meaning and meaningful action—which depends on being able to set "death in a series of meaningful and consecrated events"—is available *only* to those who live life as soldiers in war or live life "in a calling." We have moved from the religious man who is a warrior on God's battlefield (*Gotteskämpfer*)— who seeks tasks and carries them out systematically, and for whom the issues of meaning and death are resolved in Godly service—to a model usable by those aristocrats of the soul who can live in their calling as secular and nonmilitary soldiers in the battle for their own god, whatever it might be. Weber has discovered what we can call "the vocational equivalent of war."

GODS, DEVILS, AND POWER

Weber's calling promises that all who can transform their lives into service (*Dienst*) and their work into a calling in this special sense of the term will overcome the meaninglessness in death and life produced by rationalization, as they are transformed into spiritual warriors. This task is essential, given the need for power in a rationalized world. Rationalization in economic life and political domination has strongly furthered the development of rational "objectivity" (*Sachlichkeit*) and the need for "human beings with a calling and experts" to fill the posts of modern life.[66] Indeed, Weber claims that "only the ethic of the calling of inner-worldly asceticism is truly inwardly adequate to the commitment to impersonal goals characteristic of the coercive structure of domination [*Versachlichung der Gewaltherrschaft*]."[67]

> "Without regard for person," "sine ira et studio," without hate and therefore without love, without free will [*Willkür*] and therefore without grace, as objective [*sachliche*] duty in a calling and not on account of a concrete personal relationship, the *homo politicus* as much as the *homo oeconomicus* carries out his task today precisely when he performs it in the most ideal degree in the sense of the rational rules of the modern order of power.[68]

Thus, all action in a rationalized world built on specialization of tasks must have "the character of 'service' vis-à-vis an impersonal *objective purpose* [*sachlicher Zweck*]."[69] This is the heart of all of Weber's uses of calling: service by the self of impersonal objectlike purposes. Service must exclude all motives of self and orientation to others; one's purposes or goals must be impersonal in the most radical sense, just as market calculations in the economic order are "impersonal," though they also "serve" personal well-being.

To Weber, only an ethos of service built around the calling is adequate to the demands of modern rationalistic culture, because only the calling makes possible service of the purposes of impersonal activity in orders of the world that have become detached from an overarching value or substantive ethical postulate. Only the calling can empower those few who are leaders in any realm to take the risks that come when they, alone among all, posit higher values for pursuit by everyone.

But service in the calling goes beyond what is necessary for personal well-being: it must be done *on behalf* of the higher goal, which now becomes the "witness" and "law-giver" for one's action.

> In every task of a *calling*, the *object* [*Sache*] as such demands its right and wants to be executed according to its own laws. In every task of a calling, he to whom it is set has to limit himself and to exclude that which does not belong strictly to the *object*, but particularly: his own love and hate. . . . And it is to strip the "calling" of the only sense which today remains still really meaningful, if one does not perform that specific kind of self-limitation that it demands.[70]

To be engaged in a calling and not involved in just short-term "goal-rational behavior" thus requires the systematization of on-going service to a cause in accordance with the "laws" of the sphere of activity, now apparently done "for its own sake." To submit ourselves (*sich hingeben*) to an object is to have our tasks prescribed to us. Their satisfactory accomplishment is our purpose; and warriorlike service to the object provides, if not a simple answer to the question of meaning, at least an end to the obsessive questioning while we feel ourselves called.

> The ascetic, if he wants to act within the world, therefore in inner-worldly asceticism, must be stricken with a kind of happy narrow-mindedness concerning every question about a "meaning" for the world and must disregard it. . . . The inner-worldly ascetic is therefore the proper "man of vocation," who neither asks nor needs to ask after the meaning of the objective performance of his vocation within the *whole* world—for which indeed, not he but rather his god bears the responsibility, for it is enough for him to be conscious that, in his personal rational action in this world he executes his god's will, which is in its ultimate meaning inscrutable for him.[71]

Serving Science

The modern ethical guide of the calling performs functions in Weber's work analogous to those it performed for the Puritans. Indeed, the portrait of the entrepreneur-hero in *The Protestant Ethic* is the prototype of the scientific worker with a calling. As Maurice Weyembergh observes, the individual becomes "a virtuoso of his profession, as the puritan was a religious virtuoso."[72] For Weber, the Puritan businessman obtained ethical justification for his activities by interpreting profit making in terms of providence. In a parallel fashion in the present, "the enjoining of the ascetic meaning of the firm calling ethically transfigures [*verklärt*] the modern *specialists* [*Fachmenschentum*]."[73]

In Weber's work, one can live meaningfully only in the natural cycle, in a relation to one's god within religion, on a battlefield in war, or in relation to the "gods" of vocation. To Weber, the modern world cannot find meaning in a group, society, work, class, or nation unless it can serve something there in a calling. No other ground for meaning exists. The revived secular calling promises a renewal of inner power based on a sanctified meaning for worldly activity, a higher significance for a life that seems potentially meaningless and certainly directionless in light of the apparently total disenchantment of the world. These unquestioned needs for sanctification persist in Weber's work in a time that lacked the compelling power of religious faith. The Weberian calling justifies the individual whose "being" alone is inadequate, as it justified the lives of the

Puritans through their "mission." The inability to find meaning outside a mission, task, or service leads to the need for a rescue from purposelessness not by a cause alone but by a cause that can be *served*. This new cause is the "last" implicit faith in Weber's universe, the god still not demystified. It provides the task or mission, the one thing certain that ends the search for meaning and lays a foundation for empowered action. Weber's vocation is thus his last magic in an age supposedly without magic, a last defense against illusionless times. Weber's ideal requires its own demystification and disenchantment, based as it is on a religious model of meaning creation rather than a sociological investigation of the social and cultural sources of meaning in human life.

Indeed, when Weber asks the question "Has progress as such a recognizable meaning stretching beyond the technical, so that thereby service to it would be a meaningful calling?" he begs the question of service. He *presupposes* that calling and service must be the bases of any meaningful solution, that service in the sense he means it is the form of relation one *must* have to purposes, "values," or activity, and that the problem for the individual is to find something worthwhile enough to give one's life to and for in such service. No doubt it is important to inquire into the value of science and the reasons for its pursuit; yet Weber's analysis of science is *not* primarily an inquiry into the grounds, possibilities, and value of knowledge, but into the worthiness of science as an object of *service*: can one find in science a cause that gives life purpose, so that service of it gives redemption from meaninglessness, like the soldier's service? In posing the question this way, Weber shows the limits of his terms for solving the problem of meaningful action: it is *his* choice *for* these concepts of calling and service, in a context where science has uncertain intellectual support, that must be questioned and understood. The question about the meaning of life and death is always urgent, but it is *not* automatically a question about the need to "serve." Only because Weber implicitly *assumes* the need for service in a calling can he pose the question of meaning in this way. The loss of a stable object to serve— god, or nature, or art, or science, or truth—is a serious problem for the person who *must* be a *servant*; hence the persistent inquiry by Weber, and Germany, into whether a given object, however demystified, can be made an object of submission and service in a calling. Mere love of or commitment to a particular activity, object, or cause will not suffice; one must serve it in a calling as redemption from meaninglessness, as religious believers served their god.

This significance of service comes out in Weber's attack on the soul/ intellect distinction that youth make in thinking of science. There is a "very widespread idea that science has become a problem of calculation . . . done with the cool intellect alone and not with one's whole 'soul.' " Nothing is further from the truth in Weber's portrait, for it is one's soul that is *at stake* in service.

> Whoever lacks the ability to put on blinders so to speak, and to key himself up to the idea that the fate of his soul depends on whether he correctly makes this, precisely this conjecture at this place of this manuscript, let him just keep away from science. He will never go through in himself what one can call the "experience" of science. Without this strange intoxication laughed at by every outsider, this passion, this "thousands of years had to pass before you came into life and other thousands of years wait in silence," dependent upon whether you succeed at this conjecture, one does *not* have the calling for science and may do something else. For nothing is valuable for man as man which he *cannot* do with *passion*.[74]

This is not about the pursuit of scientific truth: it is about the pursuit of salvation, and it is not merely a convenient metaphor. In Weber's vision, science—or some other cause or goal—must become so important that the fate of one's soul can be imagined to hang in the balance. Nothing can be adequately served, and the individual cannot be adequately satisfied, by anything less. But with such significance conferred on science, the question of its ultimate meaning becomes moot.[75]

Devotion to a god in the calling is so mysterious that it is "laughed at" by outsiders, because none outside it understand its real importance. For the practitioner, however, service of science or any other cause must carry the weight formerly carried by religious belief and its sacred tasks, so that both the individual and science can be rescued from their modern fate. For Weber, no activity is worth the effort, and no activity can become a calling, unless it can become such a service. Implicit in this understanding is that only what one *can* serve deserves attention, for only service provides the possibility of more than mere success: the "faith" to which one gives oneself, and the service of the purposes of its "god," provide salvation and inner strength. But faith is not enough; although faith may produce desired results in the short term, only hard, selfless labor assures the visible signs of grace in the fruits of work, work committed to the greater glory and enhancement of the god one serves.[76]

The calling binds one to relentless labor in exchange for the legitimating power of successful service. One becomes an empowered warrior on the battlefield of rationalization, in exchange for an end to the dilemma of meaning. The fate of the times, Weber believes, must lead everyone to this idea of "calling."

Redefining and Rediscovering Personality

In making possible redemption from meaninglessness, service in the calling transforms the self. Paradoxically, "impersonality" in service leads to "personality"; abnegation of the self leads to elevation of the self; lack of regard for the "personal" aspects of the task allows one to become a "person" in the fullest sense. Anyone who wants to become a "personality" must perform his work as a calling, with the unitary devotion and the impersonality that a calling requires. In this way, such a person "dies" to the natural self and is reborn as "personality." Weber's understanding of the tradition of personality and of its significance for Occidental development is here mobilized prescriptively. "Only he has 'personality' in the scientific field who serves *purely the object* [*Sache*]. And it is so not only in the scientific field. We know no great artist who has ever done anything other than to serve his object and only it."[77]

Weber's idea of personality, like Kant's, demands the overcoming of the natural self, not the working out of its "inner" law, as in the tradition of *Bildung*. It is an ideal opposed to the distorted cult of personality and vain advancements of self that Weber finds so prevalent within German society. In particular, society is confused about the supposed contrast between the specialist (*Fachmann*) and the personality. Everyone seeks to escape specialization and recover the older, more fully rounded possibilities of *Bildung*, hoping to become "something higher." But to Weber personality today can be found *only* in specialization and a narrowing of focus, in the self-limitation and submission to the object that the calling demands. There remains no other avenue.

> In the field of science, . . . he is quite certainly no "personality" who steps onto the stage as the impresario of the object [*Sache*] to which he should submit himself [*sich hingeben sollte*], who wants to legitimate himself through "experience," and who asks: how do I prove that I am something other than just a "specialist," how do I manage to say something, in form and content [*Sache*], that no-one has yet said as I have? Today, this is a phenomenon appearing *en masse*, which has a petty effect everywhere, and which degrades the one who so asks.[78]

Being a personality is *not* a matter of exhibiting the self. "It is indeed *not true* . . . that the 'personality' is and should be a 'unity,' that it must get lost, so to speak, if one does not make it visible on every occasion."

Nor is it a matter of asserting what is "personal" in one's relation to an object of service, for this reverses the proper relation of self and object, making objects serve *our* purposes. Inverting Nietzsche, Weber maintains that service must go in the other direction, for the "object" (*Sache*) and its demands and laws must dictate our action: "the inner submission to the task and only to it" can raise someone "to the height and dignity of the object that he pretends to serve."[79]

> And it is *not true* that a strong personality reveals itself in that it asks first about a completely "personal touch" of its own at every opportunity. Rather, it is to be wished that precisely the generation now growing up would again, above all, become used to the thought that "to be a personality" is something that one cannot want intentionally, and that there is only one way to become it (perhaps!): the unreserved submission to an "object" [*Sache*], however it and its derivative "demand of the day" may appear in the individual case.[80]

Weber's standards imply that, since a truly "called" person does not seek confirmation through popularity, one can determine who is "genuine" and who is not. The true personality must remain vigilant over himself, aware of the "fleshly" temptations and seductions coming from self and others. At the same time, others must be on their guard lest they be misled or seduced by someone who is not a true personality but a clever actor, through whom the spirit of the calling does not speak but who masks the desire for acclaim by pretending to be called. Thus, personality and calling can serve as badges of authenticity within society, a basis for the mutual recognition of the elect and for the reconstruction of society.

The true source of personality, then, is submission or devotion to the work or object as an ultimate value, coupled with systematic, rational effort in the calling to realize these values in the world. To Weber, the "dignity of the 'personality' lies settled in the fact that for it there exist values which it applies to its own life," and these values give life "meaning and significance."[81] Thus the "essence" of personality lies "in the constancy of its inner relationship to definite ultimate 'values' and life 'meanings,' which are stamped into goals in its conduct and thus translated into teleological-rational action."[82] This "relationship" must be shaped in service within a calling.

The link between "calling and the inner-most ethical core of personality" as an "unbroken unity" was created by the Puritans, but the world has traveled far since then. Many of capitalism's opponents in Germany, Weber says, take their stand against capitalism not only on social and political grounds, but also "on account of its linkage with the spirit of the men with the calling [*Berufsmenschentum*]."[83] Weber's substantive ideal, in opposition to these critics, is the *recovery* of the unity of calling and personality whose historical role had been so significant and which, as a source of strength in confronting obstacles, has, he believes, no rival. But even before the war he noted that the barriers to its realization were everywhere. "In the present, which operates so very much with the concept of 'life,' 'experience' [*Erlebnis*], etc., as with a specific *value*, the *inner unravelling* of this unity, the proscription [*Verfehmung*] of the 'men with a calling' [*Berufsmenschen*], is quite evident."[84]

Serving the Gods

Although Weber says that science, in its capacity to dethrone magic, contributed to the modern disenchanted condition in which a single religious vision no longer holds sway over society, the results are actually quite surprising.

> It is as in the ancient world, still not disenchanted of its gods and demons, only in another sense: as the Hellene sacrificed one time to Aphrodite and then to Apollo, and above all everyone to the gods of his city, so is [the world] still today, disenchanted and stripped of the mythical but inwardly true plasticity of its behavior. And over these gods and in their struggle fate governs, but certainly no "science." It can only be understood *what* the godly is for the one and for the other order, or in the one and the other order.[85]

Despite the effects of disenchantment, in other words, Weber believes science not only has left the world still governed by "gods," but also has made possible the return of an old order of gods! It is not simply that there is no shared purpose or clear ideals, or that everyone works in different directions within the "orders" of life: it is that the world remains in the hands of "gods." These gods do not simply coexist as the ancient gods coexisted, sometimes uncomfortably but with their relationships relatively clear and stable. They are engaged in a struggle that only "fate" can determine.

What are these gods? Christianity and the domination of the Christian god overthrew the ancient gods, but with the weakening of Christianity's hold, the old polytheism returns. "The many old gods, demagified [*entzaubert*] and thus in the form of impersonal powers, emerge from their graves, strive after power over our lives and begin among themselves again their eternal struggle."[86] It is this polytheism that the young, in

Weber's opinion, find hard to bear and that challenges their manliness: they want the return of a "monotheism" of absolute answers, or a leader to prescribe direction. Failing that, they flee into stimulation or "experience." Yet these alternatives do not confront the hard fact that "struggle is not to be excluded from . . . cultural life."[87] For Weber, the struggle now is not between anthropomorphized embodiments of the holy, but between "impersonal powers," "the gods of the individual orders and values." The most dangerous form of this struggle is that between political "gods," like the nation, the proletariat, pacifism, democracy, and socialism; or between different cultures, like the French, German, and Russian; or between different ethical systems. "Here also various gods struggle with one another and indeed for all time," and there is no easy resolution.[88] But Weber's picture is rigid and oversimplified, for one *can* draw on elements or aspects of other cultures, discover their riches and use them with value. They are not enemies, as Weber supposes, except in time of real war, when they fight for supremacy or survival. Why does Weber not recognize this?

For Weber, human life, committed to different standpoints toward the world, reveals "the undeniable disparity between ultimate formulations of the picture of the world," "the incompatibility and therefore the inability to settle the struggle of the ultimate generally *possible* standpoints toward life." Indeed, Weber says, echoing Nietzsche, those who live in the world cannot help "experiencing in themselves nothing other than the struggle between a plurality of ranks of values." Yet the real question is "finally everywhere and always not only [one] of alternatives between values" or cultures—that would be manageable—but rather of something involving very dark powers: the "unbridgeable deadly struggle, as between 'God' and 'devil.'" Between "gods" and "devils" there can be, of course, no "relativizations and compromises." As long as life "is founded in itself and is understood from itself" alone, it knows "only the eternal struggle of these gods with one another." According to one's ultimate standpoint, one position is the devil and the other god, "and the individual must *decide* . . . which *for him* is god and which is the devil." "You serve . . . this god *and offend the others*, when you choose for [one particular] position." Most people "are not conscious and above all also do not *want* to be conscious" that they must make such a choice. But Weber claims the world *must* recognize that each must choose "which of these gods" to serve or "when he wants and should serve the one and when the other." This awareness brings one into a "struggle against one or several of the other gods of this world," for "life as a whole . . . means a series of ultimate decisions, through which the soul, as in Plato, *chooses* its own fate—which means the meaning of its action and being," and only choosing lifts life above the course of nature, making it something consciously guided.[89]

As Weber observes, one can serve one god at one time and another at a different time. There are, of course, real compromises made in everyday life, for "in almost every single important point of view of real human beings, the value spheres indeed cross and intertwine themselves." Yet, for psychological and pragmatic reasons, people are not aware, and do not want to become aware, of the mixture of "values which are deadly enemies [*todfeindliche Werte*]." The superficiality of everyday life consists in persons' avoidance of "the choice between 'god' and 'devil' and their own ultimate decision about which of the colliding values will be ruled by the one and which by the other."[90] But Weber observes that the Occidental man of antiquity worshipped Apollo or Dionysus, depending on circumstances, and that the southern Italian worshipped competing saints and religious orders as well; in China, people paid respect to or withdrew it from the Taoist mantic or Buddhist religious rites according to need and religious efficacy.[91] Thus, Weber actually reveals that a crucial cause of shifting worship, despite the increasingly abstract nature of sublimated and rationalized religion, is practical need and flexibility in the light of circumstances. Yet this contrasts sharply with the absolutist need, born from Protestantism, that Weber preaches—that is, to serve a god and identify the devil.

If we use this pragmatic model, it is obvious that every god does not automatically have a devil standing against it, as the Greeks and Chinese knew. Indeed, the Greeks do not even *have* a conception of "devil" as the enduring enemy of all one believes to be good or holy, though they do have notions of Hades—who in fact is the brother of Zeus, not his opponent—and punishment, as in the pit of Tartaros.[92] Thus, the survival and coexistence of the various members of the order of the gods should generally be possible, as it was for the Greeks. In some cases, of course, the strife between these gods is obvious; but even when it is, the strife is not conceived by the Greeks as a struggle between forces of light and darkness, between opponents eternally at war. Therefore, the division of "god" and "devil" cannot be made a *universal* basis for value choice— as Weber wants to make it and insists everyone must make it—in light of the radically different nature of divisions in Greek polytheism. In fact, his view reflects an admixture of Christian metaphors into metaphors of polytheism—drawn from Greek religion, which was not a salvation religion—despite his claim that the unitary vision of Christianity has been overthrown. The transformation of the world into god and devils at war must be recognized, when it happens, as a product of *particular* circumstances, conditions, and events. Absolutized, it reflects a language and a conception borrowed from the Judeo-Christian tradition, where the Hebrew god struggled against idols, and Christ, like every Christian (according to Paul), struggled against the devil.

The Greek gods, in contrast, when they had attained stability under the rule of Zeus, lived together, and though they often struggled in myth, they did not demonize one another, nor struggle to the death with one another, except in the struggle between the "generations" of the fathers, Ouranos, Chronos, and Zeus, which Zeus won. As Walter Burkert notes of Greek polytheism, "However much a god is intent on his honour, he never disputes the existence of any other god; they are all everlasting ones. There is no jealous god as in the Judeo-Christian faith. What is fatal is if a god is overlooked."[93] Instead of demonizing one another, the Greek gods had rivalries and jealousies of a very human kind, and at times they seemed to use humankind, according to Greek self-interpretation, essentially for their sport. Yet the Greeks recognized *all* the Olympians as their gods and none as devils, and knew each had to be appeased lest their wrath be aroused. Nor did the Greeks see themselves in general as *serving* the gods. Thus Weber's absolutizing and demonizing of the orders of the world, understood as gods demanding service, is false to the Greek metaphor and incoherent: it is a fusion of disparate vocabularies, based on a Christian foundation and showing the Christian origin and elements—indeed, more precisely the Protestant origin—of his thinking.

But why does Weber, "speaking figuratively," turn values, forces, and causes into gods at all and turn the enemies of these values into devils, urging his compatriots to do likewise? The hidden logic of "value" shows itself here as a logic of devotion to gods, the logic of what Nietzsche and Heidegger call "metaphysics." Values are made into gods by individuals dominated by the need to serve, submit, worship, and be devoted, because, for cultural reasons, that is the only way they know to find meaning, purpose, and inner strength. They must deify the forces of the world and enroll themselves in service, seeking to fulfill a god's demands or war and struggle on their god's behalf, because they need a god, however impersonal, to provide meaning and direction, in the way that service of the Protestant god once did. With the old gods gone but the need for worship as strong as before, the need for something to submit to impels the search for a substitute. As Nietzsche observed, "It seems to me that indeed the religious instinct is powerfully in growth—but . . . it refuses precisely the theistic satisfaction with deep mistrust."[94] For

Weber, service alone—the clear choice and selfless, systematic action on behalf of an overarching value or cause understood as a god—can provide meaning and strength in a time when a single shared vision is attenuated; all must seek their god and their calling if their lives are to be consciously directed and not simply the playthings of powers they do not understand.

But there is more to Weber's world of gods and devils than submission: there is fighting. Empowerment requires the spur to combat that comes from belief in the existence of devils. Only when one can become the tool of a god and oppose a devil will empowerment of the self become a reality. In Weber's universe, only by forcing a dualistic and oppositional structure on the world of meaning and value can one create strong selves empowered for the tasks of the present. The language of Christian gods and devils created the first personalities, the innovators and empowered individuals of Puritanism, and only a discipline like theirs and a secular metaphysics modeled on theirs can do the same in the present.

In Weber's moral universe, the service of gods who confront devils is inescapable: all positions *must* be lived as service to one god or another, and the meaning of service, hence the meaning of life, derives from the object or value to which one submits oneself and for which one fights. This form of service, in which one becomes a soldier on the battlefield of warring gods or values in "deadly struggle," ends doubt about the meaning of death and hence of life. This is Weber's definitive answer to Tolstoy's question and to the dilemma and crisis of culture, and this is why Weber can say that only a "hair-fine line separates science and belief," for all service, even of science, is a matter of enrolling in the service of gods. For Weber, our ultimate choices are not "merely" values or causes or objects: they must be seen as something in the service of which we give our lives. Indeed, "the highest ideals, those that move us most powerfully, take effect for all time only in the struggle with other ideals that are just as holy to others as ours are to us."[95] This is not relativism, in Weber's understanding: it is not based on an "organic ethics of calling" of the kind found in Hinduism, where conflicting and contradictory forms of service and calling coexist and are positively appreciated, and in which all spheres of life not only have their own law but are also given independent, if not equal, value.[96] This is war.

Serving Society

For Weber, teachers perform a moral task in using knowledge to bring to the awareness of students the multiplicity of positions not their own and the existence of facts that run counter to their positions, especially in politics.[97] This is particularly important for Weber's goal of teaching submission to gods and values. Students are thereby able to realize exactly what they reject when they affirm a value or position, and are brought to the necessary realization that there are positions that cannot be harmonized with their own. Their choice reveals the "for" and "against," the terms of the battle they must undertake, and the potential weakness of their own positions. This is why reason alone cannot settle such conflicts.

But the necessity of choice also reveals why the imposition of political and other values in the classroom is threatening to the task Weber wants teachers to undertake. For to Weber, the task of the teacher is to show students their *need* to enroll in service, to bring them to enlistment, and to reveal to them the nature of the battlefield on which they must do combat. At the same time, the classroom itself is *not* a battlefield with winners and losers, for *all* must come out winners, that is, all must develop into champions of one goal or another. The classroom should enable transformation and development inside, without the need to take sides in the battle that must be fought outside. To turn the lecture room into a battlefield deprives science of its one and essential claim to social service: the service of helping others find their gods and their own service. Science *alone* can do this. It *must* remain untainted for social well-being. To turn it into an instrument of war is not only impossible, owing to its nature and the irreconcilability of the value spheres; the very attempt is destructive of its calling, which demands impartial clarification of value positions for the purpose of serving the true interests of students.

This view of the polytheism of the universe and the need for service gives science a new life and task. In Weber's view, science makes an enormous contribution to a life with many gods. Its calling is to teach the reality of the *war* of the gods and the need to enlist in combat. This is Weber's substantive lesson in the guise of formal truth. Science can provide a special kind of clarity, for it can reveal what the "godly" is in each order of the world, and thus it has a special possibility of service. The real calling of science in society is now revealed: having left behind its role as provider of privileged access to what is universally essential, valuable, and true, science is now to be used to understand what the different gods are that rule the various orders of the world. This or that practical position "may be derived according to its *meaning*, with inner consistency and therefore integrity, from this or that ultimate foundation as a *Weltanschauung*—it can be from only one or there could be perhaps several—but not from this or that other one." Science can thereby help to give to an individual an "account . . . of the ultimate meaning" of his conduct. Thus, to Weber the scientist reveals the hidden axioms of an individual's life, the service the individual is engaged in, even unbeknownst to him, and the meaning of this service. This makes the person aware of his god and its demands, along with the appropriate devils, allowing him either to affirm his god consciously and serve it deliberately or to reject it and find another. The teacher using science thus makes it possible for individuals to discover and carry out their own calling, and therefore "stands in the service of 'ethical' powers: to create duty, clarity, and the feeling of responsibility."[98] Science can once again have a significant and meaningful position within culture and society.

But despite Weber's claims, this teaching is not formal. The student must be taught "to resign himself to the simple accomplishment of a given task," to distinguish facts from evaluations, "to put his own person behind the object" of his efforts, and "above all" to suppress his desire to "exhibit" his personal tastes and sentiments.[99] That is, the student must learn to *serve*: to submit himself to the object and the task and put aside the demands of the self. Only thus can the service be truly a calling and the self be truly overcome and formed into a personality.

Though this passes itself off as a merely formal task, it is obviously thoroughly substantive. The key to substance here is *not* the particular value one serves but the *fact* and form of *service* to this value, the obligatory mode of conduct toward what one prizes. The way one *must* live, the way one *must* serve, the way one *must* relate to what one values: there can be little more substantive than this. So much for the neutrality of Weber's science. Here the formal, which Marcuse has remarked on in the case of technical rationality, has flipped over into the substantive. And here, in Weber's presentation, we see that for him the task of science goes beyond its technical ability to reveal the "gods" of the different orders and value positions through an axiomatic reduction. Weber's science and scientist claim that everyone serves gods, like it or not, and that all relations to these gods must take the form of service. They assert, further, that *every* god is matched with a devil or devils. They teach, finally, that the only correct form of serving one's gods is ascetic submission of self in a calling, to the god one serves. This can hardly pass for an ethically neutral position toward ultimate questions, for the answer to the most ultimate question—the character and constitution of the individual and what ways exist to find meaning and strength—is clearly *prescribed* here, even if the particular calling is unspecified.

Weber's earlier work does not speak of service of gods or devils, but uses an idealist and materialist language of choices and costs. The scientist's task was to show the "significance" of choices and positions, that is, to show the "ideal interests" that underlay given ends, by making explicit the ultimate standards on which action was based, revealing what values were espoused and what rejected. The scientist could show the consequences of a position and its costs, leaving the task of choosing to the actor alone.[100] By 1910, gods and devils begin to appear in letters, and they appear too during the war, in the essay on value freedom and the lecture on science, though there remains alongside them a more neutral treatment of the function of discussing value judgments.[101] By this time, the form of calling and service, rescued from religious tradition, has become the definitive framework, the only possible form, and a sine qua non for all secular searches for meaning and empowerment. It is the fundamental presupposition of Weber's lecture on science, with service being linked to the schema of gods and devils. And yet, to Weber it seems that this framework of meaning is a purely logical answer to a technical question, the obvious and only form of life remaining in rationalized society through which the modern human being can hope to find meaning.[102] An ascetic cultural and social tradition that has been chosen and affirmed passes itself off as the outcome of a scientific investigation of the modern condition and the available solutions to its dilemmas. It is this presupposition and form that must be questioned.

Weber is unaware of this determining supposition and continues to claim that ultimate value questions cannot be settled by scientific means and that science does not have sacred values to dispense or meanings regarding the universe to suggest. To Weber, the calling of science may allow one to pursue science with the submission and commitment of the believer and may help others find their own service, but one cannot prescribe it, or anything from it, for the restoration of any larger social and cultural direction for others. "The prophet, after whom so many of our youngest generation long, is indeed *not* there"; indeed, it is modern Germany's "destiny to live in a time alien to god and without prophets." For "the technical and social conditions of rational culture" themselves make the possibility of new religious visions or a return to a prophetic and brotherly religion unlikely, in that new religious conceptions rarely arise in a "rational culture organized for work in the calling." Yet even though Weber's science is predicated on and teaches the inescapable fact that all *must* serve, whatever the gods may be, only a prophet or savior, he says, could prescribe for people which *set* of the warring gods to serve.[103] The larger guidance may yet appear, but in the meantime we must "go to our work and do justice to 'the demand of the day'—humanly as well as in our calling. This, however, is plain and simple, if everyone finds the daimon and obeys it, which holds the threads of *his* life."[104]

Weber's implication is clear: when the people as a whole has no prophets, each must find his own daimon, his own service, and thus his own calling. Still, for Weber, the search for one's daimon and obedience to it are the only guides in a time with no revelations or leaders. Collective fate may be obscure, but if so, everyone must turn to his own calling and everyday duty. Weber's fundamental assumption is that each must become in his own way a warrior on behalf of a higher cause, even if no science can prescribe which cause. Service alone makes it possible to stand individually against the emptiness of the time.

CONCLUSION: THE MASTERY OF RATIONALIZATION

The Protestant ascetics, without certain knowledge of their god's plan, channeled their activity nonetheless toward the enhancement of his glory. For them, worldly activity could be transformed into a calling, providing visible signs of grace for those who served. The soldier in war, on the other hand, became a champion of the nation that sent him and sanctified his death, which made his life and death meaningful while he fought. Weber, however, condemned to be without a revelation that would sanctify everyday duty and guide action toward a higher, perhaps collective, purpose, and unable to draw regularly on the actuality of war, strove to sanctify life instead by the revival of the calling in a secular and individual way. The individual with a calling rescues himself from a routine attitude toward activity and from the emptying of value from the world due to rationalization by setting the desires of the self into the background and giving himself over to meeting obligations as if they were religious or military tasks, thus lending them the sanction of higher purpose. But although enhancing and legitimating what one does and who one is by converting life into a selfless calling and oneself into a champion may protect the self from anxiety and empower it for struggle, it also conceals the extremity of the threat to self and society inherent in the disappearance of reliable transcendental ideals, undermined by the advance of rationality. Instead of confronting this threat, service in a calling makes one a hero and gives one the capacity to withstand the pressures of others and the desires or weaknesses of the self that might force one to diverge from the proper path; it also orients one to struggle and provides strength for overcoming the resistance of the world.

In Weber's view, the advance of rationality has ripped humankind out of nature and left it to act in a world without completion or overarching shared value. At the same time, rationalization has produced a series of spheres of human activity governed by autonomous standards and laws that resist ethical and substantive control. Weber claims we must accept the dominance of rationalization and the rule of autonomous spheres and submit to them "for their own sake." But we have seen that it is really for our "soul's" sake, the sake of personal redemption from meaninglessness, that we submit. Yet even though the rule of rationalization is here to stay, and although its value is rooted in the needs of both its staff and those it administers, Weber recognized that human beings dominated by such spheres were in danger of being reduced to mere functionaries carrying out objectively specified tasks and duties. They lack any sense either of dwelling in a natural harmony or of acting on behalf of higher purposes they themselves posit or that are posited by "leaders," purposes that could tame and "materially" or even ethically direct the specific spheres in which they act.

Indeed, as rationalized culture progresses, the place of any personal relationship that actors in such spheres might once have had to a master, lord, or ruler—a relationship characteristic of prerationalized culture—is filled by surrogates for the worldly or otherworldly personal masters that then provided direction and guidance for service. These surrogates are values that replace what has been lost through impersonality. They are "ideologically transfigured" and embodied in a community in the form of " 'ideas of cultural value': 'state,' 'church,' 'community,' 'party,' 'enterprise.' "[105] Yet a calling that wants merely our submission is not enough to rescue the world of rationalization from sterility and immobility. To submit passively even to such culture values, to accept blindly the autonomy of these activities and yield passively to them, is to remain merely obedient, and it leaves politics to bureaucracy without leaders, economics to bureaucracy without entrepreneurs, science to technique without innovators.

It is Weber's more inspired concept of the calling that, he believes, gives him a means of overcoming this dilemma. Where such autonomous spheres rule, it is not possible to do more than simply submit to them and accept disempowerment *unless* we are able to reappropriate and master them through an impassioned calling. We must choose an ultimate value to guide our service to them, taking up their banner, following their laws and fighting for them as the path to our own redemption, thus apparently ending our transcendental quest for meaning, to find what we need in the given conditions of our world. We must generate the empowered actors required to master these realms, the new "heroes" of the soul who are daring, fortified to take risks, oriented toward world mastery, and capable of commanding others to follow, in order to make the rationalized spheres more than a collection of mere technical tasks.[106]

The prescription of service in a calling as the universal solution the times require shows that Weber did not merely accept the conditions of rationalized spheres as the ultimate conditions of the world. In fact, if these spheres became totally autonomous, he suggested, the world would be lost, for then everything would be merely a form of technical control and individuals would have lost all hope of finding meaning. For Weber, meaning and power can be found in only one way: through the transformation of ultimate values into "gods," through submission to them as sources of salvation, and through enlistment in combat on their behalf. This might make it clearer why Europeans in 1914, confronted with the loss of compelling religious faith and with the dominance of these "bourgeois" spheres of life, welcomed so overwhelmingly the advent of war and the service of their nations.

Although Weber acknowledged that a concrete individual's *Weltanschauung* will usually show a strong "elective affinity" with his class and status interests, his model of the individual in the abstract requires that the person make the choice for an ultimate value without the help of science. The potential actor dwells in a lonely place, in which, supposedly unaided, he must make a decision and a choice of value, the submission to which and service of which make him a personality.[107] Yet it is not those who serve who prescribe laws to themselves, as in the Kantian situation where freedom results from self-imposed laws of reason. The world, as Weber interprets it, is not and cannot be governed by reason; rather, it reflects the struggle between impersonal "gods," with persons acting only as the champions and warriors of these gods. Weber's "disenchanted" world still retains gods; worse, it retains devils. The service to these many and conflicting gods may not necessarily destroy the possibility of social life or common purposes. However, when the human relationship to ideals and purposes is one of service in a calling, and when human redemption from meaninglessness and impotence is possible only in a struggle carried on in behalf of gods, there is danger. If consensus or acknowledgment and acceptance of others should fail, then we have, facing one another in Weber's world, a set of champions serving gods who see their opponents as agents of the "devil," who may have difficulty discussing articles of peace, even of the Hobbesian variety, since they have been making spiritual war in a service that is the source of life's meaning. For, as Weber says: " 'Peace' means a shifting of the forms of struggle or of the opponents of struggle or of the objects of struggle, and nothing else."[108]

The danger in Weber's formulation lies in converting purposes, causes, and positions into overarching gods whose "validity" must be defended because one has staked the fate of one's soul on them, and because one knows no other way to find meaning, justification, and strength in life except through service of powers that demand one's all. It is true that Weber argued there was an alternative to "absolutist" commitment to one's god, to "conviction" (*Gesinnung*) of the intrinsic and absolute value of the calling: a commitment based on the notion of "responsibility," which prescribed that the good "intention" in fulfilling the calling absolutely must be modified by a standard oriented toward practical success and toward a reasonable calculation of consequences and costs that might lead the actor to modify or abandon his intention.[109] In Weber's science, however, an "ethic of responsibility" in the calling can no more be justified "scientifically" or absolutely than any other ethic that guides action. It, too, by Weber's logic, must remain a matter of faith. Science cannot tell whether ends "sanctify" the means.[110] Thus, the choice of whether to act "responsibly" or purely on the absolutist basis of "conviction" must remain completely up to the actor; it cannot be resolved by Weberian science. It is this situation that creates the social danger of service: if all must have a service that is central to their life's meaning, and if service in the calling need not necessarily be performed "responsibly," then the need for validating "gods" and for a warrior's life on their behalf may lead to a conflict of churches and to spiritual or civil war.

Weber did not expect that his time, in conditions of rationalization, could share a common vision or purpose except in war and the defense of the nation. He hoped that, with the aid of a restored and now-trusted science, individuals not only would find their own form of submission and calling, but would also "understand the godly" in other spheres of life, hence acknowledge and understand what others—and that others—must serve. There was clearly the danger that some would always be ready to refuse acknowledgment of the legitimacy of others' "gods" or service, despite Weber's urging that science and the scientist act in the service of understanding, and despite the fact that each must act in the service of the god he has chosen. And indeed, nonacknowledgment was the general experience of imperial Germany, where Jews, women, and socialists were excluded from positions of learning, war was made on Catholicism and socialism, and a chauvinist nationalism that brooked no criticism was stolidly defended.[111] The contemporary experience of nonacknowledgment did not offer much hope to such a proposal as Weber's for the future. Yet Weber intended that the affirmation of one's own calling be a preliminary to at least a modest recognition of the vocation and service of others. Still, despite his own recognition of the common plight and need of others, Weber did not desire peaceful co-existence: the world of service is a world of conflicts and struggle, and it cannot, and should not, be otherwise. To Weber, one could now at least recognize those who "authentically" served their god and distinguish them from the merely vain and self-advancing. Yet in a world where one must serve gods in struggle as the only means of finding meaning, the danger of radical attempts at "solution" is only too obvious.

For Weber, the vocation was not only a way of acting and living. It was, for him, the last and only resort in a time with few shared ideals and no true prophets. Weber's understanding and proposals reach the limit of their value and validity in their pervasive and unquestioned devotion to calling and service as the only remaining source of meaning and self-empowerment for those without religion or war. Basing his ideal on a religious "mystery" and drawing on war to confirm it, Weber confronted a supposedly "demystified" age with one last mystery, thus preserving one last "enchantment" and illusion while trying to live a life without illusions.

4   The Identification of Self and Nation

During World War I, while Weber was retaining and reviving a form of enchantment for the purposes of identity and inner power, Thomas Mann was generating his own magic or "enchantment," and for similar purposes. The inadequacy of Mann's prewar solution to the problems of the artist's identity and of the relation between "life" and spirit—life understood as bourgeois life, and spirit understood as the critical consciousness of art—was visible not only in the meagerness of his artistic achievements between *Tonio Kröger* in 1903 and *Death in Venice* in 1912. It was also expressed by Mann himself in worried letters filled with fear of artistic sterility and in his post-1912 reflections on the end of a phase of his career, an end marked by the story of Gustav Aschenbach. Self-absorption, obsession with aestheticism, defensive attachment to the bourgeoisie, overrefined self-observation, and insecurity—all reach their high point in the story of artistic exhaustion, repressed desire, and distorted apprehension of reality contained in *Death in Venice*.

The period following the outbreak of World War I, however, was a pivotal one for Mann. It brought celebration and release for Germany and its intellectual classes, but it also brought a crisis of the ruling order and ideology, and a struggle for self-understanding and self-justification in the face of massive European enemies east and west.[1] Though he claimed that "1914 was his rebirth into community," Mann underwent his own crisis.[2] Already at work on *The Magic Mountain*, he grew increasingly angry and frustrated at the attacks leveled at Germany and the legitimacy of its initiation and pursuit of the war. The attack that affected him most deeply and provoked him to put aside his manuscript for more than two years was the one launched by his brother Heinrich, for Mann saw in it not only an attack on Germany, but also a thinly veiled attack on himself, his personality, his artistic beliefs, and his support of the German war effort. Yet Mann turned this attack to his own purposes, for good and ill, by defending both Germany and himself, defending himself as Germany and Germany as himself. He thus achieved an identification between them so strong that it transformed his artistic creativity and laid the basis for the powerful interpretations of German culture and society that emerged in *The Magic Mountain* and *Doctor Faustus*.

In his wartime *Reflections of an Unpolitical Man*, Mann turns a conflict within his family into a symbolic battle of Germany against the West, a battle of German *Innerlichkeit* against reason, of culture against civilization, of aristocratic individualism against politics and democracy. Through the waging of this conflict, Mann invents a new intellectual history of his origins, identifying and connecting himself to his intellectual forebears and to a new German identity, specifically to his own identity as a German, fighting Germany's cultural battles as his own, fighting his battles with his brother as a form of Germany's battles for identity.[3] This spiritual combat effected an extension of Mann's artistic self that made possible the expansion of his art into political and cultural themes not accessible to him before. He saved himself from the sterile self-absorption that threatened his creativity before the war by objectifying his struggles outward, not just artistically but culturally and politically. In this way he transcended the earlier form of his representativeness and identity through the fusion of self and nation.

The *Reflections* are, symbolically, Mann's second plunge into the "family" for the purpose of self-understanding. The first was *Buddenbrooks*, which saved him from the fate of Hanno Buddenbrook and the hero of "The Joker" and freed him for the accomplishment of *Tonio Kröger*. Experiencing the failing power of the bourgeois calling and the bourgeois decline into decadence, Mann finds new strength in the calling for art. But experiencing also a decline of power within the artistic calling, Mann turns to a reempowerment through identification with the nation. In the *Reflections*, Germany becomes his true family, and this frees him for a second release from death and powerlessness, frees him for *The Magic Mountain*. Through the *Reflections* Mann discovered both his spiritual family and what he considered his essential identity—and the identity of the true artist—with Germany.

But in the *Reflections*, Mann also takes a temporary step backward. In the first place, he takes up, as his own positions, attitudes he criticizes in *Death in Venice*.[4] By defending art as war and declaring his ideal to be the Prussian ethos of *Durchhalten*, or "hold fast"—derived from Friedrich the Great and defended by Aschenbach—Mann reidentifies himself with Aschenbach and supports an oppressive and rigid attitude toward reality and work.[5] In the second place, Mann's *Reflections* are driven by a hysterical defense of himself and of *Deutschtum* (Germanness) in its worst form against the criticisms of his reflexive, bourgeois, and unthinking nationalism leveled by Heinrich.[6] It is sibling rage—not just the defense of Germany's war but of his own symbolic war on behalf of injured self-worth—that fuels the immoderate and poorly thought out arguments of the *Reflections* and makes their political positions so extreme: Mann fights symbolically for his life against both his brother's literary successes and his criticisms of him. This hysterical rage underlies the third problem with the work: its transformation of Mann's personal struggle into a Europe-wide struggle between hypostatized cultural essences—embodied in nations—that take their place in his vast symbolic construction and interpretation of the war. Although the process of identifying self and nation had enormously positive artistic consequences for Mann's later writing, the other issues at work undermine any larger value of the *Reflections* except as an important way station on Mann's own road to creation and a symbolic indicator of the new roots of identity and meaning in his work.

ART, WAR, AND SERVICE

In his first defense of the war, Mann cast the struggle of Germany with the West in terms of the opposition between culture and civilization—a distinction with a long history in German thought[7]—and elaborated the beginnings of his view of self and nation.[8] "Culture is inclusiveness, style, form, self-control [*Haltung*], taste, a certain spiritual organization of the world. . . . Civilization, however, is reason, enlightenment, softening, modesty, scepticism, dissolution—spirit [*Geist*]. Yes, spirit is civilian, is burgherly: it is the sworn enemy of the instincts, of the passions, it is antidemonic, antiheroic." For these reasons, and ignoring the creativity of other, essentially "civilized" nations, Mann argues that the spirit of civilization is opposed to the spirit of art. "Art, like all culture, is the sublimation of the demonic. . . . Art is far from being inwardly interested in progress and enlightenment, in the comfort of the social contract, in short, in the civilizing of humankind."[9] But what makes art so uninterested in civilization is not only that it belongs to the demonic and perhaps the heroic: it is that art is war! Here, despite his claim to have gone beyond the "dead end" of *Death in Venice*, Mann affirms as his own the view of art he had attributed to that story's hero. "Are they not completely similar relations which bind art and war with one another? For me at least it seemed all along that he would not be the worst artist who recognized himself in the portrait of the soldier. That triumphing warlike principle of today: organization—it is indeed the first principle, the essence of art."[10]

It is not surprising in wartime and in Germany that citizens would regard soldiers as exemplary. But it is surprising to find an artist arguing that his discipline is soldierly and that living like a soldier is a model for his life. In fact, Weber's and Mann's tendency to think of soldiers as models precedes the war, though it is fully developed only in wartime.[11] But art has more in common with war than organization.

> The weaving together [*Ineinanderwirken*] of enthusiasm and order; systematic manner; creating, building further, and forcing forward of the strategic foundations with "lines of communication"; solidity, exactness, circumspection; bravery, steadfastness in the endurance of exertions and defeats, in the struggle with the tough resistance of the material; contempt for what is called "security" in bourgeois life ("security" is the most loved concept and loudest demand of the burgher), the habituation to an endangered, tense, careful life; pitilessness toward oneself, moral radicalism, submission [*Hingebung*] to the most extreme degree, martyrdom, complete application of all the primary forces of the body and the soul, without which it seems ridiculous to undertake anything at all; finally, a taste for adornment, for the lustrous, as an expression of breeding and honor. All of these are, in fact, military and artistic at the same time. With great justice has art been called a war, a grinding struggle: the German word, the word "service" [*Dienst*], looks more lovely still, and indeed the service of the artist is more closely related to that of the soldier than to that of the priest.[12]

Of course, in the great tradition of concealed self-quotation, it is Mann *himself* who called art a war in *Death in Venice*, and here he covertly invokes himself as authority. What is remarkable is that, in Mann's eyes, the image of the soldier and of military service supplants, and is here even opposed to, the older ideal of the burgher and the burgherly calling as the model for the artist. This new ideal is the beginning of the search for an identity that will connect him more strongly with the nation. The dichotomy that had ruled his self-understanding has been replaced. "The antithesis of artist and burgher, literarily cultivated with pleasure, has been characterized as a romantic inheritance—not with complete understanding, as it seems to me. For this is not the opposition that we mean: burgher and gypsy, but much more: civilian and soldier."[13] The artist even shares the sentiments of the soldier and, though a civilian, identifies with his feelings and experience. "How should the artist, the soldier in the artist, not have praised god for the collapse of a world of peace, that he had his fill, so completely his fill of? War! It was purification, liberation that we experienced, and an enormous hope. . . . And today Germany is Friedrich the Great."[14]

The model of Friedrich provides an answer—embodied anew in the German war—to the loss of inner power, decay, and decadence that dominate German culture at the turn of the century. "I belong spiritually to that race of writers spread all over Europe who, coming out of decadence, appointed to be chroniclers and analysts of decadence, at the same time bear the emancipatory will toward its renunciation—let us say pessimistically: the inclination toward this renunciation—in their hearts and at least *experiment* with the overcoming of decadence and nihilism" (201).[15] Praising Protestant, Prussian, and supposedly Kantian attitudes toward duty, Mann idealizes Friedrich, who represents the manly, strong, heroic response to the hatred of enemies, the experience of weakness, and the need to defend oneself alone against insuperable odds.[16] Friedrich is a symbol of the *Leistungsethiker*, embodied earlier in *Buddenbrooks* and *Death in Venice*, the man with an ethos of achievement, able to bear up under great pressure and in isolation under the burden of his destiny, contradictory though it is. Friedrich's character is full of oppositions, yet "there is irony toward both sides, a radical scepticism, a fanaticism of achievement [*Leistung*] fundamentally nihilistic and a sovereignty as much evil as melancholy."[17]

In symbolizing Germany through Friedrich, Mann not only defends its conduct in war, but also interprets that conduct as the product of a forward-driving destiny toward greatness and maturity. "He was a sacrifice. . . . But he was mistaken if he believed that he was free to perform differently. . . . He had to do wrong and lead a life against his thoughts, he could not be a philosopher but had to be a king, in order that the earthly mission of a great people be fulfilled." This situation "remains incomprehensible . . . if one does not grasp his feeling of duty as a kind of possession and himself as a sacrifice and tool of a higher will."[18] Thus the king, the nation, the artist, Mann himself, are similarly situated as tools of a higher power and sacrifices for a higher good. They cannot choose differently, but must violate the norms of the dominant powers and the values of bourgeois normality. These symbolic equivalents confront their destiny with skepticism and determination, and war is their field of struggle.[19]

ART AND ARTIST, SELF AND NATION

Reflections of an Unpolitical Man has puzzled Mann's critics and admirers alike. Given the moderate, progressive, "Western" character of the Mann the world knew after 1933, the hysterical, antidemocratic, and reactionary quality of the *Reflections* seems hard to square with that exemplary defender of reason and enemy of National Socialism. Some have gone so far as to maintain that the work is a spiritual tract, whose "ultimate problem is . . . religious, not . . . political."[20] Even in the 1920s, when Mann spoke in defense of the Weimar Republic—though initially in tepid tones—his listeners, especially the conservative admirers of the *Reflections*, thought he had changed his views and gone over to the other side. Mann himself maintained that his views had not changed, that he upheld the same values he had enunciated during the war, and his remarks should not be dismissed lightly.[21]

The continuities between the Mann of the *Reflections* and the Mann of the 1920s and after are extensive and profound, but they are not political continuities in the sense of positions either for or against the republic. They are continuities, rather, of his commitment to the concept of the German nation and to his conception of his own identity. What was forged in the war years was not a political thinker but a new kind of artist, one whose understanding of self and nation produced a new field for art and a new basis for the artist's identity. "What else then is this long monologue and written work than a backward glance at what I was, what I was for a while justly and honorably, and what I, without feeling myself *old*, obviously can no longer be?" (216). Mann reveals his true purpose when he writes: "I wonder whether a world turning-point . . . is not precisely the moment to go into oneself, consult with one's conscience and launch a general revision of one's own foundations" (69). He did revise these foundations, but the outcome was more complex than he imagined.

Given Mann's earlier literary and essayistic portrayal of the artistic calling in terms of service, it is hardly surprising that in wartime he should have written the *Reflections* from a desire to find an activity "like service in the field" (160). His artistry was a kind of service, of course, but a service of art alone, not of the nation. The national enthusiasm for war could not be satisfied in him by his going about his business in the usual way, nor could his embarrassment at not being a soldier be easily overcome.[22] After his tentative engagements in the ideological defense of Germany, Mann needed to put his "thinking and striving in the service of German self-understanding, of a positive German self-critique" (176). "I wanted to serve" (161), but "it was not state and army that 'drafted' me but the time itself: to more than two years of service of ideas [*Gedankendienst*] under arms" (9).[23] Although his project was complicated and intensified by his struggle with his brother, Mann's need to serve the nation was more than just another component of his engagement with the German cause. It led ultimately to his putting the nation in place of his previous objects of service. Acceptance by Germany replaced his striving for acceptance by the bourgeoisie.

The Identity of Germany

Mann defines the "true" Germany, the cultural essence of the nation, initially in terms of what it is opposed to: the West, civilization, enlightenment, politics, democracy. At the same time Mann, unable to serve in the military, struggles to legitimate himself as truly German, indeed, as *the* true German. But precisely because he identifies himself so strongly with those cultural features of Germany he considers essential to its identity as a nation, and because he feels so personally implicated in Heinrich's critique of German politics and culture, everywhere Mann defends Germany he is implicitly defending himself, and every defense of his own character is likewise a defense of German identity. This defense is complemented by an exploration of what Mann considers to be Germany's essential reality and mission, its own calling and destiny. Finally, he comes to see Germany not only as the battlefield of European spiritual struggles, but also as the mediator of these struggles, a resolver and synthesizer of these conflicts on a higher level. Through this resolution of German identity, Mann makes it possible to establish the parallel roles of the artist and the nation as mediator. Germany and the true artist are one.

From the start, Mann defines the war in cultural, rather than political, terms, as the war of "the union of the Western world, of the heirs of Rome, of 'civilization' *against Germany*" (48).[24] Germany is not so much "England's power-political competitor" as "its spiritual opponent" (33). Yet the war is only the latest outbreak of an age-old struggle. "The spiritual roots of this war, which is called quite correctly 'the German war,' lie in Germany's indigenous and historical 'Protestantism.'" The war is "a new outbreak of the ancient German struggle against the spirit of the West as well as the struggle of the Roman world against obstinate Germany" (47–48). It is "in the grandest sense an irrational struggle against the world-entente of civilization which Germany has taken upon itself with a truly German obedience to its destiny, or ... to its mission, its true and native mission" (52). Mann construes the war in terms of great spiritual forces struggling for control of the future and the continuation of their own culture. "For isn't it true," he wrote a friend in 1915, "that it is ultimately nothing less than the *social reorganization of Europe* that matters—a task that the West obviously is not equal to and in which equally obviously the German mission consists."[25] In fact, to Mann the fundamental spiritual contradiction of recent European history is the conflict between the eighteenth and nineteenth centuries: the dilemma of modern Germany is that the twentieth century takes after the eighteenth, hoping to erase the remnants of the nineteenth century and the spiritual ideals it stood for. Mann sees himself as the representative of the nineteenth, and casts Heinrich as the representative of the eighteenth. In this defense of a nineteenth-century identity against the eighteenth century and the eighteenth-century dimensions that are found in the twentieth, Mann provides a historical and political interpretation of what is in fact a *Bruderkrieg*, a civil war, a war between brothers. In so doing, Mann claims to be the tool of the national spirit, the bearer of its tasks and the tasks of the nineteenth century (31).

Germany, the home of the Lutheran Reformation, is in protest not only against the West and Catholicism, but also against everything it thinks derives from this inheritance, including politics and democracy as defined by France and England—although just how Protestant England fits into the picture of the Roman enemy is never clarified. It is not politics and democracy as technical devices of self-government that Mann, and Germany, oppose. It is politics as part of the identity of western Europe, shaped by the Enlightenment and given over to utilitarian, calculating choices rooted in Enlightenment reason. To Mann, the essence of the German nation excludes politics, so much so that "in Germany the affirmation of the national contains in itself the denial of politics and of democracy" (264).[26]

There is now a spiritual-political contradiction added to the other contradictions that beset him: art versus life, *bohème* versus bourgeois, spirit versus life. The contradiction of East versus West becomes the fundamental spiritual contradiction within the European soul and the artist's soul, recognized first by Dostoevsky, who observed "German loneliness between East and West . . . Germany's offensiveness to the world . . . the antipathy . . . the hate that it has to bear and against which it must defend itself" (49). These sentiments about Germany's position were not unique to Mann, and even a liberal like Weber asserted Germany's duty to history and posterity in resisting a world that would be divided up between "the decrees of Russian officials on the one hand and the conventions of Anglo-Saxon 'society' on the other, perhaps with an admixture of Latin 'raison.' "[27] As Mann says:

> The world people of the spirit, strengthened to effusive physical strength, had taken a long drink at the spring of ambition; it wanted to become a world people, as God had called it to become, *the* world people of reality—if necessary (and obviously it was necessary) through a violent breakthrough [*Durchbruch*]. Had

Spain, France, England not had their world hours and hours of honor? When the war was unleashed Germany believed ardently that its own hours had come, the hours of affliction and of greatness. (338)

The myth of Germany's encirclement, of the efforts of the great powers jealously to deny her what they had claimed for themselves, appears here in the fantasy of a "breakthrough" to power, greatness, acknowledgment—much like the longing of a younger sibling for the attention already obtained by an older one. Again, this interpretation of German reality was expressed not only by Mann. The flames of popular feeling had been fanned since at least the turn of the century by the German government and by imperialist and conservative groups longing for a world political role and filled with resentment of the "enemies" that stood in the way of German ambitions. What is interesting is how Mann draws on these conventional sentiments to effect an even closer identification between himself and Germany. The analogy of self and Germany, of the artist and the nation, of the individual longing for connection and the German people striving for breakthrough and redemption from isolation, reemerges later—and in the same terms—in the great allegory of twentieth-century German history, *Doctor Faustus*.

To Mann, the West's essence is "politics," meaning public participation in self-government. "Progress" and development, if they took hold in Germany, would mean "the democratization of Germany," which would be the same as "the loss of its Germanness [*seine Entdeutschung*]" (67). Thus "the present war" is not only about balances of power, trade, and political order. It is also about ideas, and war brings out the essential nature of nations and of their culture (194).

> [War] is the great means against the rationalistic disintegration of national culture, and my participation in this war has nothing at all to do with world and trade domination, but rather is nothing other than the participation in that passionate process of self-knowledge, self-limitation, and self-fortification which German culture was compelled to through a terrible spiritual pressure and assault from without. (116)

To Mann, the war is yet another example of Germany's unique place within Europe. Germany is a land "where the spiritual contradictions of Europe confront one another almost without common national coloring, without national synthesis." From this fact, Mann makes an unusual conclusion: "Germany is no nation" (194). It is rather a "people" (*Volk*), next to which "nation" is an artificial import from the West, without roots in German experience. "The national principle is the atomistic, the anarchistic, the anti-European, the reactionary principle. Democracy is reactionary, for it is nationalistic and without any European conscience. . . . European conscience, supra-national responsibility is alive uniquely and alone in the unpolitical and antidemocratic people, in Germany." Indeed, Germany is "the most cultivated *Volk*, the most just, and the one that most truly loves peace" (207).

Thus Germany, unlike other combatants, is not fighting only for its own vision against the visions of others, since its nature as an "all-European" entity, so to speak, distinguishes it from the merely national identity of other nations. Germany is a microcosm of Europe, containing within itself and as its essence the complexity and contradictoriness of Europe generally. This nature prevents Germany from becoming a nation and makes it more urgent that it resist the efforts of the Allies to turn it into just another nation.

> There is . . . a land and people that is not a nation, and can never apparently become one, in that certain sense that the French or the English are nations, because the history of its formation, its concept of humanity [*Menschlichkeitsbegriff*] stand against it; a land whose inner unity and completeness are not only complicated but practically overcome [*aufgehoben*] through spiritual contradictions; a land where these contradictions appear more violent, fundamental, evil, less open to compromise than anywhere else. . . . This land is Germany. The inner spiritual contradictions of Germany are hardly national, they are almost purely European contradictions. . . . In Germany's soul *Europe's* spiritual contradictions are settled. . . . This is truly its national destiny. No longer physically . . . but spiritually Germany is still the battlefield of Europe. (54)

Germany is thus both different from Europe and a microcosm of it. How it can be both Mann does not make clear.

But this feature of Germany is also personal. "And when I say 'the German soul,' I do not mean in general the soul of the nation, but I mean in particular the soul, the head, the heart of the German individual: I mean also even myself. To be a spiritual place of struggle for European contradictions: that is German" (54). To be German, therefore, for Mann the German, is to have one's self be the locus of struggle for the spiritual conflicts of Europeans and their cultural ideals, to experience in one's own soul and work the conflict between the alternative paths and cultures of Europe. Germany's fight is identified with, and is an extension and projection of, his inner struggle, and is identified too with the fight within his family between himself and his brother. At the same time, his inner struggle is exalted as a microcosm of Germany's struggle.

Of course, to Mann, Germany has contradictions that belong only to it, and they are embodied in its struggle with the *Zivilisationsliterat*, the type of intellectual Mann sees as his main adversary—who must therefore also be Germany's main adversary: that is, his brother Heinrich.

> There exist in Germany spirits who not only do not share in the "protest" of its community against the Roman West, but who rather see their actual task and mission in the passionate protest *against* this protest and who advance the close annexation of Germany with the imperium of civilization with all the strengths of their talent. . . . Their patriotism manifests itself in such a manner that they see the precondition of greatness . . . not in its disturbing and hate-arousing "particularity," but rather in its unconditional union with the world of civilization, of literature, of . . . democracy—which world would in reality be complete through the subjugation of Germany. (55–56)

This betrayal of German uniqueness is aimed at destroying Germany. "Whoever's efforts would make out of Germany simply a bourgeois democracy in the Roman-Western sense and spirit, would want to take from it its best and most difficult thing, its problematic, in which its nationality most really consists; he would want to make it boring, clear, dumb, and un-German, and would be therefore an antinationalist, who insisted that Germany become a nation in a foreign sense and spirit" (54–55).[28]

But to Mann, identification with the West and longing to transform Germany do not derive from regard for the beneficial effects of Western Enlightenment and democracy. They derive from longing for the old, noble world of the Western past, blind to the German present. In a temporary reversal of conventional evaluations, Mann, in Spenglerian fashion, makes romanticism an attribute of westernizing, democratizing interests. "Do the Western powers not appear to us today chiefly as *old*, yes, old-fashioned? In that they represent world-political and civilizing legitimacy, they function aristocratically, and I believe that much of the sympathy that is alive among us for the West, allegedly from democratic motives, is in truth aristocratic sympathy, sympathy with the old, noble, declining worlds, romanticism, 'sympathy with death.' "[29] A few years later, in *The Magic Mountain*, Mann was to use romanticism and sympathy with death to stigmatize not the West and Heinrich, but reactionary resistance *to* the West. Here romanticism is made the enemy of German reaction, while the German refusal of Western culture and politics is upheld as the realistic and modern choice.

Yet the oppositional quality of the *Zivilisationsliterat* is not so foreign. "I do not completely forget here, that it almost belongs to German humanity to behave as an un-German and even as an anti-German" (52). The *Zivilisationsliterat* "is not un-German, he is only an astounding, remarkable example of how far, still today, in post-Bismarckian Germany, the German can succeed in self-disgust and alienation, in cosmopolitan devotion and self-renunciation. . . . The structure of his spirit [is] *un-national*" (58). Only someone "unnational" would try to rob Germany of its cultural essence in order to make it like a Western nation.

> To literarize, radicalize, politicize, westernize Germany means: to rob it of its Germanness. . . . We are more something like Europe in essence [*im Auszuge*]. . . . There is no national German solidarity and synthesis—at most in music, our homeland, but not and never in the spirit and in politics: on account of which it is a foolish and unnational undertaking to want to replace the musical atmosphere of Germany with a literary-political one, as the *Civilisationsliterat* [*sic*] wants to.[30]

The unique German people also has a unique calling. The Germans, "like Hamlet, were not actually born to action, but were unavoidably called to it. To be called, whether to a knowledge or to an action, to which one is not born, that always seems to me the meaning of the tragic" (148). Their persistence can be seen in Friedrich the Great's "reverence for the Schopenhauerian equation of courage and patience, the love of 'nevertheless' [*Trotzdem*], or . . . of the ethos of 'hold fast' [*Durchhalten*]" (148). Here, Mann not only defends Aschenbachian ideals for himself, but also makes them the key to Friedrich's and Germany's calling and heroism. Of course, heroism is a virtue always, and understandably, extolled in war. But it is not heroism as such that is the issue in Mann's wartime writings or *Death in Venice*, but a specific ideal of heroism, whose model is the naturally weak individual who persists despite exhaustion. Mann defends this type as the paradigm for the nation and the self.

Thus Mann analyzes Germany in terms that mirror those he uses about himself. His confusion of the national and personal symbolic levels and his intensely symbolic perception and interpretation of the war prevent an evenhanded understanding of its events and of the stakes being fought for. They lead to his irrational defense of German politics, institutions, and reaction on behalf of fidelity to the symbolic construction. In this respect Mann dwells, as Aschenbach did, in symbols, seeing reality as a projection and representation of his inner reality and sibling rivalry. The need to map his two struggles onto the war, and his inability to separate Germany's struggle and political reality from his own need for vindication and identity, lead Mann to a gross submissiveness to the least admirable aspects of German culture and politics. While this confusion of self and nation became liberating for his artistic self, it was, at least in the war years and the early 1920s, mystifying for his understanding of the nation and of a war that became a bitter ideological struggle.

The Identity of the Self

Mann became more explicit about his cultural origins as he strove to show himself as deeply German and worthy of the attention of patriots, for his feelings of illegitimacy and of being a "bohemian" among the bourgeoisie carried over into a sense of his illegitimacy within Germany. But in defending Germany and himself, he actually argues for the existence of a "true" Germany and maintains that what shaped him also shaped that Germany. Mann confesses his loyalty to and identity with the nineteenth century. "I am, in the spiritually essential, a true child of the century in which the first twenty-five years of my life fall: the nineteenth. . . . Romanticism, nationalism, *Bürgerlichkeit*, music, pessimism, humor—these elements of the atmosphere of the past age form in the main the impersonal constituents of my being" (21–22). That atmosphere formed the air in which Hanno, the victim of decadence, developed: "The refractoriness, the sensitive-moral revolt against 'life as it is,' against the given, the reality, against 'power'—this refractoriness as a sign of *decline*, of biological insufficiency . . . that is the nineteenth century, that is the way in which this century saw the relation of spirit to life" (25).

The founders of his "spiritual-artistic *Bildung*" are Schopenhauer, Nietzsche, and Wagner (71–72). They made him "a psychologist of *decline*," he claims, with Nietzsche, the greatest "psychologist of decadence" and champion of "the idea of life," as his master (78–79). "Does Georg Simmel not rightly maintain that since Nietzsche 'life' has become the key concept of all modern *Weltanschauungen*? . . . It was Nietzsche who, with incomparably deeper and more passionate cynicism, for the first time questioned philosophically the highest moral ideals, the truth itself, in their value for life" (84). Indeed, the understanding of the link between Puritanism and the bourgeoisie that Mann shares with Weber, Troeltsch, and Sombart he attributes to their common heritage in Nietzsche, the "godless Calvin" with his "heroism of weakness." "Our agreement about the psychological series 'Calvinism, *Bürgerlichkeit*, heroism' emerges through a higher, the highest spiritual means: by means of *Nietzsche*; for without this experience that dominated the time ... the social scientist would have hit upon his Protestant-heroic thesis doubtless as little as the novel writer could have seen the form of his own 'hero' as he saw it" (146).

Yet Nietzsche's legacy is ambiguous, for, Mann claims, his works are in many respects un-German, even anti-German.

> Education through Nietzsche is as little a real and unobjectiona-
> ble German education as that through Schopenhauer and Wagner.
> ... Nietzsche, notwithstanding the deep Germanness of his spirit,
> has contributed more strongly than anyone else, through his Euro-
> peanism, to the critical education, to the intellectualization, psy-
> chologization, literarization, radicalization or ... to the *democra-
> tization* of Germany. ... The powerful strengthening of the
> prosaic-critical element in Germany that Nietzsche produced
> means *progress* in the most doubtful, most political sense, in the
> sense of "humanization"—progress in the Western-democratic di-
> rection and ... education by him is not exactly what one may call
> an education in the spirit of preserving Germany. (86, 88)

Since even Nietzsche furthers democratization and progress by chastising Germany and holding it up to its better self, Mann claims that anyone admiring him, if only unconsciously, embraces modernizing elements as well as purely German ones. Yet this revelation does not lead Mann to embrace the modernizing elements of his brother or other critics of Germany. Some forms of criticism are acceptable only when they come from pessimistic moralists like Schopenhauer, Wagner, and Nietzsche.

> The Nietzsche who really mattered to me ... [was] the one who
> marked out *one* picture with lasting love among all plastic art—
> Dürer's "Knight, Death, and Devil"; the one who expressed to
> Rohde his natural pleasure in all art and philosophy in which "the
> ethical air, the Faustian smell, cross, death, and grave" is to be
> felt: a word that I seized immediately as a symbol for a whole
> world, *my* world, a nordic-moralistic-Protestant, i.e., *German* one.
> (541)[31]

Mann had been unable to legitimate himself to the bourgeoisie, he felt, because the content of his calling, in however bourgeois a form he pursued it, always put him outside bourgeois respectability. Now, in recovering his intellectual and German roots, both spiritual and social, Mann seeks to legitimate himself as a German before Germany.[32] But to do so is also not simple. He is not a "good and proper German," being partly of "Romanic, Latin-American blood," and since youth oriented more "European-intellectually" than "German-poetically." Nor is novel writing a very German calling, because the novel is "not really German" or a "proper German species." Thus it is unimaginable that "a writer of novels could rise to a representative position in the consciousness of the nation, like the poet, the pure synthesizer, the lyricist or the dramatist is able to do" (70). Yet Mann turns this apparent confession of illegitimacy on its head.

> Still I have not completely forgotten here too that it practically belongs to German humanity to present oneself as un-German and even anti-German; that, according to authoritative judgment, a tendency toward cosmopolitanism destructive to the sense of nationalism is inseparable from the essence of German nationality; that one must possibly lose one's Germanness in order to find it; that without an addition of the foreign no higher Germanness is perhaps possible; that precisely the exemplary Germans were Europeans and would have felt as barbaric every reduction to the nothing-but-German. . . . To such national untrustworthinesses of our great ones we have therefore become accustomed to make a good face and have simply decided to receive such a thing into the concept of higher Germanness. (71)

Thus, although it may *seem* that a man with foreign admixture and worldly interest is illegitimate, in fact such persons are not only acceptable, they are absolutely necessary to the development of Germanness. Indeed, they may be the true Germans! Here Mann again converts a perceived inadequacy, lack, and inferiority of his own into a sense and source of *superiority*. Having blamed the *Zivilisationsliterat* for not being a true German, he confesses that he is himself not a pure German, yet he transforms his impurity into a higher rank, while denying that rank to the *Zivilisationsliterat*. Still, having affirmed this superiority, he becomes nervous at his audacity.

> Meanwhile I am not so mad as to connect the Europeanization of my taste with my rank (but about that of course there should be no discussion). It is no merit, if it is also no reproach, that intimate and exclusively German things were never enough for me, that I did not know how to begin much with it. My blood needed European stimulations. Artistically, literarily my love of German things begins precisely there where it is possible and valid for Europe, capable of European effects, accessible to every European. (71)

What began as a confession of impure Germanness has ended as a criticism of Germany, a description of Germany's inadequacy to stimulate the best work and higher *Deutschtum*, and of Mann's need for stimulation from outside. Instead of *him* being inadequate, *Germany* is inadequate. And if this might seem to a German audience arrogant and condescending, Mann outflanks such criticism by discussing those "not intimately German, but rather European events": Schopenhauer, Nietzsche, and Wagner, whom no defender of *Deutschtum* can fail to acknowledge.

Mann admits that his "own being and essence are much less foreign and opposed to the *Zivilisationsliterat*" than his critique would indicate. "It is certainly not at all the case that he is a bad burgher and patriot who does not care about Germany. On the contrary! He cares about it with all his strength, he feels himself to the highest degree responsible for its fate." But he furthers progress—something Mann admits he too does inadvertently, though with "conservative opposition." Any accusation that Mann is simply opposed to progress and the West he believes is refuted by the critical elements in his artistic work. Even his own conservative nature contains elements that further progress, despite inner opposition. This is his "literary" part, for "literature is democratic and civilizing from the ground up; more correctly: it is *the same* as democracy and civilization" (40). Thus, part of him is disloyal to the old Germany and inevitably advances the new one. Indeed, since even its opponents advance its cause, however unwittingly, "progress has everything for it" (67).

The *Zivilisationsliterat* is thus patriotic, as Mann is, and Mann furthers progress, as the *Zivilisationsliterat* does. He has chronicled the "moral-political-biological process" of decline in *Buddenbrooks*, knowing his work promotes decline while the *Zivilisationsliterat* wants to hasten it. "Only that all along, in contrast to the radical literary man, I have also cultivated restraining counter-tendencies in myself and, without understanding myself politically, expressed them early. The concept of life did this, which I had from Nietzsche, and my relationship to this concept" (586–87). Indeed, in contrast to the West, the concept of life, *Leben*, best sums up German culture, this "most German, most Goethean, and in the highest, religious sense conservative concept" (84). In Mann's view, *Tonio Kröger* demonstrated his countertendency by transcending the decline in *Buddenbrooks* with a new resolution, taking the concept of life out of philosophical and sociological debates where it was embedded abstractly and linking it to bourgeois life: "And the name of life, yes, that of beauty found itself here, sentimentally enough, transferred to the world of *Bürgerlichkeit*, the world of the ordinary that is perceived as blessed, of the opposite of spirit and art" (91). For Mann, the specifically German theme has become a German *and* bourgeois theme.

The Nature of Art

Mann's efforts to legitimate himself as German did not stop with his origins and character. His artistic production had to be legitimated as well.[33] Thomas Buddenbrook, for example, should be seen as a very German "sufferer who resisted bravely, the moralist and 'militarist' after my own heart" (72).

> "Buddenbrooks" . . . is certainly a very German book . . . above all in the formal sense—by which with the formal I mean something other than the actual literary influences and sources of fertility. . . . It became, it was not made, it grew, it was not formed, and precisely through this it is untranslatably German. . . . Precisely through this it has the organic fullness which the typical French book does not have. It is not a proportioned work of art, but life . . . *Gothic*, not Renaissance. (89)

Though his first novel engages his family past, Mann claims it reveals the mood of the time and the tenor of protest against Germany. Indeed: "The literary—if not also spiritual—cosmopolitanism of *Buddenbrooks* marked me as a proper offspring of this epoch. A culturally revolutionary epoch, the name of whose essence was insubordination against just that Germany that the lonely Nietzsche had decried" (238–89).

Buddenbrooks interested the educated middle classes, but *Tonio Kröger* attracted intellectual and radical youth. "In *Tonio Kröger* the Nietzschean element of *Bildung* broke through. The lyrical philosopher's dithyrambic-conservative concept of life and his defense against the moralistic-nihilistic spirit, against 'Literature,' became . . . an enamored affirmation of all that was not spirit and art, that was innocent, healthy, respectable-unproblematic and purified of spirit" (91). In its Nietzscheanism, in Mann's view, *Tonio Kröger* is another sign along the path of Mann's German development, while also part of the love affair between art or spirit and bourgeois life.

But to Mann the most important feature of his work and the link to German experience is not its form, nor its debt to Nietzsche. It is his concern with a certain type of hero, a certain kind of self. This hero, he argues, is linked to Weber's *Protestant Ethic* and the man of vocation exemplified by the Puritan entrepreneur. He is the bourgeois *Leistungsethiker*, the man who takes achievement and performance as his ethos, and to Mann he is the embodiment of the modern German individual.

If I have understood sympathetically anything of my time, it is its type of heroism, the modern-heroic form of life and life-conduct of the over-burdened and over-coached *ethical man of achievement* "working on the edge of exhaustion." . . . And I may say that I have written practically nothing that might not be a symbol for a heroism of this modern, neo-burgherly type. Yes, seen in this way, Thomas Buddenbrook is not only a German burgher but also a modern bourgeois; he is the first figure in whose formation this decisive experience had a part; and over the main figures of the Renaissance play [*Fiorenza*], over all the life of the prince novel [*Royal Highness*] until Gustav Aschenbach this experience operated formatively and was creative of symbols in my work. (144–45)

Indeed, it is the "bourgeois men of acquisition and achievement" with whom Mann has "psychical-symbolic sympathy." This sympathy, he suggests, allowed him to understand the world and underlies his solidarity with Germany in the time of its greatest need.

I see now for once that the tragic-ethical Nietzsche experience played a role in my experience of the burgherly man of achievement [*Leistungsethiker*], even if it was also not at all the case with the learned psychologists of capitalism. I see further that even this insight of feeling into the connection between capitalistic neo-burgherliness and the Protestant ethic originates in a certain modernity of my work that is critical of the times. And I see finally that my "patriotism" of 1914 was quite essentially a sudden and quite properly temporary politicization of this sympathy, of this symbolic participation. (147)

Thus, to Mann, the work most important for understanding his Germanness is *Death in Venice*. What is noteworthy, however, is that it is precisely those virtues held up to apparent criticism in *Death in Venice*—"in its own way something final, the late work of an epoch" (212)—that return in Mann's reevaluation of the work as the exemplary German virtues. Those qualities that he claimed to have surpassed Mann now admires and attributes to Germany. Indeed, the critique of Germany on behalf of freedom is misplaced, Mann argues, because "the deepest longing of the world . . . is directed not at all at wider anarchization through a concept of freedom but at new obligations [*Bindungen*]" (515). He describes the times and his own experiment in *Death in Venice*:

The longing, striving, and searching of the times, which is *not* by any means directed toward freedom, but toward the eager desire for an "inner tyranny," for an "absolute table of values," for constraint, for the moral return of certainty [*Wieder-fest-Werden*]—it is a striving after *culture*, dignity, for self-control [*Haltung*], for form. . . . In a story I engaged in experiments with the renunciation of the psychologism and relativism of the dying epoch, I allowed an artist to dismiss "knowledge for its own sake," to renounce sympathy for the "abyss" and to turn toward will, toward value judgment, toward intolerance, toward "resolution." I gave it all a catastrophic, that means, sceptical-pessimistic ending. That an artist could win *dignity* I placed in doubt, I allowed my hero, who had tried it, to experience and to confess that it was not possible. I know well that the "new will" that I allowed to be frustrated would certainly never have become a problem for me if I had had no part in it. . . . To allow it to be frustrated, however, this "new will," and to give this experiment a sceptical-pessimistic ending: precisely this seemed moral to me—as it seemed to me artistic. (516–17)

Here, Mann underscores his difference from and continuity with Aschenbach by using Aschenbach's language.[34] The narrator in the story had remarked that Aschenbach's work and ideals helped an exhausted generation endure its sufferings beyond the limits of its strength, and Mann's identification with Aschenbach can be seen in the claim that he had performed a similar service. People growing up on *Buddenbrooks* and *Tonio Kröger*, he said, let him know that these works "have *helped* others to *live*" (220). Thus, Mann believes he has portrayed the plight of the modern German hero, showing how well attuned he is to the experience of failing power that fights on, which he takes to be the reality of Germany.

Of course, it was not Puritan entrepreneurs who "labored at the point of exhaustion," but the modern men of the calling Weber describes, not the early religious men but the later secular men struggling to find a cause and a source of empowerment. The Puritans were exhilarated, confident world-builders, who may have been anxious about their otherworldly fate but who mastered this world literally and, through their achievements, mastered the next symbolically. By portraying the outcome of the *Leistungsethiker*, not its origin, Mann thus reveals its modern fate.

Bürgerlichkeit

Although Mann's task of relegitimating the self and connecting himself with Germany takes him beyond his traditional confrontation with the burgher class, *Bürgerlichkeit* remains a central concern to him. Indeed, in defining *Deutschtum* and making the nation the key referent of his identity, Mann links the nation to the *Bürgertum*, the formerly exclusive anchor of his identity. "The *Bürger* is national according to his essence. . . . If he was the carrier of the ideas of German unity, it was because he has always been the carrier of German culture and spirituality" (116). In fact, "the German and the bourgeois are one; if 'the spirit' is actually of bourgeois origin, so is the *German* spirit bourgeois in a special way, German education [*Bildung*] is bourgeois, German bourgeois nature [*Bürgerlichkeit*] is *human*, from which follows that it is not, as the Western one is, *political*." Indeed, one obtains "a bourgeois education [*Erziehung*]" even from Schopenhauer and Wagner (107). Yet, Mann claims, this is not only his inheritance: the whole of German culture is indebted to the *Bürgertum*. "The deepening of the German type . . . is the work of this unpolitical burgher culture . . . [which grew in] a time of the upswing of German individuality" (114). Regrettably, Mann says, he was compelled to become the chronicler of the decay of the burgherly class, of its vitality and essence.

> Burgherliness [*Bürgerlichkeit*], therefore, and indeed patriarchal-aristocratic burgherliness as life mood, life feeling, is my personal inheritance. . . . My actual experience, however, that enabled me to give to literature a work characteristic for the history of the German *Bürgertum* was the "degeneration" of such an old and true burgherliness into the subjective-artistic: an experience and problem of overrefinement and loss of proficiency, not of hardening. . . . What I experienced and formed . . . was *also* a development and modernization of the burgher, but not its development into the bourgeois, but its development into the artist. . . . The problem . . . was not a political one but a biological, psychological one. . . . The psychological-human concerned me. (139–40)

To clarify his relation to *Bürgerlichkeit*, Mann draws on Kierkegaardian distinctions made by Georg Lukács in *The Soul and the Forms*, and in the process revises his earlier understanding of the relation between life and the calling.

> Lukács . . . distinguishes above all between that foreign, violent and dissimulating, ascetic-orgiastic bourgeoisie [*Bourgeoistum*], whose most famous example is Flaubert and whose essence is the mortifying denial of life in favor of the work—and the truly burgherly artistry of a Storm, Keller, Mörike, which first actually realizes the paradox of its adjective in joining a burgherly conduct of life, founded on a burgherly calling, with the hard struggles of the strictest artistic work and whose essence is "the proficiency of the artisan." . . . He regards this ethical-artisanly mastery, in con-

trast to the monkish aestheticism of Flaubert, whose burgherly conduct of life was a nihilistic mask, as the Germanic form of the burgherly artist type. Aestheticism and *Bürgerlichkeit*, he gives us to understand, represent here a complete and legitimate form of life, and indeed a *German* form of life; yes, this mixture of artistry and *Bürgerlichkeit* forms the actual German variation of European aestheticism, the German *l'art pour l'art*. (103–4)

Fichte, in fact, claimed that "the German—and only he—practiced art *as a virtue* and a religion—which says the same thing and is an ever valid translation of the *l'art pour l'art* formula *into German*" (316).

But whereas Lukács merely contrasts Flaubert's artistic ethos with the artistry of German burgherly artists, Mann wants to make this contrast a feature of the superiority of German culture and the inferiority of French culture. He isolates and criticizes a life-denying artistic ethos he believes characteristic of the French bourgeoisie on behalf of what he considers the healthier burgherly ethos of the German craftsman, with which he identifies himself and through which he affirms *Bürgerlichkeit*.

> "Burgherly calling as a form of life," Lukács writes, "means in the first place the primacy of ethics in life; that life is dominated through what is systematically and regularly repeated, through what returns in conformity with one's duty, through what must be done without regard for desire or lack of it. With other words: the domination of order over mood, of the lasting over the momentary, of quiet work over genius that is fed with sensations."
> (103)

Of course, Mann admits, he himself lacks a proper "burgherly calling . . . as the real form of life and order of life"; yet so did other writers. "But should this critical condition really be indispensable? It is of course clear that the spirit loves to put the symbol in place of reality. One can live like a soldier [*soldatisch leben*] without in the least being fit to live as a soldier. The intellectual lives in the image [*Gleichnis*]" (104).

With these reflections Mann revises his conception of self and acknowledges the symbolic value of the calling as the solution to the problem of identity. Without a proper bourgeois calling—and thus unable to live *as* a "soldier of the calling" in the bourgeois sense—he can nonetheless live *like* a soldier of the calling within art. He has replaced literal adherence to the bourgeois calling with a symbolic substitute, modeling himself on the called individuals of the bourgeoisie in order to live like those symbolically whom he cannot live like actually. He has learned to live in symbols, since reality denies him the possibility, he believes, to live as a real person anywhere else. In the *Reflections* this symbol is further redeemed by being made to stand for the "ethical" aspect of bourgeois life rather than for the aesthetic aspect of the artistic life.

In claiming that his calling is an ethical symbol, an ethos and practice that is burgherly but with an aesthetic rather than a traditional bourgeois content, Mann identifies himself more strongly with the upright, bourgeois side of his identity, separates the form of the calling more completely from any determinate content, and recognizes the significance of the calling as a justification of life. The justification of Mann's life as an artist, as for Aschenbach, now takes the form of an "ethical" role, but ethical here simply means embodying the bourgeois virtues of hard work in a calling. This alone Mann construes as responsible living, as opposed to the irresponsibility and purported beauty-seeking of mere art. Of course, Mann had *always* opposed aestheticism on behalf of respect for and adherence to a bourgeois calling. Thus Mann here merely restates and reembraces the bourgeois dimension of the calling more self-consciously and fully, by arguing that the aesthetic concern of art—art as a sphere of life with a value all its own—cannot legitimate, cannot empower, and is, in fact, suspicious, with nothing redemptive about it. The artist's life can be redeemed *only* when lived "ethically," as the bourgeoisie lives in the calling. Here Mann makes more explicit his adherence to the forms and values of bourgeois life, while minimizing his devotion to purely artistic ends. His artistry borrows burgherly forms of life for the craftsmanly purposes of art, affirming the superiority of burgherly life to art.

> That primacy of the ethical in life of which the critic speaks—does he not mean the superiority [*Übergewicht*] of the ethical over the *aesthetic*? And is this superiority not present when life itself, even without a burgherly calling, possesses primacy over the *work*? An artistry is burgherly owing to the fact that it transfers to the exercise of art the ethical characteristics of the burgherly form of life: order, continuation, rest, "diligence"—not in the sense of assiduousness, but of faithfulness to the craft. (104)

Previously, Mann strove to justify his life through achievement, to prove his bourgeois nature by accomplishing something, though in art. At that point, his life was something to be given up in order to achieve something through which his life might be redeemed in the eyes of inner and outer bourgeois judges. Thus, his artistic achievements were visible signs of his worth, so much so that his elevation of the ethical over the artistic seems at first to be mere rationalization and a crude attempt to justify himself.

It was a romantic delusion of youth and allure of youth when I imagined formerly that I was sacrificing my life to "art" and that my *Bürgerlichkeit* was a nihilistic mask; when, certainly with sincere irony toward both sides, I gave art, the "work," precedence over life and declared one may not live, one must die "in order to be completely a creator." In truth "art" is only a means to fulfill my life ethically. My "work" . . . is not the product, meaning, and goal of an aesthetic-orgiastic denial of life, but an ethical form of expression of my life itself. . . . Life is not the means to the achieving of an aesthetic ideal of perfection, but the work is an ethical symbol of life. The goal is not some kind of objective perfection but the subjective consciousness that I "could not have done it better in any case." (104–5)

Once he casts the alternatives as ethical expression of life, represented by the bourgeoisie, versus "aesthetic-orgiastic" denial of life, represented by the fantasy bohemians, then, of course, the choice is easy. The point is that Mann has moved from commitment to the products of art to commitment to the calling as such, as form of life and as ethical symbol. Indeed, the life lived in the calling itself, not its products, is now recognized as the essence of bourgeois identity and of the identity Mann covets. For the older adherents of the calling, work was certainly an ethical symbol of life: they saw their achievements as expressions of grace. Neither art nor any other worldly achievement could be given primacy over life, because what life seeks is God and justification, not achievement. Yet the paradox of the calling and the fulfillment found in work is that in order to justify and legitimate life, the called individual denies the value of life on behalf of work, so that at the end he may feel justified. "Natural" life is sacrificed so that a higher life may be attained. One saves one's life by overcoming it, and at the end one can believe in life, but it is a life religiously transformed, justified because it has been uplifted by God and transfigured through self-sacrifice for a higher ideal. Work is not elevated over life, for that would be idolatry of the flesh—or, in Mann's terms, aestheticism, which is life-denying in the sense that it rejects bourgeois life, and it is this life that must be defended.

Thus, Mann is telling the truth when he defends the primacy of ethics over aesthetics in his life, the primacy of the search for "redemption" over the search for beauty. Indeed, because he "saw through" beauty, he actually sought deformity and decay as symbol.

I was never concerned with "beauty." . . . [It] was nothing German fundamentally and especially not the object and taste of an artistic German-burgherliness. In this sphere the ethical outweighs the aesthetic, or more correctly: a mixture and identification of these concepts takes place which honors, loves, and cares for *the ugly.* For the ugly, illness, decay, *that is the ethical,* and I have never felt myself in the literal sense as an "aesthete," but always as a moralist. (106–7)

Regard for the ugly proves his credentials as something other than an aesthete, proves his concern for the ethical and moral problems of bourgeois life, which is not only bourgeois but German. "I feel myself to be German by virtue of this belonging to a burgherly-ethical artistry that is German. . . . Because I, coming personally from an old-burgherly German sphere, despite all modern questionableness and Europeanizing needs, am connected in my way with those representatives of German-craftsmanly artistic mastery" (105–6).

Thus Mann forges a link between Germanness, his burgherly heritage, and the tradition of the burgher craftsman. "Ethics, *Bürgerlichkeit,* decay: they belong together" (106). In equating Germany and *Bürgerlichkeit,* Mann not only identifies them, but also shifts the focus of his self-identification from the bourgeois class to the German-bourgeois class, for now the essence and significance of the bourgeoisie is linked completely to its Germanness, in a Germany whose spirit and *Bildung* derive from burgher traditions. Mann's criterion for belonging and identification is now *Deutschtum,* which is a higher form of *Bürgerlichkeit,* while the bourgeoisie itself is identified with, but transcended by, Germany. Mann now feels entitled to a German identity by virtue of his identity as a member of a *Bürgertum* that is German through and through and whose contributions to Germany are unique and valuable. The unpolitical burgher has become the unpolitical German.

Art and the Artist

It is not only Germany and the bourgeoisie that mediate and stand in the middle, but the artist as well. Yet the artist first comes to his task out of uncertainty and inner conflict. "To what point, whence, after all, writing, if it is not a spiritual-moral effort for the sake of a problematical self [*Ich*]?" (20). In fact, art is self-protection. "Artistry is something *one withdraws behind* when the objective is a little upside down" (546). An artist like himself directs his critique "inwardly . . . into one's own individuality. . . . He insinuates his own self as carrier of the universally human and loves as well as censures, affirms as well as denies humankind only on the way to his own self" (296).

Mann takes this problematical self with its ambivalence to be a universal feature of artists. "Someone who is accustomed to making *art never takes* the spiritual, the intellectual, *completely seriously*, since his task was always much more to treat it as material and a plaything, to plead for points of view, to practice dialectic, to let whoever is speaking always be right" (228–29). The artist "tolerates no settledness in any truth, no dignity of virtue. The artist is and remains a gypsy, even supposing that it is a question of a German artist of burgherly culture. Since it is his object to speak out of many souls, he is necessarily a dialectician" (402–3). Yet art is not just ambivalent: it is "an irrational power, but a great power" (396–97). Indeed, it is a major *source* of the irrational: "war, heroism of a reactionary kind, all the disorder of unreason will be thinkable on the earth and therefore possible as long as art exists" (399).

The situation of art and the artist have been changed by Nietzsche, because of whom art has become the "critique of reality by the spirit."[35] This connection with spirit means art's departure from the world of the "naive."

> Art was a stimulus, an enticement to life. . . . What made it problematical, what made its character so very complicated, was its connection with the *spirit*, pure spirit, with the critical, negative, destructive principle. . . . It connects the most intimate, sensually most gifted creative affirmation of life with the finally nihilistic pathos of radical critique. Art, poetry stopped being naive, it became, to use the older expression, "sentimental" or, as one says today, "intellectual"; art, poetry was and is now no longer simply life, but also *critique* of life. (569–70)[36]

In this modern condition, the artist, in his "Protestant rather than antique" character, "is of problematical essence and is impure."[37] Indeed, Mann wrote *Death in Venice* precisely to prove that "an artist's life is no dignified life, the path of beauty no path of dignity" (573). Aschenbach is punished just for striving for dignity. In fact, "an artistry without that touch of charlatanry, that inclination to feminine lying, has perhaps never existed" (197), and one must mistrust the artist, for artists are always useless and charlatans (573–74).

The artist's troubled self and lack of dignity, coupled with the modern situation of art, seem to leave Mann only one alternative.

> In a spiritual-poetic respect there are two brotherly possibilities that the experience of Nietzsche produces. The one is that aestheticism of wickedness and Renaissance-aestheticism, that hysterical cult of power, beauty, and life. . . . The other is called *irony*—and I speak here of my case. In my case the experience of self-denial of the spirit in favor of life became irony—a moral attitude.

... Above all, however, it is throughout a *personal* ethos, not a
social one. (25–26)

For an artist whose nature is as flawed as the artist Mann has described,
the ironic pose is not only an artistic device, but a psychological and
ideological position and a relation toward the world. "I wonder ... if
ironic modesty will not always remain the truly *decent* relationship of
the artist—no, not to art but to artistry" (574). This means that to Mann
the emergence of art from its naive period into its sentimental period is
not a difference in kinds of *art* but marks the change from an artist
without guilt and a problematical self to one burdened by guilt, worthlessness, and illegitimacy.

The crucial thing is that art rightly understood, ironic art, has a special
relation to certain other human activities.

> Its mission lies in ... its middle and mediating position between
> spirit and life. Here is the source of irony. ... But here is also, if
> anywhere, the relationship, the similarity, of art and politics: for it
> too, in its way, occupies a mediating position between pure spirit
> and life. ... But to want to make the artist into a politician be-
> cause of this similarity of situation would be a misunderstanding;
> for his task, to awaken and keep awake the *conscience* of life, is
> absolutely not a political task, but still more a religious one. (571)

To Mann, being "in the middle" is common to both art and politics,
despite the difference of their tasks. Though they do not perform the
same functions, they occupy a similar position in the moral economy of
life—the artist and the politician, and also the burgher and Germany are
"in the middle." Because they are related positionally, it will be possible
to join their different tasks in the same person and identity.

It is important to remember that Mann does not interpret the experience of worthlessness and the problematical nature of the artist in terms
of himself alone but in terms of the nature of art and artistry as such.
He can accept his situation and condition only by objectifying them and
defending himself as the true artist, the only one who understands what
true art requires and demands. Since he can feel justified only by an
elevated sense of himself, he is compelled to criticize not only the demands his brother made on art and on him but also the practice of art
in all cultures but his own. "Art—is it not always a critique of life practiced by a little Hanno?" "The sensitive exception cannot be politically
decisive, but despite this ... represents the conscience of humankind."
Yet the artist is redeemed for an even higher role. "In a higher, sharper,

aesthetic-moral sense ... precisely against its will, [he] is *its suffering leader*" (575). Thus, as he has always done, Mann puts the artist in a lesser place with one hand, while aggrandizing and making him superior with the other. The artist never has a place *among*; to Mann he is always outside, below, and *above* at the same time. The problematic self turns itself into an imperial self to cope with its sense of inadequacy and its rage at the accusations of inadequacy leveled from outside and inside.

Personality *and* Bildung

"[The German] will never mean society when he says 'life,' never place the social problem over the moral one. We are not a people of society and not a rich source for strolling psychologists. The self [*das Ich*] and the world are the objects of our thinking and poetizing, not the role that a self sees itself playing in the world" (35–36). With these words Mann proclaims that, whatever rootedness the German self may have in its own culture, nation, or *Stand* (status group), the French category of "society," unlike the German conceptions of culture and *Gemeinschaft*, cannot be a frame of reference for understanding life or the person in Germany. Society is a collection of "roles," performances, "movement," politics, democracy, progress. What is more important is the direct relation of self and world, though what Mann means by "world" is not clear. Instead of society, he uses categories of class, people (*Volk*), culture, and nation, as well as essences or attributes like *Bürgerlichkeit, Bildung, Persönlichkeit*, and *Deutschtum*. He will not accept the newer world of bourgeois "society" as the world a German would desire. Society might triumph in Germany, but if it does it will be foreign to Germany, a product of defeat by the West and the Enlightenment, not a natural development or evolution.

To Mann, the antisocietal German traditions of personality and self-formation have their origins in burgherly culture, which has also "caused *Bürgerlichkeit* and intellectuality, *Bürgerlichkeit* and artistic mastery, to remain words intimately related in meaning" (114–15). And yet, because the older burgherly culture was not a democratic, liberal, egalitarian sphere, but an elite and aristocratic one, the German conception of the individual, too, is quite unlike the Western one. "For individualism in the German sphere is not so much a liberal as an aristocratic world view—as was evidenced later by the case of Nietzsche" (132). Yet Mann wants to uphold the distinction between individual and personality. "The person is not only a social, but also a metaphysical being; in other words, he is not only an individual but also a personality. It is therefore wrong to confuse the supraindividual with the social, to misplace it completely within the social; one ignores thereby the metaphysical supraindividual; for the personality, not the mass, is the actual carrier of the universal" (248). Personality, according to Mann, is "always a product of mixture and of conflict: times, oppositions, contradictions bounce against one another, become spirit, life, form. Personality is being, not asserting [*Meinen*], and if it tries even once to assert, so it becomes noticeable to it that it consists of opposites" (491).

What is curious about Mann's formulation is that the German concept of personality was actually built around the *unity* of the self, not its contradictions. It is true that Kant sees the self in two worlds, the world of personality and the world of nature. But for him the person is at home in both and transcends the natural world by achieving personality on the basis of pure practical reason. The notion of personality dear to Weber is a notion that unifies and empowers the self to act, to assert itself, to defend what it holds dear, and to submit itself to an ultimate ideal for which it becomes a tool and warrior. Mann seems to recognize this when he asserts: "It is passion . . . from which alone the new and thus not yet existing comes—pain, therefore, suffering, sacrificing devotion [*Hingabe*] to something purifyingly suprapersonal" (203). Yet by defending the contradictory nature of the self, full of oppositions, belonging to two worlds and at home in neither, therefore never univocal, always ironic, and by clinging to the need for some concept of personality, Mann is obliged to identify personality with conflict and unwillingness to take a stand, and not with the empowering unity and decisiveness the tradition actually bequeaths. The other alternative would be to reject unity *and* the traditional notion of personality, in order to defend a more open conception of self. This was to come in *The Magic Mountain*.

Service and submission still belong to Mann's conception of personality. Mann accuses the modern social orientation and democracy of undermining the possibility and discrediting the value of every kind of service, *Dienst*. Even if the democrat finds the "service of God" acceptable, he cannot endure the notion of *Menschendienst*, service of human beings.

> Originally . . . in predemocratic times, the desire to serve was something universally human, at least universally European. Goethe asserts: "There is also in the human being a wish to serve." . . . [Now] it is more and more counted unworthy of a human being to serve, even then when it is not a matter of serving human beings but is or ought to be a matter of serving an *object*, for example the humanly still important object of art. (482–83)

Mann has recognized the truth that service of a cause and an authentically "social" dimension of life *are* indeed in conflict, and since for Mann the democratic ethos threatens the possibility, indeed the necessity, of meaning that lies in service to a cause, including "the cause of art," democracy at this point threatens Mann's whole project of meaning.[38] "Despite everything, that 'wish to serve' in the human being is certainly something undying. . . . That there are no more servants lies in the fact that there are no more masters—which means none of those, to serve whom is possible with good aristocratic conscience" (484). To Mann, progress and democracy, whose leveling effects and egalitarianism destroy order of rank because they destroy order of merit, are hostile to aristocratic notions of service rooted in the nondemocratic burgherly past of Germany. This is the real danger of the new order. Human instincts, Mann imagines, rather than social arrangements, remain oriented to service, personal or impersonal, but when difference cannot be recognized, merit acknowledged, superiority adored and served, then service ceases.

For Mann, aristocratic individualism is reinforced by the whole legacy of German culture.

> The German was free and unequal, that means aristocratic. The Reformation was certainly a democratic event. . . . But Luther's true and deepest effect was of an aristocratic kind: he completed the freedom and self-majesty of the German person, in that he internalized them and thus removed them from the sphere of political quarrel forever. . . . We have from Kant the belief in the superiority of "practical reason," of ethics, we have from him the social imperative. But the phenomenon of Goethe was a new confirmation of the legitimacy of the individual being, the greatest artistic experience of Germany, after the metaphysical-religious one that Luther brought: an experience of *Bildung* and sensuality, completely human, foreign to all abstraction, enemy of all ideology, of patriotic ideology first and of political ideology in general. (279)

To Mann, "aristocratic" means free, self-determining, self-willing. It stands for a self that is self-moving, autonomous, and possessing dignity. Mann draws perhaps on Nietzsche's notion of the noble, but his regard for the aristocratic is really based on its superiority. For Mann, the aristocratic heritage is not only central to German culture; it is the only thing that can withstand the "socializing" of Germany. "The most loving culture and care of the aristocratic-individual, the highest curiosity and sympathy toward the unique individual soul, the special spiritual value—

are indispensable as a counterweight to the organized socialism in the state of the future: or life will no longer be worth a schilling" (282). The essence of Germany must be preserved, and since the artistic self believes it shares this essence and is modeled on it, preserving Germany is the only way of preserving the self.

CONCLUSION: THE IDENTITY OF SELF AND GERMANY

"Chronicler and commentator of decadence, lover of the pathological and of death, an aesthete with the tendency toward the abyss: how did *I* come to identify myself with Germany?" (153). With this question Mann raises the fundamental issue of the *Reflections*. But the real question is how he made that identification so firm and sure. "I clung to a pessimistic ethos whose essence was 'nevertheless' [*Trotzdem*], fortitude, holding out under hard conditions, and I saw in Germany a land that lived under difficult external and internal conditions, a land that had it hard, as an artist has it hard. I identified myself with it—that was the form and the meaning of my war patriotism."[39] A man who can say that in his opposition to westernizing tendencies "the national essence [*Wesen*] itself operates out of me" (31) does not have far to go to the equation of himself and Germany.[40]

Actually, it was Heinrich who first identified Mann with reactionary Germany. In making the case against Germany's actions in the war and against its political and social system, Heinrich saw Mann as a microcosm of the values and attitudes standing in the way of progressive German development. Mann was not mistaken in seeing Heinrich's critique as a barely concealed attack on himself, though that is not all it was. And Mann understood the war with Germany as a war also within Germany, symbolized by his brother and himself, a war that could have no harmonious, synthesizing resolution. To what extent he understood this before the war is unclear, despite the manifest sibling rivalry at work and despite his own testimony. "It is not megalomania but only the need and habit of an intimate point of view if for a long time I have seen this destiny symbolized and personified in my brother and myself. . . . There is no German solidarity and ultimate unity. European wars will no longer be carried on on German soil? Certainly they will! There will even always be German civil wars [*Bruderkriege*]."[41]

To Mann, the key to *Deutschtum*, Germanness, but also to the burgher, the artist, irony, and even politics, lies in the idea of the "middle." And this shared nature, this quality of middleness—positioned in the middle but also mediating extremes—makes possible his identification of himself with Germany as well as the identification of all of these "positioned" activities with one another.

> It is the old song of *Tonio Kröger:* "I stand between two worlds, and am at home in neither and consequently have it a bit hard."— But is one perhaps precisely thereby *German?* Is not German essence [*Wesen*] the middle, the intermediate and mediating one and the German the intermediate human being in the grand style? If it is already German to be a burgher, so is it perhaps still more German to be . . . something between a burgher and an artist. (111)

The burgher, in other words, is the fundamental "middle" *Stand.* Indeed, the burgher is not only the representative German, but the carrier of Germanness. "The *Burgher* is German, more German than prince and 'people': this human being of the geographic, social, and spiritual 'middle' was always and remains the carrier of German spirituality, humanity, and antipolitics" (31). The essence of the burgher as representative of Germany lies in its unpolitical past. "To German *Bürgerlichkeit* inviolably belongs a romantic element: the burgher is a romantic individualist for he is the spiritual product of an unpolitical or still prepolitical epoch" (136). Yet to maintain the ethos of the German burgher in a time when the burgher has disappeared is to remain attached to a bygone era long after it has lost its resonance. As Mann has an imaginary interlocutor remark: the burgher has been deprived of his humanity and soul and been hardened "into the capitalistic-imperialistic bourgeois . . . the *hard* burgher: that is the bourgeois. There is no more spiritual burgher" (137). And Mann confesses: "It is true, I have overslept a little the transformation of the German burgher into the bourgeois" (138). Still, the burgher represents Germany. "German *Bürgerlichkeit*, that was always German humanity, freedom, and *Bildung*. The German burgher, he was actually the German human being, and toward his middle position [*Mitte*] strove from above and below everything that strove toward freedom and spirituality" (137).

Politics, too, stands in the middle. "Politics is necessarily the will to mediation and to the positive outcome, is wisdom, flexibility, politeness, diplomacy" (578). Art and the artist also stand in the middle. Art has a position "between spirit and life. . . . This mediation is the source of its irony."[42] And in art, Mann affirms, "irony is always irony toward both sides, something intermediate" (91). The artist has "a *mediating* task," a "hermetic-magical role as mediator between the world above and the world below, between idea and manifestation, spirit and sense."[43] Indeed,

Tonio Kröger's name was a symbol for "the middle position" (91), and Nietzsche, too, was "at home in *both* houses, in decadence and health" (92).[44]

In the *Reflections*, therefore, Mann defends *Deutschtum* as "the idea of the middle," and he identifies himself—as the representative of art as the idea of the middle, and of irony as the ethos of art—with the ideal of Germany, born from the burgher class, the class of the middle. But while the former representative of Germany, the burgher class, has now vanished, that does not mean that Mann himself, heir of that class, cannot become the new representative of Germany, identified even more closely with it and bearer of its ethos. Mann has gone from wounded narcissism to the grandiosity of the imperial self.

In one sense, it is quite reasonable that Mann would see himself as the representative of Germany. Every self is, in some way, a representative of its own culture, embodying and expressing its traits, habits, mores, but also its contradictions and dissensions. But to make oneself the *supreme* embodiment of the national culture is excessive, especially given that Mann excludes from the community women, the left, the working classes, Jews, expressionists and radical art, and radical political and social movements. In fact, Mann represents a Germany made more bourgeois and harmonious by the spiritual exclusion and delegitimation of these groups.[45] Thus, it is a narrow interpretation of Germany that Mann here seeks to represent, though he later tried to accommodate Germany's truth more completely in the 1920s and after, as he became more secure in his own identity as a German, an artist, and a brother.

In the *Reflections*, Mann, like Gustav Aschenbach, sees the world symbolically. He elevates Germany's struggle to a position of colossal significance and value. The battle fought here is over the most ultimate things, the deepest and the highest, over identity, power, meaning, essence. This identification of Germany's fight with his own inner fight and the fight against his brother, however, distorts Mann's picture and representation of the external world. He sees that world only as an extension and projection of self and the self's deadly struggle over insecure identity. This accounts for the hysterical and irrational tone of the work. That is also why Mann is correct, though perhaps not in the way he meant it, when he says later that there is no discontinuity between the *Reflections* and his political views after the war: the substantive positions have changed, but he stands in the same relation to Germany. Mann's interpretation of Germany remains a projection of his inner struggle over identity. Bound to a sense of self identified with German fate, politics, and soul, his formal relation to German politics and the German nation remains the same after the war as during it.

This confusion of self and nation may have been liberating and empowering for the self, but it is mystifying for the nation. It mystifies Germany's struggle, projecting inner needs outward onto it, interpreting German struggles through the hysteria experienced within. Mann reifies Germany, making what it is at present its essence, defending its every aspect against the onslaught of the Roman West (that is, his own brother). Mann thus makes the war an even more bitter ideological and spiritual struggle through his own megalomania, and gives Germany a megalomaniacal role by making it the key to Europe's spiritual battles. But as Mann adopts a more patient relation to his inner struggle, Germany becomes *The Magic Mountain*. As he fights against the devil outside and within himself, Germany becomes *Doctor Faustus*. In *Doctor Faustus* the artist is identified with the Germany of the *Reflections*, a Germany that has remained wrapped up in this older version of identity and turned to devils for support. For some—including Mann's old friends Ernst Bertram, Hans Pfitzner, and Gerhart Hauptmann—this devil was Hitler. Now Mann does not just project his identity crisis outward: he takes Germany inside. He represents Germany and becomes its model, the two-sided Germany, in which the good must be defended against the evil, even though it recognizes the evil in itself. But this process, too, freezes Germany in symbols, no longer seeing its reality as separate and complicated, different from the self. In the *Reflections* Mann casts out the "doubters" of German identity who disagree with him, who gang up on him and on poor Germany. Because he is so identified with Germany, he has only a symbolic relation to it—the self symbolic of the nation, the nation of the self—and self and nation cannot relate as genuine others, with difference as well as likeness. It took the assassination of Walter Rathenau and the mellowing of Mann's own positions for him to overcome the reactionary version of himself and Germany. Still, although he came to defend the concept of Humanity as his definitive and final ultimate ideal, he never overcame his identification with Germany.

5   Illness as a Vocation:
The Magic Mountain

The Magic Mountain, completed after Mann's discovery of *Deutschtum* during World War I, is suffused with the language of illness and weakness, used symbolically to express the disability and disempowerment that Mann now believes is produced throughout bourgeois society.[1] It shows the complicated relation of an individual to his own loss of power in terms of its origin, his struggle to interpret it, and the failure of all attempts to reempower the self. *The Magic Mountain* creates a place that "gives permission" to powerlessness to express itself and be experienced, and it symbolizes allegorically Germany's lack of inner strength and its struggle for self-understanding. In the simplest terms, it tells the story of an ordinary young man who visits a sick cousin in a tuberculosis sanitorium in the Swiss Alps, intending to stay three weeks; he ends up staying seven years. The outbreak of World War I brings him down from the mountain to disappear in the chaos of fighting on the battlefields of France.

The Magic Mountain raises questions directly about the crisis of work and calling in bourgeois society as bases of identity and sources of strength, but it symbolizes everything in terms of devotion to, and service of, illness. It also embodies novelistically Mann's overcoming of the isolation of the artist's calling and personality through the identification with Germany and its spiritual problems developed in the *Reflections*.[2] Indeed, Mann's political writings of the 1920s and beyond reflect an ongoing revaluation of the relation of self and Germany, a working out of his interpretation of the nation in terms of his own personality and his interpretation of self through the nation's development and experience.

The Magic Mountain is Mann's first embodiment of the widened problematic in which the expanded self reflects and absorbs the nation. In the novel, Germany is explored as if *it* were a self, and its principal character, Hans Castorp, is explored as a self whose development draws on and reflects issues crucial to Germany. But the self's issues have changed, and traditional cultural meanings and sources that once guided self-development and *Bildung* are recognized as no longer adequate for the shaping and development of the self, as Weber had recognized long before. Hans's *Bildungsreise* takes him into the nation and culture from which he has, ironically, been cut off in the "flatland." The formation of the German self and identity now demand such a journey. Experience of the bourgeois class exclusively, or of calling, or even of falling away from the class or nation, can no longer be the sole source of development. The self has no alternative but to develop and acquire *Bildung* through a confrontation with the social, political, and cultural issues and conflicts of today. *Bildung* is to be found in the strife of ideological opposites in the present, in the present's conflicts and desires, and in the encounter with forbidden objects: these form the stuff of a new foundation of self.

But *The Magic Mountain* not only marks a shift in the set of materials and experiences the person seeking *Bildung* must confront and assimilate; its bourgeois hero actually requires illness and withdrawal from bourgeois life as prerequisites to this development, illness and withdrawal that, at the same time, express the lack of meaning of that life. Mann himself calls *The Magic Mountain* "the renewal of the German *Bildungsroman* on the basis and under the sign of tuberculosis," and for that very reason, it is "a parody."[3] The novel shows that the cultural purposes and direction once sought in the ordinary bourgeois world of work and achievement, the older ideals of self and the sources of inner power, are now exhausted. It is this situation that is reflected in the search for new means and possibilities of *Bildung*. Mann's hero "falls ill" from lack of the nutrition that the cultural world is expected to provide. His illness is also, of course, a reflection of his own weaknesses and incapacities and of his estrangement from bourgeois life, an estrangement interpreted as unhealthy by the book's representative of "civilization" and the West, Settembrini.[4] In Mann's earlier vision, bourgeois life and the "children of light" had always been healthy, though generally unreflective and insensitive. But in his later work illness becomes a reflection of the infirmities and inadequacies of the bourgeois world itself, which no longer empowers by offering a reliable path toward certainty, truth, and identity even to the healthy. To be healthy in this world is now to share in *its* illness, to be as weak, unanchored, unstable, and unreliable as *it* is. The ill, therefore, now reveal the limitations of bourgeois life itself, and not just the ways that they as individuals are unfitted for it or unaccepted by it.

Here Mann's early preoccupation with illness and deformity—which reflected his estrangement from and sense of inadequacy in life—fuses with romantic, but mocked, idealizations of illness as a sign of genius and the exceptional self. Now the ill person is no longer simply an outsider who cannot measure up to the healthy demands of life. He is singled out and even distinguished by his illness, though ironically, and this incapacity is initially taken to be a mark of talent and gifts that offer the possibility of rare insight and experience, even of penetrating understanding or exceptional creativity. Yet also present, as part of the subtext of Hans Castorp's educational journey, is the intra-German struggle over romanticism and Mann's own process of what he called *Entromantisierung*, his overcoming of his own romanticism.[5]

Self-fashioning is as central to *The Magic Mountain* as to the *Reflections*, but now it is problematized and made the object of a search. Here, reflection on work in a magical world that inverts it is central to the clarification of identity. The key to the cultural tendencies in the time that the novel exposes lies in the struggle for identity, meaning, and a relation to work symbolized by Hans Castorp. With his un- and antibourgeois impulses, Hans finds a haven of the estranged and well-to-do, not only outside Germany in the Swiss Alps, but effectively without Germans, except for the cousin he comes to visit. In the *Reflections*, Mann had said that Germany was the spiritual battlefield of Europe. In *The Magic Mountain* non-Germans fight out cultural, political, and ideological struggles as a battle for a German's soul: Italian Freemasons, Eastern European Jews, seductive Russian women, Dutch colonial adventurers, Swiss medical specialists, Russian psychoanalysts.[6] Mann's hero turns his back on capitalist civilization and the world of progress, a world Mann had criticized in the *Reflections*. But what is radically new is that Hans also turns his back on work in general—the essential symbol, in Mann's symbolical world, for bourgeois society and proficiency, meaning, and commitment within it. Hans thus embodies a critique of the bourgeois world, though a critique in the process of reflection. Indeed, the narrator stresses Hans's typological and symbolic value and attributes "a certain supra-personal significance" to his fate. "The person lives not only his own personal life as an individual [*Einzelwesen*], but, consciously or unconsciously, also the life of his epoch and contemporaries."[7]

The Magic Mountain is an expression of the crisis of bourgeois life in Germany, understood through the disruption of a meaningful relation to work and through a quest for meaning that finds no answers in bourgeois life or the time as presently given. It thus deals with a man and an epoch "lost" to life below: bourgeois life. Indeed, the man and his times do not become lost through the experience of being on the mountain: they are lost to life before the book begins. *The Magic Mountain* tells their story, which is in many ways a continuation of the crisis of "life" first set out in *Tonio Kröger*. The early works on art now open up to a perspective centered not on art but on bourgeois life in Germany and *its* crisis. Mann himself described the novel as a "literary counterpart to *Buddenbrooks* . . . a repetition of this book at another stage of life."[8] The world of the flatland, from which Hans comes to the mountain, is decadent, like the world of Thomas Buddenbrook. The question of life's purpose, which in Mann's world is also always a question about the meaning of work, receives no more satisfying answer in the flatland of pre–World War I Germany than it received in the old Hanseatic trading town in which Thomas Buddenbrook was an important figure.

> All sorts of personal goals, purposes, hopes, outlooks may float before the eyes of the individual person, out of which he creates the impulse to higher exertion and activity. If the impersonal around him, the time itself, at bottom lacks hopes and outlooks despite all outward activity, if it inwardly discloses itself to him as hopeless, without outlook, and helpless, and opposes a hollow silence to the question about a more than personal, ultimate, absolute meaning of all exertion and activity—a question posed consciously or unconsciously, but still somehow posed—then precisely in cases of more honest persons a certain laming effect of such circumstances will be inevitable, which may extend along the path through the spiritual-moral part straight into the physical and organic part of the individual. To feel like achieving something important exceeding the measure of what is simply required, without the time knowing a satisfying answer to the question "What for?" [*Wozu*], requires either a moral loneliness and directness that appears rarely and is of a heroic nature, or a very robust vitality. Neither the one nor the other was Hans Castorp's case, and thus he was quite average [*mittelmässig*], though in a truly honorable sense. (50)[9]

Mann remarked in his diaries on 6 June 1919 that "it is necessary to show H.C.'s spiritual determination by the times, his spiritual-moral indifference, lack of belief, and hopelessness."[10] Hans is not in the midst of a crisis of the kind Thomas Buddenbrook experienced, however. Thomas tried, unsuccessfully, to sustain a calling he once held dear. Hans goes to the mountain before he has a calling. Indeed, because he can withdraw from "normal" bourgeois life to the mountain, Hans does not have to confront his crisis within the flatland at all, nor keep up a social facade in the midst of failing inner strength, as Thomas did. Without consciously intending to leave bourgeois society, he goes to a haven where everyone has money but no one has a calling, but which has its own kind of service and order.

Hans is able to seek answers outside the established bourgeois realm to questions the bourgeois realm can no longer even pose.[11] Intruding directly into the novel, the narrator ventures his "private thoughts" about Hans's dilemma, suggesting that Hans would never have stayed so long on the mountain "if to his simple soul there had come from the depths of the time some information, somehow calming, concerning the meaning and goal of the service of life [*Lebensdienst*]" (321). It is important to note that the narrator does not speak here of the meaning and purpose of life, but of the *service* of life. As Mann says elsewhere: "No metamorphosis is more familiar to us than the one at whose beginning stands sympathy with death, at whose end stands the decision for service of life [*Lebensdienst*]."[12] This choice of words underscores the novel's contrast and dichotomy, stressed many times by Mann, between service of life and service of death—meaning service of impulses that go against what bourgeois society takes to be life-enhancing and life-sustaining. But the more important issue is that the question of life and death is posed here, as in all of Mann's works, in terms of service—submission and devotion to a higher principle or entity with its own purposes, goals, and demands. Human choices are not understood in terms of service or refusal of service, or in terms of aspects of life that individuals may choose or reject. Choices must be *between* one form of service and another, for life is understood always and only as service and as a choice between realms and forms of service. The need for service and submission is never questioned.

This dilemma is posed at an even higher level in *Doctor Faustus*. Although *The Magic Mountain* is an achievement of the first rank, it is also a bridge from Mann's earlier artistic period to *Doctor Faustus*. Indeed, it could be argued that *The Magic Mountain* makes the later novel possible, because in it Mann links a hero's identity to the identity of Germany, his first allegory of the cultural problems of the nation before World War I. Themes and characters from this earlier work will return: from Nietzschean views of culture and life, to humanists, devils, and those who long for power, to the problems of order, terror, and meaning.

The Magic Mountain raises serious questions about the nature of modern *Bildung*, yet it also casts doubt on itself through its problematic ending and that ending's role in the "lessons" of the work. Indeed, its ending raises questions about Mann's own relation to the hero and to Germany's plight in general, conceived through Hans Castorp's experiences. Hans is largely confronted by teachers who are laughable caricatures and self-discrediting symbols, which seems to leave him space to find a different path beyond them. But Hans does *not* have a grasp of any solution to his problem, and the question is whether the *novel* has such a grasp.

THE ESCAPE FROM WORK

Why Hans Castorp stays on the mountain for seven years can be answered only by considering his problematical experience of everyday work in the flatland and those qualities of his character that incline him to leave bourgeois life. Hans's background is similar to that of the hero of "The Joker" (*Der Bajazzo*), Thomas and Hanno Buddenbrook, Tonio Kröger, and Mann himself. Each comes from the Protestant (sometimes Calvinist) commercial patriciate of a north German trading city, with forebears who were principled and successful adherents of a calling in bourgeois society. Yet none is able to carry on a bourgeois calling like his forebears. Like the hero of "The Joker" and Thomas Buddenbrook's brother Christian, but unlike Hanno and Tonio, Hans is inclined to laziness, idleness, and the indulgence of his appetites and pleasures. But he lacks the artistic inclinations, gifts, and sensitivities that set Hanno and Tonio apart as unusual representatives of bourgeois decline: that is, he is incapable of mobilizing "nonbourgeois" talents to find a new path in the bourgeois world. Yet in this way he is even more "representative" of bourgeois life in Mann's symbolic universe, for he is an ordinary hero whose story is more important than he is. Hans's character is the stuff not of tragedy or melodrama, but only of comedy.

Despite his search "for a calling with which he could stand before himself and his people" (51–52), Hans is not really "called" to anything except idleness and love of pleasure. His calling is merely an occupation, without relation to his identity, a reflection of the need to fill a place before the external "witness" of the community. He lacks an internal witness or center strengthened by a particular task that the discipline of a calling would provide. For him the calling is purely a *role*: it cannot become a means of personal identity and direction. It will therefore be much easier for Hans to put aside the ethos of the "person with an ethic of achievement" (*Leistungsethiker*) than it was for Thomas Buddenbrook or Gustav Aschenbach, since he has never been imbued with its values. He has never experienced devotion to accomplishment of tasks as a way to inner power, resolution of identity, and sense of self. The "bourgeois nature of life" (*Lebensbürgerlichkeit*)[13] that conveys the world of effort and distinguishes men with a calling in bourgeois society has not been passed on to him. In his efforts to be "finally free of the pressure of honor ... enjoying forever the boundless advantages of shame" (116), Hans is still a confirmed heir of Thomas Buddenbrook and Aschenbach, though in humorous fashion. But unlike them, he gives up before he has submitted to a calling and found it leading only to emptiness. For him the calling and the struggle of work are empty before they have begun. Yet unlike Hanno, Hans is not sensitive enough to be defeated mortally. His mediocrity is, ironically, the great strengthening quality that, although it cannot fit him for a serious bourgeois life, protects him against the total disability of the overly sensitive decadent outsider.

More importantly, *The Magic Mountain* suggests that it may be precisely Hans's problematical relation to work, one of the "impairments of his personal life by the times," that is the cause of the physical impairment expressed in his "illness."

> How should Hans Castorp not have respected work? It would have been unnatural. As things were, it had to be valued as the thing certainly most worthy of respect, there was fundamentally nothing more worthy of respect beside it, it was the principle before which one stood or did not stand, the absolute of the time, it justified itself [*beantwortete ... sich selbst*], so to speak. His respect for it therefore was of a religious and, as far as he knew, indubitable nature. But it was another question whether he loved it; because that he could not, as much as he respected it, and indeed on the simple grounds that it did not agree with him. Strenuous work strained his nerves, it exhausted him soon. ... This conflict in his relation to work required, strictly speaking, resolution. Was it thus possible that his body as well as his spirit—first the spirit and through it also the body—would have been more enthusiastic and persistent toward work if, in the foundation of his soul, there where he himself was not aware of it, he had been able to believe in work as an absolute value and a self-justifying principle [*sich selbst beantwortendes Prinzip*] and to calm himself with it? (52–53)

This passage points to the centrality of work for the health of the person and the relation to life. Work is the center of identity, but, crucially, this passage reverses Mann's earlier understanding of the direction of causality. In the early works, biological decline, diminished capacity for life, came first, and their manifestation was revealed in spiritual deviance from the bourgeois pattern of life and in diminished capacity for the bourgeois calling. Now *spiritual* decline has become primary and the source of the biological illness of the body. The body expresses and manifests spiritual illness. More important, the source of *all* decline, first spiritual and then physical, now derives from a defect in the "times," whatever the source of the times' problem. Much of the novel takes place in exchanges that struggle to define this defect—the source of the weakening of the commitment to work—and to lay out the remedy for an age lost to life and gone astray. The essential symbol for life, health, and return to the world of the flatland remains the positive relation to work as a self-justifying principle.

Lack of commitment to work, lack of a center for the self constructed on justification of the self through devotion to a calling: this is the manifestation, the spiritual expression, of the illness of the times, and through it first the spirit, then the body, lose power and become weak. Physical illness has not interfered with Hans's calling: the physical illness, whose reality we are led to doubt throughout the novel, is an external symptom, within the body, of the spiritual illness within the soul. The inability to find meaning and identity in a calling from among the materials given by the "times" has caused illness in the body, though this inability is a symptom of the illness in the times, an individual illness produced by the times' illness, which, though harder to diagnose, is the emptiness and purposelessness of bourgeois life itself. As Hans says: "I would have to be lying if I wanted to claim that work agreed with me so excellently. . . . Actually I feel truly healthy only when I do nothing" (86). But whereas Hans is merely disinclined toward labor through affinity with repose and attraction to illness, rather than through ideology, he finds a powerful theoretical defender in the Jewish Jesuit Naphta. Indeed, it is no accident that in the first debate between Settembrini and Naphta, work is a principal issue. The relation to work is not only an index of health, but to Settembrini—and the novel—it is also an index of the differences between "cultural realms," East and West, stasis and progress, which uphold different views of work and influence individuals in opposite directions. Cultural difference is thus made to center on different approaches to work. The Settembrini-Naphta debate seems increasingly a debate over the value and meaning of the Western bourgeois world and its valuation of work, against the newly emergent threat to that world symbolized in different terms and ultimately embodied in Naphta's fusion of proletarian order, jesuitical faith, and terror.

Interestingly, there is no spokesman for the Protestant work ethic in *The Magic Mountain*, despite the fact that Protestantism is Hans's background and that of the world he falls away from. Settembrini and Naphta represent two different Catholic traditions, with an admixture of Jewish millenarianism. Perhaps that ethic has no defenders in the symbolic world of the mountain because the Protestant world is in crisis and cannot be argued for. This is not to say that bourgeois values are not struggled over or defended. In fact, the novel suggests they are attacked by, and must be defended from, romanticism and the obsession with death that attack that world from within. German romanticism is in tension with the Protestant work world, though it is also part of and perhaps even partly engendered by that world. But the bourgeois world of work portrayed in this novel is as defeated as in *Buddenbrooks*; indeed, nowhere in Mann's works does it have a credible defender, except perhaps in the alienated Tonio Kröger. Even later, it will be no accident that the narrator of *Doctor Faustus* is a Catholic humanist and not a Protestant man of the calling. Mann cannot write a voice that argues this position credibly, though many of his characters struggle to embody it.

The world from which Hans is estranged is the world of Thomas Buddenbrook. "As I lie here and see it from afar, it seems to me crass . . . hard, cold. And what do hard and cold mean? They mean cruel. There is a cruel atmosphere down there, pitiless. If one lies here and sees it from afar, one shudders at it" (277). This awareness is what made Thomas Buddenbrook quake, despite the vitality and capacity for life he showed at an earlier time, when he took hardness and standards for granted. Hans, however, has never believed in them.

> One must have a rather thick skin to agree so completely by
> nature with the way of thinking of the people down there in
> the lowland and with questions like "Does he still have some
> money?" . . . To me it was never completely natural. . . . I notice
> belatedly that it always struck me as strange. Perhaps it was con-
> nected with my unconscious inclination toward illness. . . . I have
> never actually felt myself plainly as strong as a rock, and then my
> two parents died so early. . . . You must understand and realize
> from such a thing that under these circumstances one cannot be
> so completely robust and cannot find the cruelty of the people
> completely natural. (279)

Lost to life, Hans speaks of people below as "those who do not know" (*die Unwissenden*) (582). What Hans seeks can be found only on the mountain, this "underworld" above the world, because the flatland lacks the "fundamental concepts" to understand him, and only on the mountain can he find "*freedom*" from an uncomprehending bourgeois world (314).

Even after years on the mountain, Hans finds the reason for his disaffection from the world of work obscure, but he relates it to his inclinations toward illness, death, and his love for the exotic Russian woman Clawdia Chauchat. "I had a civilian calling [*Zivilberuf*] . . . a sturdy and reasonable calling . . . but I was never particularly attached to it, I admit, and indeed for reasons about which I only want to say that they lie in darkness. They belong with the reasons for my feeling" for Clawdia (847). The novel does not explore these reasons further.[14] It treats Hans's illness and his love of a "forbidden" object as the products of the same defect in the times and the expression of the same rejection of bourgeois life, thus confusing bourgeois life with life as such, a confusion endemic to Mann's work. The novel attributes Hans's illness and love to a metaphysical cause—sympathy with death—which is made to account for his preference against life and for withdrawal, but the origin of this sympathy remains unexplained. It is the metaphor for loss of power, and stands in the novel as a given, as if it were something that need not be accounted for further, though much of the task of the novel is aimed at overcoming precisely this sympathy, at least by limiting its effects. But in leaving the social and cultural reasons for illness and misguided love in obscurity, and in taking sympathy with death as a misguided yet autonomous fact, *The Magic Mountain* remains too much on the level of symptoms and effects, leaving the problems of bourgeois life in as much obscurity as Mann left them in before.

THE CALLING OF ILLNESS

It was not only for romantics and decadents that illness had special significance and presented unusual opportunities.[15] In *Ecce Homo* (1888), an extraordinary account of an even more extraordinary *Bildung*, Nietzsche claimed that even though "being ill *is* itself a kind of ressentiment," his liberation from ressentiment and his understanding of its nature were due to a long illness of his own.[16] "Illness [*Krankheit*] *slowly disengaged me. . . .* Illness gave me at the same time a right to a complete reversal of all my habits; it permitted, *it commanded* me to forget; it presented me with the *compulsion* of lying still, of idleness, of waiting and being patient—But that means of course thinking! . . . Never have I had so much happiness in myself as in the sickest and most painful times of my life." Illness prevented reading, thus freeing his "undermost self, as it were buried and become quiet under a constant *obligation to listen* to other selves (—and that is what reading actually is!)." But under the compulsion and limitation of illness, this self "awakened slowly, shyly, doubtfully—but finally *it spoke again*."[17]

For Nietzsche, forced withdrawal from life during which "the *nourishment* of my spirit had come to a standstill"[18] meant reviving a self virtually extinguished, thus beginning his real education and self-examination. For Hans Castorp, not a reader, illness and enforced idleness do not free for such introspection and reawakening. They free him to listen, for the first time, to the diverse and conflicting voices or "selves" of an unharmonious culture. What revives in him during his illness is not a self drowned by listening but a self starved for opportunities *to* listen. That is also why Hans is so attractive to the pedagogues who seek to influence him. The commitment and devotion to the calling that rule in bourgeois life inhibit the social, political, and personal reflection that occurs on the mountain—which, it is imagined, would be seen as waywardness and the undermining of vitality within the flatland.

Yet because the *cure* for illness is itself a discipline imposing tasks and demanding obedience, illness on the mountain makes possible a *counter*vocation. It frees the person from the callings of the flatland but enrolls him in a new service. Freedom from the purposelessness of the flatland is found in the service of illness—physical *and* spiritual—and its cure.[19] In becoming ill, Hans finds a calling *out* of life, serving the physical cure on the mountain while actually serving the "educational" cure of comprehending life, the spiritual cure for the illness of the flatland. "Being ill" is a form of weakness that frees not just from but for: for reflection about the flatland, and still within a discipline. The world of the mountain we can thus call the realm of "illness as a vocation." Indeed, to the inhabitants of the mountain, illness is "the common vocational interest [*Berufsinteresse*] of everyone" (597). The world of the mountain gives time away from the world's demands, bought at the price of illness, as later the devil gives time to Adrian Leverkühn in *Doctor Faustus*, but at a much stiffer price.[20] Of course, Hans is not physically ill; indeed, he is the only patient on the mountain who is not sick at all. Yet because he is impotent in life, detached and uncommitted to the bourgeois world of work, his true home is with the sick.

Hans embraces his "weakness" once it seems to have shown itself physically and interprets his life in terms of it.

> I have been lying here since yesterday and thinking over . . . how I behaved toward the whole thing, toward life . . . and its demands. A certain seriousness and a certain disinclination toward robust and boisterous ways has always been in my nature. . . . Everything, I think to myself, comes from the fact that I have a defect myself and am at home with illness from the start—it shows itself on this occasion. (260)

That he interprets his life in these terms is quite telling. Bourgeois life is taken as the standard of health, and Hans situates his problems within his own constitution, thus interpreting his weakness and embracing his estrangement. Yet his defect is the very lack of connection to bourgeois life as it is given, a lack that he tries to believe is biological but that part of him knows is spiritual and inward. "The thing was—and Hans Castorp also definitely knew this—that the shameful manifestation with which he was struggling was not only of physical origin . . . but expressed an inner agitation" (190).

The world of the ill is an exclusive fraternity, and the spirit of illness is felt to be aristocratic, a form of elevation over mere bourgeois life, which makes a superiority out of an inferiority. To Hans, illness is a means of elevating and refining the self:[21] "One thinks a stupid man must be healthy and ordinary, and illness must make a man distinguished and clever and exceptional" (138). But in this Hans fetishizes the loss of power, weakness, and disqualification, showing that he suffers from the romantic disease from which Mann himself once suffered.[22] He draws a strong reply from Settembrini, speaking in a Nietzschean vein: "Illness is absolutely not noble [*vornehm*], absolutely not venerable—this conception is itself illness or it leads to it" (139). Illness is "spiritual backsliding [*Rückneigung*]. . . . Illness means much more a *degradation*. . . . To honor it is an *aberration* . . . and the beginning of all spiritual aberration" (140–41).

Naturally the defender of illness is Naphta, who justifies the disdain the "aristocracy of illness" has for the healthy and the mildly ill and locates the essential character of humanity in illness. "In the spirit therefore, in illness resided the dignity of men and their nobility; the more ill he was, by so much higher a degree was he a man, and the genius of illness was more human [*menschlich*] than that of health" (642–43). To Naphta, "spirit" is as it was for the early Mann: a product of illness as estrangement from life. But to Naphta this is not a burdensome fate. The ill are more fully spiritual and separated from the dumb healthiness of mere nature and the philistinism of *Bürgerlichkeit*, whose domain is life and bourgeois work. Indeed, for Naphta the only path to real health is *through* illness and the sacrifice of self on its behalf. In this respect, Naphta is a precursor of the devil in *Doctor Faustus*, elevating illness not just to a special, even exclusive, source of genius, but to a form of Christ-like self-sacrifice, through which humanity, and the person who sacrifices himself to illness, may be redeemed and restored to health.

> As if progress, as far as it existed, was not owed to illness alone, that means: to the genius—which as such is nothing other than illness! As if the healthy of all periods had not lived from the achievements of illness! There have been men who consciously

and voluntarily have gone into illness and madness, in order to win humanity knowledge which would turn into health after it is obtained through madness, and whose possession and use is no longer determined through illness and madness after this heroic act of sacrifice. That is the true death on the cross. (643)

The costs of the willful embrace of so romantic a view are not lost on Hans, though it takes time to realize them. "I have subordinated myself to the principle of unreason, to the ingenious principle of illness. . . . I have forgotten everything and broken with everything, with my relatives and my calling in the flatland and all of my opinions . . . so that now I am completely lost to the flatland and in its eyes am as good as dead" (848). Dead to ordinary life below since long ago, Hans finds in illness a refuge for himself, "to whom only a hollow silence had been the answer to definite, if also unconsciously posed, questions" (321). He is not deluded, however, into thinking himself an enemy of bourgeois life. Reflecting on Clawdia's description of him as "a pretty bourgeois with a little moist spot," he asks himself "which element of this mixture of his being would show itself to be stronger, the bourgeois or the other" (486).

But the mountain mirrors the flatland in many respects, particularly as a place where healthy people "perform their service [*Dienst*]" (209). The flatland and a life lived in service are identical, and Hans has fled to escape service. Yet life on the mountain is also conceived in terms of *Dienst*, a regulated, consoling, and purposeful service, as in a cloister, and Hans says, "I . . . have the 'rules' at my fingertips and observe them quite precisely" (272). The predominant activity of those on the mountain is the service of lying down, the *General-Liegedienst* that takes place on the balconies of the sanitorium and requires no activity. After less than two weeks on the mountain, Hans realizes that the cure "was becoming almost a substitute for the fulfillment of duty in the lowlands and a substitute calling. . . . Yet still he felt fully its curbing, restraining effect on his civilian mind" (289–90). His cousin Joachim, a "piously serving" (*dienstfromm*) soldier who longs to return to service in the flatland, sets a "good example with regard to faithful duty in the service of the cure" (208) and is "dependent quite completely on service [*Dienstlichkeit*] and discipline" (480). Indeed, beyond the cure's value for health, Joachim serves it "also a little for the sake of the service of the cure, which ultimately was a service like any other, and fulfillment of duty was fulfillment of duty" (207). But in his adaptability and cheerful embrace of the cure, Hans proves more suited spiritually than Joachim for both the mountain and the cure.[23] Even Hofrat Behrens remarks that to be ill "takes talent" (68). And Hans cannot leave this counterservice on the mountain, for reasons he tells Clawdia: it would be desertion "to want so directly to serve utility and progress in the flatland. That would be the greatest ingratitude and disloyalty to the illness and its genius and to my love for you" (826).

But although he is enrolled in a service that fuels his education, Hans learns nothing on the mountain to drive him back to bourgeois society or equip him for a calling of even a nonbourgeois kind. It is no accident that the only thing that can bring about his return is war, which always shatters normality. Yet whereas war frees him from his distance, it does not free him *for* anything in everyday life, but only for an activity that negates and threatens everything society normally cherishes. In this way, Hans shares the fate of his epoch: to be liberated and motivated only by war; unsatisfied with bourgeois society's possibilities, feeling powerless and directionless; eager to escape the confines of society but unable to find the strength to change it or resign himself to its purposes and hopes—hence, lost to "life" from the start.[24]

If Hans's illness is a symptom of the illness of the times, a product of the unsatisfying answers or silence that bourgeois society provides to the question "Why?" in what exactly does the illness of the *times* lie? Why do the times no longer give an answer? Despite the debates of Settembrini and Naphta, these are the unasked questions of *The Magic Mountain*.

SYMPATHY WITH DEATH AS SYMPTOM

Mann uses the expression "sympathy with death" in the *Reflections*, where he remarks that Hans Pfitzner used the phrase to describe his opera *Palestrina*. He notes there that in the "little novel" he had begun before the war, *The Magic Mountain*, "a kind of pedagogical story," the expression "sympathy with death" was a theme. Mann claims it is a formula, motif, "key word" for and "basic mood" of, romanticism, a definition reinforced by the conception of illness he found in Novalis and the German Romantics.[25] Before the war, Mann wrote that his new work would form "a kind of counterpart to *Death in Venice*. In style it is quite different, easygoing, and humorous (although death is loved again)."[26] In 1915 he announced the theme of death and the themes of *The Magic Mountain* as he had conceived them thus far:

> Before the war I had begun a longer story that takes place in the high mountains in a tuberculosis sanitorium—a story whose fundamental purposes are pedagogical-political, in which a young

man comes to terms with the most seductive power, death, and is led, in a comic-horrible manner, through the spiritual contradictions of humanity and romanticism, progress and reaction, health and illness, but more for the sake of orientation and learning than deciding. The spirit of the whole is humorous-nihilistic, and the tendency swings rather toward the side of sympathy with death.[27]

Hans's fascination with death begins with loss following the early deaths of his parents and grandfather, which leave him with an urge toward repetition, apparent in his love of funerals, and an elevated conception of the dying. "I find that the world and life are so suited that one should in general wear black, with a starched ruff instead of a collar, and associate with one another seriously, subdued, and formally, in thinking of death—that would be right to me, it would be moral" (410–11). Against Settembrini's moralizing defense of "practical life work" (411), progress, and the elimination of suffering, Hans defends mournful regard for death as the true occupation of the living.

Mann suggests it is preoccupation with death that estranges the person from life and work. Settembrini expresses it thus: "You want to say . . . that the early and repeated contact with death produced a fundamental mood in your soul which makes you irritable and sensitive to the hardness and crudity of unthinking worldly life, let's say, to its cynicism" (279–80). The novel, and Mann elsewhere, tries to claim that since "sympathy with death" is the cause of estrangement from life and the calling, the obligation of a world caught up in a romantic preoccupation with illness and death is to limit it and, for the sake of life, restrict its influence. But this claim reverses the connections between things that the novel elsewhere reveals, for Mann repeatedly suggests that it is to the times and their lack of purpose that we must look to find the source of Hans's illness. Since the times are the reason for Hans's preoccupation, his sympathy with death must be, not a cause, but a symptom of estrangement, an expression of loss of vitality, life, and power. It is withdrawal from bourgeois work that leads to preoccupation with death, for sympathy with death is the quintessential antiwork, antibourgeois ethos. Settembrini, too, is deluded about the primacy of this sympathy, but his hostility and fear far exceed both Hans's and Mann's. "Death as an independent spiritual power is a highly dissolute power, whose wicked power of attraction is doubtless very strong, but sympathizing with which signifies just as indubitably the most horrible aberration of the human spirit" (280). To make it Hans's task to overcome this sympathy directly is not to overcome the cause of obsession with it; it is merely to treat the symptoms, not the illness of the times itself. Mann does seek a spiritual explanation, rather than a biological one, for the "falling away" from bourgeois life, but he does not seek a social explanation, based on the disappointments and limitations of bourgeois life, for the limitations on what bourgeois life has to offer are not directly addressed. The fascination with death is understood as the product of disaffection not with bourgeois life but with life itself, whatever that is, and bourgeois life emerges once more from a novel of Mann's identified with life as such.

Estrangement and withdrawal from work and other values of bourgeois society, whatever *their* cause, are what always lead to preoccupation with death in Mann's spiritual universe. Take Thomas Buddenbrook's absorption with death, which occurs only when his inner commitment to his calling fails; thus it comes after the inner loss of power, not before it. Or Hanno's willing embrace of death when he is faced with defeat by the masculine demands of bourgeois life and work. Or the death-centered preoccupations of antibourgeois aesthetes in "At the Prophet's" and "Tristan," whose heroes' obsessions with death and decay are part of their hostility to the vitality and insensitivity of bourgeois life. Or Gustav Aschenbach, the failure of whose calling and estrangement of whose life lead him to seek death and a dying city.[28]

Preoccupation with death is an implicit critique and explicit consequence of a world of work whose purpose, focus, and interest can no longer give individuals meaning or empower them for life. On the one hand, death is the symbolic negation of bourgeois life. On the other hand, it becomes a principle relative to which work and the concerns of bourgeois life become unimportant and distracting. Of course Hans, unlike Naphta, is never commited to such a principle wholly. He toys with it, rather, titillates himself with it, experiments with it, as Mann suggests, but never goes over wholeheartedly to it. Still, he is so in thrall to it that even after later revelations about it he is unable to hang on to his lesson clearly and returns to his sympathy again. The cause of this return is obvious: the symptom must recur as long as the cause is not confronted. Even his return from the mountain is in the "service" of death in the form of war. Sympathy with death is the mark, symptom, and symbol of disappointment with bourgeois life and its understanding of work and meaning, of its failure to impart strength. It is the expression of decadence, not its cause, and Hans is a living critique of the values of the bourgeois world, though not its uncompromising enemy. He is the embodiment of desires and needs that the world cannot satisfy. To focus only on sympathy with death misses the problem that gives rise to it.

Illness and sympathy with death are thus consequences of the failure of the world of work. The failure of life is portrayed in two ways: as estrangement from work that answers no inner needs—and so is transformed into illness—and as preoccupation with death, which locates a sacred, though inverted, value in an otherwise disenchanted world. Sympathy with death leads to the wish to wear mourning and be worshipful, in devotion to, in service of an object whose importance and value cannot be denied. Indeed, later *Doctor Faustus*, taking up the themes of *The Magic Mountain*, will radicalize this preoccupation with inverted sacred values and will portray it as darkly empowering rather than debilitating, by turning death into the devil.

Yet the dying people on the mountain have little ennobling about them, as Herman Weigand points out.[29] This realization acts as a damper on Hans's enthusiasm and prevents him from finding sacred objects among them, from finding an unambiguous source of value in their suffering and end. The extremity of Naphta is another disillusioning force that leads Hans to turn to life, at least temporarily, while still experiencing death as sacred.

After his later epiphany in the snowstorm, however—where he wakens himself from a dangerous sleep and intellectually turns away from death— Hans sees death somewhat differently. Rather than embracing it as the alternative to life that he has taken it to be and as the position from which he might maintain a critical distance toward life, he makes it into a vehicle of return to life—or so he claims. "For a long time I stood on an intimate footing with illness and death. . . . For death you know is the principle of genius . . . and it is also the pedagogical principle, for love of it leads to love of life and of humanity. . . . There are two paths to life: one is the usual one, direct and honest. The other is evil, it leads through death, and that is the path of genius!" (827). Death is now the path to inspiration, the god of genius, reserved for those unable to take the common path to life. It is the path of enlightenment and also of a symbolic return to life as conquering genius. But whatever Hans may claim for his new insight, his sympathy does not lead him back. If he finds life at all, it is only in the form it takes on the mountain, far from the demands and conflicts of any form of life below, bourgeois or otherwise.

Only the cataclysm of war—not an inner process of development and understanding, but an external event—leads him back to life. When it happens, he thanks the heavens for showing him the path home, which, whatever his learning and experience, he was unable to find by himself. He returns to life, bourgeois society, in military uniform, as far removed from the world of the bourgeois calling as any magic mountain. Yet the disaffection from the realities of bourgeois life experienced by the soldiers returning from the trenches and by post–World War I Europe generally, in both the defeated and the victorious countries, proves that war was no return to life at all and held in its bosom no possibility of a new relation to society, to work, or to living.

THE CONFLICT OF THE TIMES

Most of the intellectual weight of *The Magic Mountain* (as well as most of the baggage) is carried by Settembrini and Naphta. In their debates about what Mann took to be the important social themes of the time concerning the future of society and humankind, they show his new intellectual concern.[30] The emphasis in *The Magic Mountain* is strikingly different from his earlier focus on the artist's identity and calling and the artist's relation to the bourgeois class. This new horizon in Mann's work overcomes the limitations of the self-absorbed artist preoccupied with the personal difficulties of his calling. At the same time, it opens up a range of issues and themes that makes the artistic works of the second half of Mann's life achievements of extraordinary depth, breadth, and power.

The incorporation of social, cultural, and political themes that Mann takes to be central to German destiny makes possible a synthesis of a new kind between the novel of society and the novel of personal identity. From *The Magic Mountain* onward, Mann elaborates an identity and fusion between the self and the nation, whether the self is an average young man or an artist. Social and cultural themes thereby become the themes of art but also the new building blocks of the identity of the artist or ordinary man. This new development is more important than whether one takes the side of Settembrini or Naphta. Hans takes both sides, in a sense, but surpasses them both by defending the capacity that can transcend them. Lacking an alternative intellectual ground that is solid, he bases himself ultimately on sympathy with the well-meaning Settembrini, who voices moralizing views of civilization that Hans considers no longer compelling but whose opponent, Naphta, is even less compelling. Hans remains faithful to the "spirit of death" that Naphta defends, while "freeing his thoughts" for the more humane concerns represented by Settembrini. Unfortunately, in this sense he has no resolution, though he finds a comfortable way to understand his position.

Mann himself became an open defender of the positions of Settembrini—and hence of his brother—in his political speeches and essays of the 1920s and after, taking over positions on behalf of civilization and reason that he had bitterly attacked in the *Reflections*. But this means that Mann, and the narrator, have no deeper understanding of the issues than does Hans Castorp. A real resolution of the intellectual and political debates the novel presents may or may not be possible, but they certainly cannot be resolved within the terms deployed by the two interlocutors, nor within the dichotomies defended in the *Reflections*. Indeed, to pose the debate of the times in the way Mann does makes real intellectual understanding impossible. As Fritz Kaufmann suggests: "Essentially this is a *philosophical* novel. . . . The unity of the work is defined by the magic circle of reflection which the young Castorp spins for himself. From this circle there can be no liberation in the work itself."[31]

Without a position outside the circle, or a middle ground, there is no way for Hans to return to the flatland, nothing to resolve him to leave the mountain. Nothing he learns can send him back to life. Only war, which pulverizes and confuses all positions, creates a field of struggle, a primitive identification, and a meaning that make the seeming return to life compelling through engagement in the higher stakes of a life-and-death struggle. The war to which Hans returns is not the real flatland, the world of work and social life. Rather, war reduces life to its most basic elements while enchanting an otherwise disenchanted generation—one that went through the conflict with romantic longings—to recapture a sense of urgency and vitality.

Settembrini and Naphta are, in general, subject only to the critique of the other, that is, to an extreme attack from a totally opposed viewpoint. It is true that the arrival on the mountain of the charismatic Mynheer Peeperkorn brings a personal dimension to Hans's experience on the mountain that overshadows mere intellect. It is also true that Mann means Hans's resolution in the "Snow" episode to stand for this middle ground, as a representative of "the German mean" (*die deutsche Mitte*). But in "Snow" Hans works with dichotomies set by Settembrini and Naphta, which are presented as if they in fact exhaust the existing intellectual universe, as if they are the real alternatives of the time. Yet the intellectual battle and self-conscious class struggle that Settembrini and Naphta are engaged in leave both positions discredited and exhaust whatever intellectual possibilities the novel can imagine. When liberation does come, it is through a Christian fantasy of redemption through death.

For Civilization

Settembrini's positions replicate many of those that Mann denounced in the *Reflections* as the views of the *Zivilisationsliterat*. Even so, Settembrini defends an ideal of humanity (*Humanität*) that bears more than a resemblance to the one Mann made his own, and despite his preachiness and the intellectual subtlety of his opponent, he is presented with sympathy and humorous affection, all of which make him, in certain ways, a precursor of Zeitblom in *Doctor Faustus*. Settembrini is an independent writer and a self-described humanist who invokes Prometheus as the first of his kind, a man for whom "literature is nothing other than ... the unity of humanism and politics" (223–24). Humanism and politics are one and the same force, and may be comprehended in a single word: "civilization" (224–25). Ultimately, "the friend of humankind cannot ... recognize the difference between politics and the non-political. There is nothing non-political. Everything is politics. ... The social problem, the problem of coexistence itself is politics, politics through and through, nothing more than politics. Whoever devotes himself to it ... belongs to politics" (711–12). Having fought so bitterly against this point of view in the *Reflections* even while predicting its triumph, Mann now gives it a prominent place in *The Magic Mountain*. He subjects its bearer to attack only by Naphta—an attack, indeed, more powerful and sharp than any Mann himself ever directed against it.

Settembrini defends "the 'world,' the interests of life against sentimental flight from the world—classicism against romanticism" (348). He thus defends bourgeois work against illness as work's negation: "Reason and enlightenment ... have expelled these shadows that camped on the soul of humankind—not yet completely, they are lodged in struggle with them still today; the name of this struggle however is work, sir, worldly work, work for the earth, for honor and the interests of humankind ... to lead them on the paths of progress and of civilization to an ever brighter, kinder and purer light" (139–40). His critical attitude toward the mountain and defense of work thus make Settembrini unable to appreciate Hans's embrace of the counterworld of the mountain, as both an escape from bourgeois life and a place for education.

Settembrini's understanding of the difference between East and West echoes Mann in the *Reflections*. There are two great principles in conflict, he says: "power and right, tyranny and freedom, superstition and knowledge, the principle of persistence and that of fermenting movement, of progress. One could call the one the Asiatic principle, the other, however, the European" (221). Therefore, he says to Hans about the East, "do not direct yourself inwardly toward it, do not let it infect you with its concepts, place rather your own nature, your higher nature against its, and keep sacred what to you, the son of the West, of the godly West— the son of civilization, what is sacred according to nature and tradition" (339–40). Even Germany—which Settembrini respects as a land of enlightenment, *Bildung*, and freedom—has its Eastern element. "Look at him, this Luther! . . . My friend, that is Asia. . . . Decisions will have to be faced—decisions of inestimable significance for the happiness and future of Europe, and they will fall to your land, in its soul they will have to fulfill themselves. Placed between East and West, it will have to choose, it will have to decide finally and consciously between the two spheres that strive after her being" (714). Like Mann, Settembrini places Germany in a pivotal position in Europe. Yet unlike Mann, Settembrini claims that Germany must choose one and renounce the other. Although Mann in World War I strove to preserve the unique qualities of Germany against the onslaught of Western values, recognizing its affinities with the East, his ultimate position—hinted at in the *Reflections* but spelled out only in talks from "On the German Republic" to "Culture and Socialism"—is to see Germany mediating dualisms and synthesizing their best qualities within itself. It is not choice that must be made, but combination, and to Mann only Germany can accomplish this task. Thinking dualistically, Hans too believes that there are only "two spiritual directions or spiritual currents . . . the pious and the free." The trouble with the free path, Settembrini's, is that "it believes itself to have human dignity so completely on lease. . . . The other also contains much human dignity" (409). That is the side defended, though in an unusual form, by Naphta.

Against the Bourgeoisie

Naphta alone in the novel has a diagnosis of the illness of the times and the bourgeois world, and his condemnation of that world and proposals for healing bring him into bitter conflict with Settembrini, who defends the bourgeois world and the fight against darkness by the forces of civilization.[32] To Naphta, the world of *Bildung*, self-development, and bourgeois work are dead ends, hopelessly decadent, and humankind can be rescued only by the radical rejection and overcoming of that world in new bonds of command and obedience. Hans listens to Naphta because he is fully estranged from the bourgeois world that has given rise to the spiritual illnesses in him and the times. This is why Settembrini's task is hopeless, for he is defending the West to an audience—both within and outside the novel—already disillusioned with it.

For Naphta, an eastern European Jew who has joined the Jesuits, capitalist Europe is "a condemned world system" on the verge of going under (524). Progress and the struggle for happiness have produced a capitalist bourgeois state that holds out no cure for the mortal illness of bourgeois society. The capitalist state and world system stand in the way of the new, and their ideals are a thing of the past. To Naphta, "The catastrophe should and must come" (528–29). The old relation of self and society is totally degenerate. "*Bildung* and possession [*Besitz*]—there you have the bourgeois. There you have the foundations of the liberal world republic" (709). Nothing sound and enduring can be constructed from material civilization as it is today. "The unconfessed but secretly quite generally diffused desire for war was an expression of it. It would come, this war, and it would be good, although it would bring to a head other things than its authors expected of it" (958–59).[33]

Well before the annunciation of his apocalyptic visions, Naphta defends proletarian rule.

> Now then—all of these economic principles and standards, after centuries of being buried, are having their resurrection in the modern movement of communism. . . . The correspondence is complete even in the sense of the claim to domination that international labor raises against international traders and speculators, the world proletariat that today sets humanity and the criterion of the city of God against bourgeois capitalist decay. The dictatorship of the proletariat, the political-economic demand for salvation of our time, does not mean domination for its own sake and for eternity, but rather a temporary overcoming [*Aufhebung*] of the contradiction of spirit and power in the sign of the cross, in the sense of overcoming of the world through the means of world domination. . . . [The proletariat's] task is to terrify for the sake of the healing of the world and of the winning of the goal of salvation, the stateless and classless filial relation to God [*Gotteskindheit*]. (559)

In these words Naphta is not announcing a new freedom for labor oppressed by the bourgeoisie or expanded reproduction within the economy and for the well-being of humankind. Rather, what stands against Settembrini is a proletarian movement that seeks salvation, redemption from the meaninglessness that has advanced under the bourgeoisie and can be ended only by the righteous purging of the world of those forces that prevent the absolute from reemerging. This is not a prescription for political and social transformation, but a call for collective religious redemption and the recovery of lost unity. For Naphta it is absurd to imagine with Settembrini that "the outcome of future revolutions would be freedom," for "the principle of freedom has fulfilled itself and is antiquated" (554). Freedom, in fact, "has ruined the world" (556). Indeed, to imagine that bourgeois ideals of *Bildung*, personality, and the flowering of the self are desirable, let alone possible, is naive. "The secret and the command of our time are not liberation and development of the

self. What it needs, what it strives after, what it will create, is—terror"
(554–55).

> A pedagogy that still understands itself today as a daughter of the
> Enlightenment and perceives its means of *Bildung* in critique, the
> liberation and cultivation of the self, the dissolution of absolutely
> fixed forms of life . . . its backwardness, for those who know, is
> beyond any doubt. All truly educational organizations have known
> all along what in truth all pedagogy is always concerned with:
> namely the absolute command, the iron bond, discipline, sacrifice,
> renunciation of the self, violation of the personality. Finally it is
> an unloving misunderstanding of youth to believe it finds its desire
> in freedom. Its deepest desire is obedience. (554)

The tradition of *Bildung* is exhausted. The times cry out for order,
direction, discipline, and belonging within an order of rank to which
humankind can submit with assurance. For Naphta as for Weber, the
proliferation of science and technical knowledge and the demands of
specialization threaten the striving for belief and redemption. Naphta
even criticizes abstract justice and scientific truth in Nietzschean fashion,
yet defends belief and religion against them. "The true is what benefits
man. . . . He is the measure of things and his welfare is the criterion of
truth" (551). Thus, Naphta defends the church and religion against modern science: "What has led man into darkness and will lead him ever
deeper is . . . 'presuppositionless,' aphilosophical natural science" (552).

What the world aspires to is an overcoming of the contradictions that
have undermined the unity and totality it once possessed. "That power
is evil we know. But the dualism of good and evil, of the beyond and
the this-worldly, of spirit and power, must, if the kingdom is to arrive,
be temporarily overcome [*aufgehoben*] in a principle that unites asceticism and domination. This is what I call the necessity of terror" (557).
Settembrini's "reverence for the individual life belonged to the most
insipidly protective bourgeois times."

> But under tolerably passionate circumstances, as soon as a single
> idea was in play that went beyond that of "security," something
> suprapersonal, supraindividual therefore—and this alone was
> worthy of men, consequently it was the normal condition in the
> higher sense—at all times the individual life would not only be
> sacrificed to the higher thought without ceremony, but would also
> be unhesitatingly risked, as far as the individual is concerned, of
> his own free will. (637)

History thus documents that the aspiration of the individual is not freedom, self-development, or wealth, but self-sacrifice on behalf of a higher

ideal or principle. This ultimate supraindividual ideal is what the time lacks and what it seeks everywhere, precisely because of the desire for self-sacrifice and self-overcoming, as the true sources of meaning and strength.

Settembrini, Naphta says, does not understand religion, which is opposed to "arch-philistinism and primitive bourgeoisness [*Urbürgerlichkeit*]" (639). Settembrini makes the mistake of transforming "God and the devil into two different persons or principles" and sees " 'life' as an object of struggle lying between them. In reality, however, they are one and united in opposition to life, to life's bourgeois nature [*Lebensbürgerlichkeit*], ethics, reason, virtue—as they represent the religious principle in common" (640). The devil's position, however much one may imagine there are grounds to oppose it, is as unstintingly critical of bourgeois life as is God's. Here Naphta again foreshadows the devil in *Doctor Faustus*: the religious critique of bourgeois life is manifest in an antigodly but still religious and redemptive power that justifies and fortifies the individual. Naphta confesses he has made it his task to undermine certainties and prepare the ground for the reemergence of absolutes in a time of crisis. "Your humanity . . . is already today an antiquated custom, a classicistic absurdity, a spiritual ennui that breeds a fit of yawning and to make a clean sweep of which the new revolution, *our* revolution, sir, is preparing. . . . Only out of radical skepticism, out of moral chaos does the absolute arise, the holy terror that the time requires" (969).

To Hans, Naphta is "a revolutionary of conservatism" (636). Yet without any clear insight of his own into the problem and bankruptcy of bourgeois society, Hans does not have a full grasp of what the issues are between the two men. He is suspended between their mutual negation. Mann, however, gives him the chance to decide and, in so doing, presents what he thinks is the only possible resolution to their conflict, if only on the level of dreams—though it is a dream in more than one sense.

False Resolution

Hans, the narrator, and Mann attempt to forge resolutions to Hans's estrangement from work, illness, and death, advancing the hope and possibility that a middle ground might be found in the conflicts of the times and upholding the standard of "humanity" as a guide to human life. Whether these new perspectives are intellectually and artistically credible is questionable. Yet out of Hans's struggle for the new ground, Mann redeems the events and debates of social and political life for the internal shaping of the individual and his actions in the external world. In this sense, as well as in the more obvious sense of a story of the hero's development, *The Magic Mountain* is a *Bildungsroman* of enormous consequence for Mann's own development and for the development of Germany.

In the course of one important experience Hans seems, however temporarily, to reconcile the opposites. One day he gets lost intentionally in the snow, despite the protests of his reason. In a dreamlike state (remarkably reminiscent of the concluding vision of Nietzsche's *Birth of Tragedy*)[34] he sees a beautiful locale surrounded by mountains and the sea, filled with lovely young people playing and wandering about. But in the midst of this scene he envisions a temple, within which two old women violently dismember a child. Out of this vivid dream of opposites, of light rooted in darkness and death—in Nietzsche's terms, of the unity of Apollo and Dionysus—Hans weaves his understanding of life and death: "Whoever knows the body, life, knows death. Only that is not the whole of it. . . . One must hold to the other half, the opposite. For all interest in death and illness is nothing other than a kind of expression for interest in life," in man and "his estate and state" (684).

This dream is the foundation of his independence from and reconciliation with Settembrini and Naphta. Hans interprets his dream as a dream

> of the estate of man and his polite-intelligent and respectful community, behind which in the temple the hideous blood feast takes place. Were they so polite and charming to one another, the people of the sun, in silent regard for just this horror? . . . I will side with them in my soul and not with Naphta—moreover also not with Settembrini, they are both babblers. . . . With their aristocratic questions! With their nobility! Death or life—illness, health—spirit and nature. Are those really contradictions? I ask: are they questions? No, they are not questions, and also the question about their nobility is not one. The frenzy [*Durchgängerei*] of death is in life, it would not be life without it, and in the middle is the estate of *Homo Dei*—in the midst between frenzy and reason—just as his state is between mystical community and empty individuality. (684–85)

To Hans, what have been presented as oppositions and dualisms are not real oppositions. The interpenetration of the opposites, typified by the relation of life and death, is the reality, and the human being, now identified as the "man of God," stands *in der Mitte*, in the sanctified confluence of the supposed opposites, by his nature contradicting these alternatives—as Nietzsche says, "worshipping . . . in the temple of both gods."[35]

[Man] alone is noble and not the contradictions. Man is the master of the contradictions, they exist through him, and therefore he is more noble than they. More noble than death, too noble for it—that is the freedom of his head. More noble than life, too noble for it—that is the piety in his heart. . . . I will be good. I will allow death no domination over my thoughts! For therein is goodness and love of humankind and in nothing else. Death is a great power. . . . Reason stands foolishly before it, for it is nothing other than virtue, death however is freedom, frenzy, deformity and desire. Desire says my dream, not love. . . . Love is opposed to death, only it, not reason, is stronger than it. Only it, not reason, gives kind thoughts. (685–86)

Thus Hans claims that humankind must not be ruled by intellectual contradictions and abstract ideas but must see itself as the master of contradiction.[36] Although death remains close to Hans's heart, it is denied dominion over his thoughts, whatever that means.[37] Yet this is not an intellectual resolution, but a solidifying of identity beyond the intellectual conflicts that rage around it. And the vehicle of this new identity is not reason, but a vision and a dream, a symbolic expression of the truth of experience, not reason. In the intellectual sense, Hans has no resolution, for although Naphta may be more "right" than Settembrini, his proposals are madness, and although Settembrini may "mean well," he imagines that reason can cure madness. Thus there is no well-grounded intellectual position in the novel, except for the vision of humankind's uniqueness. Hans does *not* in fact transcend and reconcile these antitheses; he just imagines that he has done so. Even in circumscribing devotion to death, only love, and not reason, can resist its attraction. Thus the association of love, death, and illness that Hans once defended to Clawdia here seems broken, at least in intention: love is separated from the unholy trinity to fortify the person *against* the seductive power of death. Yet the only love that the novel shows us or that Hans evinces is the intoxicated love of illness and the exotic.[38]

I will hold true to death in my heart, yet remember clearly that faith in death and the dead is simply evil and dark lust and hostility to humankind, when it determines our thoughts and governing. *For the sake of goodness and love man should allow death no domination over his thoughts.* . . . For a long time I have sought for this word. . . . Now I have it. My dream has given it to me most clearly, so that I will know it for ever. (686)

But because the events of "Snow" happen only in "thought" and not in the heart (even though they occur in a dream), and because love in the novel is so unreal, their effect does not last, and the heart reasserts itself, drawing Hans back to the seductive idleness and inebriating illness of the mountain. The symptoms of illness are not overcome as long as its real cause is left untreated. Thus, while the personal position of *die Mitte* is a crucial part of the intellectual ground Mann believes he has conquered in the novel both for himself and for Germany, Hans cannot, in fact, take its lessons to heart, and its effect begins to fade. "The highly civilized atmosphere of the 'Berghof' caressed him an hour later. At dinner he fell to it powerfully. What he had dreamed was fading. What he had thought, he understood this very evening no longer so correctly" (688). Whatever it means to hold true to death in one's heart, its effect is too strong—and its cause too unchallenged—for any vision to overcome without some other reinforcement for its lessons.[39]

Though Mann himself called the italicized words of the "Snow" episode the "sentence expressing the upshot" of the whole novel,[40] the lessons of the snow are remembered only by the novel, not by the hero, and thus are only for the narrator, the author, and the reader.[41] Mann wrote of Hans in "Snow": "Here he dreams a dream of beautiful humanity [*Menschlichkeit*], in which the synthesis of the Naphta world and the Settembrini world is, as it were, anticipated. He is a sacrificed forerunner. It is not truly allowed to him to experience the new concept of *Humanität*. He disappears in the war. Still, before he disappears he has a presentiment of something."[42] These remarks reveal Mann's ideological purpose, a purpose confirmed in his own interpretations of the novel and in his speeches of the 1920s. Despite his claim of having his hero, and himself, find a middle ground beyond the contradictions posed in the novel, Mann was to embrace one side of the opposition as his own higher unity and ultimate principle.

Because the allegorical purpose of the novel is to reveal the various forces, powers, and ideas struggling for Germany's soul and the soul of its citizens, it would be premature for Hans and Germany to return to their tasks with their *Bildungsreise* incomplete. In fact, of course, it can never be complete. The stasis of the mountain world is just an excuse for the deployment and examination of the modern German cultural and political scene. It cannot reasonably be subject to the same demands that could be made of a realistic novel. As a consequence, however, *The Magic Mountain* undermines its realistic level not only by parody but by its allegorical purpose as well. For the novel, and Mann, also ask that the narrative be taken as a real story, however parodied, of *Bildung*. The question is whether these two levels of allegory and realism can coexist in the same work, or whether the needs of one undermine the successful realization of the other and impose demands on one level that the work cannot fulfill without discrediting or making less credible the other level. On the one hand, to interpret the novel from the point of view of Hans's personal development is to raise questions about the coherence of his experiences and to doubt the efficacy and influence of any and all of his experiences for his real development and return to life. On the other hand, to interpret the novel from the point of view of the cultural and political allegory of Germany is to make unreasonable the question of Hans's own learning and the evaluation of these experiences for their effect on a real life. These tensions in Mann's allegory will become even more compelling in the allegory of *Doctor Faustus*.

The Magic Mountain allows a fusion of the self of Hans Castorp with the reality of Germany and raises the question of their identity in tandem and inseparably. But the problem of levels remains. Some interpreters—including even Mann himself[43]—have tried to resolve it by emphasizing the autobiographical nature of the novel, thus assimilating both its hero's story and the story of Germany to Mann's own *Bildung*. But while this perspective illuminates some themes and makes more comprehensible the changing nature of the novel as it was written, it does not necessarily illuminate the structural problem of the novel or provide a standard by which to judge its principles of selection or the reasonableness and coherence of its main character. The novel's conclusion, in the explosion of war, complicates the issues even further.

DEATH AND THE DREAM OF POWER

Whatever Hans may have learned in seven years on the mountain, no single event or person, nor all of his experiences together, move him even one step closer to "life," understood as a willingness to abandon his retreat from the flatland and return to the bourgeois world in some capacity. With the self-discrediting of Settembrini and Naphta, *The Magic Mountain* in fact supports no intellectual ground, despite the apparent revelations of "Snow." Without such ground, Hans has no means of return, except as the object of circumstances and demands beyond his control. Neither confrontation with the intellectual conflicts of Europe, nor his researches into the nature of life, nor his romance with the East, nor his experience in the snow, nor his encounter with Peeperkorn, a "personality," does more than merely enrich his fund of experience.[44] Perhaps some decisive experience is still missing that would shift the balance or transform him. But perhaps no experience on earth is capable of returning him to bourgeois life, either because of the total bankruptcy of that life or because of Hans's total and unmitigated estrangement from it.

Hans has turned to metaphysical reflections on life and been critical of the unquestioned validity of forms of knowledge and the importance of reason—but only, we are told, in order to set boundaries to reason so it does not overstep them and betray its own task. Thus, Hans gives credit abstractly to the value of the "service" of life, while his own experiences and understanding inhibit him from embracing it concretely through a return to the flatland. As the narrator says, "The meaning, purpose, and goal of the critical principle can and may be only one thing: the thought of duty, the command of life. Yes, while law-giving wisdom laid out critically the boundaries of reason, at precisely these boundaries it has planted the flag of life and proclaimed it the soldierly duty of man to serve [*Dienst zu tun*] under it" (757). But service is something Hans still cannot do in the flatland. In the meantime, the tedium of life on the mountain grows heavy.

> Hans Castorp looked around himself. . . . He saw throughout the uncanny, the malevolent, and he knew what he saw: life without time, life without care and without hope, life as industriously stagnating depravity, dead life. . . . He was afraid. It seemed to him as if "the whole thing" would come to no good end, as if a catastrophe would be the end, a rebellion by patient nature, a thunderstorm and storm wind that would make a clean sweep, that would break the spell of this world. . . . He longed to flee. (872, 880)

Death and Self-Sacrifice

A longing for the end, which led so many to welcome war in 1914, is the setting for the final events of the novel. In Hans's case, he discovers, one evening while listening to Schubert's song "Oh, Lindenbaum," that his heart has in fact remained very true to death, and he is carried away by intoxication with the song and its expression of death's world. Indeed, the narrator tells us, "his destiny would have turned out differently if his temperament had not been amenable in the highest degree to the charms of the sphere of feeling, the general spiritual attitude, that the song embraced in so intimately-mysteriously a way"; yet through his sympathy he had become as well "a critic full of misgivings" (904–5). The narrator again affirms the profound effect on Hans of attraction to death as a cause rather than a symptom of his choices. But whatever Hans's doubts and misgivings, they do not detract from his love of death; rather, they enhance his passion for it.

Hans's enchantment with death goes beyond simple fascination, however, for it contains an extraordinary dream of power that is here revealed. Only a process of self-overcoming, Hans imagines, can cope with "this enchantment of the soul with dark consequences! . . . Oh it was powerful."

> We were all its sons, and we could accomplish powerful things on earth by serving it. One needed no more genius, only much more talent than the author of the Lindenbaum song in order, as an artist of the soul's enchantment, to give that song enormous proportions and therewith to subjugate the world. One might probably even found empires upon it, earthly all too earthly empires, very solid and rejoicing in progress and actually not at all ill with homesickness. (907)

Here Hans's vision of the kingdom of death is one not of retreat and escape from life but of the domination of life and of the power that service of death can give. Indeed, this vision of conquest was to prove all too true to life in the decades after the novel's appearance.[45] The puzzle is its appearance in Hans's reveries shortly before the outbreak of war. But the explanation is not far to seek. Theoretically, there are three paths one can follow when confronted with the longing revealed in this fantasy. The first is to recognize and interpret it as a fantasy of domination and power, indeed a fantasy of ressentiment. But this meaning of the fantasy of death remains uncriticized in the novel; it is understood neither by the hero nor the narrator. To understand it would be to grasp the attraction of death as the attraction to an antibourgeois power, promising a world in which the failed and disaffected bourgeois may triumph over bourgeois life in terms more consistent with his own feelings and identity. Such an understanding would make it possible to experience truly the failure and disappointment with bourgeois life that Hans feels and the impossibility of satisfying that life on its terms. It would mean that he accepted his powerlessness and failure within it, and that he hoped to find a new path, alone or with others, not dominated by bourgeois life's exclusive terms and understanding of success.

The second alternative is the one lived out in Germany and Mann's other fiction, for his fantasy shows that Hans Castorp is a forerunner, in parodied and less threatening form, of Adrian Leverkühn! Even this mediocre young German contains within himself, though as a possibility unrealized, the source of a devilish pact that, it is imagined, can lead to a "breakthrough" into life. But, lacking Adrian's talent, will, and determination, Hans sinks back into passivity and waits for events to determine the direction of his life. Since Adrian experiences his estrangement and powerlessness more painfully and his desire to belong and be redeemed through submission to a calling more intensely and urgently than the escapist Hans, he is driven to take more active steps to protect himself against bourgeois life, to oppose it, and to conquer it. Still, the inclinations toward devilishness that Mann saw in himself as a young man and recovered for his Faust story as an old man are present, though in ineffective and humorous form, in Hans and the world of the mountain. Its ineffectuality soon became the murderousness of National Socialism.

The ultimate outcome of Hans's intoxication with death forms a third, quasi-religious path, a vision of self-sacrifice that finds its fulfillment on the battlefield at the novel's conclusion, and in his encounter with the Schubert song that end is foretold. The overcoming of sympathy with death is to be accomplished through a real death, a Christ-like, self-sacrificing death that supposedly upholds a new possibility of love and the future, which Hans only just senses but cannot call by its real name, whatever it might be. This, too, anticipates Leverkühn. The true message of the "magic song" in Hans's view is to inspire not intoxication with death, but its overcoming through a return to life as love—a return, however, that can happen only through his own death. Here, finally, is the bridge back to life of which Hans once spoke to Clawdia in the "*Walpurgisnacht*" episode. It is real death that leads to a vision of love, the new, and the future, though what the new is and how death is to lead to renewal remain unclear despite the novel's ending, which tries to reveal the process at work.

> But its best son might still be the one who in his overcoming consumed his life and died, on his lips the new word of love that he still did not know how to speak. It was so worthy to die for it, this magic song [*Zauberlied*]! But whoever died for it, yet that one actually died no longer for it and was a hero only because he already died at bottom for the new, the new word of love and of the future in his heart. (907)

Taking to heart Naphta's vision of Christ-like self-sacrifice through immersion in illness on behalf of a future redemption, Hans's imagination conjures up a vision of redemptive death and self-sacrifice, though on behalf of an ideal very different from Naphta's. Yet despite the difference of ideals, the only hope of higher meaning that Mann gives his hero is through sacrifice of self and life for a greater cause.[46] This greater value cannot be found in bourgeois life, because that life's ultimate principle has become too empty to satisfy even the unrefined Hans.

The alternative to the emptiness of the civilian service Hans was unable to pursue in the flatland but pursues in substitute form on the mountain is soldierly service, not of death, but of a "higher" principle on the battlefield. In Mann's universe, that ultimate principle is not now the nation, as it was for Weber's archetypal soldier, but an ideal drawn from the nation's past, a vision of love for humanity, which, frankly, seems even sillier amid the exploding shells of World War I than other more mundane ideals. Indeed, the swan song to love and humanity that the narrator sings at the end of the novel threatens to make him seem more absurd than Settembrini, who at least defends the cause of freedom from absolutism along with baser territorial concerns. Perhaps Mann saw the need for the enslaved generation to "go under," like the Hebrews of Egypt, before a new generation of spiritually free people could enter the promised land. But it is hard to conceive of the bloodletting of World War I as the prelude to a vision of love and humanity. Instead, of course, it was the prelude to something much darker.

War and Disenchantment

The climactic event of the novel and its passage through death, then, is the imagined passage to life through war. As Hermann Kurzke understatedly remarks, in the war Hans "dies in sympathy with death, but the following generation will devote itself to the new. The shape of this perspective on the 'new' remains, it is true, more than vague."[47] Hans has been on the mountain for seven years when war breaks out. He "long ago no longer knew at all anymore where else to go" and "was on the whole no longer capable of grasping the thought of return to the flatland" (982). Indeed, "all contact between him and the flatland had been completely abolished"; he had totally immersed himself in "this hermetic magic for which the enraptured one had shown himself pleasurably receptive and which had become the fundamental adventure of his soul" (984).

Then comes war, and its effect is stunning. For Hans, the man who paid no heed to events below, who, according to the narrator, occupied himself with the shadows of things but not the things themselves, the outburst of war "blows up the magic mountain and sets the seven-sleeper harshly outside its doors." But the effect of the outbreak of war on Hans is even more radical and liberating, and dates "from the moment of his awakening" (989).

> He saw himself disenchanted [*entzaubert*], redeemed [*erlöst*], liberated—not of his own power, as he had to confess with embarrassment, but turned out by elementary external powers, under whose

> guard his liberation quite accidentally crept. . . . It could happen
> that life was taking back its sinful delicate child once again—not
> in a cheap way, but perhaps only in a serious and strict way, in the
> sense of a trial that perhaps might mean not life, but precisely in
> this case three salvos of honor for him, the sinner. And thus he
> sank down then on his knees, face and hands raised to a heaven
> that was sulphurously dark but no longer the grotto ceiling of his
> mountain of sin. (988)

In this moment, a new light is cast on Hans's condition, both for the
reader and for himself. The spell of the mountain and the spell on the
hero are broken by a deus ex machina. Hans thanks the heavens for a
liberation of which he was not capable himself and for the chance to
be readmitted to life for a man who now sees himself as a sinner against
the spirit of life. Yet he foretells his own doom, perhaps even seeks it,
when he casts in religious language the whole process of his salvation
and "sin" and, unable to ask the god of life for complete forgiveness,
submits himself to a trial by fire from which he may not recover but
because of which he would at least no longer be a sinner.[48]

"Where are we? What is this? Where has the dream driven us? . . . It
is the flatland, it is the war. . . . It is a regiment of volunteers, young
blood, students mostly, not long in the field" (990–91). "There is our
acquaintance, there is Hans Castorp. . . . What, he is singing!" (993). The
words and song on his lips are, of course, refrains from Schubert, the
song of death that Hans had imagined was a path to power over life.[49]

> And thus, in the turmoil, in the rain, the twilight, he goes out of
> our sight. Live well, Hans Castorp, life's guileless delicate child!
> Your story is over. . . . We told it for its sake, not for your sake,
> for you were simple. . . . Fare well—you may live now or may
> remain here! Your prospects are bad. . . . Moments came when,
> ominously and in governing, a dream of love sprang up in you out
> of death and the body's lasciviousness. Out of this world feast of
> death, out of this evil feverish passion that ignites the rainy
> evening sky all around, will love too some time ascend? (994)

Indeed, the vision of war on the last two pages of the novel is not
even heroic; it is a scene of random violence where life and death occur
by chance. In this way, Mann's brief, dehumanizing picture of battle at
least sees farther than Weber's heroizing of the effects of war on the
meaning of life on the battlefield. The narrator leaves Hans to his fate,
a not too hopeful one. Hans likely dies having only glimpsed what might
yet arise from his dreams of death. This is his return to the flatland.

The life to which Hans returns when he goes to war cannot be taken as a symbolic return to life. War is freeing, yet it gives no model for life. Despite Mann's hope for love as the outcome of war, the novel reveals war as false liberation. Nothing about the picture of war we are given reveals a responsible and active relation to life. Life as portrayed in the novel is concretized in the bourgeois order, and that order still has no answers to the question of meaning, purpose, or identity. War is the negation of all order, bourgeois and otherwise. Thus, while experience on the mountain may eventually draw Hans away from his intense attraction to death, illness, and the exotic, it leaves him passive. He has nowhere to return to in the flatland as it is presently constituted. This is the real reason why Hans cannot live the new synthesis, the new idea of humanity, although he may have an inkling of it: that idea has no place or support in the flatland.

Yet it is *not* a new idea that is missing from "life," nor is it this particular one that is needed. If *The Magic Mountain* shows anything, intentionally or not, it is that mere ideas, no matter how intensely experienced, are not enough to shape life and form meaning. What is required is a genuine conception of purpose and identity grounded in a changed and vital social order or in a form of life with roots in society, and along with it a new relation to work, self, and society. Can the old world really find again its meaning in the synthesis of antiquity and Christianity, of Marx and Hölderlin, of East and West that Mann calls for elsewhere, the new ideal of humanity? Hans is not simply between positions: he is between *worlds*, with one world going down and the other not yet arisen. Perhaps this accounts for Mann's flirtation for a time with Spengler's vision.[50] Unfortunately, the new world was not to be that of Mann's next work, about the biblical Joseph and the worldly salvation of his people; rather, the new world was to be one of devil's pacts, Hitler, and madness.

CONCLUSION: THE ALLEGORY OF SELF AND NATION

In describing his novelistic task after the war, Mann provided insight into the intellectual structure of his novel:

> In the war it was too early, I had to stop. The war first had to become obvious as the beginning of the revolution, its result not only had to be there, but had to be recognized as an apparent result [*Schein-Ausgang*]. The conflict of reaction (friendliness toward the Middle Ages) and humanistic enlightenment [is] thoroughly prewar historically. The synthesis appears to lie in the

(communistic) future: The new subsists in essence in a new conception of man as a spirit-corporeality (overcoming of the Christian dualism of soul and body, church and state, death and life), also moreover a conception already prewar. It is a question of the perspective on the renewal of the Christian state of God [Gottesstaat] at home in the humanistic state, on a somehow transcendentally inspired human state of God, therefore, arranged spiritually-corporeally. . . . Hans Castorp's release into the war thus signifies his release into the beginning of the struggle for the new, after he pedagogically experiences fully the components: Christianness and paganism.[51]

For Mann the analysis of individual meaning and the path of the calling, of the synthesis of the *deutsche Mitte*, is the bridge between the crisis of culture and the crisis of self-shaping embodied in the dilemma of *Bildung*. The cultural elements from the German experience of war and crisis are incorporated into a revised ideal of self and service by Mann, as they were into an applied ideal of self and calling by Weber. "Man, cultivated [gebildet] as a member of a cultivated [gebildet] state: now that is political *Humanität*."[52] Thus, Mann maintains the possibility of synthesis, and not simply of the overcoming of contradictions by human transcendence. He connects the idea of German culture and *Humanität* as the *Mitte* with the ideal of the German artist and self. The crisis of National Socialism, in *Doctor Faustus*, later shows divergence from the *Mitte*. Yet the standard of the *Mitte* is always present in Mann's work. "It is the idea of the middle [Mitte]" that Hans Castorp discovers and that appears to him "as the idea of life itself and of humaneness [Menschlichkeit]."

> This is, however, a German idea. It is *the* German idea, for is not German nature the middle, the mean, and mediating, and the German the man of the middle in the grand style? Yes, whoever says *Deutschtum* says middle; but whoever says middle says *Bürgerlichkeit*. . . . Here *Deutschtum* itself means *Bürgerlichkeit* . . . world bourgeoisness [Weltbürgerlichkeit], world middle, world conscience, world prudence, which does not let itself be carried away and which maintains critically the idea of humanity [Humanität], of humaneness [Menschlichkeit], of men and their *Bildung* toward right and left, against all extremes.[53]

Through the idea of the middle ground or way, Mann combined his analysis of Germany as the mediating element and middle ground between East and West with the view of the artist as mediator between life and spirit. This view is now enriched by the addition of an orientation to identity that makes the average German as well as the artist, indeed the human being as such, ideally the mediator between conflicting and irreconcilable oppositions that, in reality, belong together, like Apollo and Dionysus. This was the meaning of Hans's Nietzschean vision in the snow, though he forgets it. The novel succeeds where Hans fails, by remembering the lesson of the middle ground, a lesson Mann thinks most apt for Germany in its geopolitical position but also more broadly.[54] The claims about human love that emerge from the explosion of shells on the battlefield, however, are a backward-looking lesson of Christian hope and charity, a lesson that is fundamentally religious and neither aesthetic nor political. Thus, the romantic and reactionary *Reflections* are superseded, but not in the way Mann imagined.[55]

Mann claimed that his book "educates to intellectual clarity about life."[56] Yet Hans Castorp, despite his lengthy *Bildung* on the mountain, his exposure to illness, love, death, personality, and debates about civilization and order, finds nothing to empower him to return to the flatland or to make a choice and act.[57] Despite his experiences, he remains unfit for "life," fit only for war, and war requires no special preparation, qualities, or spirit of *Bildung*. But how could it be otherwise? A spell cannot be lifted by learning, unconsummated love, flirtation, or conversation. If Hans's condition is truly enchanted or bewitched (*verzaubert*), then only an extraordinary power can disenchant him (*entzaubern*), and all the efforts of *Bildung* in the world, or on the mountain, must go for naught. *The Magic Mountain* actually tells of the powerlessness of *Bildung*, though it wants to tell of the emergence of a new vision of life beyond education in death. Weber's notion that faith and involvement in magic are undermined by advancing rationality and technical understanding is here contradicted. The power of magic is too great for that. Only war can free Hans from magic, and for what? The bourgeois order that hovers around the magic mountain is still unattractive and without a place for Hans, except in uniform. Indeed, the novel has let us know that the times are at fault for Hans's disaffection, though it is his own intoxication with death that pushes his destiny down its peculiar path. Although Mann himself was to take over much of Settembrini's credo as his own, if in a less pompous and simpleminded way, the novel persuades us very little of the attraction of this conception.[58] Hans cannot return to what Weber called the "slow boring of hard boards" that is the life of building the world of the flatland. His resolution remains on the level of fantasy and imagination, not action.

With the exhaustion of cultural purposes and grounds for identity within the bourgeois world of work and achievement, Hans has taken a side road away from commitment to that world and its ideals. He immerses himself in illness, love, death, discussions of politics. Yet none of these return him to "life"—understood as the existing social order, though a return could in principle include opposition to or disaffection with the social order.[59] In fact, the brilliant, though unintended, message of the novel is that *no* amount of *Bildung* can eventuate in reempowerment and a return to life when life is as it is in the flatland. Even the newer form of *Bildung* has no answers for the failure of the social world to provide meaning. No self-education can overcome that failure, because, whatever one imagines about creating meaning oneself, one actually creates within and with the means of a given world. Hans's experience is thus an implicit critique of the world of the flatland, but neither the hero, the narrator, nor Mann himself imagines any alternative to it, that is, a different orientation toward work, identity, or social life. All they have is the vaguely religious and antiquated idea of humanity, an idea that, no matter what its value, cannot by itself rescue Hans or the world.

The Magic Mountain thus leaves us in profound ambiguity over the real "cure" for the illness of the times. Unlike some earlier Mann stories, where illness "leads" to something, however cut off from "life" its victim may be, the routinization of illness on the mountain, its presence among the ordinary, leads to nothing. It remains an excuse to step back from life and art, to listen, flirt, and wander in service to illness and its cure. Whatever the changes Hans undergoes, whatever the experiences that enrich his personality, they are bought at the price of a commitment to change the world, and he is no better equipped for life than before, despite the fantasy of a new love for which he may be prepared to die. He has found something to die for, and this is his resolution for life. In this sense, the novel is a critique of *Bildung*, but not in any way Mann intended. It is a vivid demonstration of the powerlessness of *Bildung* in a period with few defensible values, purposes, and goals. The dead end of this process shows the impossibility of reconstructing a replacement for *Bildung* from the time's materials as an alternative path to the one Hans has abandoned. No form of *Bildung* can lead to human regeneration in a time of disillusionment about society, identity, and work, any more than can Weberian notions of positing one's ideals and shaping the personality while serving them like a soldier on the battlefield.[60] Only through analyzing the corrupt and corrupting social sources of decline and changing the social world can the emergence of other sources of inner power, identity, and resolution become possible.

Mann does claim that Hans in fact glimpses the first form of the new idea of *Humanität*, though he is unable to live it.[61] This ideal, which Mann had already defended publicly in his lecture "On the German Republic," comes straight from the *Zivilisationsliterat* Settembrini.[62] Mann seemed to defend the transcendence of antitheses, and even claimed that *Humanität* was "in truth the *deutsche Mitte*";[63] yet, in the same way that he seemed to stand between the *bohème* and bourgeois but always favored the bourgeois and adopted crucial aspects of its modes of identity formation, the consequence of *The Magic Mountain*'s apparent middle ground is yet another substantive commitment largely on behalf of one polarity. Mann is not so relativist and neutral as he claims.[64]

Despite Mann's hints of a resolution in *The Magic Mountain*, however, and despite his defense of *Humanität*, the vision of the human sketched out and forecast in the novel was a vision with *no* social support or understanding, except among certain intellectuals and *Vernunftrepublikaner* and, in a somewhat different form, among socialists.[65] Mann's views in the novel are cast in abstract terms of reason and unreason, overlooking the social setting and context for change and development, turning politics and love into the keys to social harmony, and looking to ideological and cultural issues as the foundation of the present, the past, and the future. Unfortunately, the *real* new idea thrown up in the course of German history was not a conception of *Humanität*, but the regressive, reactionary, bloodthirsty, nationalistic, irrational form of identity characterized by Hannah Arendt as tribal nationalism, itself a product of profound shifts in the economic and social life of Europe, of intense crises over domestic social change and the international competition between nations.[66] These social factors helped spawn the ideological positions that exerted so profound an influence over European life; but the diagnosis of *The Magic Mountain* is blind to them.

In the 1920s Mann thus resurrected *Humanität* from the trash heap onto which he had thrown it in the *Reflections*. It is the revival of a conception drawn from the German Enlightenment, vivified, in his view, by Novalis and the Romantics, and ultimately derivative from humanism.[67] Mann defends "a higher unity as humanity's goal . . . *humanitas*" and, using the language of the Russian visionary Merezhkovsky, looks forward to "a redemption of the race of mankind," one "which is no longer Christian and yet not pagan either."[68] Mann restores the element of *Humanität* from the now-displaced tradition of *Bildung* and elevates it to the position of a governing value in the name of which humankind and the individual may be redeemed. He does so out of the need for a new ideal to "serve" as an ultimate cause and to sacrifice oneself for, one that fuses the old and the new. Yet at the same time, the novel itself undermines faith in this ideal by having Settembrini its main defender and leaving Hans with only an abstract vision of love for the human. No other ideals emerge from the novel except "meta-novelistic" ones having to do with the identity of self and nation. Thus the novel shows that, in its world, war overrides all other lessons, but that, apart from the intervention of war, the rescue for a man lost to his time remains unknown.

6 Ascetic Politics and the Empowered Self

Mann's portrait of the crisis of work in German culture ends on a redemptive note that remains abstract and idealized. In fact, the honesty of *The Magic Mountain*, which Mann completed after Weber's death, undermines the hopefulness with which its narrator, and Mann himself, view the new ideal as one that empowers the bourgeois individual. Weber, however, was not so circumspect. Despite the growing weight of the crisis of German bourgeois life and of its ideals of self and action, Weber continued to rely on the capacity of the calling to empower the self, master the potentially autonomous orders of social life, and restore meaning and significance to its devotees in culture and society. Moreover, he turned to it to solve Germany's power-political needs and sought to create a charismatic individual, what we can call a "political self," to counterbalance and control the "bureaucratic self" being fabricated by German culture. Thus Weber linked the political crisis to the cultural and social crisis through an analysis that places the disempowerment of the self and the need for its reempowerment at the center of efforts for reform.

The immediate conditions and background of Weber's reflections on the calling for politics are well known, and Weber himself spelled them out in many critiques of German politics. These conditions included, first, the political infantilization imposed on the German public by Bismarck and his absolutism, his unwillingness to permit parliament any power or responsibility, his obstruction of the emergence of strong and independent political parties, and his refusal to allow autonomous political talents to develop outside of his control; second, the dominance of the German bureaucracy over policy and leadership positions after Bismarck's fall; third, the political supremacy of the Junkers in a time of their economic decline; fourth, the inability of any other class or political movement to display the political maturity needed to supplant the Junkers and become the leading political class of Germany; and fifth, the swaggering and weakness of a monarch whose principal advisors came from the court. Weber noted further the degeneration of independent public and national ideals brought about by the ideological manipulations of the government, the imitation of Junker social habits by the bourgeoisie, and the rantings of what he called the "literati." To Weber, Germany lacked reliable political standards for judging the integrity and capacity of leaders and was the scene of a desperate search for authoritarian personal masters. Finally, there were the bitter experiences of war and then defeat, the public discussion of war guilt, betrayal, and self-blame, and the convulsions of revolution at home.

Weber's institutional proposals for Germany are also well known.[1] They include his insistence, first, that domestic policy and political forms be subordinated to a "national" point of view and to Germany's international political needs in its struggle with other nations for a share of global power and markets; second, that an effective parliament be established, one based mainly on the British model for the training and selection of leaders and for the supervision of the bureaucracy; and finally, that a plebiscitary leader be made head of state, elected directly by popular vote and having real power based on the transformation of parties into political machines. Of course, the tradition of subordinating domestic politics to international policy already had a long history in Germany, not least among academics.[2] Further, proposals for generating new leadership were not unusual in Germany at the time, nor was the attempted imitation of British parliamentary models. The leadership vacuum had long been obvious, more so after the military dictatorship imposed on Germany by Hindenburg and Ludendorff during World War I. Finally, Britain's role as a "pattern state" had strong support among liberal political theorists in Germany and elsewhere, if only as a device to make possible the rise to power of talented political leaders.[3] Yet the new and difficult economic conditions of Europe, Germany's historic rivalry with Britain, and the persistence of a reactionary social order and institutional apparatus were about to make the liberal parliamentary and reform project more difficult, if not impossible, to accomplish fully.[4]

Weber proposed a vast tripartite solution for German political problems—a new type of leader, new political institutions, and a new political culture. But what is surprising and, ultimately, quite problematic is Weber's attempt to link each part of his proposals to the discipline of the calling. Weber made the problem of the generation of leaders not only a technical and institutional matter but what we can call a "characterological" or cultural one as well. Furthermore, he cast the problem of leadership partly in political and military terms—as Thucydides, Machiavelli, and other power-political thinkers had done before him—but also partly in a language borrowed from Protestantism, using a vocabulary not normally associated with modern "disenchanted" politics. "Creaturely worthlessness," "devotion" and "submission" to a cause or object, "deadly sins" against the "holy spirit" of the calling, contracting with "diabolic" forces and powers, the "salvation" and fate of the soul, the "serving" of the "gods"—this is the language of Weber's political essays.

In using these terms, of course, Weber is speaking figuratively. But the nature of these particular figures reveals the extent to which Weber's political calling relies on his earlier treatment of the Puritan discipline of the calling and his analysis of the form of personhood shaped in that discipline. In importing such notions into politics, Weber produced dangerous implications for public life, shoring up ideologically, if unintentionally, a potentially authoritarian conception of leadership and greatly restricting the means for demanding responsibility and accountability of leaders to the constituents they are usually supposed to represent. To Weber, leaders must have unrestricted responsibility to their *idea* of the nation, unlimited by the demands and needs of the real nation except when voting occurs. This conception is fortified by a narrow emphasis on the problem of domination (*Herrschaft*), by a misleading interpretation of English political institutions based on a problematic ideal type, and by his unwillingness to consider the deeper social and cultural difficulties of creating parliamentary institutions in a country whose social order and political culture were hostile to them. Weber's proposals would have contributed inadvertently, but just as easily as the actual reforms did, to making the "transition" of Germany from authoritarianism to democracy easily supplantable by a later "transition" to national socialism.

It is not our purpose to question the need for leaders, or responsibility, or the value of commitment to political goals and causes. What we are criticizing is Weber's conception of an empowered ascetic leadership elite whose devotion to the "service" of their cause is a means of strength and empowerment similar to the Puritan calling. This conception conceals a quasi-religious relationship to the political cause, prevents and mystifies reciprocal relations between leaders and followers, and is in other ways an unreasonable alternative to the loss of aristocratic leadership in Germany, dependent more on Weber's understanding of the loss of strength and meaning than on a "matter-of-fact" regard for the actual political problem.

THE "PRINCE" AND THE BUREAUCRATIC SELF

There have been reflections on the nature of the political leader in the West ever since the ancient Greeks. In fifth-century Athens, Thucydides' portraits of Pericles and Themistocles provided dramatic as well as analytical examples of independent leadership in action, and it is no accident that Weber describes Pericles as the forerunner and prototype of the modern demagogic leader whose personal qualities are the source of his leadership position.

> The actual leader of politics that the fully realized democracy created, the demagogue, was regularly the leading military official in Periclean Athens. But his actual power position rested not on law or office but completely on personal influence and the trust of the *demos*. It was therefore not only not legitimate but not even legal, although the whole constitution of democracy was just as tailored for his presence as for instance the modern constitution of England for the existence of the cabinet ruling likewise not by virtue of legal competence.[5]

Thucydides emphasizes Pericles' great political foresight, but talent is not enough for a leader, as the example of Alcibiades showed. Good leaders must not be corrupted by private interests, ambition, greed, passions, or desires, nor must they give in to self-display or manipulate popular passion, private greed, or rivalries. Pericles was independent, always honest, and never flattered. Hence his reputation for being able to contradict the multitude with relative impunity, coupled with his extraordinary political judgment, the capacity to know what was needful (*ta déonta*) in every political situation.

Plato's *Republic* brought a more systematic reflection on the leader's self or soul, emphasizing the possibility of forming a just person as a foundation for political character and a prerequisite to good leadership. This reflection is the ultimate source of the tradition of "mirror of princes" or advice to princes literature, which began in the Hellenistic period and continued through the Middle Ages, often in the form of addresses to rulers by philosophers.[6] Despite Christianity's greater interest in the inner structure of the self of the believer than in politics, the Christian tradition, too, with its strong relations to Platonism and the Stoics—Augustine, Aquinas, and Erasmus, for example—occasionally considered the nature of the good political leader, though it tended to focus more on standards of conduct for princes and their need for Christian virtues and purposes than on the actual formation of political character.

In the early Renaissance the mirror of princes literature became the vehicle of humanist thinking on the importance of *virtus* and on the best type of education for future governors. But the form culminated in Machiavelli, who reversed what was thought to be the obvious and natural relation of character and political action when he argued that the prince's character had to be suited to the needs of maintaining a political realm.[7] The prince must be shaped to perform the tasks of power, and that requires audacity, foresight, adaptability, flexibility and mobility of character, and ability to manipulate appearances, even his own. The character of the leader must allow itself to be defined by his political tasks within the constraints of honor and glory, freeing itself from the limitations of the morally good in order to be free for politics. Thus Machiavelli's prince "wins" his followers not through the visible force of his character but through its apparent nature and the tactical moves he makes based on his knowledge of human nature, of politics, and of the actions of successful leaders from the past. He also puts aside any effort to cultivate the soul of his constituents or to perfect human beings. This leads Sheldon Wolin to remark that Machiavelli broke "the old alliance between statecraft and soulcraft" and created a "post-Christian science."[8] But after Machiavelli's time, the changing conditions of politics shifted political discourse from the character of rulers to the structures and institutions of the emerging absolutist states and the bases of power, obligation, legitimacy, resistance, and political rights, all transformed by the Reformation and later by revolutionary activities in politics and society. With the exception of Hobbes's advice to rulers in *Leviathan*, reflections on leadership all but disappeared.

With Weber, however, reflection on the nature of political leaders begins in earnest again. Although Weber provides neither simple advice to rulers nor techniques of political action, "Politics as a Vocation" is his version of *The Prince*, an attempt to persuade the German nation of the need for a leader with an ascetic and empowered self, independent and autonomous, capable of giving energy and direction to the nation in its political struggles. Indeed, despite the tendency to see Weber as a power-political Machiavellian, Weber actually *reconnects* "statecraft" and "soulcraft" and is thus more reminiscent of Plato and Christian thinkers before Machiavelli. Weber wants to shape persons and institutions for "domination," given the realities of mass politics and imperial competition. In the process he lays out what he takes to be the inner standards and demands a leader must fulfill to be allowed to try his hand at politics. Outside of the philosophical tradition of Plato, such inner standards for leaders and the means to their establishment had not been a real issue for political thought, despite regular condemnations of envy, greed, ambition, and the other personal weaknesses that undermined leaders and the achievement of their causes.

Weber accomplishes this new beginning (though with problematic

consequences) by drawing on the calling to create an ascetic leader devoted to his cause, systematically pursuing the realization of his object
in a rational and responsible fashion. The peculiar condition of German
politics, in Weber's view, makes it necessary to generate a new source
of leadership, now that the possibility of a "leading" economic class that
also leads politically is ended: neither the aristocracy nor any other class
is capable of producing adequate forms of responsible rule. Yet because
of his exclusive focus on the inner shaping of leaders and the technical
requirements for generating them, Weber was unable to envision and
embody a more profound set of political ideals that might have guided
German politics. Thus, despite his version of *The Prince*, he created no
equivalent of the reflections on liberty and republics that Machiavelli
achieved in his *Discourses*. In this respect his political thinking did not
attain the depth and wider significance of the great power-political
thinkers.

The Loss of Aristocracy and the Failure of Class

Weber's proposals for an ascetic solution to the German leadership problem are a response to the decline of the aristocracy as a ruling class and
the search for a replacement. Weber saw the historical Western conflict
between an economic system dominated by traditional enterprise and
one dominated by capitalism as more than an economic conflict in its
German form: it contained, he believed, the crucial political question of
whether "the small rural centers of political intelligence" would be supplanted by "the cities as the only carriers of political, social, and esthetic
culture." This was more than just a geographical and social shift. "This
question is identical with the question whether people who have been
able to live for politics and the state, for example, the old, economically
independent landed aristocracy, shall be replaced by the exclusive domination of professional politicians who must live off politics and the
state."[9] Weber believed that the old aristocratic leaders of Germany, like
aristocrats elsewhere, had had an economic independence that enabled
them to devote themselves to the nation's interests unmotivated by mere
self-interest. They possessed bases for autonomy, we can say—both inner
and outer—and could thus live "for" politics, because they had the tendency of superior classes everywhere to believe in their deserved place
in the social order and to develop a sense of responsibility and a perceived
right to rule. In Germany, the coincidence of their economic interests
with the general interests of the state, as well as their role in the military
unification of the nation, also gave them confidence in their judgment
and their political "intelligence" and skill: "the strength of their political

instincts was one of the most powerful funds that could have been used in the service of the state."[10]

The economic and political decay of this aristocracy was the problem. The aristocracies of Europe were everywhere in economic and political decline and in many ways ill equipped, by themselves alone, to lead their countries. In Germany in particular, first, "under the influence of capitalism, the landed aristocracy undergoes a serious inner transformation, which completely alters the character of the aristocracy inherited from the past."[11] But second, there is a growing disharmony between the aristocracy's economic needs and the national need for capitalist expansion: the Junkers' fortunes were in decline, and their interests were actually opposed to the fundamental economic interests of the nation. Thus, the aristocrats "have done their work and lie today in an economic death struggle, out of which no state economic policy can lead them back to their former social character."[12] Yet the Junkers remained in their ruling positions, supported by the social and political structure of the state, ruling mainly through the nonparliamentary means of the army, the dynasty, and the bureaucracy.[13] But they were gradually degenerating into a collection of bureaucratically trained ministers and narrowly oriented successors of Bismarck, poorly equipped to wage the raging political battles. To Weber it was "dangerous and in the long term incompatible with the interests of the nation" to allow the representatives of an economically "declining" class to make a claim on leadership once the nation "changed its economic structure."

Thus it is not surprising that in 1895 Weber initially agrees with Marx on the necessity for "leading" economic classes to rise to political leadership and put forth the particular claims of their class as the general claims of the nation. "It has been the *attainment of economic power* in all times that has allowed the idea of its *qualification* [*Anwartschaft*] *for political leadership* to arise within a class." Nonetheless, Weber concluded that it would be worse for Germany to have a leadership elite drawn from the current economically leading class, the bourgeoisie, than from the declining aristocracy, for, as a class, the bourgeoisie lacked "political maturity" and judgment owing to decades of political impotence followed by lengthy subservience to Bismarck. The bourgeoisie was too narrowly interest-oriented, submissive, and politically inexperienced. "The reason lies in its unpolitical past, in the fact that the work of political education of a century cannot be made up for in a decade, and that the domination of a great man is not always a means of political education." One section of the *Großbürgertum* longs for "a new Caesar," while another is sunk in "political philistinism." Many of its leading members also aped the habits and sought the privileges of the Junker nobility, further weakening their class's identity and competitive attitudes. Finally, opposition to the bourgeoisie by both the educated strata and the working-class movement weakened its political power and strengthened aristocratic power despite the aristocracy's decline. As a candidate for rule, the working class, though not yet leading, was self-confident and relatively mature economically, but it was too bureaucratically disciplined to be capable of action, initiative, and responsibility, and its leaders had neither "*national* passion" nor "the great *power* instincts of a class called to political leadership."[14] Consequently, none of these potentially alternate ruling classes possessed the adequate "inner" empowerment for rule, so to speak. To Weber, "this is in truth the key to the present danger of our situation."[15]

What an elite must have to qualify it for leadership, Weber claims, is "*political maturity*," and that means an "understanding of" and "actual ability to place the lasting economic and political *power* interests of the nation above all others." Thus, Weber concluded—as Marx had earlier in the *Eighteenth Brumaire of Louis Bonaparte*—that the question of the "political calling" of the classes waiting in the wings was more complicated than the simple relation between leading class and ruling class revealed, for "*economic power and the calling for political leadership do not always coincide.*" In Weber's view no single class in Germany was capable of advancing its own interests on behalf of the nation and making a claim for leadership. Thus, although Weber had already diagnosed the problem of political disempowerment before the turn of the century, at that point he lacked the language for completely understanding it and the means for its solution. Indeed, he had originally left open the question of which class might become eventually mature; by the time of World War I, however, he has ceased to speak of it, evidently no longer believing that such a capacity for leadership could develop from the "natural" process of class accession.

At that point, Weber turns instead to technical means and the creation of inner requirements for leadership. Even though no class automatically generates leaders from its midst, Weber believed it possible to create them by persuading men of the need for submission to the discipline of the calling with an ascetic concern for and commitment to the nation and its economic and power-political interests. Weber's ultimate proposal requires the transformation of a select group of human beings through service, devotion, and submission to an ultimate value. The discipline of the calling, so important historically, would not only create autonomous men, he imagined, distant from the natural desires of self and others and adhering to the cause alone; if such men had the opportunity to develop their political talents in the arenas of parliamentary struggle, the calling would also empower and fortify the self of the new men, training them technically, orienting them toward action, initiative, and struggle to realize their cause by grounding their life meaning in the "holy" practice of the political calling.

In reality, the aristocratic ruling elite had not itself been in any way ascetic or self-denying, devoted only to its "mission." That is, Weber's ascetic ideal, which he proposes as the only possible basis for political character, is a deliberate *break* from the previous model of political character and empowered self. In contrast to the ideals of the ascetic character, the aristocrats' sense of self-worth, as Weber often remarked, had depended only on their sense of their own "being," independent of any mission or task that they strove to carry out. "Strata in solid possession of social honor and power tend to shape their status legend in the direction of an inherent special quality: it is their (real or alleged) *being* that gives nourishment to their feeling of dignity."[16] The nobility's feeling of dignity, "their 'rank' therefore, rests on the consciousness of their qualitative 'being,' residing in itself, not referring beyond itself."[17]

But Weber set aside the aristocratic model in proposing a discipline for generating leaders. He evidently believed that the presuppositions for the emergence of aristocratic character were disappearing, and that consequently aristocratic capacities and qualities were gone for good, incapable of being recreated. He thus rejected the possibility that nonascetic modes of self-fashioning could equip for rule. Therefore, he shifted the issue and the language from "being" to "mission" and from "interests" to "cause"—or, we might better say, from "material interests" to "ideal interests"—opting for a deliberately antiaristocratic ethos, the Puritan one, to create a new political elite. Although he hoped such an ethos would be attractive to talented members of all classes, he had to know that only certain members of the educated bourgeoisie (*Bildungsbürgertum*) might find it appealing or be capable of it. To create political leaders with Puritan attributes, Weber sought to "convert" talented individuals by demonstrating the collective necessity of the ascetic calling for Germany's political needs and by arguing for the individual necessity and value of a political "faith" and the personal "gifts" that living in a calling could bring. Believing he was providing merely formal guidance, he even attempted to lay out the ethos, or principles of conduct, appropriate to "serving" a political god. Finally, he argued for the necessity of transforming national identity and sought to teach the nation the "calling" of followers, hoping that a populace driven to follow leaders would make it more likely that such leaders would arise and be able to rule in the interests of the nation. But despite his efforts, this project was stillborn in almost every respect.

The Rise of the Bureaucratic Self

Beyond analyzing the sociologically determined transformation of the class situation, Weber attacked the politically imposed obstacles to the development of leaders. The first was Bismarck's domination of German politics and the nation's subservient attitude toward him. From his earliest letters to his latest political writings, Weber held the submissiveness of the German nation responsible for its inability to generate adequate leadership, revealed in the "unmanly glorification" evident in its "completely unpolitical kind of hero worship." "Nowhere else in the world has even the most unrestrained admiration of the personality of a politician caused a proud nation to sacrifice to him its own substantive [*sachliche*] convictions so completely." But despite his own paeans to Bismarck's political genius, Weber faults him for his lack of concern with the future of German leadership. In fact, Bismarck tolerated no autonomous power anywhere in ministries or parliament, no "inwardly independent minds" or persons, and he conducted his domestic policy precisely to turn parliament, party, and party leaders into a "political nothingness." He sabotaged the most important bourgeois party, the National Liberals, even though they supported him strongly, and strove to destroy the trade unions, "the only possible carriers of a substantive [*sachliche*] interest representation of the working class," thus driving the workers into radical positions while at the same time trying to buy them off with welfare benefits. Thus, because of "his Caesarist nature," Bismarck left behind "a nation *without any and every political education*"—indeed, at a *lower* level than it had reached twenty years before—"a nation *without any and every political will*, accustomed that the great statesman at the top would take care of politics for it. . . . The great statesman left behind *absolutely no* political tradition . . . [and] a *completely powerless parliament*."[18]

With Bismarck's downfall, the second obstacle to leadership arose: rule over Germany by men trained for bureaucratic office. In Weber's view, of course, bureaucracy is an essential component of any modern socioeconomic and political order, provided it is confined to administration, and the Germans surpassed all others in their development of "the rational, functional, specialized *bureaucratic* organization of all human associations of domination, from the factory to the army [*Heer*] and the state."[19] But in positions of political rule and not just administration, bureaucrats were disastrous. "What was lacking was the *direction* of the political system [*Staatswesen*] by a *politician*—not by a political genius, which one can expect only once every century, not even by a significant political talent, but *actually* by a politician." The bureaucracy had a stranglehold over the highest levels of political office and was a principal area of Junker power. Further, Bismarck had "thought it expedient to *cover* his Caesarist regime *with the legitimacy of the monarch. . . .* As a result the nation allowed itself to be talked into accepting something as 'monarchic government' which in truth meant only the uncontrolled rule of the bureaucracy, within which, if they are left under it, political qualities of leadership have never and nowhere in the whole world been born and come to the top."[20] Thus, in Weber's view, "*politicians* must give the counterweight to domination by officials."[21]

Despite bureaucratic ideology, rule by career officials cannot, in any event, be construed as neutral, impartial rule "above party." In reality, "the party interests of the conservative bureaucrats positioned in the seat of power and of their affiliated circles of interest groups alone dominate the government," and they hide their "politically fully disoriented behavior" behind the monarch as if it reflected his wishes.[22] Thus, Weber suggests that the political rule of the bureaucracy is actually the rule of a party masking itself as the executors of the monarch's policy above party. It protects its own power and conservative positions at great cost to the national interest in terms of the nation's reputation and in terms of the exclusion of other party positions and political leaders from power and responsibility.

To Weber, however, the problem of bureaucracy and rational forms of domination goes deeper than institutional obstacles: it is at the very heart of the identity crisis of society and culture. His early fear for the fate of society was that obsessive capitalistic material striving might lead to "mechanized petrifaction."[23] But he soon came to fear the bureaucratic hardening of society and its debilitating and disempowering effects on culture and action. On the most basic level, Weber argues that bureaucracy is a form of domination almost impossible to displace, thus excluding other forms of organized politics. The "bureaucratic '*agency*' [*Behörde*]" and the "bureaucratic '*enterprise*' [*Betrieb*]" in the modern state and capitalist economy are "much more *inescapable*" than any other "historical carrier of the modern rational order of life." "Where the bureaucratization of administration has been completely carried through, a form of relations of domination has been created that is practically as good as unbreakable."[24] While this was not inevitably disastrous, Weber argued that, together with the machine, bureaucracy "is at work setting up the shell of bondage of the future," which men will be forced to live in "if a purely technically good, that means, a rational, bureaucratic administration and public welfare is the ultimate and only value to those that should decide about the kind of direction of their affairs." And thus the question is: "In the face of this superiority of the tendency to bureaucratization, how is it *above all still possible* to preserve *any* remainder at all of 'individualistic' freedom of movement in *any* sense at all? . . . How can . . . *any* guarantee be offered that powers are available which restrain and effectively control the enormous superiority of this stratum steadily growing in importance?"[25]

Still, despite frequent attacks on the fetishists of bureaucratic control, Weber applauds bureaucracy's usefulness and indispensability, provided that it is restricted to administration and, most important, that people can be found to direct and control it for the larger purposes of political struggle for the nation. "Bureaucracy purely in itself is a precision instrument which can be placed at the disposal of very different interests in domination, as much purely political as purely economic ones, and as any other kind."[26] But whatever the possibility in theory, the prospect of practical control is problematic, for Weber believed modern culture was fabricating as its fundamental cultural product and prototype a "bureaucratic self," what he calls the *Ordnungsmensch*, the person oriented toward "order."[27] This type is an unavoidable consequence of "the growing demands for administration dependent on the increasing complexity of civilization."[28] It is also a product of Germany's emphasis on diplomas, technical training, and expertise, its admiration for the "high moral standard" of its bureaucracy, and the culturally widespread socialization and habituation to functional, obedient action—by both the functionary and the subject—on the basis of rational norms.

These worries were not new in Germany. They had been expressed as far back as the Prussian reform period. " 'I know,' mourned Fichte, 'that the state has always worked in every way to accustom us to be machines, not independent beings.' . . . 'The exaggerated solicitude of the state,' Humboldt deduced, 'weakens energy and activity in general, and the moral character [turns] into national uniformity. . . . *Goods* [are produced] at the expense of *vitality*.' "[29] More recently, the novelist Theodor Fontane had castigated a society that valued only the officer and the bureaucrat and that pursued tokens of approval from state power in the form of examinations passed, degrees received, and offices, titles, and medals conferred.[30]

In *Discipline and Punish*, Foucault speaks of the "creation" of individuals through the disciplinary methods of modern power.[31] Weber's examination of structures that produce officials "in the spiritual sense of the word" reveals a similar process of self-fashioning.[32]

> The individual official cannot extricate himself from the apparatus in which he is harnessed. The professional official [*Berufsbeamte*] is . . . chained to his activity with his whole material and ideal existence. . . . He is through all this above all forged tightly to the community of interests of all the functionaries integrated into this mechanism. . . . The "files" on the one hand and on the other the discipline of the official, that is, the adjustment of the official to precise obedience within his *accustomed* sphere of action are becoming . . . increasingly the foundation of all order. Above all, however, . . . is "discipline."[33]

As Weber observes, within the bureaucracy "the adjustment [*Eingestelltheit*] of *men* to the observation of accustomed norms and rules persists," despite every attack on the apparatus. The "adjustment to obedient accommodation cultivated in the officials on the one hand and the ruled on the other" is precisely characteristic of bureaucratic order.[34] Apart from functional accommodation, the "personal position" of the official is shored up by "a specifically elevated *social esteem* of 'status' vis-à-vis the governed," and even measures of discipline and control must be "considerate of the feeling of honor" of the official. Indeed, "status consciousness" is the "inner compensation for the self-feeling of the official" ready to subordinate himself to his superior "without the slightest will of his own."[35]

Yet the notion that officials are satisfied with devotion to "an impersonal *objective goal*" like rationality is not true. Weber notes that "behind this objective goal there naturally stand usually imagined 'ideas of cultural value' realized in a community, ideologically transfiguring [the goal], as a surrogate for the earthly or supernatural personal master: 'state,' 'church,' 'community,' 'party,' 'enterprise.' "[36] This is one reason why it is hard to dispel the "charm" of the *Ordnungsmensch*: the bureaucratic self may be submissive and without daring, devoted to rationality and functional competence, but it is frequently so in a situation where its devotion is sanctified and uplifted by a treasured suprapersonal object and supreme value toward which its reverent feelings engender conservatism when it comes to action or change.

Thus to Weber, the significance of bureaucratic rational order for modern culture and politics is found not only in the actual use and function of its formal apparatus but also in its capacity to use discipline, rewards, and sanctified cultural objects to transform individuals into appropriate and obedient functionaries and subjects. Yet such fabrication of the bureaucratic self has even more far-reaching social consequences, and in 1909 Weber gave definitive expression to this problem.

> It is an even more terrible thought that the world should be filled with nothing other than those cogs, thus with nothing but men who cling to a little post and strive for a somewhat greater one—a condition which you find again, as in the Egyptian papyri, advancing thus in the spirit of present-day officialdom and above all in its *rising generation*, present-day students. This passion for bureaucratization . . . makes one despair. It is . . . as if we *should* become, with knowledge and will, men who need "order" and nothing but order, who become nervous and cowardly if this order wavers for a moment, and helpless if they are wrenched out of their exclusive adaptation to this order. That the world may know nothing further than such *Ordnungsmenschen*—we are engaged in this development all the same, and the central question is not how we can promote and hasten it still further but rather what we have *to set against* this machinery to keep a remnant of humankind free from this parcelling out of the soul, from this exclusive mastery of the bureaucratic ideal of life.[37]

Bureaucratic order, in the state and capitalist industrial organization, thus breeds throughout society, and not only within its own apparatus, a pervasive attitude of addiction, adaptation, and submission to order. "It exercises over men and their 'style of life' far-reaching specific effects entirely peculiar to *itself*."[38] It breeds *Ordnungsmenschen*, men dependent on order and structure in private and public life for the direction and support of their lives. At the same time, it undermines their strength and power to act independently of that order, to guide it, give it purpose and direction, and attract others to those purposes.

The emergence of the *Ordnungsmensch* and of the cultural practices that shape him are a product of the same historical struggles over rationalization that formed the modern world. Weber claims that "it is decisive for almost all of cultural development" how the struggle for power between chiefs and their subsidiary power holders came out and what "the character of the *stratum* of officials" was that aided the chiefs in these struggles, for "the direction of *education* was decided through it, and the kind of *status group* formation was determined through it."[39] In the West, education became a matter of imbuing individuals with the technical expertise required for functioning in the different spheres of rational life—in the economics of the firm, the workings of the law and administration, or in the scientific method. The whole edifice of what Simmel called "objective spirit" makes its demands and imposes its specifications on individuals, defining their roles without consideration for their particular talents, cravings, or motivations. Specialized training (*Facherziehung*) has thus displaced *Bildung* and the cultivation of self-development as the object and content of education, reflecting the demands of the existing rationalized material and political order for expert personnel.

As we have seen, Weber agreed that *Bildung* was no longer an adequate educational goal in a world requiring technical expertise. But to Weber, technical education alone is also not adequate to meet the full range of society's needs, needs that go beyond the technical to the necessity of purposes, values, causes, and goals defended and championed by fortified individuals who can rescue society from mere functional specialization. Still, we cannot look to *Bildung* to meet these needs, for *Bildung*, Weber implies, *does not empower*. In Weber's view, only empowered selves can make choices and commitments and can reappropriate the mechanized spheres for human purposes, leading them forward and providing the dynamism to mobilize action and solve specific problems. Otherwise the spheres will drift into rigid impersonal rationalization with no values or purposes to motivate them.

To Weber, then, since the social and educational consequences of bureaucratization and rationalization—the broad disempowering cultural effects of these processes—cannot in general be prevented for the mass of humankind, it is essential to generate empowered leaders to offset the pervasive effect of the ideal of rationalized *Ordnung* and its generalized subjection of society. But power embodied in rationalized social and political structures is fabricating, and simultaneously disempowering, the social self, embedding its own order and functional needs in the psyche and habits of individuals, so that the person cannot imagine functioning outside or without that order. The question remains whether, given Weber's diagnosis, a countervailing power can be found to set against it or be put in control of it, and whether culture can produce an ethos and motivating force to generate an empowered self.

POLITICAL LEADERSHIP AND POLITICAL SELF

Given the social, political, and cultural obstacles to the emergence of empowered leaders, Weber rethinks the nature of political leadership in terms of the calling. But since changes of character and self-ideal are not adequate by themselves, he proposes to join those leaders to a set of institutional changes: to create responsible parliamentary government, strong party machines for winning over the democratic electorate to specific policies and perspectives, and plebiscitary leadership selection to bring to office the kind of politicians that can command followers and guide the nation in its worldwide economic and power-political struggle.

What Weber does *not* do is rethink the social structure and political culture of Germany in terms of their ability to sustain representative institutions and the kind of political struggle that Germany had never before experienced, except in fantasy, for dealing with its political needs. Nor does he propose more extensive democratic changes, normative arguments, or a defense of interests that could mobilize the populace against the existing, antiparliamentary elites and institutions, for Weber does not want mobilization, except within very narrow limits. Weber did not recognize that his political proposals were in advance of what crucial social groups would support over time—unless, that is, the social structure were seriously transformed, the ruling elites in bureaucracy and army were purged, economic prosperity were maintained for an extended period, or masses of people were to become politically mobilized to defend reforms. Even if such conditions had been met, the attacks that were made on the Weimar Republic and its leaders, from putsch to assassination to depression, might have been too severe to permit the republic's survival. The "superstructure" Weber proposed simply could not be supported by an unchanged social, economic, and cultural "base" unless greater political mobilization and involvement could be generated by potential supporters.

In presenting his purely political proposals, Weber does not adequately analyze the links between German society and culture and his intended reforms. This shortcoming reflects his exaggerated reliance on conceptions of "domination" and their legitimations of themselves as the key to politics; as a result, the importance of social groups, political culture, popular participation, and the habits, mores, and customs so crucial for political development become obscured. Thus, in the important political "transition" in which he was involved, Weber's approach prevented him from seeing the problems that a purely institutional arrangement could not address.

The Calling for Politics

In Weber's analysis of the nature of empowered leaders, the calling and "charisma" are inextricably linked. According to Luciano Cavalli, "charisma constitutes a 'calling' in a strong sense."[40] Conversely, according to Weber, at the foundation of *every* calling for politics is charisma, "the authority of the extraordinary, personal *gift of grace*."

What interests us here above all is . . . the domination by virtue of devotion [*Hingabe*] of the followers to the purely personal "charisma" of the "leader." For here is rooted the idea of the *calling* in its highest expression. The devotion to the charisma of the prophet or of the leader [*Führer*] in war or of the great demagogues in the *ecclesia* or in the parliament means that he is personally valued as the inwardly "called" leader [*Leiter*] of men, that they submit to him not by virtue of custom or statute, but because they believe in him. . . . These [men are] politicians by virtue of "calling" in the most precise sense of the word.[41]

Thus charisma is to be considered not only in its purest form—as the unique possession of "carriers of specific gifts of the body and mind *considered* 'supernatural,' " meeting "all those needs that go *beyond* the demands of the economic everyday"[42]—but also as the crucial element in all genuine leadership, that is, leadership in which the personal devotion of followers to the leader's "person and its qualities" is the central fact. For "every charisma still claims some remnant of magical origin, therefore is related to religious powers, and therefore 'the grace of God' always resides in some sense within it."[43] Like the calling of the Puritans—whose ultimate cause was God and who thereby obtained his "charisma," the gift of his grace, as well as strength and the capacity to command followers—Weber's version of the secular political calling is predicated not only on the service of an ultimate cause but also on that special kind of engagement with others that constitutes the personal domination by one person over others.

In Weber's analysis, the leader's calling can be understood only by contrasting it with other callings, in particular the calling of the official. The notion of a calling proper to a specific sphere of social life is not confined to politics, for all callings have the same form. An "official's office is [also] 'a calling,' " and it manifests itself "in the character of duty belonging to the position of the official, through which the inner structure of his relationships is determined."[44] But the callings of the official and the leader, in every realm, embody and represent two fundamentally different "spirits" of work and thus something different "in terms of the meaning" of their positions. The official should be "above the parties, but that means in reality, outside the *fight* for personal power. Fight for personal power and the personal *responsibility for his cause* [*Sache*] that results from this power is the life element of the politician as of the entrepreneur."[45] Indeed, in a more politically pessimistic moment late in life, Weber remarked that in a situation where "bureaucratic administration means: domination by virtue of *knowledge*, . . . usually *only* the person interested in private acquisition, therefore the capitalist entrepreneur, is *superior* to bureaucracy in knowledge, technical knowledge and knowledge of facts, within *his own* sphere of interest. He is the *sole* authority [*Instanz*] actually *immune* (at least relatively) to the inescapability of bureaucratic rational domination."[46]

> The *leading* spirit—the "entrepreneur" here, the "politician" there—is something different from an "official." Not necessarily in form, but certainly in substance [*Sache*]. . . . If a *leading* man is an "official" according to the spirit of his performance, no matter how capable—a man, therefore who is accustomed to perform his work dutifully and honorably according to rule and command— then he is useful neither at the top of a private economic organization nor at the top of a state.[47]

Thus, empowered leaders and officials represent two very different kinds of "selves," fashioned through the socialization processes of the realms they inhabit, processes revealing that the discipline imposed in rational administration "in its inmost essence is foreign to charisma."[48] According to Weber, every analysis of bureaucracy must consider this "ethos" or "spirit" of the bureaucrat, his "inner" as well as his "outer" position."[49]

> The genuine official . . . according to his actual calling, should not practice politics, but rather "administration," impartial above all. . . . *Sine ira et studio*, "without anger and bias" he should discharge the duties of his office. He should therefore not do precisely what the politician, the leader as well as his following, always and necessarily must do, *fight* [*kämpfen*]. For partisanship, struggle, passion—anger and bias—are the element of the politician. And above all of the political *leader*. *His* conduct stands under a completely different, precisely opposite principle of *responsibility* than that of the official.[50]

The problem of German politics was that the conservative bureaucracy in Germany "in decisive moments put people with the *spirit of officials* [*Beamtengeist*] in leading positions in which *politicians* belonged"— where politician means "people who had learned in political struggle to weigh the significance of *public words* and who above all had had the feeling of responsibility of a *leading politician* and not the feeling of duty of subordination belonging to an official, which is proper in its place but is here pernicious." An "abyss" separates these different feelings of responsibility, though "each is suitable in its place but *only there*. . . . The official has to sacrifice his own convictions to his *duty of obedience*.

The leading *politician* has to *reject* publicly the responsibility for political actions when they contradict his conviction and has to sacrifice his position to it." Thus, what the official lacks is "what one in the purely political sense of the word calls 'character,' which has nothing at all to do with private morality." However, it is lacking "not accidentally, but as a consequence of the *structure of the state*, which had *no use* for it."[51] Not only do the practices of "office hierarchy" put up obstacles in the way of whatever leadership talents that do appear; "the [very] essence of the position of a modern administrative official is on the whole highly unfavorable to the development of *political* autonomy (which is to be well distinguished from the inner independence of a purely *personal* character)."[52]

But Weber does not want to separate the leader altogether from rationality or rule-governed behavior. It is true that the real home, so to speak, of rationalization in the state is the bureaucratic apparatus, which carries out its business according to calculable rules, without regard for persons, objectively [*sachlich*], in a "spirit" of "formalistic impersonality," pursuing an "impersonal *objective goal*."[53] Yet some of these qualities are also important for the modern leader and entrepreneur, for both "the bureaucratic state apparatus and the rational *homo politicus* integrated into it" are governed by rationalistic rules and must do their tasks "objectively"—meaning here, independent of ties to persons.[54]

> The *homo politicus* just like the *homo oeconomicus* executes his task today precisely when he carries it out in the most ideal degree as defined by the rational rules of the modern structure of power, "without respect for person," "*sine ira et studio*," without hate and hence without love, without free will [*Willkür*] and consequently without grace, as an objective duty and not as a result of a concrete personal relationship.[55]

What this means is that an empowered leader must fight for his cause and make it real but that this cannot be accomplished simply by devotion to the cause. Not only must the politician act "impersonally," in the sense of devoting himself to an impersonal cause and never a person;[56] but if he is responsible, he must also make *calculations* based on the supposed objective laws of power relations, and not on mere conviction of his ethical rightness. That is, the realization of the cause requires the use of technical, rational means, and "objective reason of state" governs politics. Like the Puritan entrepreneurs, who combined the charismatic inspiration of God's cause with a *praxis pietatis* that was systematic and rational, the modern leader is two-sided. He must be a bearer of charisma, yet he must try to realize his cause systematically and rationally, in conformity with rules of power, without being affected by personal considerations that might go beyond "objectivity." How is the politician to be shaped to these two roles in a culture that prizes the bureaucratic spirit? Weber's belief that there is an enduring conflict between charisma, on the one hand, and the permanent institutional structures that arise through "routinization" to deal with the weight of everyday needs and pressures, on the other, reflects the difficulty of permanently attaching his conception of leadership to the demands of a bureaucratic state.[57]

The Life for a Cause

If the problem of leadership is defined as a question about sources for the empowering of the political self, and if the leadership qualities of aristocrats cannot be recreated—because neither their economic and social position nor the sense of worth and "being" that grounds the aristocratic self can be duplicated—how can the political calling, as Weber understands it, meet the needs of the present? "Through what qualities can he hope to do justice to this power (however narrowly circumscribed it may be in the individual case) and therefore to the responsibility that power places upon him? ... What kind of person must one be, to be allowed to lay one's hand on the spokes of the wheel of history?"[58] How can a calling modeled on the form and innovative spirit of the Puritans, those opponents of aristocratic values, generate the power required?

The central feature of Weber's political calling is the special relation of the leader to his cause or object. Service of a cause, in Weber's sense, provides, we can say, four kinds of "redemption." The first is redemption from meaninglessness, the discovery of a meaning for the life of the called individual and for his action.

> [The politician] lives for his cause [*Sache*], "strives for his work,"
> if he is more than a narrow and vain upstart of the moment. ...
> Whoever lives "for" politics, makes "his life from it" in an *inner*
> sense: either he enjoys the naked possession of the power which
> he exercises, or he feeds his inner equilibrium and self-feeling
> from the consciousness of conferring a *meaning* on his life
> through service of a "cause" [*Dienst an einer "Sache"*]. In this inner sense, every sincere man who lives for a cause also lives from
> this cause.[59]

To Weber, service of a cause gives meaning to the life of him who serves, in the same way for the servant of politics as for the scientist or religious believer. Thus the central feature of the life of the servant is not the *particular* cause to which he is committed, nor even that he *has* a cause, but that his life obtains meaning only in a particular *relation* to that cause, a relation of devotion and ascetic service. A life of service is an absolute necessity, and to Weber there is no other path to meaning. The power to redeem life from meaninglessness is conferred exclusively on ascetic service of the cause, whether by the politician or by any other practitioner of an ascetic, active calling.

The second redemption provided by service to a cause is redemption from weakness, through the acquisition of a strength similar to the active powers acquired by the Puritans, in the form of a self empowered by the securing of meaning. Weber claims that "the final result of political action" is very often out of all relation to "its original meaning. But consequently, this meaning—the service of a *cause*—must not in any way be lacking, if action is indeed to have inner firmness [*Halt*]." The commitment to service of a cause is the fundamental anchor of the political actor in a world whose outcomes are uncertain. To Weber, "the 'strength' of a political 'personality' " is the most essential measure of a leader.[60] Only the conversion of a particular cause into an object of service in a calling—and of the politician's life into a tool for realizing that object— can provide the politician with the strength needed to face a political world that is hostile and combative and may defeat his cause. Indeed, only such a meaning and its resultant strength equip the politician to resort to means for realizing his cause that might bring him moral condemnation.

Third, service to a cause provides redemption from a worthless self. Behind Weber's understanding of the need for a cause is a view of the self as essentially base and potentially dissolute. The self is vain and creaturely, and the dangers to political service posed by this unreliable self are grave, threatening the success of the cause and thus the other forms of redemption to be found through the calling. "The politician daily and hourly has to overcome in himself a completely trivial, all-too-human enemy: quite common *vanity*, the deadly enemy of all objective [*sachliche*] devotion and all distance, in this case, distance toward oneself." Self, that is, threatens to put itself in the foreground, intruding on devotion—as the "idolization of the flesh" once intruded on Puritan piety—to the point of being a "deadly enemy." Therefore, in Weber's view, the politician needs the "strong taming [*Bändigung*] of the soul"— that is, conquest of the unruly self. Taming, however, is possible "only through the habituation to distance—in every meaning of the term . . . distance toward things and men." This means detachment from the worldly temptations encountered in all involvement with and concern for others. Service of the cause is a personal and solitary matter, and too great an involvement with the "world" of others tempts one away from ascetic accomplishment of the tasks set by the object. But not only distance from the world and other persons is needed: one must be just as distant from the self and *its* demands, for the self importunes as much as (or more than) the world outside. Drawing on religious figures again, Weber claims that lack of distance is "one of the deadly sins of every politician."[61] Indeed, "*distance* and *reserve*" are the "presupposition of all personal dignity."[62] In Weber's analysis, the politician, like the Puritan, carries within himself the greatest threat: the self and its base nature are the enemy.

The politician thus must subject the self through service of a cause (*Sache*) in order to overcome personal desire and the corrupt self. "*How the cause must look*, in whose service the politician strives for power and utilizes power, is a matter of belief [*Glaubenssache*]. . . . There must always be some kind of belief. Otherwise the curse of creaturely worthlessness [*Nichtigkeit*] actually weighs down—this is completely true—even the outwardly strongest political successes."[63] To Weber, *no* political action is possible without redemption from the worthless self through service. Indeed, the calling loses its meaning if we do not honor "the specific kind of self-restraint that it demands."[64] Faith in a cause and submission of the self's powers to its service are, to Weber, the only means of constraining the defects of self that, it is feared, would otherwise explode and overpower even the best works. Weber does not believe that there is any other means for the self to restrain itself; he acknowledges no other cultural or ethical habits or views or any sense of responsibility that could be relied on to limit "selfish" or "weak" impulses. Belief and faith, linked to ascetic service, are the *only* things that can curb the potentially unruly self and the only obstacle to the self's breaking out and running wild.

The fourth kind of redemption provided by Weber's service to a cause is redemption from mere subjectivity through the acquisition of a sanctified standard of judgment and of what we can call an inner "witness" for action. "With every task of a *calling* the *object* as such demands its right and wants to be carried out according to its own laws [*nach ihren eigenen Gesetzen*]. With every task of a calling he to whom it is assigned has to restrict himself and to exclude what does not belong strictly to the *object*, and most of all, his own love and hate."[65] Thus, every cause has its own *Eigengesetzlichkeit*, whether an individual cause or the causes of the "autonomous" spheres of rationalized society.[66] To Weber, the object and the calling actually "demand" specific actions in accordance with a systematic rational analysis of the procedures and requirements for realizing them. Indeed, for strength in service to be effective, Weber claims, a true warrior for his cause must have three other qualities that are "particularly decisive for the politician: passion—a feeling of responsibility—a sense of proportion."[67]

The "strength" of a political "personality" requires such qualities, but what do they mean? These qualities all seem to be founded on loyalty to the "demands" of the cause. Passion means "passionate devotion to an 'object' [*Sache*], to the god or daemon who is its master." Given Weber's worry about the intrusion and the worthlessness of the unruly, desiring self, it would seem that he should want to curb passion. But in fact he wants only to focus and channel it, for, in his view, what German politics lacked when conducted by officials was not only responsibility but also the passion that *makes* politicians want to fight. "Politics is made with the head, not with other parts of the body or the soul. And still the devotion [*Hingabe*] to it . . . when it is genuine human action, can only be born and nourished from passion."[68] Thus to Weber the question is how to encourage and engender passion for a cause while restraining passion for the self's vain strivings.

Yet in Weber's interpretation mere passion, or what we might call "love" of the cause alone, is not enough to create an adequate calling for the politician, any more than it was for the Puritan believer. The cause gives strength and redemption, but in exchange it "wants" to be realized. Purity of heart, single-mindedness, and submission can by themselves neither satisfy its demands nor accomplish the ascetic tasks it sets for its devotees. That is why "warm passion and a cool sense of proportion" require a commitment to the *realization* of the cause, not just to its adoration. "[Passion] does not make one into a politician if it does not make *responsibility* toward precisely this cause into the decisive guiding star of action."[69] Only responsible service, not a devotion that merely "testifies" to one's faith in the cause, can "realize" the cause. Thus, in Weber's view, the *mode* of devotion is crucial. Mature self-restraint and responsible service, ascetic and systematically controlled labor on behalf of the cause, are the political equivalent of Puritan *praxis pietatis*. Here the danger of the self that does not understand the need to subject its strivings for power to the exclusive service of the cause becomes a threat to the redemptions offered by the cause served in a calling.

> The sin against the holy spirit of his calling . . . begins there where this striving for power becomes *unobjective* [*unsachlich*] and an object of purely personal self-intoxication, instead of entering into

the service of the "object" [*Sache*] exclusively. For there are ultimately only two kinds of deadly sins in the field of politics: lack
of objectivity [*Unsachlichkeit*] and—often, but not always identical
with it—lack of responsibility. Vanity, the need to enter as con-
spicuously as possible into the foreground, leads the politician
most strongly into the temptation to commit one of the two or
both. . . . His lack of regard for the object [*Unsachlichkeit*] urges
him to strive after the glamorous appearance of power instead of
real power; his lack of responsibility, however, [urges him] to en-
joy power exclusively for its own sake, without substantive goal.[70]

Thus the self is not merely a danger; it is a devil that surrounds us
with constant temptation. "Objective," the translation of *sachlich*, here
means loyal to or totally focused on the object to be served and the
means to realize it. Although intoxication with the object is permitted,
self-intoxication undercuts service by undercutting commitment to the
object. It turns the politician away from the imposed laws and demands
of the cause, thus undercutting "objectivity" as well as responsibility, for
the exacting demands of the cause are sacrificed if the self makes a pact
to be satisfied with only the "impression" it makes or the feeling of
power it experiences. Yet the politician "cannot and may not reject or
transfer the ultimate *personal* responsibility for that which he does."[71]
His person must be *used* and sacrificed for the cause; he is its tool, not
its master. He must not use the cause for himself or his other purposes.

The four forms of redemption granted by the secular political calling
are necessary and sufficient conditions for the creation of the secular
equivalent of Puritan personality.[72] Indeed, to Weber, if the politician is
ever to become a personality like the Puritans before him, with their
strength and unity of self, it must be through completely overcoming the
self and living for the cause. "There is only a single way (perhaps!) to
become [a personality]: the unrestrained devotion to a 'cause' [*Hingabe
an eine 'Sache'*], however it and its derivative 'demands of the day' may
appear in the specific case."[73] Thus, although Weber speaks of the "Caesarist" leader as the "master" or lord (*Herr*) of his followers,[74] he is in
fact only partly right: the true political vocation is, in fact, not only about
masters but also about mastered men—mastered by their *impersonal*
service, though they control followers through their *personal* qualities.
The true political calling dominates and subjects the person.

As in the case of the Puritan saint, the genuine politician, in Weber's
view, cannot find the proper "witness" to political action in the populace
at large or even among his devoted followers. All personal or popular
human witnesses and all acclaim of others, except as means to power,

must be disqualified and excluded as reflections of vanity. The "correct" witness to action can only be the internalized impersonal cause itself. One must turn one's eyes away from others' needs and from the impression one makes. Only the vulgar demagogue is concerned with his "effect" (*Wirkung*) and with "vain self-reflection in the feeling of power," which is a product of *lack* of strength: "inner weakness and impotence" hide behind it.[75]

Weber implies that the problem in politics is that all commitment by leaders to real persons in fact conceals longing for adulation of the self. It interferes with devotion to the cause as the ultimate witness and ignores the "laws" of the cause's fulfillment as the standard of political action. Because of the self's latent desire, attention to others always threatens to seduce it away from exclusive devotion to the cause. Thus, Weber's conception of the empowered self requires that the politician *must not serve others* except indirectly: he must serve the *im*personal cause alone. The gratifications of relations with others in politics threaten the cause by making possible a love affair with the self, which is a devilish object. To Weber, evidently no self can resist such temptations unless *all* desire, *all* service of real others, is excluded absolutely. Only total abandonment and forgetfulness of self permit a potential leader to be redeemed for politics through ascetic devotion to the cause. Because of his conception of the desiring self, Weber is forced to adhere to the ascetic discipline of the calling to both empower and restrain it and make it fit for politics.

Weber's politician, thus, must renounce personal attachments, even to himself, and remain devoted exclusively to an impersonal end. The political man must "carry out his task as objective [*sachliche*] duty of the calling and not on account of a concrete personal relationship."[76] Others not only threaten the capacity to judge: they interfere with the absolute and unmediated devotion to the cause. It is only on the basis of the absoluteness of his devotion alone that the political leader is entitled to command the confidence of others and experience redemption and the charismatic "gift of grace."

It is ironic that, in Weber's view, to become a leader and draw followers the leader must, in effect, shun the service of others and cleave to the cause alone. It is obvious, therefore, that to Weber, real autonomy and strength are obtainable only through asceticism. Only in this relation to an object can the inner "core" of the man be shaped and fortified by total reliance on that object or cause. Wherever this kind of charisma appears, Weber says, "it constitutes a 'calling' [*Beruf*] in the emphatic sense of the word: as 'mission' or inner 'task.' "[77] Only the service of an impersonal cause can return the politician to what is essential, constitute the new person, and be the standard for judging the worth and effectiveness of the self and its actions.

Note that such subservience is not to any *particular* cause but to ascetic service of *some* cause. It is *service* that subjects; the actual object is irrelevant. Only the acknowledgment and acceptance of such an object and devoted service to it can free the self from its weakness, inherent worthlessness, and self-intoxication. In this quasi-religious solution to the problem of creating political leaders, the language and conception of the Puritan calling—worthless self, systematic active asceticism, visible signs of grace, total submission to a "god," the calling itself—generate the language and conception of the political calling. The Weberian politician must defeat all other impulses and sources of satisfaction, for neither a life in politics alone nor the "love" of one's cause makes self-overcoming and -empowerment possible. To Weber, only politics lived as a *calling* can lead to that goal and to the sanctified tasks it dictates. Only this path to leadership remains for a social world without aristocrats: to rely on the discipline of the calling and of service to create the character and self-empowerment needed for the tasks of politics and the nation.

ASCETICISM AND THE CALLING OF THE NATION

As a solution to the problem of politics, Weber did not limit the need for asceticism and service to leaders alone, but extended it to the collectivity as well. Indeed, as he wrote to Adolf von Harnack in 1906: "That our nation has never in *any* form gone through the school of hard asceticism is . . . the source of all that I find hateful in it (as in myself)."[78] To Weber, the history of Germany had been a story of passive submission, not active asceticism. The reason for this, he thought, lay in a culture shaped by Lutheranism and Pietism, which was unlike the culture of formerly Puritan peoples. In Weber's view, Puritanism and its mode of self-empowerment bred a "*relatively* great immunity" against "Caesarism" in England, even disrespect for authority, and an "inwardly free" attitude that prevented the idolization of great men or political obedience out of "thankfulness" to the leader—something very different from the German experience, especially under Bismarck.[79] Indeed, "Puritanism enabled its adherents to create free institutions and still become a world power."[80] Thus, it is "the power of religious movements first—not alone, but principally—[that] has created here those differences that we sense today."[81]

Whereas Puritanism showed a "naturalistic, rational inner attitude and inner point of view toward the state" and regarded offices and officials as functionally necessary rather than as objects of adoration, the German attitude was one of worshipful submission and obedience to officehold- ers. Lutheranism sanctified the state and enjoined submission to it. Pie- tism, too, put a premium on submission and duty and, though rooted in Calvinism, favored primarily the virtues of the faithful official, clerk, worker, domestic, and patriarchal employer.[82] These two religious tra- ditions were combined with the German brand of "unpolitical . . . ed- ucation, metaphysically oriented,"[83] leading Germans to endow officials with "God-given authority," which Weber brands an "emotional state metaphysics."[84] Given Germany's cultural and sociological background and the lack of practical political experience and sophistication bred by the German nation's inner powerlessness and subservience under Bis- marck, Weber's question is whether national political culture can be reshaped to equip Germany to make itself over into a disciplined political body capable of standing relatively united behind a leader with a calling.

Weber implies that Germany's ascetic calling as a nation must be the service of the nation's power-political tasks—as defended by the leader— and the shaping of its men and women for the challenges ahead. On behalf of this service, domestic policy and forms of government must be fashioned to develop increased commitment to the nation. Weber's wife reports a speech he gave in 1916: "Weber did not wish to speak as a member of any party, for '*I have always regarded politics from a national point of view—not only foreign policy, but all policy*'—exactly the same view that he had already held as a young man. Accordingly the ultimate yardstick was not domestic policy but *foreign interests*."[85] In- deed, as Weber noted elsewhere, "Only he who is capable of adapting domestic policy to foreign policy tasks can be called a politician in the national sense."[86]

Some form of social integration is essential to making Germany ca- pable of this calling. Weber claims that this effort of integration has been widespread; indeed, the "necessity of winning over the proletariat for foreign conflicts and the—disappointed—hope in its 'conservative' char- acter in opposition to the bourgeoisie" is what first led rulers everywhere in Europe to promote equal suffrage.[87] Social life must be reformed and working-class integration specifically achieved so that social unification of the classes may make possible a greater sense of involvement, and willingness to be involved, in the nation's tasks and accomplishments. This kind of integration is visible in England and France, where the work of economic education has gone on long and a position of world power has given the working classes a stronger national stake. "The goal of our socio-political work is not world happiness but the *social unification* of the nation ... for the difficult struggles of the future."[88] Economic policy must be adjusted out of concern for the future and in order to "breed" future generations with the "physical and spiritual qualities that we would like to maintain for the nation."[89] Suffrage, institutions of government, and training of leaders must be changed to make possible the rise to power of genuine political talents.[90] Only this higher purpose and a regard for its responsibility to the future can give Germany the inner unity and inner power it requires to carry out its calling in world struggle.

Even the question of internal political reform must serve the nation's power-political interests first, however vaguely the nation is understood.[91] To Weber, as to the many *Vernunftrepublikaner* of the twenties and after, the nature of reform must be dictated by "the historical tasks of the German nation," which "in principle stand *above* all issues of the *form* of the state." Thus, in defending the need for a working parliament, Weber asserts that finding the appropriate state form means asking "simple questions of technique for the formation of the will of the state. ... For an *objective* [*sachlicher*] politician which of these [forms] is expedient [*zweckmäßig*] for his state in each case is an objective question to be answered according to the political tasks of the nation. ... For the vital interests of the nation stand, of course, even above democracy and parliamentarism." Even so, no political transformation can, by itself, produce political capacity or success for the nation in its struggles. "Technical changes in the state make a nation neither proficient nor happy nor valuable. They can only clear away mechanical obstacles for it and are thus solely means to an end."[92] The reform of the nation, as well as its mobilization and education for service, must be handled culturally and socially.

Thus, in Weber's analysis, nationalism becomes the asceticism of Germany. Just as the calling makes it possible for the individual to overcome the hateful divided self, so too does Weber intend the ideology of the nation—the true "cause" for Germans and the highest object of their service in a calling—to make possible not only the regulation and channeling of party strife, class war, and interest-group domination but also future economic struggle. Conversely, it is only through social reforms that admit all sectors of the nation into its benefits and obligations that the nation can attain the unity that alone will make it possible to act as a single whole.[93]

Unfortunately, Weber's attempt to idealize as the sole common good the nation and service to it, by constructing a unitary object of national devotion in a time of deep-seated, hard-to-reconcile conflicts, obscures the nature of the divisions within the polity. It imagines that there can be real social unification, ideological and political, without the serious social reform that alone can make it possible. Moreover, it leads to the dangerous fantasy, indulged by Germans of every kind, that the proper thing is always for the nation to be united, above party, always sacrificing individual or sectional interests to the good of the whole in joint struggle against the common enemy. This belief led, in an unsophisticated form, to the continual need of individuals to prove that their concerns were truly national and not merely a matter of "interest" or party. But it was one thing to see the fantasy become mass hysteria in the heady opening days of World War I[94]—war, after all, has this effect everywhere—and quite another to imagine that it could be a peacetime condition. Yet Weber claims it is a "delusion" to think that "the political feelings of community [*Gemeingefühle*] could not tolerate a severe test of strength through divergent economic daily interests. . . . This is approximately true only in times of fundamental social upheaval." Although the experience of socialist support of World War I still lay in the future, Weber could say that whereas the masses do not normally possess the instinct for power and prestige, "in great moments, in the case of war, the meaning of national power also passes before their soul—then it is shown that the national state rests on primeval psychological foundations even in the broad economically dominated strata of the nation and is by no means only a 'superstructure,' the organization of the economically dominant class." In "normal times," however, when this instinct is unconscious in the masses, "the economically and politically leading strata" must be "carriers" of this political sense.[95]

But that power-political sentiments of the masses come out in war is no proof that they can be mobilized and maintained reasonably by rulers in peacetime. Peace unleashed social and economic struggles in a rapidly developing country like Germany, and an appeal to foreign policy interests—where reactionary classes and corrupt, repressive bourgeois elites rule—is not credible unless the social and economic order is transformed to give disaffected social interests a greater expectation of satisfaction and participation and to create domestic political values that bind the other classes to the state and its purposes. In 1895 Weber claimed that the masses in England did have reliable power instincts because there "the dependence of its economic blood on its political power position is demonstrated daily."[96] But Weber undervalues the more complicated English political culture that led the population to support political struggles abroad often for "moral" reasons—as in the case of the Bulgarian agitation in the late 1870s, for example—or that led to the formation of a nonrevolutionary Labor party. In Germany—despite the increasing bureaucratization and "normalization" of Social Democracy—without a political culture or networks of integration to support solidarity with adventures that seemed nakedly aggressive, and with ideological division in the country and reactionary political leadership, a situation like the one in England was not possible—as the years 1929–33 were to show in the antirepublican movements that developed then and crippled Weimar.

Consistent with his support of these goals and following the tradition of Ranke that looked at nations and their states as individualities struggling on the world stage, Weber claims that "the whole of politics is oriented to objective *Staatsräson*, to pragmatism [*Pragmatik*], and to the absolute end in itself . . . of the preservation of the external and internal distribution of power."[97] Indeed, even "the inner-political functions of the state apparatus" are regulated on the same basis. "*Staatsräson* follows closely, toward the outside as toward the inside, its own inwardly determined laws [*Eigengesetzlichkeiten*]," and "success . . . naturally depends ultimately on relations of power and not on ethical 'right.' "[98] The idea of *Staatsräson* thus always implies the expression of the interests of the unitary nation or of the nation wishing to be unitary.[99]

> For us in this national state the ultimate standard of value even for reflection on political economy is "*Staatsraison.*" . . . With this slogan we want to raise the demand that for the questions of German economic policy . . . the ultimate and deciding vote in this particular case should belong to the economic and political power interests of our nation and its carrier, the German national state.[100]

But despite Weber's claim, reason of state can be a false unity that masks national division. Weber wanted to use social reform to make the nation "one" for its foreign political tasks, and reason of state certainly takes the nation as one, putting external relations first, making domestic politics subsidiary. The notion of a nation as a unity, however, worked best when monarchs ruled as the embodiment of the nation and their interests were mapped onto those of the nation, as if the nation's interests were the same as theirs. But in times of parliamentary rule and democratic participation, this mapping of interests cannot remain unchanged. Imperial rule and rule by Prussia were imposed by Bismarck on all of Germany, and reason of state was often nothing but an ideological halo to justify Prussian ambitions and Prussian wishes at the expense of other democratic and political aspirations. In fact, in the period after unification and the attacks on Catholicism and Social Democracy, this ideology became more than acceptable to the bourgeois classes as they rushed to sacrifice their political ambitions to their fear of the working class and their wish for identification with the military and power-political successes of Bismarck. Imperialism, then, became the ultimate expression of reason of state.

Weber felt that imperial ventures had educated the British working class and taught it an uplifting obligation to both the future and empire. He wanted to involve the German working class more in social rewards to obtain their support for imperial struggle and, if necessary, war. In the case of war, which is a limiting case, reason of state unites all in principle—though any examination of the cost to the German working class of the government's imposition of the *Burgfrieden*, the labor peace in World War I, must recognize that unity was obtained at real cost to labor. In any event, war is not the footing for domestic life, yet Weber wanted to make the kind of unity that war brings the condition of peacetime life. Thus, despite his usual defense of politics as conflict, Weber's ideal here is the unified state acting on the basis of a reason of state modeled after war. Peace, in short, becomes war carried on by other means. But in peace real social questions arise, based on conflict, competing interests, and struggles, and they cannot be harmonized except through political negotiation, war, or repression. Weber did not want to suppress them. On the contrary, he wanted a more open and legitimated struggle to bind groups to the state and its promises of benefits. But he provides no justification for why such struggles are beneficial or necessary, other than his appeal to the foreign policy tasks of the nation. The social and political pacts that built Weimar unraveled when powerful interests sabotaged institutions for which there was no mass support. These institutions proved unable to cope with the economic crisis of 1929, and the mass of the citizenry could not see them to be in the interests of their freedom, given the lack of development of political norms and ideals within German political culture.[101]

Weber himself was not deluded by the obstacles to social integration. Arthur Mitzman argues that Weber's belief that aggressive *Realpolitik* could teach political responsibility disappeared after 1900.[102] But Weber's notion of the nation and its needs and the ideal type of national struggle continued, providing a pattern of giving priority to international needs over domestic political ones. The tradition in which Weber fitted himself was formulated by Leopold Ranke in his defense of the primacy of foreign policy (*Außenpolitik*) in the 1830s. In his "Political Dialogue," Ranke argued that politics belonged to "the field of power and foreign affairs." The parceling out of the world required that a nation achieve genuine independence to attain its rights and rise to "universal signifi-cance." "The position of a state depends on the degree of independence it has attained. It is obliged, therefore, to organize all its internal resources for the purpose of self-preservation. This is the supreme law of the state." To the criticism that such a position would seem to favor a military tyranny above other forms, Ranke confessed that for the beginnings of a state's existence, "when independence must be fought for," such a tyranny was preferable. But gradually, he maintained, "the need for peace in human nature will assert itself; then a balance will be struck."[103] But once one accepts Ranke's hierarchy of political values, where the needs of the nation outwardly are always superior to its inward and domestic needs, the political debate is then so severely restricted that it cannot address other genuine political demands. No question is raised about who decides what the outward needs are and how they are to be met. Further, questions of political form cease to be subjects of struggle and interests and take on aspects of the "emergency" situations of war, where the life-and-death struggle of the nation is invoked to curb debate. This atmosphere excludes every other standard or demand, whether of free-dom, participation, or political rights.

Weber's analysis of the political forms appropriate to modern Germany is completely a product of this hierarchy of values, not of any fundamental commitment to political liberty, democratic and republican forms for their own sake, or participation. It accommodates itself to the realities of mass democratic electorates only as an objective condition for leaders to work with and is too often most impressed with the imperial successes of Britain rather than her freedoms. It is hard to build a viable and vigorous political order on such a basis. Despite defending parliament, for example, Weber could also say, as he did in 1917: "Forms of state are to me techniques like any other machinery. I would attack parliament and defend the monarch if I were a politician or would promise to be one."[104] In more distressed times and with less brilliant heads at work, this kind of thinking led to attempts aimed at forcibly overcoming internal national divisions, in order to create a purified cause and nation and so restore a sense of higher purpose.

In elevating the nation over the state, Weber was, of course, reacting to Hegelian and Rankean overvaluations of the state as such and its "supreme idea," "principle," and role, as well as to the romanticism and state worship that more vulgar admirers of Bismarck, Prussia, and the war indulged in. To Ranke, states were the individualities: "Instead of the passing conglomerations which the contractual theory of the state creates like cloud formations, I perceive spiritual substances, original creations of the human mind—I might say, thoughts of God."[105] During the war Weber remarked of the state that "it would be almost inevitable that the conclusion would be drawn that it must be also the ultimate '*value*'—especially for valuations that touch the area of 'politics'—in whose life interests all social action is ultimately to be measured." But this is an "inadmissible interpretation" from facts to valuations.

> In the sphere of *valuation*, however, a standpoint is quite mean-
> ingfully defensible that would like to see the power of the state
> increased to the maximum thinkable in the interest of its usability
> as a means of force against obstacles, while on the other hand
> however denying it any value of its *own* and stamping it as a
> purely technical resource for the realization of completely differ-
> ent values from which alone it derives its fief and can therefore
> also keep it only as long as it does not try to renounce its calling
> for action [*Handlungsberuf*].[106]

To want to downgrade the status and value of the power state, as Weber does, is one thing; to reduce in value all other attempts to reform political order on behalf of rights or democratic interests is something else entirely. The first downgrading could make the state reformable as an object of human fabrication, by depriving it of its fetish character. But the second downgrading, which Weber supports, undercuts and de-legitimates grounds for reform that are not about foreign policy tasks and makes resistance to the state on purely domestic political grounds impossible. It is hard to square this position with Weber's recognition of enduring aspects of the political inheritance—for example, the idea of "fundamental rights," which he cites as something "to which ulti-mately we owe not much less than *everything* that today hovers before even the 'most reactionary person' as the minimum of his individual sphere of freedom."[107]

Thus, the elevation of the nation into a holy cause, without a mean-ingful confrontation of its social divisions and political inequities, pre-vents reform of the nation on both the social and political levels. Weber's thinking about the relation of political reform and the nation's needs cannot offer adequate arguments to support more genuinely democratic regimes.[108] Germany, unlike England, had no tradition of principled strug-gles for liberties and moral causes represented in bourgeois parties or leaders, as in English liberalism and radicalism, or in Gladstone. Nor was there, as in France, a tradition of republicanism, on behalf of which a perhaps lesser sociologist but much greater republican, Emile Durkheim, enlisted to support republican political education. Nor was there a tradition, as in America, of political culture based on democratic society and an established constitution that, whatever its corruption or vulgarity, prized political rights and popular sovereignty.

Weber remains an advocate of expansionist political nationalism, in a time when other potential political values of participation, freedom, and equality had so little credit in Germany that he as a privileged bourgeois could not defend them as essential to a polity for other than foreign policy reasons. Such an attitude might have been understandable, if not defensible, in an earlier period, like Ranke's, that focused on *Außenpolitik* because there was no domestic political life and foreign policy was the only outlet for political sentiments, the desire for political glory or success, and identification with the nation. But it is much harder to defend in Weber's time, when new political possibilities were emerging in Germany. Thus Weber was often left to argue for his version of the nation and *Staatsräson* on grounds of "manliness," a criterion that certainly had appeal among German elites but that reveals the fusion of identity issues with their symbolic resolution in expansionist adventures. Weber remains a liberal, but still politically authoritarian, nationalist, and imperialist.

THE "CAESARIST" LEADER

In 1918, Weber wrote that "our prevailing form of fashioning the will of the state [*staatlichen Willensbildung*] and the form of the political machinery [*Betrieb*] must doom to failure *every* German policy, no matter what its goals are."[109] Weber, in fact, made his proposals for political reform primarily to create a more adequate arena for the selection of qualified leaders on the basis of mass support and to check rule by bureaucracy. Taking equal democratic suffrage for granted, Weber demanded the creation in Germany of a parliament with real power, in which potential leaders would learn the business of politics through membership in committees—formed both for the purposes of legislation and to monitor and control the bureacracy—and would vie with one another for political supremacy and the mandate of the populace. But his hope for the possibilities of leadership selection by means of parliament were tempered when he became convinced that even a renewed German parliament would be given over to fractiousness, interest group struggle, and party machines hostile to leaders; he therefore turned elsewhere for the ascetic politicians with a calling he thought absolutely necessary to the modern political struggle.[110] He began to advocate the popular election of a president with preeminent authority, brought to power on a "plebiscitary" basis—though he continued to believe that "the effective co-domination of powerful representative bodies" with such a leader was the best defender of the constitutional guarantees of public order and of political continuity.[111] But Weber's understanding of the political calling interfered with his understanding of leadership in a modern society, for he envisioned the called leader as the sole possessor of autonomous political personhood and as the captor of his followers, an idea that followed unavoidably from his conception of the necessity of a calling and of what the calling entailed.

The Nature of the Caesarist Leader

Weber's language for describing leaders in the later part of his career is filled with numerous references to "Caesar" and "Caesarism." Though he had earlier criticized Bismarck for his "Caesarist nature" and the German bourgeoisie for its inability to resist Caesarism and its longing for a new Caesar, Weber came to characterize his *own* ideal leader as a Caesarist "dictator" of the "electoral battlefield." Indeed, he claimed to see such Caesars everywhere. For example, "English parliamentary domination" inclines toward "the development of . . . Caesaristic features. The leading statesman gains an ever more paramount position over against the parliament from which he comes."[112] In America too, Weber claimed that reform mayors were "municipal dictators" brought to power by reform movements, who "had to be conceded their *own* free appointment of their additional assistants." These "revolutionary dictators" ignored both traditional and formal legitimacy.[113] The changes in city politics were carried out by elected mayors with enormous power.

> [They] worked with an official apparatus *appointed* by them—therefore "Caesaristically." Looked at technically, the efficiency of "Caesarism" as an organization of domination often growing out of democracy rests above all on the position of the "Caesar" as a free confidant [*Vertrauensmann*] of the masses (of the army or the citizenry), liberated from tradition, and precisely on that account as an unrestricted master [*Herr*] of a cadre of highly qualified officers and officials selected personally by him freely and without regard for tradition and other considerations. This [is] "domination of the personal genius."[114]

These Caesars and dictators are products of the "antiauthoritarian interpretation" of charismatic leadership, where recognition of the leader by followers is not a consequence of claims of legitimacy made *by* the leader but is the basis of the legitimacy *of* the leader, what Weber calls "democratic legitimacy." This is the form typical of modern party politics, embodied in "plebiscitary domination," present "where the leader [Herr] feels himself legitimated as the confidant of the *masses* and is recognized as such. The appropriate means for this is the plebiscite . . . *formally* the specific means of the derivation of the legitimacy of domination from the (formally and according to pretence) free confidence of the *ruled*." This form of "plebiscitary democracy—the most important type of leader-democracy [*Führerdemokratie*]" is the key to Weber's conception of modern leadership, and he makes it the center of his reform efforts. It is "in its genuine meaning a type of charismatic domination that hides itself under the *form* of a legitimacy derived from the will of the ruled and continuing only through it. The leader (demagogue) actually rules by virtue of the attachment and the trust of his political following for his *person* as such."[115]

But there are difficulties in Weber's usage. Is it really appropriate to label such leaders "Caesars" and "dictators," despite the fact that they must be responsible at the least through regular elections, legislative control, judicial investigation, and the organs of "public opinion"? This set of categories lumps together irresponsible and responsible forms of leadership, authoritarian and uncontrolled domination with elected officials with a "mandate," giving theoretical ammunition to those who would adapt those categories to more literal dictatorial forms of control by claiming to unmask all leadership as, in its essence, dictatorship. This language does not distinguish between degrees of control over politics by politicians and by the public; thus it leads to an *authoritarian*, not an antiauthoritarian, interpretation of leadership, despite the fact that historical example is considerably more ambiguous and complex. For Weber the essence of all charismatic leadership of a plebiscitary kind *is* dictatorial, authoritarian, Caesarist—making politics the struggle between heads of rival armies, whose outcome in its first incarnation at the end of the Roman Republic is too well known to be recalled here.

Further, what Weber calls the "charisma of speech," associated with these demagogic leaders, has problematic consequences. It began in Athenian democracy and has reached its height in the "stump speeches" of modern campaigns. To Weber, modern campaign rhetoric has become less important for "the meaning of its content" and more important for its purely emotional quality, intending only to impress the masses with "the power and certainty of victory of the party and above all of the charismatic qualification of its leader."[116] But even Weber recognizes that such a situation means that the "political *danger* of mass democracy lies indeed in the first instance in the possibility of a strong preponderance of *emotional* elements in politics," for "the 'mass' as such . . . 'thinks only till tomorrow.' "[117] Thus Weber acknowledges potential drawbacks of plebiscitary leadership but has no prescription for limiting them, preferring to attribute them to the nature of mass democratic forms in general rather than to his *preference* for plebiscitary leadership creating "dictators of the electoral battlefield. . . . The naturally *emotional* character of the devotion and the trust of the leader is nevertheless characteristic of leader-democracy in general, from which usually arises the inclination to follow as leader the extraordinary one, promising the most, working most strongly with stimuli."[118] Because some of the emotionality of the masses can be controlled through organizations, one needs "rationally organized parties" to channel "the *un*organized 'mass': the democracy of the streets," as "a very important counterweight to the immediate and irrational domination of the streets typical of purely plebiscitary peoples"—a counterweight that, in Germany, the unions and the Social Democratic party have been providing.[119] Yet despite the controlling function of specifically mass parties and their organizations, which can do things that leaders alone, evidently, cannot, Weber continues to endorse for Germany, without reservation, what can only be called the potentially "mis-leading" nature of this leadership.[120]

To Weber, rationalization and specialization within politics have clearly not obviated the need for leaders; rather, they have made leaders an absolute necessity, not only for controlling bureaucracies but also for carrying out the proper business of party struggle itself. The consequence for "the political enterprise" of the "progressive democratization of the political means of struggle and organization of struggle" is "the *politician with a calling*," a man who "makes the political enterprise within a party the content of his existence. One may now like this figure or hate him— he is in his present form the undeniable product of the rationalization and specialization of political party work on the basis of mass voting." It is furthermore a historical fact, says Weber, that "mass democratic parties everywhere have had to subordinate themselves more or less unconditionally to leaders who had the trust of the masses if these parties saw themselves placed before great tasks." Democratization thus inevitably calls forth the plebiscitary leader. "Democratization and demagogy belong together. But: *completely independent*—let this be repeated—of the type of state constitution, as long as the masses can no longer be handled purely as a passive object of administration, but in their point of view are somehow actively of importance."[121] Hence, it must be remembered that "the *demos* in the sense of an undivided mass never itself 'administers' in larger associations but rather is administered and changes only the kind of selection of the ruling leaders of the administration."[122] These objective conditions require the politician with a calling and cannot be circumvented.

The Technical Approach to Parliament

In his defense of new institutions and political development Weber again allows the argument of "objective conditions," drawn from his social scientific analyses, to overwhelm any potential substantive grounds. Given that "a certain minimum of inner consent at least of the socially important strata of the dominated [*Beherrschten*]" is absolutely required for any form of domination, it is parliaments that are today "the means to manifest outwardly this minimum of consent."[123] Further, as the example of England shows, they are means for preserving civil and political rights, supervising the bureaucracy as well as the political leader, and dealing with the "succession" question either by peacefully deposing "the Caesarist dictator" who has lost the confidence of the masses or by guaranteeing continuous rule at times when no strong leader emerges.[124]

But to Weber the principal justification for a parliament is that it is a space in which genuine leaders—"personalities" with the appropriate training—can emerge and develop and "mass leaders" can be selected "not purely emotionally" to prove themselves as "statesmen."[125] "For political leadership only those personalities are well-trained that are selected in the political *struggle*," because "the essence of all politics is ... *struggle, recruitment of allies and of a voluntary following*."[126] Only competition for real power attracts the right types and rewards their struggle. "Every parliamentary struggle is obviously a struggle not only over substantive [*sachliche*] oppositions, but even more so over personal power." Only if party majorities are automatically rewarded with power and the responsibility for governing will "the people with great political instincts and with the most pronounced political leadership qualities ... fight it out and ... also have the chance to arrive in the leading positions," for the parties must elevate those who will take their party to success, those, that is, having "a personality equipped with attributes of a *leader*."[127]

Yet although such possibilities of power make possible, or at least do not hinder, the "selection" of leaders, such selection is still not assured, for "only a *working* parliament ... can be the ground on which ... genuinely *political* leadership qualities grow and ascend on the path of selection. A working parliament, however, is one that, *continually collaborating, controls the administration*."[128] This form of supervision and training guaranteed through the parliamentary right of inquiry, legislative committees, and governmental agencies is not only necessary for making parliament an effective power; in Weber's view, it is the prerequisite for making parliament an "educational influence" as well and the "selection place" of political leaders. Here again, the experience of the British Parliament bears witness, for "this body became the place of selection of those politicians who understood how to bring a quarter of humankind into subordination under the domination of a tiny politically astute minority. And indeed—the main point!—to a still considerable extent into *voluntary* subordination."[129]

For the success of parliamentary politics, therefore, Germany requires "the development of a dedicated *corps of parliamentarians with a calling* [*Berufsparlamentariertum*]. The parliamentarian with a calling is a man who exercises the mandate of the Reichstag not as an occasional extra duty but rather . . . as the primary content of his life's work. One may love or hate this figure, he is purely technically indispensable, and he is therefore *already present today*."[130] It is here that Weber again turns the argument for parliament into an argument of technique, a formally rational, means-ends argument based on technical necessity. To be sure, he is arguing principally, he believes, with defenders of the old order. "Whoever, on ultimate grounds of belief, puts *every* form of authoritative domination for its own sake over *all* political interests of the nation, he may declare himself for it. He is irrefutable."[131] Yet the same argument can be made against those who defend democratic and parliamentary forms of domination. One could conceive, according to this view, of needing an authoritarian government when conditions lead to a situation where the nation's political interests so require, because Weber gives no other grounds to justify a form of government than the fact of its being technically most suitable. The issue is not whether a "best" form of government exists; rather, it has to do with being allowed to defend one's choice on other than technical grounds, through an appeal to other political values and principles that can engage the sentiment and convictions of a following and serve as an argument not just for "dispassionate" intellectuals and writers of constitutions but for potential adherents of parliament.

Following Weber's view, one should feel no hesitation at abandoning political institutions when new technical needs arise. One need not be a Burkean to see the danger in such feeble support, on the basis of "technical necessity" alone, for democratic institutions. For a nationalist like Weber, that may be persuasive (it certainly gives new meaning to the notion of *Vernunftrepublikaner*), and it seems to support those who believe that Weber's notion of reason is purely instrumental, but for a mass following the consequences are cold institutions with little shoring up of political rights or convictions on any other basis, rational or cultural. Since arguments for new political means are permitted *only* on the level of rational technical reason, everyone is obliged to become a Hobbesian. This follows directly from Weber's conviction that disputes about values cannot be discussed, since they embody struggles between "gods" on behalf of whom the individual chooses his cause and service. There can naturally, therefore, be nothing more to discuss in politics than in science—only implications of positions, implicitly held values, and techniques for realizing one's goals. At least Weber is consistent in this respect for every sphere of life.

Yet even on the technical level there are problems with this argument. "The whole inner structure of parliament must be tailored for such leaders, as that of the English parliament and its parties has been in its way for a long time. Its conventions are certainly not capable of being transferred for us. But the structural principle indeed is."[132] Britain as a "pattern state" was always influential on plans for parliamentary reform. But the mere adoption of such institutions is not the heart of the technical problem, because real political technique must involve *wedding* a political form to the existing social and cultural order or changing that order to accommodate a new form. To hope to transform politics without transforming the social order, political ideology, and culture that sustain it—and that may fundamentally oppose the changes—is folly. Yet Weber puts this concern aside: "Not the problem of social democratization but rather only that of democratic—therefore of equal—*suffrage* must concern us here in its relationship to parliamentarization."[133] This self-limitation is precisely the problem with Weber's position, revealing the limitations of his liberal ideology and political understanding—that is, the refusal to confront the social sphere because of its threat to the existing organization of property and production.[134] In fact, before Parliament could become supreme in seventeenth-century England numerous preconditions were necessary: a unique medieval inheritance, isolation from the continent, civil war, the deposition of two kings, and serious social transformation. Thus Weber's technical calculations even by themselves are incorrect, because the changes he proposed would have required a change in institutions, mores, habits, and social roles that could obstruct the changes—and this obstruction is what happened in Weimar.

Further, despite Weber's evident Hobbesianism, which appears as a critique of all grounds for political reform except formally technical, rational ones, Weber also expects—indeed, believes in the absolute necessity for—some personalities to go beyond the merely technical to conquer the realm of the rational for motivations that are oriented strictly to higher ideals. These individuals must be able to act with force in the world and to tame the apparatus of rationality that, in the form of bureaucracy, wants to defend itself and its rule everywhere on the basis of purely technical considerations and arguments, excluding the influence of other ideals and goals. Weber's arguments, then, seem to be between different devotees of pure nationalism, who share a higher goal and hope to think rationally on behalf of that goal. But politics, notwithstanding Weber's view, cannot be supported only by the champions of higher values who deploy cool technical arguments; political action requires the engagement of masses of people, especially in periods of revolution or regime collapse. Great leaders did not create democratic institutions simply because of their demagogic capacity to sway the masses to follow them everywhere; rather, because leaders in fact embodied popular aspirations, values, and projects, both material and ideal, they were able to win and then act with the full support of the populace. It is ironic that Weber, admirer of the Puritans, would strive to reduce this political debate and struggle to a fight over techniques, that he would opt to rationalize further a structure of politics that men and women of great passion believed in and fought for, often linking their techniques to higher purposes as well as their own personal power.[135]

Thus Weber is himself like the *Vernunftrepublikaner*, persuaded of the need for democratic institutions only for the purely utilitarian purpose of generating leaders. This view is typified by the historian Friedrich Meinecke: "Parliaments can become useful means to an end, if they make possible the rise of significant talents to power; and for this reason, not because parliamentary rule as such is our ideal, we consider the extension of parliamentary rights a demand worth discussing."[136] Such men were obviously unable to inspire any mass following or support for such institutions in Germany—outside of the Social Democrats, whom they generally disdained; indeed, it is not surprising that the great defenders of the republic were the Social Democratic faithful, who, though they were becoming ossified and impotent owing to bureaucratization within their own ranks, remained committed to popular political forms. Hence it is *not* just bureaucrats who undermine the political realm, but also ostensible defenders of the "political" like Weber—people who ultimately represent a pure rationality in political discourse and state building and who, because of their disbelief in any conception of democratic rule other than the form of domination they defend, cannot recognize the need to embed institutions in popular sentiment, participation, and rewards, mobilizing masses of people with political ideals based on self-interest, equality, and genuine participation.

The Subjection of Followers

We cannot understand Weber's conception of the calling of politics without analyzing its companion component, what we can call the "calling of followers." As we noted above, devotion to the charisma of a leader "means indeed that he is valued personally as the inwardly 'called' leader of men, that [followers] submit to him not by virtue of custom or statute, but because they believe in him."[137] Like the earlier religious and entrepreneurial practitioners of the calling, the modern politician with a calling must be able to create and command the confidence of those around him, making them *want* to subordinate themselves to him, for "the politically passive 'mass' does not beget the leader from itself, but the political leader recruits himself a following and wins the mass through 'demagogy.' "[138] Yet Weber's description makes clear that one of the crucial characteristics of his notion of the political vocation is to be found not only in the adherence and devotion to an *impersonal* cause *by* the leader but also in the development of a "calling of followers" in their *personal* devotion *to* the leader. Plebiscitary devotion to leaders means "the confession of a 'belief' in the calling for leadership of him who lays claim to this acclamation."[139] It is not only that parties want to win power and gain the benefits of office. Party followings also gain satisfaction "from working in faithful personal devotion for a man and not only for an abstract program of a party consisting of mediocrities." Party "officials," unlike notables with their own political fiefdoms, "submit relatively easily to a leading personality [*Führerpersönlichkeit*] that has a strong effect demagogically," for "work for a leader is in itself inwardly more satisfying."[140] Thus domination by virtue of charisma has to be understood as the attachment to calling by leader *and* followers, where the leader serves his cause and his followers serve *him*. This type of domination provides a calling for everyone and, in this sense, is Weber's more "democratic" foundation for meaning and personhood in modern society.

Moreover, the community of the faithful is unified as a community by its devotion and submission to the leader, and the bonds between adherents are based on shared "attachment to and trust of his political followers in his *person* as such."[141] There is no "appointment" of followers but "only the call [*Berufung*] at the inspiration of the leader,"[142] who calls his followers as God once called his flock. Thus Weber's politician looks upward to his impersonal cause, not around himself to others. Similarly, his followers look upward to *him* who is their personal cause, not around *them*selves to the collective or even individual positing of their own autonomous goals and service. Their service is to him while he serves his cause effectively. Weber's ideas of charisma and the calling are, hence, each bipolar.

Thus, in his analysis of the kind of party and parliament needed to support a genuine politician, Weber reveals the necessary substantive consequences that follow for those who "serve" the leader. Of course there are, he claims, no fundamental principles of state and participation, of democracy and rights, to be specified or instituted from the start, and the nation's political tasks have to do with foreign policy. But Weber's "technical" and formal answer nonetheless implies certain substantive positions and precludes others, independent of the question of their worth or effectiveness as positions. Indeed, the nature of politics as a calling *itself* limits the range of political options.

> The direction of parties through plebiscitary leaders necessitates the "soullessness" [*Entseelung*] of the followers, their spiritual proletarianization, one could say. In order to be usable for the leader as an apparatus, they must blindly [!] obey, be a machine in the American sense, not disturbed by vanity of notables and pretensions of personal opinions. *Lincoln's* election was possible only through this character of the party organisation, and with Gladstone there happened . . . the same thing in the caucus. This is simply the price with which one pays for direction by leaders. But there is only the choice: leader-democracy with "machine" or leaderless-democracy, that is, the domination of "called politicians" [*Berufspolitiker*] without a calling, without the inner charismatic qualities that precisely make a leader. . . . For the time being we have only the latter in Germany.[143]

This insistence on the "spiritual proletarianization" of followers is surprising, considering that among the justifications Weber originally advanced for a responsible parliament were the education of the nation to independent political thinking, the development of its political will and judgment, and the training and recruitment of responsible political leaders through experience in government agencies, committees, and parliamentary inquiry into government affairs.[144] Whether a transformation of suffrage and the public scrutiny of parliament and government can, by themselves, "educate" the nation politically or not is an open question.[145] But how can independent political talents develop in a parliament based on Weber's idea of parliamentary submission?

This form of subjection is evident also in the role and structure of parties as Weber conceives them. In England the parties "are forced by the 'Caesarist' tendency of mass democracy to submit to men with real political temperaments and gifts as leaders, as soon as they show themselves able to win the confidence of the masses. . . . Precisely strictly organized parties . . . must *subordinate* themselves to the men who hold the confidence of the masses, *if* they are men with the nature of leaders."[146] Parties must be organized not like "guilds" but "in the manner of 'followings,' " whose political chiefs are real leaders.[147] Any party interested in sharing government power must act this way. Indeed, parliaments as such never "rule" or make policy, not even in England. "The great broad mass of the deputies functions *only* as a following for the 'leader' or the few 'leaders' that form the cabinet, and obeys them blindly *as long as* they have success. *This is the way it should be.* . . . This 'Caesaristic' strain (in *mass states*) is ineradicable." It is a product of "the superior political manoeuvering ability of *small* leading groups," but it also guarantees that responsibility can be clearly fixed on "specific personalities," because, Weber claims, in a large governing assembly responsibility would otherwise "evaporate."[148]

Nevertheless, although Weber claimed to be modeling his proposals on the British Parliament, such blind following was not the case in Britain, despite the fact that party cohesion, expressed in strong party-line voting, increased through the end of the nineteenth century. Obviously, of course, any leader, confronted with a contentious and uppity parliament, might *want* such submission to increase his capacity to affect policy as he wishes. But if blind obedience is the rule, how can Weber imagine that younger politicians will emerge and learn responsibility? How are their "selves" to be shaped for the political calling by such tutelage? If followers in parliament are essentially captives of the leader, as Weber describes them, then despite what parliament may be able to do to protect popular political and other rights and to guarantee the smooth deposing of unsuccessful leaders, the development of newly called leaders from the ranks of such an institution is suddenly an open question again.

Gustav Schmidt has already shown that Weber, despite his reliance on a theoretical understanding of the English system, did not take the crucial step of "the recognition of the opposition as an integral component of political life."[149] But even on its own terms, Weber's authoritarian reading of party submission—ignoring the collaborative nature of association with the leader and the effect of disparate pressures, arguments, and constituencies on the shaping of policy—leads to the complete undermining of the tasks of parliament he had originally prescribed. In fact, in ignoring differences of degree and kind in the nature of obedience to leadership, Weber's description better defines later developments in the Bolshevik party than it does the Liberal or Conservative parties of Britain.

It is hardly surprising, given his view of the requirements of leadership, that Weber became more and more pessimistic about the possibility or desirability of a parliament on the British model and advocated more and more strongly a "plebiscitary-charismatic" leader elected by national suffrage. "The president of the Reich could become the only safety valve for the demand for leadership if he were elected in a plebiscitarian not a parliamentarian manner."[150] But such a preference then also effectively displaces parliament as an arena for training leaders, and in fact Weber begins to focus on it largely as a vehicle for controlling bureaucracy rather than anything else. Thus, despite his original advocacy of a politically effective and powerful parliament that recruits talent by offering real opportunities for power and a training ground for political talent to develop and sharpen its skills, Weber ultimately leaves true charismatic talent once again to arise at least as much outside parliament as within and to develop political knowledge and judgment on its own.

Weber's thinking on leadership thus leads to a circle of reasoning that undermines his original intent and makes it necessary to discover a way out. Beginning with the need for strong capable leaders, Weber argues that genuine parliamentarization is the only realistic source of training for rule. But since parliament might undermine a leader's capacity for control and initiative, it must actually become an arena of blind obedience and support of leaders who prove themselves to the mass. Consequently, parliament is defeated as an arena for training, and Weber's solution to generating and training leaders is undone. There were of course, in principal, potential alternative sources of leaders with experience in leading—for example, mayors in municipal government—and Weber was prepared to avail himself of them.[151] Yet even then the generation of leaders would be left largely to chance, rather than to careful training.

This inability to find a regular institutional source of leadership—due to what Weber believes is a formal requirement of leadership, namely, that it dominate everyone so fully that it must render all neighboring political talents obedient and blind—makes Weber's reliance on the substantive requirement of the ascetic calling for politics even more central to his political thinking. Only the ascetic calling can insure that, even without adequate national political training, a leader will have the prerequisites of character and the appropriate relation to an object of service that guarantee that he can be trusted to act politically, without the intrusion of destructive motives of self. Only the ascetic calling for politics, as a discipline for empowering the political self and a standard for judging leaders, can shore up the politician and reassure the populace while the leader acquires on-the-job training. Yet the very belief in the need for such a calling helps to undo Weber's practical proposals for institutions of leadership. It remains Weber's "spiritual" guarantee of the authenticity of leadership, even as political guarantees evaporate.

THE BRITISH PRIME MINISTERIAL MODELS

The British parliamentary system was the "pattern state" in the eighteenth and nineteenth centuries for Europeans—and certainly for German liberals—hoping to modernize their governmental systems.[152] It is thus not surprising that in the process of constructing his political reforms Weber based certain of his proposals on the British model and supported his argument about plebiscitary leaders with the examples of prime ministers like Gladstone and Lloyd George. But Weber was highly selective in the details he selected from this model to support his conceptions of the ideal types of leaders and organization, ignoring crucial elements that made British politics more complicated than he acknowledged and skewing it in an authoritarian direction. In his proposals to produce politically called leaders from parliament, Weber thus misappropriated the British parliamentary model and misrepresented the successes of Gladstone and Lloyd George, seeing them as individuals constrained only by the force of their own charisma, inspired only by their own political cause, capable of extraordinary independence, and standing at the head of a fully tamed Parliament. It is not surprising that he called them "dictators" of the electoral battlefield, for that is what he wanted them to be and imagined they were. Certainly, the personal gifts and charismatic power of Gladstone and Lloyd George are not in dispute; but their total effect depended on more complex political workings than Weber acknowledged, and the consequences of their actions in many ways undermine Weber's evaluation and indeed show more similarities to Bismarck, whom Weber had so strongly criticized, than to an ideal leader.[153]

Gladstone and Caucus Politics

The paradigmatic example of political leadership and charisma that Weber regularly invoked was Gladstone's capacity to draw most of the Liberal party behind him through his personal sway over local Liberal organizations—the "Caucus" first created in Birmingham by Joseph Chamberlain—in the fight for Irish Home Rule in 1886, against the party's publicly held views. The Liberal party of the 1870s and 1880s was a party of property-owning leaders, supported by an army of small-property- and non-property-owning local activists, and having a predominantly non-propertied and working-class base.[154] Its leadership was largely divided between old-time Whigs, whose power lay in land, investment, and traditional occupations, and Radicals, who included the rising middle classes, industrialists, and the defenders of religious nonconformity against the established church. Irish nationalists, led by Charles Stewart Parnell, had become a powerful political force in Ireland and in Parliament, thwarting legislation on many issues and occasionally having the seats to make or break a government, especially after the elections of 1885. With economic crises and violence in Ireland and Parnell pressing for a fundamental change in the legislative relations between England and Ireland, Gladstone secretly became a convert to the cause of Irish Home Rule in the summer of 1885, but that December his support was prematurely revealed by an indiscretion of his son, long before he himself intended to make it public. Parnell then threw his support to Gladstone, who formed a ministry in January 1886 and brought up a Home Rule Bill in April. Although nearly all of the Liberal caucuses supported Gladstone, the bill was defeated in June by a combination of Conservatives and a centrist revolt among the Liberals, consisting of ninety-three Radicals and Whigs from Gladstone's own party, including Joseph Chamberlain, the Radical leader, and many leading Whigs. Gladstone thereupon dissolved Parliament and called an election, which he lost overwhelmingly. In 1893 he brought up another Home Rule Bill, which passed the Commons only to be defeated in the Lords.[155]

Weber's enthusiastic evaluation of Gladstone is based on his conviction that Gladstone won the Caucus over to Home Rule solely through the force of his personality and the personal devotion that Liberals maintained toward him. In this, Weber thought, the caucus apparatus of the party "blindly" obeyed Gladstone, just as an American "machine" would have done, undisturbed by its "personal opinions."[156]

> The fascination of Gladstonian "grand" demagogy, the firm faith of the masses in the ethical substance of his policy, and above all in the ethical character of his personality, was what led this machine so quickly to triumph over the notables. A Caesaristic-plebiscitary element in politics—the dictator of the electoral battlefield—entered the lists. . . . In 1886 the machine was already so completely, charismatically oriented to the person, that, when the Home Rule question was unrolled, the whole apparatus, from top to bottom, did not ask: Do we stand substantively on Gladstone's ground? but rather, simply on Gladstone's word, veered off with him and said: Whatever he does, we follow him.[157]

Although devotion to Gladstone was a significant factor for many Liberal militants in the fight within the caucuses and the party, there were in fact numerous other political reasons and forces that moved so many to support Gladstone on Home Rule. Further, and ironically, rather than being a testimony to great leadership, the triumph over the caucuses and the ensuing election in the Home Rule struggle were a valiant but *losing* cause, a product of the *failure* of Gladstone's political efforts, not their success, a struggle prematurely announced and poorly prepared for. While some historians have claimed that the struggle actually radicalized Liberalism and created a more cohesive party than existed before, others have argued that Gladstone's defeat at the polls, despite triumph within the party, in fact paved the way for a twenty-year Tory supremacy and so marked the beginning of the end of the Liberals as one of the decisive mass representative parties of Britain.[158] However one evaluates it, the election was badly timed and fought on a single issue, based on inaccurate judgments about the electorate, and without any proposals or positions other than Home Rule to win voter support of the Liberals. To get a proper critical perspective on Weber's understanding of leadership, we must examine the historical background of these events that were so pivotal for his conceptions and prescriptions, in order to disentangle the myths and assumptions from the actual course of events.

William Gladstone, a High Church landowner and originally a defender of the "aristocratic principle" in government, was prime minister of Britain in 1868–74, 1880–85, 1886, and 1892–94.[159] Despite his background and inclinations, he became the idol of the middle classes from his first term as chancellor of the exchequer in 1859, when he put through free trade and many other middle-class goals. But he had not sought this role. "He had not chosen [his middle-class constituents]: they had chosen him, and their faith in him lasted no longer than the policies by which he deserved it." Still, "as long as entrepreneurial society lasted in a form still recognizably true to its ideal, it found its chief political expression in Gladstone and the Liberal Party." Soon, however, the Liberal party started to attract working-class and Irish peasant voters and to support certain of their interests, and at the same time landed and business interests began to converge; therein was prepared the "geological shift" that took so many businessmen and landowners into the Tory party. Indeed, according to Harold Perkin, far from being a group that upheld the "old, virile, ascetic and radical ideal of active capital," the British capitalist class after the 1860s "submerged" itself in the older, "supine, hedonistic," and conservative ideal of passive property. The British bourgeoisie, that is, like the German one, lost its "inner principle of self-justification," began to emulate the landed aristocracy, and then threw its lot in with it, as its interests changed and as the protection of the public, in measures like the Factory Acts, began to take precedence in the state's legislative practices over freedom of industry. Just when many Whigs on the right were growing disaffected with Gladstone's interest in democracy and faith in the people, some businessmen among the Radicals felt they had accomplished most of their original agenda. A good part of the business class was thus poised for the Liberal party split over the "apparently extraneous question" of Irish Home Rule, and quickly shifted into alliance with the landowners against measures that both groups considered democratic and socialistic. The Home Rule crisis was thus not the main cause of a Liberal split; it was in fact as much an excuse as a genuine reason for the break.[160]

Still, Gladstone's personal power and political leadership cannot be overrated. In the period of his political supremacy, in fact, an extraordinary cult had developed around him, which, following his reemergence from retirement a few years after an electoral defeat in 1874, seemed to regard him less as an ordinary politician than as a hero. Indeed, D. A. Hamer argues that, given Gladstone's theatrical instincts and the real drama of his later career, "the myth and its dramatic requirements . . . controlled the course of his career. . . . His nature had to imitate his hagiography." His home at Hawarden became the goal of political pilgrimages, and the biographies that emerged while he was still alive and active "make Gladstone appear the chief protagonist [of British politics], not subject to any of the normal restraints on the ability of a politician to control circumstances."[161] Gladstone thought of himself as having a great mission, "a strong sense of personal call," based on God's special care for him.[162] He viewed the issues that arose for his attention as the "continually unfolding pattern of God's purpose for him." This purpose he discovered in the "voice of the people," which indicated to him "where his duty and his work were to be found." He himself said of the role of the great orator in history: "He cannot follow nor frame ideals: his choice is, to be what his age will have him." Indeed, Walter Bagehot said of him that he was "a man who cannot impose his creed *on* his time, but must learn his creed *of* his time."[163]

In a very Weberian description of Gladstone, Hamer has argued that Gladstone did not believe in overly close organizational ties between leaders and followers or in the imposition of particular policies by leaders on the party or by the party on its leaders. He was unwilling to intervene in organizational matters or to settle intraparty disputes, a detachment that only enhanced his political authority and seemed to make it more pure. Gladstone preferred that action and unity arise spontaneously from within the party, rather than because of the imposition of his leadership. Still, he often took the initiative when he thought the time ripe, without cultivating or consulting the party, his followers, or even his closest colleagues, thus leaving them to support him or not on a purely voluntary basis. With his evangelically based sense of duty and mission, he began to seek a "great cause" after his 1874 defeat, one he hoped would establish order in the party. In his view, such a cause could not be a creation of the party but must arise of itself and find its instrument in the party. The cause would then overcome the party's mere "sectional interests," making the party the tool of a lofty purpose. Indeed, because Liberal sectionalists substitute their own "predilections" for the "paramount weight of the object itself," Gladstone felt, "all proportion of judgment is lost." Praising Gladstone's own "sense of measure" and "acute sense of proportion and relationship," Hamer argues that Gladstone had the imagination and rhetorical power to convert his single issues into larger centers of interest, and with his political personality and personal approach "he was the best substitute for a creed, a system of thought, that the party possessed."[164]

T. A. Jenkins, in contrast, believes that Gladstone often acted only when it was clear there was sufficient support for his position. Although Gladstone did consider the party as only an instrument for " 'a great work to be carried out,' " his leadership was exceptionally autocratic and dictatorial, the product of his earlier religious views and development. Jenkins suspects that Gladstone's demand for internal party discipline and obedience "concealed an inability to tolerate resistance to his leadership" and that his intolerance of disunity and predilection for great causes indicate shortcomings, not strengths, in Gladstone's leadership. Indeed, he thinks Gladstone was temperamentally too impatient and inadequately conciliatory to be a leader when his party was divided, and agrees with party regular Lord Selborne that Gladstone lacked proportion and breadth, which made it impossible for him to serve "except when it is the time for some 'heroic' measures." Even though Gladstone thought he had the "mass of feeling" and public opinion behind him, he felt he could come out of retirement and displace the sitting Liberal leader only as the consequence of "a nearly unanimous" call "with the appearance of a sort of national will." After the elections of 1880, Gladstone headed the government because of his unique capacity to be a balancing force between the Whig and Radical wings of the party, each wing wanting to prevent the other from controlling the party. But he and others assumed during the period 1880–85 that his retirement was imminent. In fact, he spoke of it so often that he undermined his own position, encouraged the avoidance of difficult policy decisions, discouraged the emergence of a clear direction in the government, and prevented cabinet unity and a clear policy direction among his political heirs.[165] For the purposes of argument, however, and to give Weber every benefit of the doubt, let us grant Hamer's and Weber's more idealized view.

It is almost certain that Gladstone had not intended his conversion to Home Rule, the great cause he hoped would unify the disorganized Liberal party, to become public so soon.[166] Although some have maintained he supported it out of personal ambition and a desire to be summoned to deal with a great national issue, it is clear that he hoped the Conservatives—who had toyed with such a policy already—would, with Liberal support, ally with Parnell to push it through.[167] When that failed, he seems to have assumed he would have time to convert the party to the cause—to prepare the ground for an internal and "spontaneous" conviction from within the party—for he did not want to push the party openly onto a track it did not want to follow.[168] Because of the premature announcement and his conviction that conditions in Ireland were converging on violence and anarchy, he determined to go ahead speedily with Home Rule, and when Parnell threw his support to him, he created a government. In his previous government he had given cabinet places to many Whigs rather than Radicals, hoping to win them for progressive legislation; even though this scheme had not worked in 1880, he tried it again in 1886.[169] Worse, in setting up the cabinet he badly mishandled and offended his major rival in the Radical camp, Joseph Chamberlain, refusing him the Colonial Office he badly wanted and giving him instead the lesser office of head of the Local Government Board. He might still have won Chamberlain over to Home Rule, or at least lessened his opposition to it, had he granted attention to features of the Radical program. Yet this he did not do, nor did he support Chamberlain's plans for local government reform, thus making it all the easier for Chamberlain to leave the government over Home Rule and the ideological disagreement over Irish policy.[170]

Weber ignored these problems with Gladstone's political judgment and actions, choosing instead to focus exclusively on his capacity to dominate the Liberal caucuses and win their support—that is, on what he thought was Gladstone's capacity to control his "blind" supporters. This capacity must be considered in more detail.

After the Reform Bill of 1867 created millions of new voters, a new provincial political organization, often compared to the political ma-

chines of America, emerged to make the system work and absorb the
voters. With the Conservative party more advanced than the Liberals in
creating extraparliamentary organization for winning elections, Radical
members of the Birmingham Liberal party, rivals of the Whig leaders in
London, organized the first Liberal associations.[171] In 1877, these various
local associations united to form the National Liberal Federation (NLF)
in Birmingham—with Gladstone, himself alienated from party leaders, in
attendance defending his Balkan policy.[172] He at once became associated
with the NLF as its champion, providing emotional coherence and a
moral appeal that was irresistible to the Radicals.[173] When the Liberals
won in 1880, the NLF, informally known as the Caucus, became a semi-
official organization supporting the new government in office. Yet although the NLF helped create party unity to support legislation, unlike
the Conservative organization, which was subservient to the Conservative
leadership, the NLF forced Liberal leaders to confront its positions.[174]

The crucial example of Gladstone's leadership for Weber was the
support thrown to him by the Caucus after he had introduced the Home
Rule Bill into Parliament in April 1886. Gladstone's supporters won over
the council of the NLF and quickly met with similar success in most of
the local caucuses, with the exception of Chamberlain's Birmingham.
According to Jenkins, the bulk of Gladstonians unquestionably obeyed
him "blindly," and it was Gladstone's "powerful advocacy of home rule
which alone convinced the liberal rank and file that the measure could
be safely conceded." Support for the measure "involved a gigantic act
of faith, and many of his followers later expressed their misgivings about
his tactics." James Loughlin, more measured, says it is "likely" that Gladstone's influence was what carried the day in the Parliamentary party.[175]
In any case, the Caucus now seemed to be exercising the kind of pressure
conservatives had feared, to "usurp the power of Parliament and transfer
it to omnipotent extra-Parliamentary bodies, or even, *via* these, to a
Parliamentary dictator."[176] Indeed, some of Gladstone's associates themselves feared the growth of servility toward him. The use of the Caucus
to defeat party notables and bring the Parliamentary party into line unified
the rest of the party on the basis of principle and devotion to Gladstone—
a development that to Weber was the hallmark of the Caesarist leader.[177]
M. Ostrogorski—on whom Weber relied for much of his understanding
of the Caucus—thought Gladstone had the "temperament of the demagogue," and he believed the development of local party organizations
loyal to leaders would pressure members of Parliament (MPs) to conform
to the leader's will.[178] Hugh Berrington, however, argues that Liberal
organizations were actually more likely to applaud MPs who defied the

leaders and the whips and stood for Radical principles. Thus, he argues, the Caucus at first made for more indiscipline, not less. After 1886, the Caucus merged with the London party machine, and its success led to its co-optation and "dull conformity" with the dictates of party politics, for the Liberal establishment never conceded the NLF real power in determining policies.[179]

Although Gladstone's personal charisma was crucial in this event, the struggle over control of the caucuses also reflected long-standing and fierce internal disputes within the party, despite Weber's attempt to credit Gladstone alone. In particular, it reflected a rebellion of other provincial locals against control by Birmingham. The NLF had been dominated by Chamberlain and his associates, and many provincial associations felt Birmingham's control of the central office housed there made it easy for them to be used and manipulated by Chamberlain to serve his personal ambitions for power. They objected to statements made on behalf of the federation issued without consultation with the locals and resented Birmingham's arbitrary behavior and resistance to opposition. Thus, provincial Liberals desired to free themselves and their organizations from this domination; in fact, the Manchester caucus contemplated seceding from the federation as early as 1882.

Of course, there were opponents of Birmingham who still opposed Home Rule, and Gladstone did lose the support of some of the Liberal center. Rich and conservative Liberals—the grand bourgeoisie and the landowners—generally found Home Rule unacceptable, as opposed to the commercial and industrial petty bourgeoisie, working-class Liberals, and Radicals outside of Birmingham, who were much more amenable to it. Indeed, there was already much sentiment for Home Rule in the country and among Liberals before 1886, and many Liberals who supported Gladstone did so either for reasons of principle or because they thought Ireland was ungovernable by Parliament and there was no realistic alternative to Home Rule. The strength of Gladstone's electoral victories in the towns shows the attractiveness of the issue for the Radicals, who saw themselves fighting the same enemy as the Irish. In addition, different pressure groups, like the Non-conformists, the National Education League, and the Liberation Society, derived serious tactical advantages for their causes from supporting Gladstone's stand.[180]

Thus it is clear that the desertion of some of Gladstone's associates coupled with the success of his supporters within the NLF "reflected rivalries and tensions which had been present since the foundation of the organization in 1877."[181] This shows the extent to which, in supporting Gladstone's break with his opponents among Whigs and Radicals, the caucuses were *not* largely moved against their interests by Gladstone's person, but, quite the contrary, used one issue where their sentiments may have been lukewarm or opposed to further other *interests* of theirs, thus providing their support and getting an outcome they strongly desired for other reasons.

Apart from the clear effect of Gladstone's personal appeal, a number of flaws in his leadership were evident in his parliamentary and electoral practice. First, according to J. L. Hammond, because Gladstone lacked tact, patience, and the talent for dealing well with men, he handled the Home Rule Bill badly in the Commons, losing patience and withdrawing concessions he had made. "It may indeed be said of him that nobody else could have gained for Home Rule anything like the support it received in the House of Commons and in the country in 1886; that was the result of his moral power and intellectual ascendency. But it may also be said that a man with gifts far inferior to his could have obtained a second reading for his Bill if once that Bill had reached the position that Home Rule Bill had reached by April, 1886."[182] Second, despite indications from Irish Nationalists that they would be satisfied with a declaration for autonomy and the creation of a parliamentary inquiry into the best approach to Home Rule, Gladstone decided to introduce his more far-reaching bill immediately, with no time for educating the public or negotiating with other powers in Parliament. His unfortunate sense of urgency thus led him to precipitate action that led to his defeat. Third, because Gladstone felt Home Rule and Ireland were blocking all other progress and reforms the Liberals might undertake, he refused to give direction from the top on anything other than the Irish issue and endeavored to shelve all further domestic legislation and constituency concerns in a virtually dictatorial manner. Fourth, after his defeat in the Commons in 1886, Gladstone trusted the advice of the NLF's secretary and pressed for a snap dissolution and quick election, which caused disaster at the polls (though the disaster would have been much greater without the NLF).

Gladstone was without peer as a campaigner, and in his great Midlothian campaigns of the 1870s he became the first major British statesman to stump the entire country for his programs, more like an American presidential candidate than a British leader.[183] But in the election many constituencies had no Home Rule candidates, and many electors were ignorant of Gladstone's case for Home Rule. Further, Gladstone's absorption in a single question, excluding all others like electoral reform or the conditions of agricultural labor, meant that in 1886 voters were asked to set aside all issues that mattered to them, including that of candidate qualifications, and vote on one issue: whether to give Ireland a parliament at the request of a prime minister who was otherwise proposing to do nothing for them at all.[184] H. J. Hanham maintains that this was not in fact so unusual, since fighting elections on the basis of a single issue had been the norm since 1868.[185] But Hammond claims that "Gladstone's ill-devised procedure had made the election a plebiscite on Home Rule. No elector who wanted anything else had much reason for voting for him."[186] Even so, the majority of Liberal constituents lost in 1886 were not Radicals but Whigs, moderates, and agricultural laborers. Most working men voted for Gladstone over Chamberlain, even though Gladstone offered only Home Rule, while Chamberlain offered social reforms, a further proof of Gladstone's authority. Still, Gladstone's miscalculation and his single-minded pursuit of his own idea of what was right and what he must do alienated many possible supporters, guaranteeing total political defeat for his original goal and ideal.

In addition to ignoring Gladstone's political failures in the Home Rule crisis and the complexity of his relation to the Caucus, Weber simplified the complex relations of Gladstone to his party and followers in Parliament, assimilating them to a model of pure obedience and leaderly command. It is true that there was a rise in party unity after the reforms of 1867, which strengthened the hand of party leaders.[187] Indeed, Samuel Beer argues that partisanship intensified, and after 1880 the new forms of party organization and pressure seem to have raised the level of party voting in the Commons as well as among electors, though sanctions for resisting were few.[188] But Valerie Cromwell maintains that increased government control in the Commons was a product of procedural changes made when the position of parties was still relatively weak. In the early nineteenth century, Parliament could check the executive through the use of private member initiatives, which were accorded precedence in the Commons. But this check was gradually eroded, and after 1882 the Commons's procedures were tailored to ministerial business through growing respect for the needs of the executive; by 1914 the system of checks had completely changed.[189]

Still, Gladstone viewed the Liberal party as a kind of federation and would not interfere with the independence of his followers. He disapproved the Conservative practice of discussing a bill at a party meeting before its introduction into the House, a stand that was matched by his great regard for the independence of ministers and their supporters.[190] Indeed, even past opposition to leaders did not disqualify someone for office, provided he had not actively opposed the party position at the election. W. C. Lubenow claims that the growth of party discipline was obtained through means other than "blind, unthinking, coerced discipline. ... The association of party with vote was produced by informal forces of ideological integration, not the crude coercive power of party discipline, or the blind devotion to various bodies of party leaders. Members accepted the whip of one party, as opposed to others, because of shared political values."[191] Yet it is also true that Gladstone would withdraw into a shell when his followers were dissatisfied with him, rather than trying to win them over with persuasion, and awaited " 'spontaneous action from within the bosom of the party' in his favor." This actually prevented him from imposing a more comprehensive program on the party at times when his leadership was secure.[192] As Alan Beattie observes, "Gladstone's concern with principle, and his temperamental preference for 'leadership' rather than 'management' ... were very much connected with the greater difficulties of cohesion which the Liberals experienced."[193]

Weber thus ignores and simplifies crucial aspects of Gladstone's actions and style in a way that reveals the problems with his conception of leaders. First, Gladstone's leadership of the party became a major obstruction to the development of Liberal policy because of his enormous authority combined with his refusal to address anything other than the Irish question or to encourage any other policy development.[194] Second, by prematurely forcing Home Rule on the party as his great cause and staking his career on it, Gladstone defeated his own policy and forced the emergence of a division among the Liberals. He concealed this failure of leadership by claiming that the "classes" had acted to thwart the will of the "masses" whom he claimed to represent.[195] His stand on Home Rule and its effect on the Liberal party guaranteed that the party could never again be reconstituted on its former basis, for his crusade alienated hesitant and uncommitted voters. Still, his authority and his incredible oratorical skills did bind Labor MPs to him and were in fact a principal obstacle to the formation of a politically independent Labor movement.[196] Third, Weber overemphasized Gladstone's role in causing the shift in the party and did not sufficiently take into account the role of different social classes, a changing society, shifting constituencies, and changing relations toward policies and leaders. Even though he could move the apparatus of the party, Gladstone lost the support of a segment of the leading classes. His ability to bring the Caucus behind him should not conceal the fact that shifting social and political interests were leading to a realignment within and between parties. Gladstone's oratory alone could not move people against their interests, even if he could move many through the force of his commitment and their devotion to him.

Weber ignored Gladstone's numerous mistakes and political miscalculations in order to isolate the leader's capacity to win a constituency through the force of personality; nevertheless, the essence of political charisma cannot be confined to this quality alone. Weber's conception of leadership thus violates his own ethic of responsibility and reveals how much more enamored he was of losing but principled causes and of those who champion them than of practical political success, which requires more skills of negotiation, judgment, and accommodation than Weber cared about. The moral appeals that so animated Gladstone's audiences were important to his success, but the attempt to focus the regard for leadership on just those features runs the risk of courting failure on behalf of a romantic and idealized picture of the lonely leader and the devoted followers.

In sum, we can say that on a number of counts Weber's use of Gladstone as a model leader is fraught with problems and makes a single compelling feature of leadership substitute for a fuller portrait of *good* leadership. It is not only that Gladstone's actions are misunderstood and then idealized; they are so oversimplified that other relevant issues are completely ignored. The point is that Weber *needs* to see these qualities in Gladstone because of his dependence on the notion of an idealized ascetic leader, devoted only to his cause, with the capacity to win followers through the purity of his devotion and the force of his personality, even against their own needs and opinions. This is Weber's romantic fantasy of power.

First, despite his severe criticism of Bismarck for undermining the possibility of his own succession and his defense of a real parliament to take care of it, Weber praised Gladstone—though Gladstone, like Bismarck, undermined his succession. He stayed too long in office, refusing to retire yet promising to retire, sowing disunity in the cabinet and the party and preventing new leaders in his party from emerging as his successors, though of course there were leaders in other parties prepared to step in. By not confronting the other difficult issues his party faced, he undermined his own success and the very future of his party.

Second, he did not accomplish a total reversal of his followers' opposition to Home Rule, simply because a portion of the country had already been moving toward it—even Chamberlain had considered the advantages of the idea. His support in the Caucus thus depended on a broad range of interests, party conflicts, and ideological issues that simply worked in his favor rather than being created by him. That is, a convergence of factors made for his success.

Third, the outcome for his party of his 1886 government and his need to appeal to the caucuses reflected his failure to pursue both the Home Rule cause and the task of constructing an effective government with the care and thoughtfulness that was required.

Fourth, Weber interpreted British parliamentary practice in an authoritarian fashion that exaggerated Gladstone's hold over the cabinet and Parliament, viewed MPs and activists as merely blind followers, and ignored ideological and practical interests, the realities of coalition building, and the aggregative practices of party governing. Gladstone's great personal qualities are not in dispute, but Weber extrapolated from them too far, using them as an argument for an authoritarian structure of leadership and control of democratic participation. To him, parties were no more than the presupposition and excuse for someone's power; they were not participants in power.

Finally, by extolling Gladstone's accomplishment in the Caucus but disregarding the consequences of his actions and the mistakes that led him to confrontation, Weber flouts his own ethic of responsibility and reveals that his model of the leader is in conflict, even contradiction, with that ethic. The ethic of responsibility demands dutiful submission to a cause in order to realize that cause and not just defend it in the abstract. It requires a calculation of costs and acceptance of responsibility for them, and it demands the abandonment of the cause if the costs are too high or in conflict with other fundamental values. It certainly demands more than just personal sway and blind obedience. Weber's idealization of Gladstone's "Here I stand" thus shows how much more invested he is in examples of personal devotion and personal power over followers and organizations than he is in the ethic of responsibility. Having recognized the problem of succession in pure charismatic rule and criticized leaders who undermine the emergence of other leaders, in the end he defends plebiscitary leaders who, in all of his own examples, never leave successors.

Lloyd George and Prime Ministerial Government

In "Parliament and Government in a Reconstructed Germany," Weber distinguishes the plebiscitary from the parliamentary mode of selection of leaders. He of course mentions the two Napoleons, Hindenburg, and Bismarck as examples of "the Caesarist mode of leader selection," but he also observes that it exists even in democratized hereditary monarchies, though in a weaker form. "The position of the present English Prime Minister is based by *no* means on the trust of Parliament and its parties, but on that of the masses in the country and the army in the field. Parliament however accommodates itself to the situation (inwardly reluctant enough)."[197] This is a reference to David Lloyd George and the extraordinary circumstances that brought him to power in 1916 and supported his rule during the war—and for four years after—with no single party behind him. In his use of Lloyd George, however, Weber again isolates and emphasizes a single moment of one man's rule, conjuring up the image of a leader, but implying behind that picture a whole conception of leadership that is meant to be both descriptive yet normative. Weber substitutes one feature for a comprehensive picture and in the process ignores other aspects of the leader's history that are indissolubly bound up with the leader's charisma in real life. Lloyd George's charismatic or Caesarist appeal was undeniable. But it was not simply a popular swing toward him that brought him to power, for it was very much in the interest of Conservative leaders, and backbenchers as well, to displace the sitting prime minister in 1916 yet not take the helm themselves. Further, in his failure to build an enduring, reliable legacy and in his attempts to exclude parliamentary consultation and coalition building, Lloyd George undercut both his own possible successes and the process of cultivating real successors. Once again, Weber's ideal type misleads him and his audience.

Through what was essentially a wartime coup within the cabinet, Lloyd George, in December 1916, supplanted Herbert Asquith, the Liberal prime minister, and came to power with support from Conservatives and Unionist MPs in the midst of a serious leadership vacuum.[198] With an incompetent government, a war going badly, and a failing leader clinging to power, the public yearned for a new champion. Lloyd George, who called himself a "nationalist-socialist," had the press and public opinion strongly behind him and, seen as the messiah of the underprivileged, was uniquely identified with mass democracy.[199] Having triumphed at a time of crisis when the country sought a national savior, and without concern for party ties or party principles, Lloyd George tolerated no rivals, ignored political demands he did not like, and thought himself indispensable.[200] Paying no attention to parliamentary need, he installed a cabinet composed largely of businessmen without department or political party ties, and his war cabinet had a directorate of only five. Distrustful of career officials, he also created an apparatus—the cabinet secretariat—that, bypassing the civil service, permeated the entire central government and was answerable to him alone. From 1916 until the end of the war, parliamentary government effectively ceased to exist. Lloyd George rarely addressed the Commons, and parliamentary debate was infrequent during this period, with the house acquiescing in its displacement. Kenneth Morgan maintains that only the press provided political dialogue and opposition during these years, since Parliament had become essentially silent.[201] In the elections of December 1918, with the war over and the tasks of reconstruction and negotiation ahead, Lloyd George, dictating the framework of political debate, won what amounted to a plebiscite on the issue of whether he should continue as prime minister. "Never before nor even since has the personality of a leader counted for so much in an election."[202] "The election was a remarkable popular endorsement of the supra-party, almost supra-political position which he had attained since December, 1916."[203]

During the war, Lloyd George had exalted his personal rule, riding roughshod over constitutional convention, and his authority steadily increased as the war went on. His control of central decision making was complete, and he attained virtually semipresidential stature, above politics. By the end of the war, "party meant nothing to him except as an instrument for furthering his own personal policies and personal ambitions."[204] Like leaders of a bygone era, Lloyd George relied not on an automatic party majority but on the support of divergent groups and alternating majorities, and he survived because of his enemies' inability to unite against him. "But over the wider political front, his position was more vulnerable. His control of parliament . . . was unpredictable. He had assumed leadership as an individual, not as party leader."[205]

He was, in essence, a prime minister without a party or organization. In mid-1918 he tried to create a pro–Lloyd George party to perpetuate his future but did not succeed. He did have a rudimentary party machine in the so-called Coalition Liberals, but he made no effort to build it up during the war, and 1918 found him with few candidates pledged to back him. By October 1919 he was forced to restore the prewar style of cabinet, though he continued his personal direction of policy despite the irritation of his colleagues. Indeed, says Morgan, ever since 1922 England has in essence reacted against Lloyd George's personal power rather than continued it—though Margaret Thatcher's rule may have been an exception. In Morgan's view, Lloyd George's concept of the premiership required that Britain become like the United States with its strong presidency, and until 1922 he had an approximation of it—but as a result of a party vacuum after the war rather than of a permanent transformation of government. Lloyd George in fact became a captive of the dominant Conservatives in Parliament; not only did he not have a party of his own, but, despite his war chest, the Lloyd George Fund, he could not offer the inducements a leader usually does to win support. Many backbenchers resented him for personal as well as political reasons, and without a national crisis to restrain them, their resentments surfaced.

Further, even though Conservative support kept Lloyd George in office, many Liberals were given positions under his coalitions; the Conservatives were thus denied a share of offices that reflected their numbers. Finally, without a Parliament, a party machine, or a reliable public, Morgan suggests, the party professionals came into their own again, and Lloyd George's achievement in the realm of governance proved transient.[206]

Lloyd George had been a natural leader in an emergency but faced growing opposition when he tried to govern in peacetime as if the wartime crisis still existed.[207] He tried to preserve the conventions of the war years, slapping down ministers who were out of line, muffling the Parliament, and bypassing the cabinet by means of secret committees. Indeed, Morgan maintains, his interference in department affairs induced in ministers "the unspoken fear of Caesarism, of dictatorship." Ultimately, Lloyd George's deliberate flouting of Parliament and his imperious methods made a strong premiership like his hard to maintain on a permanent basis. His ascendency was ended when the Conservatives reasserted the autonomy of party. Thus the problems of his rule actually insured that Parliament and party would continue to serve as checks on central government.[208] This is not a task that Weber would have hoped the parliament he was proposing would provide.

It is this model of leadership that Weber apparently endorses. In the case of Lloyd George, as with Gladstone, Weber isolates a single aspect of leadership yet claims it characteristic and decisive for leaders in general. The extraordinary popular appeal and support that Lloyd George commanded is beyond dispute. But even though there were other leaders who were pleased to supplant him after 1922, Lloyd George, like Gladstone and Bismarck, did not provide for his own succession, nor did he allow any independent talents to develop around him. His type of rule may be effective in wartime, but it cannot be a model for peace, and it leaves behind no enduring institutions. Further, despite what Morgan— and Weber—believe, even a strong presidency like the one in the United States depends on the ability of the president to forge coalitions and build consensus: hence lead, not just command and rule.[209] The Lloyd George example, like that of Gladstone, thus exposes the limitations of Weber's views, not their strengths.

In both cases, therefore, Weber's use of the undeniable charismatic appeal and political success of leaders he considers paradigmatic oversimplifies the political realities such leaders confronted, ignores the variety of reasons for their successes, and discounts consequences of their actions that, in German leaders, Weber would have staunchly criticized. Weber used these examples to support his critique of more democratic approaches to governing and leadership, arguing that even in Britain democratic controls were relatively limited. When we confront the way he uses such leaders as examples and models, with a fuller historical investigation of their action, we can see the extent to which Weber's interpretations reflect an idealized view of commanding leadership and political character, based on assumptions and convictions quite independent of, and even contradictory to, historical realities.

CONCLUSION: THE EMPOWERED POLITICIAN AS HERO AND SAINT

Weber's conviction about the necessity of creating a specific kind of ascetic empowered self for the tasks of German politics led him into two serious errors. First, as we have seen, he misinterpreted and misappropriated the model of British prime ministerial politics. Weber thought of Gladstone, an unquestionably "called" politician, as the ideal type of the empowered modern leader, constrained only by his own charisma, inspired only by his political cause, consulting no others, and dominating a fully tamed Parliament. In this purist vision of politics, purged of the play of social classes and diverse interests, of political culture, other personalities, and the motivations, ideologies, and alliances of many constituencies—which in fact necessitated careful coalition building—Weber attributed to Gladstone a more authoritarian power and to Parliament a more submissive role than is justified by the historical record. He ignored the interests that led MPs and other followers to support a particular leader over others, apart from personal devotion. He imagined a politics inspired only by the purity of higher causes, where lone champions struggle against one another at the head of armies of followers to impose visions of national greatness. He thus ignored many aspects of the social foundation and complexities of British interest politics, isolating the leader's capacity to win a constituency through the force of personality and substituting a single compelling vision of leadership for a comprehensive analysis of politics. He did this precisely because of his dependence on the notion of an ideal, ascetic leader, which he projected onto Britain.

Second, in his proposals for the transition of Germany from authoritarianism to democracy, Weber focused again on leaders, failing to reckon with the social and cultural bases of the existing order, overlooking the hostility, conservatism, and political bias of institutions like the army, judiciary, and bureaucracy, and ignoring the problem of building mass support for parliamentarism—some of the many factors that in fact contributed to the eventual collapse of Weimar.[210] Yet Weber's interpretation of German political development and his project for German democratization at the end of World War I were test cases for the limits of his political and historical sociology. Indeed, Weber's inadequate attention to the social foundations of modern political order and the significance of mass political culture underlies his excessive reliance on the notion of domination as the principal tool for thinking about politics and social order, an overreliance that in turn limits the value of his practical proposals. This one-sidedness in his use of Britain and in his program for Germany reveals the excessive influence on his thought of the German problem of leadership and the limits imposed by his commitment to the ideology of calling, and underscores the need to pay more attention to the social bases of modern politics and the interaction of politics, culture, and institutions.

Weber made the politician with a calling a man above his followers and made politics a form of redemption in the service of meaning and worldly strength for the called man and the called following. The *Berufspolitiker*, thus, has to be a person who can survive without conventional absolutes or roots in a noble class. He must be a man who lives only for his guiding idea and cause, not for others or for serving *them*. He is utterly alone and is able to persist by his capacity to exercise domination through the sheer force of his personality. In Weber's view, only total submission to the cause through adherence to vocation can give him the requisite force of character to lead and make judgments as he must, since such a man and such a conviction can never depend on others. Indeed, unlike the Puritans, who—despite the fact that their path to salvation was personal and lonely—were together in a community and church that shared one faith in God, Weber's politician has little support from the shared faith of a community of equals. He has no one to lean on except his own "god," for his followers can provide him no personal strength, and his equals are his competitors. This is a heroic, solitary strength without relief.

In reality, once Weber's politician gives himself over to the calling and builds an identity, personality, and inner power on the conquest of the creaturely weakness that threatens to cripple all human beings, he becomes a prisoner of his ascetic devotion to a cause. The only possibility for him to be accepted and acknowledged by others is as a hero, a champion, a defender of a cause who will lead the army of his followers to the promised land. If he goes unacclaimed and is left to stand alone with his devotion, his calling is impotent, for although he serves only his cause, he cannot move without the army of his followers and their backing. He will never permit himself to be accepted *except* for the purity and intensity of his drive, and thus he must make his followers *his* prisoners, devotees who may make no claim on him and whose only destiny and own cause is to follow.

In a discussion between Weber and General Ludendorff at the end of World War I, in which Weber fruitlessly—and absurdly—tried to persuade Ludendorff to give himself up to the Allies to save the honor of the nation and the German officer corps, the following exchange about democracy took place, as reported by Weber's wife.

> WEBER: In a democracy the people elects the leader that it has confidence in. Then the elected one says: Now shut up and obey. The people and parties may not lecture him [*hineinreden*] further.
>
> LUDENDORFF: I could like such a democracy.
>
> WEBER: Afterwards the people can judge. Has the leader made errors? To the gallows with him![211]

The possible reciprocal relations between politicians and followers are here forbidden: in the guise of refusing to compromise himself, sell himself, or pander to the needs of others in order to be chosen, Weber's politician in fact knows how to draw no line and make no real compromise with others; he knows only the refusal to budge supported by the calling. In exchange for his followers' obedience, the politician will accept complete responsibility, but he will not countenance demands. One may reject him totally or condemn him to death, but one may never take exception to his policies while he is working. Only his own calculation of costs may dissuade him from pursuing his goal, never the needs of others as such. For the man who sees no possibility of a political life except under these circumstances, to go unacclaimed is to be excluded totally from politics—as Weber himself discovered in his own brief political efforts. This is the risk that Weber and his politician with a calling must take: the ascetic vocation gives the strength of iron, but the consequences for the politician and his followers must be total subjection, total isolation, or domination.

Weber's version of the ascetic political vocation is not simply a practical guide to the qualifications for politics that turns out to be impractical. It is the foundation for a new heroism and a new sainthood, an ascetic political soldiery marching into the political world to do the "cause's work" responsibly and with inner power. Indeed, Weber argues that a truly called politician must actually embrace both an "ethic of responsibility" and an "ethic of conviction," thus showing the complementary nature of the two ethics but also showing that only the calling can actually hold the two together. "Insofar as this is true, an ethic of conviction and an ethic of responsibility are not absolute opposites but rather supplements that only together constitute the true man, he who *can* have the 'calling for politics.' " Weber ends up taking his archetypical statement of "manly" political faith from yet another religious reformer: " 'I can do no other, here I stand.' "[212] "It is completely true, and all historical experience confirms it, that one would not have reached the possible if one had not again and again grasped at the impossible in the world. But he who can do this must be a leader, and not only that, but also—in a very plain sense of the word—a hero."[213] Weber's politician can empower himself and make his life and action meaningful to himself and attractive to his followers, but only by finding the kind of cause—and the right relationship to that cause—that can justify his solitary commitment, strengthen him, and motivate his sacrifice of self to create "personality." The battle against the self and the world discovered and inaugurated by the Puritans here finds its political form.

Precisely because Weber believes that—apart from bureaucratization—systematic social and political innovations are possible only by the action of called individuals acting on behalf of a higher cause, his work discovers and acknowledges no other sources of innovation, autonomy, and action, collective or otherwise. Collectivities cannot be empowered except as the tools of charismatic domination, which is purely personal and ascetic. This view makes it impossible within Weber's scheme to envision innovative social and political action originating in social movements, mass efforts, or associations, or the public creation of purposes and goals. Further, to Weber, there can be no individual strength or inner power except in some variant of an ascetic calling. "Where all reaching beyond this world is lacking, so must all independent weight against the world be wanting."[214] To be sure, strong and empowered selves appeared before the Reformation and elsewhere than in the West, but Weber interprets them in terms of the structure of self he found in the Puritans, because he understands his model as the *essence* of the empowered self. By severely restricting the conception of the kind of person capable of acting in innovative and commanding ways, and restricting the understanding of what demands and processes of self-fashioning can *make* the self such an actor, Weber makes it impossible to imagine an autonomous and strong self not structured identically to the ascetic Puritan's.

Despite Weber's disdain for those who would defend absolutes in practical life, his leader with a calling is the empowered ascetic saint reborn in politics. This implicit need to find renewed power and meaning in the worship of "higher" values and to ground personhood in service, devotion, and calling was a public and private disease whose real and unfortunate consequences were not fully seen until thirteen years after Weber's death.

7   The Nation, the Devil, and Power: *Doctor Faustus*

The artist usually sets out—or used to—to point a moral and
adorn a tale. The tale, however, points the other way, as a
rule. Two blankly opposing morals, the artist's and the tale's.
Never trust the artist. Trust the tale.

     D. H. Lawrence, *Studies in Classic American Literature*

Weber did not live to see the advent of National Socialism, nor did he
therefore have an opportunity to rethink his own, and Germany's, "foundations" in the light of so extreme a development. His diagnoses of
culture and politics and his prescriptions for renewal thus remain within
a circle of concepts and themes that are firmly situated in the late nineteenth and early twentieth centuries, that never confronted the most
shattering of twentieth-century, and of German, experiences. Thomas
Mann, in contrast, did go through that experience; yet he, too, generally
retained and revived concepts worked out long ago, despite the challenge
posed to the German tradition by the rise of Hitler.

Doctor Faustus is Mann's interpretation and evaluation of German
history and culture from 1885 to 1945, yet when he came to write it in
1943, he used as its basis a sketch from a notebook of his from 1905.
This indicates two things. First, conceptions of calling and the artist
derived from that earlier period are the foundation of the "personal"
dimension of the novel, thus bringing Mann's work full circle, unifying
its late political themes with its early individual ones. Second, Mann
needed the National Socialist "outcome" of the post–World War I period
in order to make the novel something more than just the struggle of an
artist against decadence and sterility—which is what it would have been
if written in 1905—just as he says he needed World War I and its outcome
in order to finish *The Magic Mountain* and resolve the antitheses of that
novel.[1] Cultural crisis and the taste for fascism thus provide the "spiritual"
dimension of the Faust story.

Doctor Faustus tells the story of Adrian Leverkühn, an isolated, reserved composer whose creative talents are inhibited by his capacity to "see through" everything, including the musical tradition, which he thinks has exhausted the possibilities of tonality as a unifying device. To overcome the limitations on the musical level, he "invents" twelve-tone composition (based on Adorno's interpretation of Schoenberg) as a new "law" for music. Yet this alone is not enough. Though he is given to parody and mockery of everything that society holds dear, what he seeks is genuine expression beyond mere parody, which can come, he thinks, only from a renewal of music's ties to a "community" and from a personal sense of being "graced" and having a true calling. Since Adrian feels intense personal worthlessness and estrangement from "God," his nonmusical needs lead him to a redemptive "pact" with the devil to realize these goals, free him from inhibition, and make possible his "breakthrough." To these ends, he contracts syphilis as the expression and confirmation of his pact. In allegorical fashion, Mann links the destiny of Adrian Leverkühn to, on the one hand, the developments of Germany in the direction of National Socialism and, on the other, the life and fate of Nietzsche. But since the work is also a Faust story, based on the sixteenth-century version of the legend, *Doctor Faustus* leads its hero to a final confession of "sins" before he plunges into syphilis-induced insanity. As Hans Rudolf Vaget suggests: "Whereas Goethe discarded the theological framework of the Faust myth almost completely, Mann and Adorno, in the light of recent history, saw fit to revalidate the original, strongly hortatory, version, in which a pact with demonic powers is tantamount to eternal damnation."[2]

In truth, *Doctor Faustus* is Mann's ultimate portrayal of the defeat of German traditions of self-empowerment and self-shaping, coupled with his own prescription of a new ideal for service as a guide for the perplexed. The inability to surmount the crisis of German *Bildung* in *The Magic Mountain*—either through a new self-cultivation or through renewal in war—is the source of the striving for its active mastery in *Doctor Faustus*, a novel filled, at the same time, with what are interpreted as the "mistaken" choices of its hero. Once again Mann seeks, but now more urgently, to make art, and Germany as well, serve the higher ideal of *Humanität*, which he had earlier hoped would be born through war. Indeed, he has Leverkühn, at the end of his life, renounce the pact and the life he has lived on behalf of precisely such a concern for humankind's future. Mann hopes to show through Leverkühn what the attempt to escape powerlessness by service of antisocial ideals in a calling breeds when divorced from the ideal of humanity, and what it did breed, he believes, in Nietzsche and Germany. In this way Mann criticizes Nietzsche, forcing him symbolically to confess the need to serve humanity—an idea that would have nauseated him. While he was writing *Doctor Faustus*, Mann saw the work as his *Parsifal*, a work of the end; but as we will see, it is his *Parsifal* in a different sense from the one he intended.[3]

Doctor Faustus completes a cycle of development that began with Mann's self-identification with the nation in the *Reflections* and proceeded through his portrayal of a passive experience of the exhaustion of the nation's culture in *The Magic Mountain*. The cycle ends in his portrait of a failed attempt at the active mastery of that exhaustion. *Doctor Faustus* symbolically sets Settembrini against Naphta once again, "bourgeois humanism" and the tradition of *Bildung* against devilishness and reaction. Settembrini is now incarnated in the narrator, Serenus Zeitblom—more worried, more helpless, and more appealing—with Naphta reemerging as the devil, more ironic and oddly more sympathetic. Their conflict is mediated this time by the struggle over the soul of Adrian Leverkühn, rather than over Hans Castorp.[4] Mann engages in another critique of the reactionary self of the *Reflections*, objectified in both artist and nation, and here completes his *Entromantisierung*. At the same time, he sharpens the problem of lost direction set out in *The Magic Mountain*, now that its "real" outcome in National Socialism is known, yet also softens it through the bond between Zeitblom and Leverkühn, two halves of a divided nation and of himself.[5] It is no accident that the narrator represents the tradition of an increasingly displaced humanistic *Bildung*, telling of the advent of the "new" antibourgeois world that will be that tradition's most bitter enemy—and of its own powerlessness fully to comprehend, resist, or master that world. Mann uses music—which "among all arts has the greatest possibility of becoming devil's art"[6]—as the vehicle for the confrontation of an artist, crippled socially and inhibited artistically, with the apparent exhaustion of a tradition and culture, an exhaustion that radicalizes his search for a solution to his powerlessness, estrangement, and failed creativity.[7]

Doctor Faustus is also an allegory of the spiritual development of the nation that gave birth to Nazism, told as the story of a composer and based on an interpretation of Nietzsche.[8] "If Faust is to be the representative of the German soul, he would have to be musical; for abstract and mystical, that means, musical, is the relation of the German to the world—the relation of a professor tinged with demonism, awkward and thereby certain through his arrogant consciousness that he is superior to the world in 'depth.' "[9] The novel portrays Mann's final understanding of the self and its link to the social and political world in a culture now no longer in crisis, but exploding. It shows the confrontation of a troubled man and troubled nation with the artistic, cultural, and political materials of their time, in a search for identity, power, and redemption in which both man and nation turn to a Faustian devil's pact to escape their dilemma. Indeed, Mann always thought that the "difference between an artist's existence and service of the devil" was "not so great";[10] now, though, the need for service is projected onto the nation as well, as Weber had projected it long before.

In World War I, the nation seemed to Mann to be in the same impasse as the artist, cut off from acceptance by the powers of "life." Thus the true artist became the representative of the embattled nation. But the appearance of National Socialism forced Mann to deal with the demonic side of the nation, of art, and of himself. Although he had fused his identity with the nation's in the period of the *Reflections*—incorporating its contradictions as his own and seeing his difficulties reflected in those of the nation—the later "madness" of Germany required that he rethink that fusion, indeed, that he "take back" the thoroughness of that identification. As the nation's evil part "split off," rejecting the demands of its good part in order to "break through" to a fantasy (and real) conquest of power, so too was there a splitting in Mann's relation to Germany and in his own identity. Mann separated parts of the nation from himself and parts of himself from himself, yet saw that he was still present in each part. The conflict of opposites was already to be found in *The Magic Mountain*, where they could coexist yet not be reconciled, only contemplated, and where they required the outbreak of war as an escape. But in *Doctor Faustus*, the opposites are more radically divided and are themselves at war, and the easy identification with the nation that was still possible in *The Magic Mountain* is so no longer. Thus, although *Doctor Faustus* once again presents the identity of the artist as inseparable from the nation and its times, an identity based on full identification between them is now problematic, if not disastrous.

The true artist—the "good" Germany—left his homeland and eventually wrote, "Where I am, there is Germany."[11] Only because he had earlier "spiritualized" Germany and "nationalized" himself was such an exaggerated identification possible. But Mann's view changed, and he came to believe that "there are not two Germanies, an evil and a good, but only one, whose best turned into evil through devilish craft. The evil Germany is the good gone astray. . . . That is why it is also so impossible for a German-born spirit to renounce the evil, guilt-laden Germany."[12] His exile forced Mann to reexamine the nation and reinterpret allegorically the roots and meaning of what now seemed Germany's devil's pact and misguided calling. In *Doctor Faustus*, he turned his back on isolated and nationalistic Germany. Initially he replaced it with a "higher," purer conception of the nation, of which he made himself the representative and embodiment. But ultimately, in the same way that he had supplanted the *Bürgertum* as his ultimate ideal, first with the aristocracy and then with the nation, now he supplanted his identification with Germany with another "higher" ideal: Humanity, "service to mankind."[13]

THE ARTIST'S CALLING AND THE PROBLEM OF FASCISM

In becoming a thinker or an artist, one "degenerates" less
than the social world from which one is emancipating
oneself believes, and less than one believes oneself; one does
not cease to be what one's fathers were, but one is rather
just the very same thing once again in another, freer, more
spiritualized, symbolically represented form.

Thomas Mann, "Lübeck as a Spiritual Way of Life"

In his notes from 1905, drafted in a period when he was obsessed with fears of decadence, weakness, and his own artistic sterility, Mann describes a Dr. Faust who, through "intoxication, stimulation, inspiration" derived from the devil, is enabled "to create brilliant wonderful works in enraptured enthusiasm."[14] By 1943, the narcissistic longing to create great works is joined to another theme.

> It concerns the desire to escape from the bourgeois [*Bürgerliche*], moderate, classical, Apollonian, sober, diligent, and faithful into the drunken-released, bold, Dionysian, brilliant, beyond bourgeois [*Über-Bürgerliche*], indeed, superhuman [*Übermenschliche*]—above all subjective, as experience and drunken heightening of the self.
> . . . The explosion of the bourgeois, which takes place in a pathologically infected and disintegrating fashion, at the same time political. Intellectual-spiritual fascism. . . . Fascism as a stepping out of the bourgeois form of life, mediated by the devil, which leads through drunken, highly intensified adventures of self-esteem and supergreatness to mental collapse and to spiritual death, soon also to physical. The extravagant existence, alternating between very painful depression, illness of every kind, and highest feeling of health, power, and triumph, feverishly elevated and accelerated productivity.[15]

What originated in Mann's plans as the isolated struggle of an artist for inspiration, creativity, and greatness has become a metaphor for a whole society's pursuit of "heightening of the self" and feelings of "health, power, and triumph," now steeped in both Nietzschean conceptions and Nietzsche's own experience of sexual infection, self-elevation, and madness—a move of Mann's from the self-involved wish to prove himself in fantasies of achievement to an analysis of the longing for escape from social norms and for a new power. "Main idea of purchased inspiration, which, in intoxication [*Rausch*], is carried away beyond it."[16] Yet there is a question whether the novel really carries through this presentation of fascism in Nietzschean terms, or whether its link to Nietzsche is more complex and even partly concealed from the narrator and the author.[17]

In *Doctor Faustus*, Mann fuses the language of calling, drawn from his conception of the artist and centered exclusively on individuals, with the language of Nietzsche, especially from the *Birth of Tragedy*, now used as the "spiritual" language of fascism. While *The Magic Mountain* had provided a vision of unifying the Apollonian and Dionysian, in the world of *Doctor Faustus* these "opposites" have now separated and become deadly enemies. In part, Mann interprets Germany's waywardness in departing from its earlier cultural promise in the same language he used to understand the waywardness of the artist in departing from the more balanced view of art enunciated in *Tonio Kröger*: Germany has shunned that middle path which "its" calling, properly understood, would have laid out for it, and that is at the root of its "devil's pact" with Hitler. But he also interprets the nation's waywardness in terms of breaking out from bourgeois, Apollonian balance into Dionysian flights of power, thus inverting *Death in Venice*, where the unwise repression of the Dionysian overcomes the weak and superficially Apollonian. The situation is no longer, as for Aschenbach, one in which staying too strictly within bourgeois bounds is dangerous for life and art; the problem, rather, is Dionysian intoxication, which takes the bourgeois world and its exhaustion as obstacles to strength and vitality.[18]

Thus we have something other than an examination of the limits of a vision of "legitimate" art tied to a dying and destructive world, as in *Death in Venice*; instead we are dealing with the link between a certain type of avant-garde artist—a type Mann had earlier bitterly criticized— and the German mentality that led to fascism. Leverkühn, of course, is no fascist, nor is he in any way political. Indeed, the narrator tells us that the Nazi regime banned his works, while Jews welcomed them. The issue is what Mann takes to be the spiritual illness and state of mind at work in different circles of society, all of which are inclined to speculate on the overcoming of the old society by a new restrictive order. Thus two stories are being told here, one about an artist and one about a nation, with two questions to ask about them: Are the parallel and the allegory between them successful? And is the interpretation of the development of either artist or nation coherent?

We have seen that in the *Reflections* and *The Magic Mountain* Mann, building on what he had achieved in *Tonio Kröger*, self-consciously carved out for himself a "middle position [*die Mitte*] between the demonic and the bourgeois [*Bürgerlichkeit*]," trying to achieve "the union of the demonic with the official, of loneliness and adventurousness with social representativeness."[19] Tonio Kröger represented the middle ground and union; Gustav Aschenbach and Adrian Leverkühn, however, each represent a different pole of the opposition, living out the consequences of their inability to find the middle way, whether of mediation or of synthesis. Although both Aschenbach and Leverkühn are on the verge of artistic sterility, Aschenbach's problems do not directly refer to the limitations of art itself or to the crisis of the outside world, while Leverkühn's are clearly the product of his own nature, his art, and the nature of the times. Still, *Death in Venice* describes Aschenbach as a hero for a time of exhaustion, just as Mann later describes Leverkühn as "a hero of our times."[20] Leverkühn's situation is more severe, for the exhaustion of art—and not just of the individual artist—puts a much greater burden on the artist and requires a more radical solution. Whereas Aschenbach rejected all illegitimacy and bohemianism in his calling and erred in the direction of self-legitimation and identification with the bourgeois, Leverkühn "errs" in the opposite direction of transgression, totally rejecting bourgeois cultural values and the public. At the same time, the personal inhibitions of the artist that, in Mann's earlier work, had equipped him for art but destroyed him for life, now also cripple his capacity for artistic creation in a culture where traditional forms seem exhausted and total subjectivity reigns. This combination of conditions will thwart inspiration and creativity unless an inner empowerment of the artist can be derived from some new source, to restrain inhibition and gain power over art. Estrangement cannot be a source of creativity by itself; it must be tied to an active ideal. The crucial thing is that, as in all of Mann's previous work, the artist *must* "represent" something to gain that power.

It is not that Mann is defending the "rightness" of bourgeois society when he portrays fascism as an escape from it, though certainly Zeitblom is its old-fashioned representative—a teacher of ancient languages, devotee of reason, "a son of the muses in the academic sense of the word, a descendent of the German humanists."[21] What Mann is defending—despite his parody of Zeitblom and Settembrini and his critique of their positions—is the ideal of Humanity that, once an integral part and pillar of the tradition of *Bildung*, had become displaced by reactionary and vitalistic elements.[22] From the 1920s on, Mann tries to revive the ideal of Humanity as an alternative to the crisis and division of Germany and to its loss of stable ideals of service—humanism as an attempted spiritual synthesis and transcendence of bourgeois society and its opponents on the right and left.[23] This is why the "breakthrough" to the "superman" (*Übermensch*), represented by Germany and Leverkühn, to the power and feeling of power they both experience through the pact is a Nietzschean solution that Mann must reject. That Mann rejects it is no surprise, for many reasons. What is surprising is his alternative, for, like Weber, Mann remythologizes the necessity of service and tries to give a calling to Germany. He ties both to an ideal of humanity attacked by the culture—even by Weber—and orients service not, as Weber did, toward battle between gods or God and devil, but toward the transcendence of oppositions, which he believes are represented by the "social" and the "human." Despite the undeniable "humaneness" of this position vis-à-vis fascist alternatives, it preserves the subjection of individuals to meaning and self-empowerment derived solely through self-legitimating service of a higher ideal, and any attempt to break out of what are essentially Christian patterns of self-understanding in order to ground meaning in something other than ascetic ideals is repudiated.

THE DEVIL AND THE UNTRUTH THAT ENHANCES POWER

Mann explicitly makes the object of Germany's and Adrian's pact with the devil the desire for power, the longing for acceptance, and the feelings of triumph and self-veneration that come from having them. But the new element that Mann brings to the Faust story is the notion of the devil's pact as service in a calling.[24]

Art, Inhibition, and the Times

Adrian Leverkühn bears a similarity to Mann's other artists, particularly Tonio Kröger, both as a person and in relation to his art.[25] In his story of the novel's origins, Mann lists the personal qualities of his exceptionally brilliant, easily bored hero: "his coldness, his distance from life, his lack of 'soul' . . . his 'inhumanity,' his 'despairing heart.' "[26] Zeitblom, the novel's narrator, adds to these "the inhibitions of mockery, of arrogance, of intellectual shame" (203). Finally, Adrian himself adds that he is "shy before the world" (*weltscheu*)—the same word Mann uses to describe Germany's relation to the world in the twentieth century—without "warmth . . . sympathy . . . love." He is estranged from bourgeois society, like other of Mann's artists, longing to make great art as they did, searching for fame and glory as a sign of social acceptance and a vehicle of self-acceptance. But unlike those others, Adrian also resembles the "bohemian" and expressionist artists that are scorned in *Tonio Kröger*—and in the *Reflections*—precisely for their negativism and lack of love of bourgeois society, for Adrian is hostile to what art has become in that society, and his hope for the future is for a revolutionized world.[27] Adrian himself doubts his fitness for art precisely on these grounds, for an artist, he says—unlike him—must be "a lover and beloved of the world" (177). Indeed, his self-hatred makes it difficult for him to find a calling of any kind.[28] "You will not believe that I consider myself too good for any calling. To the contrary: I have pity for anything I make my own." He has even studied theology, he says, in an effort "to humble myself, to submit myself, to discipline myself, to punish the conceit of my coldness, in short, out of *contritio*" (175). As Mann remarked elsewhere on the meaning of the German's estrangement: "In his shyness before the world [*Weltscheu*] was always so much longing for the world; at the bottom of the loneliness which made him wicked, is—who did not know this—the wish to love, the wish to be loved."[29]

Although Mann claimed that art is "a vampire, when we stand in its service,"[30] his artist-hero Tonio Kröger was able to reconcile himself to his coldness, his loneliness, and the depletion of his life through art, precisely by selfless service of art (an art for which he made the grandiose claim that *his* art was the *true* art) coupled with love for the society that treated him as an outcast. But Adrian's sense of his own inhumanity, negativity, and worthlessness, his feeling that everything he prizes is worthless, his hostility to bourgeois society, his mockery of everything serious in the art and society of the time, and his rejection of all romantic conceptions of the artist to the point of disliking even the words "art" and "artist" make it impossible for him to serve art or love society as Tonio, Mann's model of the "good" artist, did. His ambitions are similar to Tonio's, but the possibility of realizing them is now greatly diminished.

The service of art in a calling modeled on bourgeois life, linked to an enhanced view of the self as "representative" of something "higher," was the principal solution Mann had defended for the artist, supplemented by identification either with bourgeois life or with the nation. But in *Doctor Faustus*, this kind of "positive" calling can no longer rescue the artist by itself, no longer empower him or redeem him from self-doubt and low self-worth by giving life meaning in the ascetic service of a higher goal. Nor are bourgeois society or the nation and the times credible to him any longer as goals or communities of identification. Instead Adrian fantasizes a community of the future as his true social world, one he will love and that will love him, a *Volk* and *Gemeinschaft* to come, rather than committing himself to Mann's—and Zeitblom's— uncomforting and abstract ideal of humanity. Nor, in fact, is art by itself, in its present condition, able to act any longer as an ultimate ideal for a "negative" artist like Adrian, an ideal that could be elevated so that service of it might generate self-acceptance and inner empowerment, reconciling him to his estrangement and inhumanity by justifying him through his fitness for art's service.

Tonio had obtained strength through an ideological defense of the "fit" between the needs of art and his own unique qualities, but for Adrian this is much more difficult to achieve—at least until that point where he makes both art and himself tools of the devil. It is his former music teacher, Wendell Kretzschmar, who begins to give him a language for redeeming his sense of his monstrosity and who provides a preliminary defense of the value of his qualities for the larger purposes of art. Art today needs a person exactly like Adrian, Kretzschmar maintains—cold, easily bored, unsatisfied with accepted pieties and practices—a person with "especially the repulsive personal characteristics [Adrian] credited himself with," which will "raise into a calling [*Berufung*] the talent bound up with them." Indeed, in Kretzschmar's view, what seem Adrian's purely personal qualities are actually "supraindividual" and show Adrian's fitness as the tool of art and the times: they express "a collective feeling for the historical consumption and exhaustion of the means of art, the bore-dom with them, and the striving for new ways" (180–81).

Yet despite the reasoned support with which Kretzschmar attempts to redeem for the needs of art what Adrian views as his inhuman qualities, Adrian can draw from reason little of the comfort he needs. A man consumed with his own negativity (and the accompanying guilt), as Adrian is, and who seeks redemption through a calling in art is driven to find a more potent, suprahuman justification for himself. The positing of his own values and a field in which to realize his own qualities are not enough: he will need—as all of Mann's heroes, Mann himself, and also Weber need—some Other as ideal and authority, to stand behind, and especially above, what he does and, as it were, authorize it. What drives Adrian to embrace an "objectification" of his negativity in the devil is what always stands behind the search for a calling: the need for a sanctified external source of self-legitimation and empowerment, a "wit-ness" whose "tool" he may become. He will, of course, seek the spirit of negativity itself, the inverse of the positive world he rejects, and within the values of this dualism—inherited from German and Christian culture—he will be consoled and empowered; but he will also be trapped.

The novel gives the external reasons for Adrian's pact with the devil as the general spiritual condition of the times and the situation of art and culture. The central issue is posed by Adrian and others in terms of the burden of freedom, and Mann described it, in language borrowed from Naphta in *The Magic Mountain*, a few years later thus:

> Almost from the moment of its birth freedom was tired of itself and was on the lookout for new obligation [*Bindung*], new limitation, something commanding absolute veneration, a centripetal system of ideas and morals. It turned out that man was unable to live in the individualistic diaspora ... for [freedom] is an alarming problem—alarming to such a degree that there is a real question whether man, for the sake of his intellectual and metaphysical security, would not rather have terror than freedom. There is much said about this in *The Magic Mountain* and also in the novel of my old age, *Doctor Faustus*.[31]

Here Mann echoes observations and concerns of his contemporaries.[32] Indeed, he echoes himself in the *Reflections*, where he was the spokesman, rather than the critic, of these attacks on freedom. There he argues, as Aschenbach had argued, that "the deepest longing of the world ... is not at all directed at wider anarchization through a concept of freedom but at new obligations [*Bindungen*]," at "the eager desire for an 'inner tyranny,' for an 'absolute table of values,' for constraint, for the moral return of certainty," and for "*culture*, dignity, for self-control [*Haltung*], for form."[33] The shift from *The Magic Mountain* to *Doctor Faustus* is thus a shift from a world that gives no answers but has time to play with possibilities, to a world desperate for answers with no sense that there is time to look, a world that interprets itself, however, not in terms of loss or bankruptcy of alternatives, social forms, and ultimate ideals, but in terms of the difficulty of choice. This world, therefore, acts as if having choice were the problem, as if it possessed too much freedom rather than too few possibilities and too little strength to endure the consequent uncertainty. In the midst of decadence, it is freedom that seems to it the cause of its disempowerment.

Freedom became a "spiritual" problem for Germany as the consequence of many converging circumstances, cultural, social, and political— from the influence of Protestant spirituality, to the undermining of traditional social roles and social ties by capitalism and social transformation, to the social and political disarray of Wilhelmian and Weimar

Germany.[34] Zeitblom stresses the cultural break with the past brought by the collapse of the authoritarian state at the end of World War I:

> The feeling that an epoch was ending, which included not only the nineteenth century, but reached back to the end of the Middle Ages, to the exploding of scholastic bonds, to the emancipation of the individual, the birth of freedom, an epoch that I quite sincerely had regarded as my wider spiritual home, in brief, the epoch of bourgeois humanism;—the feeling, I say, that its hour had struck, a mutation of life was taking place, the world wanted to enter into a still nameless constellation,—this persistent feeling, listened to most attentively, was indeed not first the product of the end of the war, it was already the product of its outbreak, fourteen years after the turn of the century. (468–69)

In the first third of the century, the problem of freedom was regularly posed by artists in terms of the new burdensome "autonomy" of art, the consequence of a traditional society undergoing the "disenchantment" of culture. Kandinsky described the cultural consequences this way: "When religion, science and morality are shaken, the last two by the strong hand of Nietzsche, and when the outer supports threaten to fall, man turns his gaze from externals in on himself. Literature, music and art are the first and most sensitive spheres in which this spiritual revolution makes itself felt."[35] Indeed, as Weber observes, with the development of modern intellectualism and the undermining of traditional religious paths to meaning and redemption "art constitutes itself now as a cosmos of ever more consciously grasped independent values of its own." In fact, it takes over the function of "innerworldly *salvation*: from the everyday and above all also from the increasing pressure of theoretical and practical rationalism."[36]

Late-nineteenth and early-twentieth-century avant-garde art turned away from art's traditional nineteenth-century bourgeois audience in the wish to purify itself of the pressures and demands of the marketplace, either to create an "art for art's sake," utterly separated from social pressure, or to oppose the existing social and cultural order and create a new one where art would have a true home.[37] The lack of adequate "integration" of innovative high culture into bourgeois society, brought about by rapid industrialization, class conflict, and social fragmentation, detached art even further from a clear role in society. As Mann put it in the *Reflections*, the "bourgeoisification of art," completed at the time of the Renaissance, "means its individualization and release from a secure association of culture and belief."[38] To Weber, in these conditions "the service of cultural goods . . . , the more it has been made into a holy task, a 'calling,' seems to become an even more meaningless scurrying in the service of worthless ends that are, moreover, in themselves everywhere contradictory and mutually antagonistic."[39] In a dialogue between members of a youth movement group in *Doctor Faustus*, one student describes the immediate consequence of this loss of the old "pre-existent [*vorgefundene*] universal orderings": "The look out for traces of new strengths for order, produced by disintegration, is general" (166–67). This sense of the loss of unity and fragmentation of culture produced that quest for reintegration so well known in works like Lukács's *Theory of the Novel* and in artists as different as T. S. Eliot and Paul Klee. As Klee put it in 1924—anticipating Leverkühn, though from the left: "We must go on seeking . . . ! We have parts, but not the whole! We still lack the ultimate power, for: the people are not with us. But we seek a people."[40]

Adrian criticizes the situation of modern culture in terms similar to Weber's. Indeed, to him the problem of culture goes back to the original "fall" that disenchanted the world and elevated culture "into a substitute for religion" (428). Culture is no longer the expression of a coherent community's self-understanding; now it is a sphere of "freedom," meaning that it has evolved into an autonomous realm, obeying its own laws and relying on no external guidance for direction, promising its "gifts" of redemption to those who devote themselves to it. But culture's rationalization, to use Weber's terms, threatens meaninglessness and permanent isolation. "Naiveté, unconsciousness, taken-for-grantedness seem to me the first criterion of the constitution" of culture, but the present stage is only one of "good manners [*Gesittung*]. . . . Technique and comfort—with that one *talks* about culture, but one does not have it" (83). Indeed, to Adrian, art had once been a device for the highest expression of the spiritual, had once been part of a larger religious unity that gave it meaning. But now the "separation of art from the liturgical whole, its liberation and elevation into the lonely-personal and culturally self-purposive" have burdened art unduly (82).[41]

Adrian's response to the dilemma of culture is a complex fantasy of redemption, expressed in the language of service. The first dimension of the fantasy is embodied in his desire, like Klee's, for an imagined community of the future to redeem art (and thus himself) from its isolation and lack of validation: he proposes that art abandon its present autonomy and grandiosity and return to "a more modest, happier [role] in the service of a higher union," which would eliminate the "idea of culture" (82). Though much of the avant-garde imagined the salvation of self and society through art, Adrian sees art not only as a "means of salvation" but also in need of salvation itself, from its "somber isolation" within culture.

Art "will soon be fully alone, alone to die out," unless "it finds the way to the 'Volk,' that is, to say it unromantically, to human beings," unless it is able "to see itself as the servant . . . of a community that would contain much more than 'Bildung' and would not have culture, but would rather perhaps be one" (428–29).[42] But this will not be possible as long as art is exhausted, insipid, romantically self-important, fit only for parody. It must somehow be transformed and subjected, tamed and shaped for service.

Adrian reveals the second dimension of the fantasy of redemption in remarks later echoed by the devil: art must not only serve the community, but also give up its role as entertainment and become the servant of truth. The development of bourgeois society, its tastes in music, and the pressures of the market have reduced art to self-indulgent "play" and "seeming," thus depriving art of a grand and ideal project and goal that can justify it and relieve it of its burden of guilty self-importance. This condition must be overcome. "The work! It is a lie. It is something the burgher would like to be there still. It is against truth and against seriousness. . . . Appearance and play have today the conscience of art against them. It wants to stop being appearance and play, it wants to become knowledge" (241–42).[43] Art, then, must have not only a community of belonging but also a sanctified project to redeem it and give it meaning, and this project must be the service of knowledge. In this way, service of knowledge—which Nietzsche criticizes as yet another embodiment of the ascetic ideal in a modern guise—becomes, for Adrian, the only hope of a higher purpose for art and the artist.

But for Adrian, the problem of art lies not only in freedom of culture and in social conditions that have produced fragmentation, loss of cultural unity, and the degradation and isolation of art. It lies also within art and music themselves, where the burden of freedom becomes palpable. Traditional musical forms—particularly reliance on tonality as a mode of organization and symbol of harmony and consonance—are exhausted as devices for the artist, partly through overuse and the resulting impossibility of producing anything new, and partly because "harmony" can no longer serve as a symbol for modern social experience. They have become clichéd, at the same time that music has left behind an idealization of the artist's creative freedom and genius, patterned on Beethoven, where the artist is imagined to be capable of conjuring art out of his own depths alone, independent of and surpassing existing artistic forms. This burden of "subjectivity," in conditions of objective crisis, makes the problem of form even more confusing: "art is at a standstill and has become too difficult and derides itself" (662). As Zeitblom remarks, Adrian feels himself threatened with "sterility" by "skepticism and intellectual modesty [*Schamhaftigkeit*], the sense for the deadly extension of the kingdom of the banal" (202–3).

In this perspective, the freedom that art and the self have obtained—through the disenchantment of culture and the development of artistic forms toward greater and greater subjectivity—is not freeing, but disempowering; it is another name for isolation, lack of certainty, and increasing pressure to create in a vacuum. Adrian observes that the modern emergence of freedom is bound up with "an age of destroyed conventions and the loosening of all objective obligations [*Verbindlichkeiten*]." In fact, it "begins to lie like mildew on talent and to show traces of sterility." Indeed, he continues, "freedom is also another word for subjectivity . . . and sometimes it doubts the possibility of being creative out of itself, and seeks protection and security in the objective. It recognizes itself very soon in restraint, fulfills itself in subordination to law, rule, compulsion, system—fulfills itself therein, which means, does not cease thereby to be freedom" (253).

For the sensitive artist, then, the cultural crisis of the times, as Mann says elsewhere, brings "despair that is innate and predisposing to a devil's pact."[44] The individual longs desperately, to the point of allying with evil, for a new rule-governed order in which to situate himself, conformity to which will mean "true" freedom. Here burdensome freedom is equated with loss of the old "gods" or rules, and true freedom is identified with new "gods"—a community, a musical form, a discipline, knowledge—that impose new rules and tasks more appropriate to the time and capable of commanding obedience, liberating the individual from anxiety and empowering for creation. As Weber once remarked about social action: "We connect precisely those actions with the highest degree of empirical 'feeling of freedom' that we know ourselves to have completed *rationally*, that is, in the absense of physical and psychical 'compulsions,' impassioned 'affects,' and 'chance' troublings of the clarity of judgment, in which we pursue a clearly known 'end' through its most adequate 'means' according to the standard of our knowledge, that is, according to empirical *rules*."[45]

Thus, in Adrian's view, if art is to produce "something necessary to the times," it must have "a system master . . . a school master of the objective and of organization, brilliant enough to unite the restored [*Wiederherstellende*], indeed, the archaic, with the revolutionary" (252). This is a necessity if one is to have "spontaneous harmony . . . between one's own needs and the moment . . . 'rightness'—the possibility of a natural unison, out of which one might create without compulsion and without thought" (320). Adrian here joins a long line of Mann's characters—Tonio Kröger, Schiller, Savonarola, Aschenbach—who aspire to "reborn naiveté" (*wiedergeborene Unbefangenheit*) to rescue them from self-consciousness and a critical intellect and send them toward guilt-free creation, without self-doubt, confident and empowered, like the Puritan saints, sure in their faith and doing their god's work. And in Mann's work there is only one way to find such strength.

In the language of the novel, Leverkühn's coldness, inhibition, and isolation and his need for self-redemption through service combine with his sense of the excessive freedom in the times, the situation of modern culture, and the crisis of an "art on the edge of impossibility" (290) to leave the artist "powerless" (*ohnmächtig*) (318). As we have observed, in *Buddenbrooks* physical decline produced weakness and decadence, while in *The Magic Mountain* social decadence became the source of weakness in the person. Whatever the root of weakness, in *Doctor Faustus* Adrian makes it his task to *solve* the problem of powerlessness and decadence definitively, and it is this attempt that generates the search for a desperate expedient to produce "an inspired breakthrough."[46]

Projecting the longing to escape his own isolation and coldness onto the situation of art in general, Adrian defends the need for art to "win back the vital and the power of feeling. . . . Whoever therefore achieved the *breakthrough* from spiritual coldness into the hazardous world of new feeling, him one should certainly call the savior of art." He would create "an art without suffering, spiritually healthy, unsomber, unsadly intimate, an art that says 'du' to humanity" (428–29), whose creators would work "unselfconsciously" (*unbefangen*) (427). Aschenbach had similar hopes, but the inner force he needed to repress the darker side of art led to exhaustion and left him only the ideal of *Durchhalten*—holding on. Adrian wants to reverse Aschenbach's path, that is, *give in*, artistically, to the barbarity and illicitness Aschenbach rejected and so reach the *Durchbruch*—the breakthrough (a common rallying cry of expressionist artists)—to the primitive and elemental that have supposedly been lost through the evolution of art and culture.[47] *Doctor Faustus* is a sympathetic critique of the artists who cannot follow the middle path of the artistic calling, as well as a critique of the longing for recovery of vitality and immersion in life and feeling that swept Germany before and after World War I.

To regain power over the materials of art, Adrian first creates a new system of musical organization (in fact, Schoenberg's technique of composition with twelve tones) that permits a unique type of control over musical raw material, yet also permits a new "freedom," at least in principle. In notes for the novel, Mann says: "After the total liberation of music through tonality, the iron constructivism of the 12-tone system. Restorative in the revolution sense and to that extent fascistic."[48] As Adrian puts it, in twelve-tone composition every note "must identify itself through its relation" to a specified tone row (255). "There would no longer be a free note," for "every tone, without any exception, has its place of value in the row or its derivations" (256, 257). Thus, like the Kantian moral individual giving himself the laws of pure practical reason, or the Rousseauan individual who binds himself to obey the general will, the composer using this system is "bound by a self-given compulsion to order, therefore free" (257). Anton Webern, a Schoenberg student and disciple, gives impassioned and unalloyed expression to this solution. In such a system, "Adherence is strict, often burdensome, but it's *salvation*." One can work "more freely, because of the unity that's now been achieved in another way; the row ensures unity." Thus: "To put it quite paradoxically, only through these unprecedented fetters has complete freedom become possible."[49]

But although the "system" creates new external possibilities of power, of musical organization and control, the longing for *inner* empowerment and self-justification remains. Disempowerment, lost dimensions of feeling, and the lack of a "serious" object of devotion—produced by social decadence, inner estrangement, and inhibition—cannot be recovered by an external system alone. A "witness" and "lawgiver" for inner organization and control are still missing.

Devil's Pact, Self-Revelation, and Redemption

A new community in which art will play a role of service, a transformation of art into knowledge to turn it away from self-indulgence and play and toward a new asceticism, a rebirth of naiveté to cure self-consciousness and guilt about identity, a breakthrough to new feeling out of personal coldness: these are the objects of Adrian's longing and fantasy. But they are not the only objects, nor are they the most profound. The imaginary dialogue with the devil, which spells out the stakes of the "pact," completes the fantasy, shifting the focus from what art must be to what the person of the artist truly needs and desires and revealing a deeper meaning of Adrian's pact with the powers of negation. At the same time, the imaginary dialogue provides the fullest statement of Adrian's self-understanding, linking him more strongly to Nietzsche.

The dialogue with the devil also repeats the pattern of how, in Mann's work, the artist is compelled to come to terms with his defects, estrangement, and sense of worthlessness. That pattern is first revealed in

Tonio Kröger, where the artist's apparently "abnormal" and inhuman qualities are redeemed in the disenchanted form of requirements in the service of the high ideal of art. The sealing of the "pact" with art eventually makes the artist akin, in his own mind, to the prince and the nation, and this pact of service, coupled with love of the bourgeois and the "normal," successfully redeems what he takes to be his loathsome qualities, despite the elaborate fiction and self-aggrandizement required to bring it about. But the pillars that supported that solution—the integrity of art and the appeal of bourgeois society, though mitigated through irony—have been knocked away by the exhaustion of art and the degeneration of society. Consequently, Adrian believes his qualities can be redeemed only as aspects of a much more "evil" bargain that makes the artist akin, in his own mind, to the criminal and to a criminal nation, a Faustian pact that will both succeed and fail: it will redeem his qualities in service of an ideal, pushing inner-worldly salvation off to a future fantasy community; but it will condemn him to damnation in his own self-understanding and, in allegorical form, in the world. Yet through the devil's dialogue, Adrian finally creates an empowering ideological justification of himself and art, analogous to Tonio Kröger's, which allows him to serve and to create.

The dialogue with the devil is provided by the narrator of the novel in the form of a transcription of a document, in Adrian's own hand, of a conversation between Adrian and the devil. Since Adrian's devil—like Ivan's in Dostoevsky's *Brothers Karamazov*—seems always to echo and express Adrian's own thoughts, the novel leads us to understand the document as Adrian's self-revelation, rather than as evidence of a "real" pact provided by an omniscient and objective source.

In his discussion of the crisis of art and of the times and his exposition of the features of the pact, the devil promises Adrian three principal things in exchange for the service of devilish ideals and unmitigated opposition to the ideals of bourgeois society: social redemption, creative release, and inner power. The first—and central external—good that the devil promises Adrian is that, although his work cannot find an audience in society as presently constituted, a community of the future will someday take that work to its breast, admire it, and appreciate its genius.

> You will lead, you will strike the march of the future, the youths will swear on your name, who thanks to your madness will no longer have to be mad. On your madness they will live in health, and in them you will become healthy. Do you understand? It is not enough that you will break through [*durchbrechen*] the para-

lyzing difficulties of the time—you will break through time itself.
(324)

This longing of Adrian's, in the guise of a promise of the devil's, reveals
that Adrian's model for redeeming his life is Christ—no wonder that it
must be announced by another. Adrian conceives his relation to the
future community as a fantasy of sacrificing himself for music, art, and
the future, as Christ sacrificed himself for humankind. As Adrian's devil
says, echoing Naphta, and as Mann repeats elsewhere: "One person must
always be sick and mad, so that the others do not need to be any longer"
(314).[50] The Christian fantasy of the believer's redemption through ascetic
service, now combined with a fantasy of self-sacrifice through sickness,
here reaches its limit in a longing to be the Christ of culture, who takes
"the guilt of the times on his own shoulders" (662), serving to the greatest
possible degree, as did Christ, the ultimate servant. Adrian, that is, makes
a Faustian pact to become the Christ of art by serving the devil.[51] He
will die in the calling of art so that others may live. His madness, ec-
centricity, and violation of existing order will be legitimated and redeemed as necessary aspects of self-sacrifice on behalf of a higher ideal.

Mann had thought of Nietzsche—as Nietzsche himself had, at the
onset of his madness—in terms of "sacrificial death on the cross of
thought" and "self-crucifixion,"[52] and just as Mann saw Nietzsche's story
as, in reality, an event *within* Christianity rather than opposed to it, Mann
and Adrian see Leverkühn's story likewise. Indeed, although some have
interpreted the Faust legend as a story of ceaseless striving, pursuit of
knowledge, and relations with dark powers—as Goethe and Nietzsche
did—the original sixteenth-century Faust legend, and the basis of Mann's
story, is a profoundly Christian tale about limits, transgression, and the
possibility of salvation. Adrian identifies himself with this version of the
Faust theme, entitling his last and greatest work *The Lamentation of
Doctor Faustus* and invoking the same theme in his dialogue with the
devil. As Adrian says, echoing Naphta, devilish fantasy is part of Christian
experience: "Apostasy is an act of faith, and everything is and happens
in God, especially also the falling off from him" (176).

The second thing the devil promises Adrian is the lifting of his inner
inhibitions for his creative work, the boon of "resplendent lack of hesitation [*Unbedenklichkeit*]" in composing (316). Adrian's devil does not
see his gift as "to make new," but rather "to unbind and set free. We
let the lameness and timidity, the chaste scruple and doubt go to the
devil" (315). That is, the pact with the devil removes the inner obstacles
to creation, the sources of crippling weakness. By making a "positive"

commitment to the service of the "negative" of existing values, by deliberately embracing and affirming his own negativity as an object of service, Adrian gains unselfconsciousness. His project is authorized by a power whose agent he becomes; his qualities are "accepted" on behalf of the project of his art; and he may thus overcome the crippling doubts experienced in his inner struggle for legitimation, for he has found his service. This service justifies him, eliminating the guilt over his devilish self, transforming his negativity into a necessity for the renewal of art and culture. He and his art become a matter of destiny and commitment to a conscious project of opposition.

The third, and ultimate, consequence of release through service of the devil is, in principle, un-Christ-like, linking Adrian instead more strongly to Nietzsche: it is the acquisition of power.[53] The language of power and powerlessness used in the novel derives from Nietzsche and the decadents, caught up in fear of weakness and failing strength. This fear appears in the dialogue with the devil, which the novel sets in 1904, thus putting responsibility for the later problematic developments of art and society onto defects and needs that arise at the turn of the century. As the devil observes, all modern artists are "powerless" (*ohnmächtig*) like Adrian, "but I believe you and I prefer the respectable powerlessness of those who disdain to conceal the general sickness under dignified masquerade" (318). The devil, as an alternative, promises that escape from powerlessness through his service will bring "upswings and illuminations, experiences of releasing and unfettering, of freedom, certainty, facility, a feeling of power and triumph . . . the shudder of self-reverence, yes, the exquisite horror of oneself" (307).

To obtain the feeling of power, Adrian must give priority to the "subjective" over the "objective" and the "true." As the devil says, "You see me, therefore I exist for you." The value of the devil to the artist, that is, does not lie in any external "reality," but in the inner need he is conjured up to fulfill. Thus the devil implies that the imagination has the power within itself to free the artist from his own burden, provided he knows exactly what "untruth" he needs. The Nietzschean notion of the value of untruth is embodied here in Adrian's need to imagine the devil as a master in whose service he can enroll. The devil says: "Is not 'really' that which works [*ist 'wirklich' nicht, was wirkt*], and is not truth experience and feeling? That which uplifts you, which increases your feeling of strength and power and domination, damn it [*zum Teufel*], that is the truth. . . . This is what I think, that an untruth of a kind that increases strength is a match for any unfruitful virtuous truth" (323). The pact of service is an untruth that promises continual increase of "your feeling of your power" to the point of feeling like "a god" (324). But as we have seen, increase of power is the truth and goal of service in *every* calling, here made explicit.[54]

The promise of renewed power is finally fulfilled in Adrian's flights of genius while composing his *Apocalypsis cum Figuris*, when "his spirit, phoenixlike, raised itself to the highest freedom and most amazing power, to uninhibited, not to say, unrestrained, in any case, incessant and rapid, almost breathless productivity" (468).[55] The issue, however, is not that, in the Nietzschean view, an untruth or lie may serve the needs of power. The issue is rather what *kind* of untruth is needed, an untruth of illness or of health, of asceticism or of nobility. In this case, the relation to the devil is an ascetic untruth that creates a devoted relation to an ideal that empowers life while confirming its devaluation, but the adoption of this untruth is a necessary consequence of the need to serve something, rather than not serve.

The price for these "gifts" of the devil is the affirmation and confirmation of the hellish aspects of Adrian's life. In exchange for power, Adrian's devil imposes not only unrelenting estrangement from "godly" powers and values, but also physical and mental suffering, the feeling of being a "brother" of the criminal and madman, and, more important, permanent estrangement from others. Adrian must remain forever as cold as he is now: "Hell shall profit you, if you renounce all that live, all the heavenly host and all men, for that must be. . . . Love is forbidden you, insofar as it warms. Your life should be cold. . . . We want you cold, that the flames of production should be scarcely hot enough to warm yourself in. Into them you will flee out of the cold of your life" (331–32). Here, Adrian's isolation from others, like his other inhuman qualities, is "redeemed" for art: it is now interpreted as a cost and requirement of his devilish agreement, rather than as an inclination or idiosyncracy of his nature or character which the "warm" world might judge harshly. It has been transformed from contingency into necessity and, in this light, is "forgiven" or redeemed on behalf of the needs of art.

But it is important to recognize that the pact with the devil is not a new twist in the relation of the artist to service in Mann's work. Psychologically, it is *exactly* like the agreement that other of Mann's artists have made with art, beginning with Tonio Kröger: renunciation of life, in exchange for creation. It is spelled out by the poet Axel Martini in Mann's *Royal Highness*: "The presentation of life lays claim to all our strengths. . . . Renunciation . . . is our pact with the muse, on it reposes our strength, our dignity, and life is our forbidden garden, our great temptation, to which we sometimes succumb, but never to our well-being."[56] Thus the *terms* of the devil's pact are not new to Mann's work; the devil is only a more explicit and more extreme version of the powers that have always demanded the aspiring artist's life in exchange for strength and redemption. Service and a pact are invariant needs to gain empowerment in Mann's work; only the object on behalf of which one renounces life changes, the "vampire" whom the artist seeks out to take his life's blood in a magical exchange for artistic power and greatness.

In this sense, *Doctor Faustus* is not a break with Mann's previous portraits of the German artist, but the culmination of his tales of failing or lost power that began with *Buddenbrooks*, a failing power now experienced by a whole society, but multiplied and more severe because no longer confined to biological decline or even to society's simple lack of answers to the question "Why?" Some of Mann's characters have power "naturally"—old Johann Buddenbrook, Goethe, and Joseph, for example. Some once had power but later find it failing because they choose "legitimacy" rather than loyalty to a darker side of personality and inspiration—Thomas Buddenbrook and Gustav Aschenbach. Some lack power in life but do not lack creative power in art, and they require a form of self-acceptance to permit reconciliation with their condition—Tonio Kröger. Some lack power in both life and art—Hanno Buddenbrook. The combination of crisis in the social world, the exhaustion of art, and the inner inhibitions of the artist now threatens loss of "salvation," because it means paralysis and sterility in work for individuals whose sense of self, meaning, and purpose depends on accomplishment and on recognition of their genius. Meaning is threatened by powerlessness, the lack of a sense of inner power as well as outer power exerted over the world, the self, the objects of creation, even over the future. Inhibitions—now crippling the artist not only in life, as in Mann's other artists, but in art as well—have become obstructions of power rather than the signs of fastidious taste and fitness for art, and thus both artist and society seek release from them.

In *Doctor Faustus*, the sickness of the times and of art are the "objective" sources of powerlessness. Yet the artist's inner sickness is transformed into a vehicle of redemption, a subjective device for release from inhibition, indeed, the necessary price of release, and a means to regain power.[57] Mann always regarded sickness as a potential source of insight and regarded Nietzsche as a "Luciferian genius, stimulated by disease," in whom "the greatest sense of power and its productive confirmation appear to be a consequence of disease."[58] Yet nearly all attempts to acquire power in Mann's works or restore it once it is lost are fraught with disaster or condemned ultimately to failure, even if they succeed in the short run, as in the case of Adrian. Here Mann, like Weber, connects Nietzschean notions of power to Christian strategies of service, devotion, and redemption, making power serve the needs of redemption. Yet he crushes "ill-gotten" power—power acquired in any way other than through a Tonio Kröger–like calling—no matter what its source. Thus, despite the opposition between Leverkühn, the Nietzschean hero, and Zeitblom, the humanist bourgeois narrator—an opposition that reflects Mann's own ironic defense of the older humanist tradition—the deeper opposition in the novel is not between Leverkühn and Zeitblom; it is between Leverkühn and Tonio Kröger, the true, though hidden, antagonist and double.

Like all efforts to attain inner power through Christian forms of service, Adrian's power is obtained through ascetic renunciation, and this is how the goal and object of the devil's pact are understood by the novel and the author. Redemption and increase of power are the ultimate purposes of all the devices of self-justification and self-delusion that Mann's artists use to further creativity. Leverkühn's solution is only a more extreme form of a common project necessitated by the persistence of a religious pattern of self-empowerment and meaning creation in a time that can no longer sustain it. The Calvinist aspect to Adrian's search, accentuated by his rigid predestinationism—"Man is made and predestined for bliss or for hell, and I was born for hell" (661)—is the reason Hans Mayer correctly observes that, despite the explicit references to Adrian's Lutheranism, the novel portrays him more as a Calvinist than a Lutheran.[59]

Leverkühn's desire for earthly redemption through a community of the future, promised by the devil, remains a fantasy—though it is important psychologically—and Adrian takes no steps to bring it about.[60] Quite the contrary: he deliberately scorns popular taste and exerts no effort to make his music accessible. The redemptive community must come into being on its own and then come to him. The rejection of bourgeois society and the desire to find or construct a new society in its place was common to expressionist and other avant-garde artists at the turn of the century, a community in which the artist could overcome loneliness and be integrated and whose culture would be "natural" and spontaneous—though Mann uses the concepts of *Volk* and *Gemeinschaft* here for the negative community characteristic of National Socialism. In *Doctor Faustus*, Mann criticizes this aspect of the avant-garde. Yet Adrian seeks not just a community of belonging, but also narcissistic acknowledgment of his greatness, because his deepest desire is *not* for belonging but for what belonging *represents* to him, namely, acclaim and pride of place for his genius, acceptance of himself and his qualities, external validation of his grace to shore up his sense of self-worth. Indeed, the conviction that redemption can come through originality and successful work, through his own personal breakthrough, is so deep that sickness in the form of syphilis and the feeling of damnation are worth enduring on their behalf.

Precisely because the devil does not "make new" but merely strengthens what is already present and removes existing inhibitions, the novel reveals the fiction of the devil as a vehicle of self-acceptance, the externalization of inner negativity that serves as a new "god" for the self, necessary for inner reasons, not musical ones. As Ulrich Simon observes, Leverkühn "is a master of composition who wields all the registers of technical *finesse*, but his genius must remain mute until he can serve a transcendental, liturgical, objective reality."[61] That is why the criticism that the devil's pact is unnecessary for the needs of the story—since twelve-tone technique alone seems to bring the artistic "breakthrough" and represent redemption—is quite mistaken.[62] The real problem of the novel and of Adrian is *not* the need for an actual breakthrough, but the *meaning* of that need and the reliance on a particular mode of self-justification for achieving the breakthrough: the only means the novel reveals and Adrian knows for the artist seeking to overcome inhibition and sterility is the solidification of identity by becoming the ascetic tool of an ultimate, if negative, ideal. For Adrian this can be accomplished only through symbolic service of the devil. That is why the devil is symbolic not merely for the novel, but for its hero as well.

Thus, it is Adrian's need for self-acceptance and empowerment through an object to serve that leads to the devil's pact. The pact allows him to accept his own devilishness in order to meet the needs of art, becoming himself the "system master" that the times require by mobilizing his devilishness for art and embracing the damnation he feels. Adrian is now free to accept as valuable what he had formerly felt to be his defects, burdens, and inhibitions, because art and fate, affirmed by his pact, demand them. Here redemption through service is heightened, though inverted: to free himself, Adrian must see himself as completely devilish, sanctifiable only by devilish power, hence servant of the devil in his calling. The struggle with his devilish self ends by affirming it and turning it to what he takes to be devilish purposes. Only the devil can give him a sense of value and purpose. Only the devil's pact for service provides a conceptual framework in which to understand himself and bring the long-sought-for release.

Adrian's experience of illegitimacy derives from his acceptance of society's and Christianity's vocabularies of good and evil and his negative judgment of his inability to measure up to them. Indeed, his devil's pact signals his acceptance of Christian conceptions of self and redemption, showing that he remains, as his devil affirms, within the orbit and dualisms of Christianity.[63] Obviously, the pact with the devil does not betoken Adrian's *overcoming* of the existing order, but his implicit *acceptance* of it through its negation. He names society and its values *as* God's order. Once he accepts the Christian universe, his inhuman qualities can find a place only among the damned, for he cannot imagine a "right" or a redemption outside of existing values except through their negation, which is a form of acceptance that conceals its truth from itself.

Adrian's self-interpretation is thus formulated totally within the scheme of God and devil. As Mann said of *Doctor Faustus* later: "It is certainly a religious book, although there is someone there who seeks and finds in theology only the devil."[64] In fact, Weber points out that the calling and conceptions of meaning through service *require* the language and conception of gods and devils: "the individual must *decide*," among the impersonal powers experienced by the self as ultimate ideals, "which *for him* is god and which is the devil . . . throughout all orders of life."[65] Weber does not say which side of this polarity one should favor. In this case, it is the devil as symbol of negativity who confirms Adrian's negative qualities but turns them into sources of power. This is the outcome of the search for service by the person who must be the tool of a greater power. Adrian gets sanction for negativity and no longer needs to escape.

The calling finds its limits in the inability of a man who feels monstrous to become empowered through service, except in the service of monstrosity. It is no accident that the expressive "breakthrough" in Adrian's *Lamentation of Doctor Faustus* is the unrestrained expression of suffering and hopelessness—a work that deliberately wants to reject, negate, "take back" (*zurücknehmen*) Beethoven's Ninth Symphony, Schiller's "Ode to Joy," Enlightenment "humanism," and the possibility of human solidarity—within the confines of a rigid musical ordering. This work expresses the truth of Adrian's condition, namely, the hopelessness of achieving redemption, self-acceptance, or acceptance by others through patterns of self-fashioning inherited from the past and deployed in a time that defeats them. Adrian here gives up on the path to redemption and accepts the defeat of his calling.

But what is truly hopeless is the whole path of service, not just Adrian's negative version of it. Thus his hopelessness is not only personal; it expresses the truth of the end of the possibility of redemption through ascetic renunciation. The search for purely personal redemption through one's own daemon, as Weber prescribes it, is here revealed as inadequate, for it turns out to require that its adherent already have not only some inner strength, but also a certain compatibility with society and culture—which in fact are more inadequate than even Weber knew. Nor are the Weberian and Aschenbachian defenses of resoluteness and persistence any longer acceptable. Both the time's materials and the inner feeling of negativity and monstrosity prevent the individual from finding a positive daemon and oblige him to conjure up a negative one as long as the need to serve exists. This is what leads to the inversion of the original object of devotion in the calling, although that inversion preserves the calling's original form and ultimate goal. Although the pact generates power, the suffering that accompanies it reveals that the deeper needs for redemption and self-acceptance have been thwarted.

Thus the trap Adrian confronts is not created by the power of evil or by a Dionysian element that drives the individual beyond the bounds of bourgeois society. The trap lies within society itself, in norms that are confining and no longer empowering but that refute any other possibilities of individual meaning. Although Adrian does oppose this society and wishes to replace it, he also inwardly accepts it; thus he is left with no way of transcending it. Adrian's inability to conceive of self and culture in terms other than the ones laid out in the dualisms of Christianity and the norms of bourgeois society condemns him to move in a circle from which there is no escape, despite the fantasy of breaking out through a new order or an admixture of barbarism. Adrian wanders in this realm of God and devil tied in a Gordian knot, which can only be escaped by cutting through it, not by untying it and hanging on to one strand. Escape, that is, requires the recognition of the exhaustion of the world as it exists, the "devaluation of the values" of the supposedly positive world—which is not a personal problem but a product of the history of the times—rather than the simple negation or inversion of that world and its values. Instead of such recognition, we have the despair of Christian longing for meaning through service, whose outcome is the confirmation of self-hatred in a fantasy bond with the devil.

Recantation and Denial

Adrian does try to escape his isolation and coldness by developing real-world relationships of love with a male friend, a woman, and a nephew, but they all end in failure, and some end in death. Before Adrian suffers the syphilitic stroke that plunges him finally into madness, Mann has Adrian invite assorted friends to his home to witness his confession and recantation, a recantation dictated by the parallel with the Faust story in the sixteenth-century *Faustbuch* that was the basis of Mann's novel and by Adrian's own identification with Faust. This confession is, in part, an admission of helplessness, an outpouring of Adrian's self-hate, his sense of responsibility and guilt, and his feeling that it was his love, forbidden by the devil and therefore evil, that caused the deaths of his violinist friend and his beloved nephew, as surely as if he had murdered them himself. The unleashing of these feelings occurs as his ability to endure his estrangement and coldness and to repress his despair and sense of worthlessness and inhumanity decline with the approach of insanity. The life that has been usable for art courtesy of an elaborate contrivance of self-acceptance and self-damnation here breaks down.

But it is not only the form of the recantation that is dictated by the allegorical use of Faust; so is much of its content, and as a consequence its ending, rather than its beginning, creates a serious problem for the novel.[66] The significance of the recantation cannot be relativized by considering it, for example, as the creation of Zeitblom, the bourgeois narrator, imposing his own interpretation of devilishness on Adrian. The recantation is an event of Adrian's life and is thus the author's, not the narrator's, choice, present in the conception of the work from the beginning. The problem with the recantation is that Adrian not only confesses his "evil" ways, his choices, and his mistakes; he also expresses regret at having served wrong, devilish, and dark things rather than the powers of light. He identifies what he believes he should have done, his view of what can only be called the "correct" object of service in a calling: not art, linked to love of the bourgeoisie, which had been Tonio Kröger's ideal, and not dark powers, linked to love of nothing and no one, which had been his own ideal and, in Mann's view, Nietzsche's. Rather, he says, he should have served precisely what he had rejected all his life and dismissed in his Faust cantata, namely, the doing of "what is necessary on earth, so that it might become better there, and discreetly to do it, so that among people such order might be established that again prepares living ground and an honest fitting in for the beautiful work" (662). Having long before claimed that Nietzsche's "roots" lay "in the earth [*Erdreich*] of bourgeois *Humanität*,"[67] Mann here assimilates his Nietzsche-figure to the final stage of the Christian pattern of Faust—in the form of a virtually Catholic commitment to "good works" on behalf of life—thus forcing Nietzsche, in the symbolic person of Leverkühn, to return to that humanistic earth from which he supposedly came, to recant and confess his error on behalf of service of humanity.[68] Yet when Nietzsche's Zarathustra urges his followers to "*remain true to the earth,*" he adds, "and do not believe those, who speak to you of supraterrestrial hopes! They are poisoners. . . . They are despisers of life, dying out and themselves poisoned, of whom the earth is weary: so let them go away!"[69]

In fact, although Adrian's confession of self-hatred confirms the true redemptive purpose of the untruth of the devil's pact, his recantation of the devil on behalf of service to the "earth" is false to the story as it has been told.[70] It artificially forces Nietzsche and Germany into Faustian and Christian patterns, and it admixes a dose of the humanism as legitimating ideal that Mann had been defending for twenty-five years and that he believed both Nietzsche and Germany should have supported. " 'There is no fixed point outside of life,' says Nietzsche, 'from which existence could be reflected upon, no court [Instanz] before which life could be *ashamed*.' Really not? One has the feeling that one is in fact there, and let it not be morality, then it is simply the spirit of men, humanity itself as critique, irony, and freedom, bound up with the judging word."[71] In the Faust cantata, Adrian, remaining true to his experience, has Faust "reject the thought of being saved as temptation—not only out of formal loyalty to the pact and because it is 'too late,' but rather because with his whole soul he despises the positivity of the world to which one would like to save him, the lie of its godliness" (650). In fact, if recantation is really called for, then Adrian recants the wrong thing: he recants the *object* of his service rather than service itself and his unquestioned *need* for it, the need for an ascetic calling that locks him into the dualism of God and devil and now drives him to renounce one object for another, to claim that he should have enhanced the good and worked for others.

Mann thus undoes the meaning of Adrian's life as well as the critique of modern society, and reveals *Doctor Faustus* to be not a Nietzsche novel, which he had maintained, but an anti-Nietzsche novel, in which Nietzsche is forced to see the error of his ways and confess.[72] Such a recantation only of the "false" god of his service leaves Adrian embracing the necessity of ascetic ideals and of self-legitimation and self-empowerment by becoming the agent of a higher power. The recantation implies that, while remaining himself and using the time's materials, Adrian could—and should—have chosen a traditional and "godly" object of service like Humanity and the earth, that other possibilities of service remained viable for someone like him in his society. Yet Adrian's waywardness—like Hans Castorp's, but unlike Germany's—is a product not simply of his defects and wrong choices, but of defects inherent in the supposedly positive world he is made to defend at the end of his sane life, defects in that world's inherited ideals of good and evil and in its practices of meaning creation, value positing, and self-empowerment.

Adrian's condition reveals the exhaustion of the times more radically than Mann acknowledges.

This is one reason why the analogy of the devilish artist with Germany is highly problematic. In *Doctor Faustus* Mann remained deeply committed to the need for self-justification through a "right understanding" of the calling. But despite his use of the calling to comprehend the nation, and his use of a "social theory" of the relation of individual and nation to rescue the calling, it is the need for the calling—for a life sanctified and empowered by ascetic submission to an object of worship—that is the problematic need in the world he describes, whatever object it serves. Adrian's recantation thus not only undermines the meaning of his story; it also forces the diagnosis of Germany's action into exclusively metaphysical and psychological terms and shows that Mann is blind to the real challenge of Nietzsche and to the danger of ascetic ideals. Mann may have hoped for this kind of confession from Germany, but it was inconceivable in this form for the artist or for the nation.

The demonic artist, once merely latent in the good ironic artist, now stands for the demonized side of Germany. The good artist is the best in Germany; the Nietzschean, devilish artist is a lost soul, like Germany, and to escape the despair of having no positive ideal to serve, to paraphrase Nietzsche, would rather serve nothingness—monstrosity, the negation of what the world takes to be positive—than not serve. The tradition of the calling leads its adherent to what Mann takes to be nihilism and what Adrian thinks is spiritual murder. The times are again revealed to have no answer to the question of meaning as long as it is posed in terms of finding service; indeed, this need for service, when the person and the nation feel themselves monstrous, leads to service of the devil. No longer is it a matter of the calling rightly understood. The imperative of calling itself and the notions of meaning and self-fashioning that lie behind it now strand the person in a wilderness with only fantastical possibilities of redemption.

The need for justification and redemption through service here reaches its end. The need to transform and empower the hated self by converting it into an instrument of a higher purpose leads the servant down the path to "hell." The person who *must* serve, yet feels monstrous, cannot achieve self-acceptance in the service of the positive ideals of a society he rejects. Mann would have us believe that only the devilish object of service is the problem and that with the correct object of service, Humanity, service would once again be viable. But what *Doctor Faustus* really tells of is the end of the possibility of meaning, empowerment, redemption, and social purpose through ascetic service in the calling and a sanctified relation to an ultimate object—whether to art, work, or a fantasy future—now that the old order of values has collapsed. In fact, Adrian lives at the end of this possibility of service, but Mann does not know it.

The issue, therefore, is the failure of a structure of meaning, identity, and self-empowerment within the cultural inheritance and the time's materials: the times have undermined what that structure once achieved. Neither Nietzschean power, nor redemption, nor meaning can be found in a genuine fashion any longer on the basis of the calling. If the self is now to find strength, it must be with new means, on a different basis, now that culture has failed more radically than it had for Hans Castorp. It must find a new relation to the social world and to itself. Knowing the impossibility of reaffirming simple devotion to God, or the bourgeoisie, or the nation as presently constituted, Mann attempts to replace those ultimate ideals with yet another mystery, supposedly secular, meant to serve the same purpose his earlier ideals had served. Mann thus leaps back over the nineteenth century he had cherished in the *Reflections* to recover a prized ideal from the eighteenth century he had scorned, to remake it into an updated "deeper" ideal for the present.

> Nietzsche . . . belongs, to be sure in an extremely German form, to a general western movement, which counts names like Kierkegaard, Bergson, and many others among its own, and which is an intellectual [*geistesgeschichtliche*] revolt against the classical faith in reason of the eighteenth and nineteenth centuries. It has done its work—or has not yet completed it, only insofar as its necessary continuation is the reconstitution of human reason on a new foundation, the conquest of a concept of humanity [*Humanität*] which has gained in depth over the self-satisfied superficial one of bourgeois times.[73]

But Humanity is as much a covertly theological ideal today as it was for the age of *Bildung*. Mann's new ideal, like Weber's, confirms Nietzsche's observation that "indeed the religious instinct is powerfully in growth—but . . . it refuses precisely the theistic satisfaction with deep mistrust."[74]

Rejecting "service" does not mean defending as an alternative the self-referring individualistic pursuit of self-interest; it means, rather, a search that repudiates self-legitimation through submission to a higher ideal and an essentially Christian solution to meaning. Yet this is the only model that Weber and Mann draw on for what they think is an alternative both to the failures of bourgeois society and, for Mann, to its fascist enemy. As Ulrich Simon says, Mann is "a creative artist who happens also to be a theologian *manqué*."[75] This religious dimension is what makes *Doctor Faustus* Mann's equivalent of *Parsifal*, that final and *religious* work of Wagner's that brought a break in relations with Nietzsche.[76] As Zeitblom, the parodied narrator, says, echoing Mann: "A work that deals with the tempter, with apostasy, with damnation, what else should it be than a religious work!" (650).

In his "breakthrough" *Lamentation*, Adrian expresses the damnation and exclusion from the "grace" of bourgeois society that he feels is his lot. Mann wrote that he proposed to make "the last despair that is *transcended* in hope" the final note of the Faust oratorio.[77] But his ongoing musical collaborator, Theodor Adorno, opposed the original ending as "too positive, too unbrokenly theological" when Mann read it to him, and he proposed instead that the despair express "the force of determinate negation as the only permitted cipher of the other," of the positive world.[78] Despite Adorno's efforts to reduce the religious hope of the ending, however, Mann ended on an essentially Christian note.

> No, this dark tone poem permits to the end no consolation, reconciliation, transfiguration. But what if, to the artistic paradox that out of the total construction, expression arises—expression as lament—the religious paradox might correspond, that out of deepest unholiness [*Heillosigkeit*], if also only as the most quiet question, hope might germinate? It would be the hope beyond hopelessness, the transcendence of despair—not the betrayal of it, but rather the wonder that passes belief. (651)

Despite the interesting debate over this question, however, the point is not whether the novel should have concluded in endless despair, in vague hope, or in the more positive Kierkegaardian "hope beyond hopelessness," with which it actually concludes: for the fact is that the Christian message and superstitious magic of the novel are present in it from the start.[79]

CONCLUSION: THE ALLEGORY OF NIETZSCHE, GERMANY, AND FAUST

"A lonely man [*Mann*] folds his hands and speaks: God have mercy on your poor soul, my friend, my fatherland" (676). In this last sentence of *Doctor Faustus*, written by its narrator supposedly at war's end, four elements come together: God, Adrian, Germany, and Mann himself. The sentence concludes a paragraph that invokes Germany's failed "pact" to "win the world" and its imminent plunge into the abyss, "surrounded by demons." This paragraph, in its turn, is the last in a postscript that describes Adrian's final years, lived in a madness like Nietzsche's. The connections, and even equivalences, are unmistakable: Adrian and Germany, Germany and Faust, Germany/Adrian and Nietzsche, all swathed at the end in a blessing for God's grace, uttered by the harmless and simple narrator but which, we know from internal and external sources, is also Mann's own watchword for the novel's circle of themes.

There are four levels of allegory in *Doctor Faustus*—Germany, Faust, Nietzsche, Leverkühn—and a hidden fifth one: Mann himself, who claims that "a secret bond of the German spirit with the demonic" is "a matter of my own inner experience."[80] All function as interpretations of one another, while Faust, Nietzsche, and Leverkühn are symbolic of Germany. There is a further symbol, embodied in Zeitblom, who incarnates, as helpless witness, a disempowered aspect of the German tradition, namely, its decaying, feeble, yet humane and decent *Bildungsbürgertum*, committed to humanism but powerless and ineffectual to reinvigorate the tradition or defend itself against barbarism. *Doctor Faustus* is thus the fusion of a *Zeitroman* and a novel of identity into an allegory, with each level interpreted with the same tropes, but also in terms of one another.[81]

As we have noted, Mann's dependence on the original Faust story and its links to German experience keeps the developments of the composer in the novel within the orbit of religiosity, God, and devil, forcing a specific interpretation of the plight of artist, Nietzsche, and Germany and blocking any other understanding of the exhaustion and crisis of the self and the times.[82] Indeed, we have argued that, based on the story alone, the confrontation of Adrian's identity with the times ought not to have led Adrian to recant, or at least not to recant in the form that he does; but the requirements of the Faust story demand it, as does the author's wish to "correct" Nietzsche and cast him novelistically as the ascetic self-crucified Christian he depicted elsewhere.

More than this, the pattern of Faust constrains the interpretation of Germany, contributing to an essentially metaphysical, rather than a social or political, interpretation of the developments of the German nation, an interpretation that, just as in *The Magic Mountain*, mistakes symptoms for causes: in fact, "affinity with death," embodied in romanticism, "which has its true homeland in Germany," is brought back from *The Magic Mountain* as an explanation of German experience—in this case, of its catastrophe. In German strength, "and in all of its organized proficiency at achievement remained and strongly operated the romantic germ of illness and death. ... And, reduced to a miserable mass level, the level of a Hitler, German romanticism broke out in hysterical barbarism, in an intoxication [*Rausch*] and convulsion of arrogance and crime." That is why "one has the impression that the world is not the sole creation of God's, but rather a communal work with someone else."[83] Ultimately, in *Doctor Faustus*, a misguided calling is projected onto Germany, spiritual fascism is projected onto Leverkühn, both are imagined to be Nietzsche, and the devil carries all of them off.

> Where arrogance of the intellect mates with spiritual ancientness [*Altertümlichkeit*] and constraint, there is the devil. And the devil, Luther's devil, Faust's devil, the pact with him, the devil's bond, in order to win for a period all treasures and power of the world, at the forced cost of the salvation of the soul, strikes me as a very German figure, as something especially obvious for the German nature.[84]

Apart from Adrian's character, which is both an extrapolation from Mann's own youthful self and a representative of Germany, there are two principal places where the parallels between Adrian and Germany are drawn more closely and the language used to speak of them is the same. The first is in discussions between Zeitblom and Leverkühn about Germany's plight in World War I. Zeitblom speaks of Germany as an outcast and outlaw, "threatened by envelopment, the poison of isolation, provincial loafing, neurotic entanglement, implicit Satanism," needing a "breakthrough" that represents its longing for unification with the world (411, 408–9). Adrian meanwhile, speaking of himself in the guise of speaking of Germany, claims that the only real problem in the world is the "breakthrough" that is certainly "worth what the tame world calls a crime" (410).[85] The second place is in Mann's description of the imagined group of intellectuals who compose the reactionary and proto-Nazi Kridwiss circle in Munich in the 1920s, characterized by *völkisch* ideology, idealization of the secure medieval order, and degenerate Nietzschean views of truth of the kind expressed in the devil's dialogue. T. J. Reed points out that there is no direct "equation" made in the novel between Adrian and the intellectuals of the Kridwiss circle, but only a parallel, and J. P. Stern adds that even "on the level of specific events and individual ideas the allegorical parallels are incomplete and intermittent."[86]

But the novel does more than present elective affinities between Adrian and Germany: it allegorizes Germany through Adrian. Adrian's embrace of a hyperrationalistic compositional system within which he hopes to recover feeling, as well as his defense of the barbaric and archaic, is certainly meant to symbolize Germany's "mixture of robust timeliness, progressiveness capable of achievement, and dreams of the past, that is, highly technological romanticism."[87] Indeed, the narrator of the novel explicitly claims that Adrian's construction of his *Apocalypsis* is a "realization" of the views of the Kridwiss circle, who, "no longer interested in the psychological, pressed for the objective, for a language that expressed the absolute, binding and obligatory and that consequently imposed on itself with pleasure the sober constraint of pre-classically strict form" (494). Of course, the narrator's perspective is not necessarily the novel's or the author's, but the "parallels" are too extensive to ignore. "A lonely thinker and researcher, a theologian and philosopher in his cell, who, out of longing for world enjoyment and world domination, sells his soul to the devil—is it not absolutely the right moment to see Germany in this picture, today when the devil is literally carrying Germany off?"[88]

Yet it ought to be permissible—and not just forgivable—to undertake certain things in art, even if a politics modeled on them would be insane or disastrous. Art and politics are not comparable realms, and just because Nietzsche once spoke of the aesthetic justification of life does not mean that even he saw the realms as equivalent, or that it would be legitimate to hold art responsible for tendencies that would undermine politics if they were realized there.[89] But Mann insists that aestheticism in art *is* like aestheticism in politics, with equally disastrous effects, so that even art is not and cannot be a guiltless and unrestricted realm of freedom. If it does not bear direct responsibility for political disaster, it is still, in its own way, not innocent, because it toys with unethical, even barbaric impulses, as Mann suggests over and over in *Tonio Kröger* and *Death in Venice*. Even though Adrian's work may outwardly be rejected and banned by National Socialism, in Mann's view it is inwardly bound up with it, if only in its spirit.

Mann's new understanding of Nietzsche, contemporary with his writing of *Doctor Faustus*, follows a similar logic. There are "two mistakes that interfere with Nietzsche's thought," he says in his critique of Nietzsche in the light of the disasters of National Socialism. First (and here turning his back on his own early views) Mann claims that it is not "life" that must be protected from "spirit," instinct from intellect, but the reverse: the "weak little flame of reason, of spirit, of justice" should be protected against "the side of power and of instinct-filled life." Second, restating his views from the *Reflections*, Mann says that life and morality are not opposed: "The true opposition is that of ethics and *aesthetics*," and ethics is life supporting, while "beauty is bound up with death." Nietzsche's problem is that he confuses morals with *bourgeois* morals, thus criticizing in general what should be criticized only in one form. Yet the strength of ethics is the reason that the ethical Jews are "children of life," whereas the "dissolute little people of aesthetes and artists," the Greeks, vanished quickly from the historical stage.[90] Rejecting his earlier view of Nietzsche's "self-overcoming of romanticism,"[91] Mann now claims that Nietzsche himself is "the most complete and irredeemable aesthete" ever known, and his aestheticism is "a raving denial of the spirit in favor of the beautiful, strong, and wicked life, the self-denial of a man therefore, who suffers deeply from life." In relation to politics, on the one hand, Nietzsche's superman "is nothing other than the idealization of the fascist *Führer*," and Nietzsche was a "co-contributor" to the creation of world fascism. On the other hand, "fascism, as a capturing of the masses . . . is foreign most deeply to the spirit of him for whom everything turned around the question, 'What is noble?' " Completely inverting Nietzsche, Mann, enmeshed in the same confused terms his whole life, maintains thus that life does require "correction through the spirit—or morality." This is why Mann claims, as we have noted before, that the goal of the present must be to provide that correction through "the conquest of a concept of Humanity that has gained in depth against the self-satisfied flattened one of bourgeois times."[92]

Aestheticism against ethics and the concept of Humanity—that is how Mann understands the opposition between Nietzsche and himself and why he makes Leverkühn turn, in his last moments, from one to the other, as he himself did in turning from youth to maturity. This is why Leverkühn's recantation is a move against Nietzsche. Indeed, Mann had already rejected aestheticism and aesthetic justification of life in the *Reflections* and even long before, thus laying the foundation for this reversal of Nietzsche and his retention of ascetic ideals and the religious point of view. Mann did clearly state that "to call Nietzsche the philosopher of National Socialism is a barbarism."[93] Yet the ways in which Mann associates Nietzsche's aestheticism and his thought of the superman with aspects and the spiritual origins of a regime like the National Socialist one is a profound distortion of Nietzsche, though Mann purports to be drawing the consequences of Nietzschean purposes.[94] His own set of purposes, however—to tell and criticize Nietzsche's story and Germany's story through the life of a composer who lives out the tale of Faust—continually imposes these distortions. Indeed, *Doctor Faustus* does not even show Adrian to be especially Dionysian in character, except in his aestheticism, though his music might be so interpreted. But that interpretation makes sense only if we equate the Dionysian with the devilish, and such a view is possible only within a scheme of interpretation that already sees Nietzsche's interests as devilish within a Christian framework. Even so, Dionysian music is hardly akin to fascism or Nietzschean flights beyond the human, as the works of expressionist, radically antibourgeois artists of the first third of the century—whom Mann is here implicitly criticizing—demonstrate. On the contrary, Adrian's plight and resolution are *completely continuous* with Mann's other artist stories and resolutions, and remain firmly within what even Mann would have to call the human.

Doctor Faustus is a novel of enormous power, passion, and artistic genius, yet it is ultimately undermined by adherence to a Christian moral tale as a model of meaning, by commitment to the necessity of "service," preferably of the "good," and by a need to "revise" Nietzsche.[95] In *Doctor Faustus*, Mann's work recovers redemptive themes announced after World War I and first developed in *The Magic Mountain*, "my thoughts about a future and nascent synthesis of Christianity and humanism, of a spirit-body humankind, which in some way also was prophesied by Nietzsche as the positive new."[96] Ultimately—and despite the novel's great compassion for its protagonist and his relation to Mann himself—Mann's highly ambivalent relation to Nietzsche and his need to assimilate him to a narrative of redemption render the novel a novel of revenge: revenge on Nietzsche, his life, and the meaning of his work. It is their "taking back" (*Zurücknahme*) (649).

Conclusion: Asceticism, Social Crisis, and the Overcoming of Redemption

Connected to the language of weakness and impotence that pervades the discourse of the late nineteenth and early twentieth centuries and generates the search for empowerment, there is another discourse that is strikingly and widely present. We might call it a discourse of social disconnection, and it generates a search for a form of reconnection and belonging.

In the midst of the official, public expressions of great confidence by the capitalist middle classes, with their faith in science, liberalism, and enlightened religion, something emerges—particularly among the children of the bourgeois victors in the economic struggle—other than expressions of hope, commitment to the preservation and consolidation of the old order, and plans for continued construction of the new. What we find is a language that speaks of release, escape, the overcoming of restraint, and the longing for freedom from old bonds, whether political, religious, or parental. Critiques of bourgeois culture appear everywhere and in a variety of guises, as do arguments about "relativism" and subjectivity; attacks on morality, paternal authority, and existing social values; and vocal obsessions with death.[1] Some feel totally "outside" of society, family, and the intellectual and artistic traditions that dominated the previous generation, while others feel they are not outside enough and try to increase their distance by rooting out from within themselves social ideals and goals they had learned to revere and pursue but that now seem to them to seal their subjection to a world they reject and feel rejected by.

But although the mood of the time reveals estrangement and suspicion of others and of old authorities, it also reveals fear—fear that, with the old authorities gone, the world will fly apart: everything will become relative, communication will cease, society will break apart into warring classes, and, in all respects, people will be sundered from one another, locked in by their own values, relative truths, and subjectivity, mistrusting and discounting others, their utterances, and their values, and being discounted in turn. Pessimism becomes a pervasive point of view, reflecting doubt about the worth and possible meaning of traditional goals in an age of disenchantment and, more important, about the possibility of overcoming them with new, more fulfilling ones.

Consequently, in addition to the struggle for release, for autonomy and independence from existing society, the language of the times gives vent to a great undercurrent of longing: the longing to be connected to others, to some kind of society, whether that means existing society must be revolutionized and replaced or the self must be transformed. The mistrust of society and the insecurity of the self go hand in hand. Attacks on society and its norms are regularly coupled with grave doubts about the legitimacy and value of the self's own work and life, judged by the internalization of those very norms. Rejection or criticism of society as it exists is often linked to the desire for acceptance and approval from a different generalized, though uncertain, external Other—who, it is hoped, will be embodied in an alternative society, present or future—or from a transformed internalized Other present in that part of the self in which, as George Herbert Mead tells us, others always reside.[2]

Weber's and Mann's works reveal, in sophisticated form, the crisis of bourgeois self-understanding, self-justification, and inner power, linked to the crisis of belonging, adherence, and acceptance. Their use of the ascetic calling is the key to and bridge between the dual projects of empowerment and reconnection. *Doctor Faustus* most fully reveals the ascetic ideal of the calling as a vehicle for redeeming the self through the acquisition of power, and how the search for power is related to a redemptive fantasy of belonging contained within it. The calling, that is, is the key to a redemptive project to empower the self while also winning it a form of social approval and connection, if only abstractly—through the substitution of an abstract ultimate ideal in place of a socially concrete one, or through acceptance in an imagined future. The need for and possibility of redemption—indeed, redemption as a project—is implied in the calling. The importance of the search for redemption cannot be overestimated, either in general or in their work. As Nietzsche observes: "The need for *redemption* [*Erlösung*], the essence of all Christian needs . . . is the most honest form of expression of *décadence*; it is the most persuaded, most painful affirmation [*Ja-sagen*] of it in sublime symbols and practices. The Christian wants to *get rid* of himself."[3]

In the German past, bourgeois disciplines and practices of the self had linked individuals—though sometimes uneasily—to their class or other social groups, precisely because those practices were generated by and rooted in that class and its confident sense of identity, reflecting values and ideals that it prized. The adopted practices provided individuals with legitimated avenues of self-development and self-understanding, which thus legitimated those individuals to themselves and before the tribunal of social, as well as internal, authority, situating them confidently within their class and lending them that class's inner power and prestige. But in the period of the crisis of the bourgeoisie and of German culture that emerged in the late nineteenth century—with the challenge posed to bourgeois hegemony on the national level and to the capacity of existing self-ideals to provide adequate purposes and a sense of inner strength on the individual level—those practices seemed increasingly empty to bourgeois intellectuals. As forms, they thus became sundered from the contents they had once possessed—namely, from the ideals and purposes of the class—and became detached, free to "wander" and be put to use in the service of other ideals.

Yet although these practices could be adapted to other contents—as they were by Weber and Mann—to serve the needs of empowering and legitimating the self, individuals were then obliged to pose the problem of social belonging in new ways: either through the positing of other, real networks of connection that they could be part of, like the nation, or through the positing of imaginary entities to which they could belong, like humanity or the future. It is the social crisis of the bourgeoisie that stimulates the intensified search for individual redemption and belonging, based on possibilities and expectations that once seemed to exist, and it is this crisis that makes the search so urgent and difficult. Yet the longing for the renewal of power and belonging do not necessarily make them possible. As Adorno says: "Nietzsche in the *Antichrist* voiced the strongest argument not merely against theology but against metaphysics, that hope is mistaken for truth; that the impossibility of living happily, or even living at all, without the thought of an absolute, does not vouch for the legitimacy of the thought."[4]

Heirs of traditions in conflict—the tradition of *Bildung* and the tradition of the ascetic calling—and challenged by a social and political world strained by social change, rapid expansion, and cultural disorientation, Weber and Mann sought to stretch what they thought were still vital aspects of their German cultural inheritance to meet the needs of personal meaning, inner power, worldly belonging, and social action. They were imaginative enough to adapt what they knew to problems their traditions had not imagined, and honest enough to expose the limitations of what they proposed, though this exposure was neither conscious nor deliberate. Yet they were hindered by a social world in crisis and by ideals that were no longer adequate to meet the changed circumstances that confronted them, ideals that had survived beyond the conditions that could have nourished them; and they were unable to separate themselves enough from those ideals to take more radical steps and create new possibilities for meaning and action.

At the heart of the older ideals was ascetic service. In the essay entitled "What Is the Meaning of Ascetic Ideals?" in his book *On the Genealogy of Morals*, Nietzsche argues that although a certain kind of asceticism— "a hard and clear habit of renunciation [*Entsagsamkeit*] with the best will"—can sometimes favor the achievement of "the highest spirituality," the ascetic ideal is, in reality, an artifice for preserving "degenerating" life, a means by which the "ressentiment" of the weak, who suffer and hate life, is turned back against them. The ascetic ideal provides the weak with faith in "a *metaphysical* value"—or, to use Weber's language, an ultimate "object" or "cause"—which gives a purpose to life and to the believer, but in terms of which life and the believer are also judged to be deficient. This elevated value represents for them the highest truth or object, and human suffering is then interpreted as deriving from the believer's—and life's—inability to measure up to the demands of that object.[5]

> If one disregards ascetic ideals, then the human being, the human *animal*, had no meaning so far. His existence on the earth had no goal; "why man at all?" was a question without answer. . . . *This is precisely what the ascetic ideal means: that something was lacking*, that a huge *void* surrounded man,—he did not know how to justify, to explain, to affirm himself, he *suffered* from the problem of his meaning. . . . Suffering itself was *not* his problem, but rather that the answer was lacking to the cry of the question "*why suffer?*". . . . *and the ascetic ideal offered him a meaning!*[6]

The ascetic ideal subordinates "mere" life to a value or purpose "outside" and above life as it is. It interprets and values life as a bridge to a higher form of existence, to a kind of true being, the achievement of which it posits as its goal: "*that* the ascetic ideal above all has meant so much to man, in this is expressed the fundamental fact of the human will, its horror vacui: *it needs a goal*,—and it will rather will *nothingness* [*das Nichts*], than *not* will."[7] Ascetic service of a metaphysical value or cause provides both the missing object of striving and the discipline in which it must be pursued.

To Nietzsche, the modern versions of the ascetic ideal are a defense against the suffering and meaninglessness produced by loss of faith in the Christian God and extended by the collapse of unquestioned cultural ideals that were linked to that faith. The essentially ascetic belief that "the things of the highest value must have another, a *unique* origin" in an unchanging, eternal realm conceals the consequences of the disappearance of faith and precludes the emergence of a strong, healthy, noble type of person who can be value-positing based on the strength of his own self.[8] "The noble type of man feels *itself* as value-determining, it does not need to be approved . . . it knows itself as that which first grants honor to things at all, it is *value-creating*. Everything that it knows in itself it honors: such a morality is self-glorification."[9] Thus, Nietzsche defends a type of self and a relation to the self far different from what asceticism demands. *"The noble soul has reverence for itself."*[10]

Unable to abandon their need for an empowered self, Weber and Mann sought contemporary and vital means to strengthen the self for the tasks of personal life and life in the world, yet they ultimately relied on devices from their past. Unable to find other forms of meaning creation than ascetic ones, they sought to reveal the *necessity* of ascetic service for all and to clarify to themselves and to Germany what ultimate ideals remained available to the modern person as objects of service. Deeply influenced by Nietzsche and the highly diverse traditions he spawned, both spent their lives in continual opposition to his most profound teachings, retaining conceptions of the self and of service that their Christian and bourgeois forebears had propounded and whose fundamental form they could see no way to surpass.[11]

Weber's and Mann's project of individual redemption through empowering service is a product of converging Christian, German, and individualist traditions of self-justification and redemption through work, heightened by the crisis of the class that had originally authorized and stood behind such projects. But Weber and Mann also felt that the changing social world restricted not only avenues of individual meaning and power, but also possibilities of active engagement with the world and the future of that world itself. But as products of so many traditions that converged on the significance of the individual—Protestantism, liberalism, *Bildung*, Nietzscheanism—they sought essentially individualist solutions to what could only have been confronted by new forms of social order and action to support individual resolutions and syntheses. Indeed, even on their own terms, their solutions were burdened with irresolvable tensions. When they did turn from their bankrupt class to another collectivity—the nation—that ideal remained too unquestioned an entity, whose serious inner divisions held out little hope for the kind of positive solutions they envisioned, and which was soon to turn to much darker alternatives. When Mann, who outlived Weber by thirty-five years, turned to humanism during the Weimar Republic, in recognition of the limitations of the nation and nationalism, his ideal remained so unrooted in social reality and so much a mirror of the ideals of the intellectual elite of the surpassed bourgeois world—despite his attempts to go beyond it—that his new ideal could offer little more hope for collective renewal than his earlier ones.

Weber's and Mann's reliance on service in a calling, in direct opposition to Nietzsche's critique of ascetic ideals, is a defense against the personal sense of meaninglessness, powerlessness, and disconnection that result from the shaking of German bourgeois ideals in the nineteenth century. It is a response to the widespread sense of cultural drift and helplessness that pervade that social world. But as a basis for individual empowerment, cultural renewal, and political reform, the ideal of service in a calling conceals the depth of bourgeois crisis, burdens the individual with a problematic form of self-overcoming, and misdirects proposals for the transformation of politics. The project of redemption and reempowerment is a project that requires sanctified objects of service in its desperation to shore up the self's power; at the same time, it must fight against internalized negative judgments of the self in order for the self to believe in itself and feel itself connected to others. By relying on outmoded and debilitating forms of self-fashioning to build these connections to the class, nation, and humanity and to empower and legitimate the self for action and meaning, Weber and Mann place severe limits on their conceptions of what can count as the self's strength and power, on their notions of what disciplines of self-fashioning might be usable to help the self, and on their capacity to penetrate the depth of the crisis they were experiencing. In that sense—and in the same way that Mann interpreted Nietzsche's life not as anti-Christian but as an event within Christianity—Weber's and Mann's lives remain events within the life and history of the bourgeoisie.

Weber and Mann use the experiences of disempowerment and disconnection to point to the human costs of rationalization and the decline of bourgeois hegemony for certain of the bourgeoisie's members and to point both to its individual overcoming and its collective control. Unintentionally, however, these experiences point to a more profound crisis of bourgeois life that Weber and Mann do not sufficiently situate in a larger structure. For Weber, the crisis of the bourgeoisie is a crisis of inner strength and capacity to rule, embedded in a larger crisis of rationalization's advance. For Mann, the crisis is also one of inner strength, reflected less in capacity to rule than in the bourgeoisie's declining capacity to fortify its own offspring and to inspire its members with ideals of service. This is as far as they go.

This leaves the deeper experience of inner weakness, worthlessness, and disconnection yet to be analyzed in relation to the social crisis and the "family romance" in which that crisis is first experienced. The hostility of the class to the natural self and the search for proof and strength equip Weber and Mann to understand the crisis of the class more generally, yet their solutions are only to find a means to "prove" themselves again, this time in more abstract ways, through service of ultimate, apparently nonbourgeois ideals, but through service nonetheless. That is, they accept central terms of bourgeois self-understanding and self-validation but at the same time displace those terms to a field in which they hope they may find a new vitality. They internalize the practices of the class so that, despite their critique of that class and its bankruptcy, they continue its practices in abstract terms, apparently unrooted in the explicit ideals of the class. In fact, despite making the practices more "impersonal"—that is, less obviously class bound—Weber and Mann continue to be trapped by the goals, ideals, and forms of those practices in their own lives, concealing from themselves the ascetic and destructive bases of their modes of self-empowerment and self-justification.

The issue is not simply one of reorienting practices toward different, more abstract, impersonal, or universal goals, as they believed. The issue is to change those practices by criticizing not only that class's explicit ideals, but also the forms of its relation to those ideals and its attitudes toward self and meaning. That is, the task is to change the attitude toward and relation to the self, to society, and to the self's relation to society. For Weber and Mann to do that would have required accepting Nietzsche's critique of asceticism and breaking more completely with the self-ideals of the bourgeois class.[12] Instead, through their continued attachment to and involvement in those ideals, Weber and Mann reconfigured them and kept them alive. Weber decided that what the bourgeoisie and Germany needed was more asceticism, rather than ideals of *Bildung* and self-cultivation that induced and rationalized complacency and self-satisfaction. Thus he was led to a vigorous defense of forms of asceticism so severe that few in the bourgeoisie were prepared to accept them. As for Mann, he was too attached to the bourgeoisie to jettison its ideals, and longed for belonging, though he recognized the bourgeoisie's depletion. Yet even when he shifted his adherence and identification to the nation, he projected onto it bourgeois qualities and identity, and when he shifted again, this time to the more "universal" ideal of humanity, he related to it as a sanctified ideal to legitimate and justify the self.

The assimilation of individual experience to narratives of gods and devils, death and redemption, creates an interpretive frame that legitimates the self and strengthens it by deriving the self's meaning and value from self-denying service within frameworks and attached to ideals that are ascribed the value normally ascribed to gods. The self's worth is then made totally dependent on the extent to which the self becomes an agent of these ideals or fits into the framework and brings its narrative goals to fulfillment. Even with the loss of the bourgeoisie and its narrative of hegemony as legitimating forces, Weber and Mann accept the principle of self-justification through submission to a higher ideal, though the source and nature of that ideal are now thrown into doubt. What was not in doubt was the relationship of service.

The adoption of the ascetic calling has implications not only on the personal level of individual meaning and capacity for action but also on the levels of social explanation and interpretation and on the level of politics. In the same way that he thought the crisis of the self could be resolved by the generation of new self-ideals on an ascetic pattern, Weber also thought that Germany's political problem could be solved by a combination of institutional reform and self-ideals intended to generate empowered selves. In the same way that he limited his probe of the social subversion of self-ideals, so too did he limit his investigation of the social and cultural subversion of his political reforms.

Despite his concern with institutions, Weber's interest in "agency" had grown stronger since the investigation of the Protestant ethic and his discovery of its power and uniqueness.[13] But rather than confining himself to the incorporation of agency as a "variable" into explanation to arrive at an appropriate level of complexity and cogency of interpretation, Weber generalized a historically specific form of agency into a paradigmatic form, making universal what had been confined to a singular historical milieu, with specific social, cultural, and religious supports. Thus, despite his great innovation of analyzing religious culture in terms of self-fashioning and his advance over Marx in revising the history of capitalism, Weber allowed his commitment to the factor of agency and to certain specific forms of it to preempt a more thorough social analysis of the modern cultural and political situation, thus making his prescriptions for its dilemmas more individualist than could possibly work, especially when confronted with the massive social changes and crises that existed. The attachment to an ascetic ideal of the person as the sole source of individual empowerment and to the nation as the sole reasonable object of collective asceticism blocks Weber's awareness of more radical, or even radically liberal, analyses of German politics and society. Weber could never take real, and more drastic, democratic and social reforms seriously, except as devices to shore up those ascetic hopes. Even when he considered the Social Democratic party's claims on power, it was only in terms of its capacity for the self-denying "deeds" of national politics, and not in terms of democratic rights or the democratic ideals it defended.

Mann's work reveals the dilemma of the bourgeois self and the ascetic ideal oscillating between experiences of grandiosity and domination, on the one hand, and of inferiority and rejection, on the other, between redemption through representation of a higher ideal—bourgeois, aristocratic, national, human—and damnation through excessive hostility to the bourgeois world as it exists. The individual struggle for legitimacy, empowerment, and belonging in Mann's work fuels a reconstitution of the ascetic calling for art that must constantly be "fed" by the provision of ever newer, more "comprehensive," higher ideals, as each in turn shows its ultimate inadequacy as a legitimating and empowering device. This ideal finally self-destructs in *Doctor Faustus*, as the imperative of service, having now exhausted the possible "positive" objects of service, leads to what its devotee believes is nihilistic inversion of the existing world as the only remaining "ultimate object." The narrative of longing, isolation, self-hate, and the search for redemption and empowerment through service here comes to a close in the inability of the individual alone to find a resolution within the circle of meanings that society provides and that the narrative which interprets him contains.

The escape from this impasse requires a Nietzschean critique of asceticism and the overcoming of belief in the necessity of service to an object in a calling as the sole source of self-legitimation and power. This in turn can be undertaken only when the sense of worthlessness of the self is accepted not as a natural fact but as rooted in a concretely existing society and family, and when the inherited strategies for redeeming the worthless self through submission are understood in terms of their social origins and significance. Only a critique simultaneously social and "psychological" can overcome the individual's alternately grandiose and submissive longings for power and lead to the search for a genuine community of belonging based on something other than fantasies of domination, of genius, or of service to gods and devils.

This critique of the project of individual redemption and the defense of a socially rooted analysis of meaning and self-ideals are not meant to push the burden of redemption from the individual level onto the level of society. Of course, for some, the crisis of the bourgeoisie was in fact a stimulus to precisely such a search for collective redemption through projects of revolutionary rebirth and renewal.[14] This kind of project even appears in Adorno, Mann's advisor on *Doctor Faustus*, who hoped for a renewal of thought, and ultimately society, based on the "standpoint of redemption."[15] In fact, the overcoming of the need for a redemptive project on the individual level must be linked to a nonredemptive vision of the social and political worlds that grounds itself in the concrete problems and tasks of society.

It is the belief in and search for redemption of any kind, whether on the individual or the collective level, that is the problem. Individual difference, divergence from the norm, and social and political change need to find their place in society, or must be fought for in concrete terms, without imagining that there is a true society or a true way to live that is to be created, a longing that is rooted in the desperate wish for absolutes and ultimate values and for the sense of security, self-worth, and meaning that they provide. These longings are not rooted in metaphysical crises and problems, however, but in the inadequacies and disappointments of life in society and in the difficulty of rescuing oneself from them, preserving a sense of worth, purpose, and belonging, and discovering an independent source of strength despite alienation from specific social forms or groups.

Of course, despite the alternatives described here, we do not mean to imply that Weber's and Mann's dilemma could be overcome simply by force of will or a greater sensitivity to the social dimension of individual life. It is one thing to call for the overcoming of the need for self-legitimation and social acceptance through empowering ascetic service, but if social bankruptcy was as stark as has here been portrayed, what alternatives did Weber and Mann actually have? Neither the self-ideals and goals of *Bildung*, personality, and humanity—fabricated for a time with altogether different needs—nor the Puritan ascetic ideal was viable. There were no widely supported, socially validated practices of the self that remained for bourgeois intellectuals, either in the bourgeois legacy or in the rest of the German cultural tradition, a fact that accounts for the endless number of oppositional movements and "countercultural" practices that did emerge.[16] Nor could "mandarin" culture adequately support identity, except in a reactionary manner that strove to preserve old privileges and thus posed its alternative still in terms of *Bildung* and the rights of a cultural elite.[17] Neither individualist and liberal ideals nor class-based and national ones seemed viable for intellectuals like Weber and Mann. Yet the apparent absence of a substitute ideal that could offer direction and garner social support is no argument for resorting to ascetic solutions or to modes of belonging that are fantastical.

Is there an interpretation of their work, however, in which Weber and/or Mann can be imagined to have *overcome* this crisis of ideals and society and to have rescued a new possibility of meaning, strength, and belonging from the dead end of the calling? Arthur Mitzman, for example, argues brilliantly that, at the end of his life, Weber was precisely on the verge of overcoming the ascetic ideal, "and was certainly more receptive than previously to anti-modernist, erotic, mystical, and aristocratic views that were incompatible both with this inherited asceticism and often with each other." This receptivity was mediated by changes in Weber's intellectual circle and by certain personal experiences, especially his extramarital affair with Elsa Jaffé. To Mitzman, there is a "break in Weber's rational asceticism around 1910," so much so that "the changed personal morality and intellectual passions of the last decade threw increasingly into question that ethic of transcendence, self-renunciation, and mastery which had for over a century served Europe as the moral backbone of bourgeois society and which had earlier been the core of his personality and work."[18]

But despite the sensitivity of this argument and the great value of Mitzman's work to any rethinking of Weber, Weber's late works do not bear out this conclusion. From his defense of ascetic callings in 1917 as a response to the crisis of meaning and inner power brought on by rationalization, to his argument for the ascetic political calling in 1919 as the only source of self-fashioning for future leaders of Germany, and finally to his revision of his "Intermediate Reflection" in 1920, with its discovery of the ascetic calling as a vocational equivalent of war in its capacity to fortify and give meaning, Weber retains and vigorously defends ideals of ascetic self-mastery as a tool of world mastery. Whatever other elements entered his private and intellectual life to open his horizon to new forms of experience and perhaps to greater tolerance of others, his public utterances and scholarly work tell a story of continuity from beginning to end. Indeed, they show the final works to be reformulations of the discoveries of *The Protestant Ethic* adapted to the tasks of the present, told, so to speak, at a "higher" stage of life.

Even if Weber remained committed to asceticism to the end, it might be argued that Thomas Mann did provide a picture of an ideal of meaning, a mode of action, and a pattern for the self not based on asceticism or the calling, particularly in *Joseph and His Brothers*. Mann says of the work in 1942:

> The artist-ego is in youth of unpardonable egocentricity. . . . But
> due to its sympathy and friendliness, which it then still never re-
> nounces, it finds its way maturely into the social, becomes the
> benefactor and provider of a foreign people and of its own: in
> Joseph the ego flows back out of arrogant absoluteness into the
> collective, the common, and the opposition of artistry and *Bürger-
> lichkeit*, of isolation and community, of individual and collective
> is transcended [*sich aufhebt*] in the fairy tale.[19]

But despite Joseph's apparent move from the individual to the social,
his story remains a humanist religious narrative of the chosen people.
Joseph draws his strength from his self-assimilation to myths and other
justifying narratives that strengthen and empower him, and whose legitimacy depends on a conception of the Old Testament God. These myths
inspire Joseph to see himself as a chosen instrument of divine purpose,
and his cheerfulness is a clear product of his trust in God's goodness.[20]
As Fritz Kaufmann says, *Joseph and His Brothers* "is the document of
a humanism that knows of what is higher than man."[21] In Mann's words,
the "theology" of the novel derives from "the Old Testament '*covenant*'
between God and man," in which the refusal of "care for God" is sin.
Care for God means care "for his will, with which our own must coincide," and "intelligent listening to what the world spirit wants." Indeed,
Mann makes the remarkable statement that "we owe the suffering
through which we now have to go, the catastrophe [of World War II] in
which we live, to the fact that we lacked the wisdom of God to a degree
which had become criminal. . . . And in the foolish disobedience of the
spirit, or, religiously expressed, of God's will, we must search for the
actual cause of the explosive storm that stuns us."[22]

Thus, far from providing an alternative to the ascetic and religious
themes of the works we have considered, *Joseph and His Brothers* is
actually the fullest, most confident expression of the derivation of
strength from service of God and of the religious interpretation of meaning, with its theology and hopefulness about God's will and plan. Indeed,
in the light of the religious "solution" presented in *Joseph*, Mann argues
that his religious interest goes further back: "The hero of [*The Magic
Mountain*] was only apparently the friendly young man, Hans Castorp
. . . in actuality, it was the *homo dei* [man of God], man himself with
his religious question about himself, about his wherefrom and whereto,
his nature and goal, about his place in the whole, the secret of his
existence, the eternal riddle-problem of humanity."[23] Mann's related theological interpretation of modern history is not only completely continuous with the understanding of the implications of the turn away from

"God" presented in *Doctor Faustus*; it also provides a "positive" ideal only in the sense of a religious message about God's will and world spirit and the necessity of bringing our own will into harmony with them as the key to the working out of history. *Joseph and His Brothers* is the perfect religiously inspired prelude to the ascetic theology of *Doctor Faustus*.

Thus, despite Weber's tribute to Nietzsche and Mann's tribute to Nietzsche and Freud—who so admired Nietzsche—what Weber and Mann require is the "unmasking" of their ideals: first, through a more penetrating "psychological" analysis of their practices of the self, an analysis that needs Nietzsche and Freud as its inspiration; and second, through a more thorough analysis of the social origins of the calling and of bourgeois self-ideals. They require, further, a more democratic and open attitude toward Germany and the crisis of the bourgeoisie, one that was posed, for example, by some members of the left wing of Social Democracy and by some avant-garde intellectual and literary circles, like the so-called "left-Nietzscheans."[24] Unfortunately, the only truly democratic plan in Germany was defended by radicals whose social agenda and critique of nationalism were unacceptable to liberal defenders of an elite republican parliamentary system. Both Nietzsche's assimilation by the right and democracy's assimilation by the left undermined both Nietzsche and radical democracy as acceptable alternatives that Weber and Mann could support.

Weber and Mann analyzed the individual crisis of meaning and work and its connection to culture and politics, linking conceptions of self-fashioning and meaning to an understanding of social and political action. Their work makes possible a renewed questioning of the relation between culturally embedded practices of the self and the problem of worldly action and social order. Despite our criticisms of that work, it remains an enduring model and inspiration for social and political thought and for the analysis of society and culture.

Notes

Virtually all notes to Weber and Mann refer to the German originals, and all translations are my own. The major editions of the works are cited in abbreviated form, as indicated below. For the convenience of the general reader, however, titles of works are usually given in English. If there exists an English translation of a cited book, story, or essay, an English title—though not an English-language edition—is provided in the notes; where no such translation is known to me, the title is left in German. For example, "Wissenschaft als Beruf" is cited as Weber, "Science as a Vocation," *WL*; *Betrachtungen eines Unpolitischen* is cited as Mann, *Reflections*, GW 12.

Although many of Weber's principal works appear in larger collected volumes in German, a number of these same works were published as separate volumes in translation in English. Because English-speaking readers will be most familiar with the English titles of the individual volumes, these works (for example, *The Protestant Ethic*) will be cited in text discussion, though note citations will refer to the German editions.

Because of the size and diversity of Weber's *Economy and Society*, and because a good English edition is readily available, notes to that work specify the sections from which the reference is taken, as, for example, Weber, "Bureaucracy," *WG*.

GRS	Max Weber. *Gesammelte Aufsätze zur Religionssoziologie.* 3 vols. Tübingen: J.C.B. Mohr [Paul Siebeck], 1920–23.
GSW	Max Weber. *Gesammelte Aufsätze zur Sozial- und Wirtschaftsgeschichte.* Edited by Marianne Weber. Tübingen: J.C.B. Mohr [Paul Siebeck], 1924.
GSS	Max Weber. *Gesammelte Aufsätze zur Soziologie und Sozialpolitik.* 2d ed. Edited by Marianne Weber. 1924; Tübingen: J.C.B. Mohr [Paul Siebeck], 1988.
WL	Max Weber. *Gesammelte Aufsätze zur Wissenschaftslehre.* 5th ed. Edited by Johannes Winckelmann. Tübingen: J.C.B. Mohr [Paul Siebeck], 1982.
GPS	Max Weber. *Gesammelte Politische Schriften.* 3d ed. Edited by Johannes Winckelmann. Tübingen: J.C.B. Mohr [Paul Siebeck], 1971.

WG   Max Weber. *Wirtschaft und Gesellschaft.* 5th ed. Tübingen: J.C.B. Mohr [Paul Siebeck], 1976.

GW   Thomas Mann. *Gesammelte Werke.* 13 vols. Edited by Hans Bürgin. Frankfurt am Main: S. Fischer Verlag, 1960; 1974.

KSA   Friedrich Nietzsche. *Kritische Studienausgabe.* Edited by Giorgio Colli and Mazzino Montinari. Munich: Deutscher Taschenbuch Verlag; Berlin: Walter de Gruyter, 1988.

PREFACE AND ACKNOWLEDGMENTS

1. Harvey Goldman, *Max Weber and Thomas Mann: Calling and the Shaping of the Self* (Berkeley and Los Angeles: University of California Press, 1988). See also idem, "The Problem of the Person in Weberian Social Theory," in *Critical Issues in Social Theory,* ed. Murray Milgate and Cheryl B. Welch (London: Academic Press, 1989), 59–73.

2. See, for example, Nancy Rosenblum and Sherry Turkle, "Political Philosophy's Psychologized Self: 'Speaking Prose Without Knowing It,' " in Milgate and Welch, *Critical Issues in Social Theory,* 39–57; Charles Taylor, *Sources of the Self* (Cambridge, Mass.: Harvard University Press, 1989); Michael Carrithers, Steven Collins, and Steven Lukes, eds., *The Category of the Person: Anthropology, Philosophy, History* (Cambridge: Cambridge University Press, 1985); Thomas C. Heller, Morton Sosna, and David Wellbury, eds., *Reconstructing Individualism: Autonomy, Individuality, and the Self in Western Thought* (Stanford: Stanford University Press, 1986); and "Reflections on the Self," special issue of *Social Research* 54, no. 1 (1987). The study of Marx is no exception, as the works of Jon Elster and Jürgen Habermas show.

3. Indeed, Foucault claimed near the end of his life that the objective of his work had been "to create a history of the different modes by which, in our culture, human beings are made subjects," and, in its latest phase, "the way a human being turns him- or herself into a subject" through "the forms of rationality applied by the human subject to itself"; see his "The Subject and Power," afterword to Hubert Dreyfus and Paul Rabinow, *Michel Foucault: Beyond Structuralism and Hermeneutics,* 2d ed. (Chicago: University of Chicago Press, 1983), 208; and *Politics, Philosophy, Culture: Interviews and Other Writings, 1977–1984,* ed. with intro. by Lawrence D. Kritzman, trans. Alan Sheridan et al. (New York: Routledge, 1988), 29. Also Luther H. Martin, Huck Gutman, and Patrick H. Hutton, eds., *Technologies of the Self: A Seminar with Michel Foucault* (Amherst: University of Massachusetts Press, 1988).

CHAPTER 1

1. See Jean Pierrot, *The Decadent Imagination, 1880–1900,* trans. Derek Coltman (Chicago: University of Chicago Press, 1981); the most

influential expression of this problem is Max Nordau, *Degeneration*, trans. from the 2d German ed. (London: William Heineman, 1898).

2. Norbert Elias, *The Civilizing Process: The Development of Manners*, trans. Edmund Jephcott (New York: Urizen Books, 1978), 27.

3. W. H. Bruford, *The German Tradition of Self-Cultivation: "Bildung" from Humboldt to Thomas Mann* (Cambridge: Cambridge University Press, 1975).

4. See Jürgen Kocka, ed., *Bürger und Bürgerlichkeit im 19. Jahrhundert* (Göttingen: Vandenhoeck & Ruprecht, 1987).

5. This concept is borrowed from Stephen Greenblatt, *Renaissance Self-Fashioning: From More to Shakespeare* (Chicago: University of Chicago Press, 1980).

6. See Michel Foucault, interview, "The Ethic of Care for the Self as a Practice of Freedom," in *The Final Foucault*, ed. James Bernauer and David Rasmussen (Cambridge, Mass.: MIT Press, 1988), 3.

7. Foucault, in Dreyfus and Rabinow, *Michel Foucault*, 250.

8. Foucault, interview, in Bernauer and Rasmussen, *The Final Foucault*, 11.

9. On the German tradition of personality, see Goldman, *Max Weber and Thomas Mann*, 120–30.

10. Foucault, *Politics, Philosophy, Culture*, 50–51.

11. Nietzsche, *The Gay Science*, in *Kritische Studienausgabe* [hereafter cited as *KSA*], ed. Giorgio Colli and Mazzino Montinari (Munich: Deutscher Taschenbuch Verlag; Berlin: Walter de Gruyter, 1988), 3:583.

12. Nietzsche, *On the Genealogy of Morals*, in *KSA*, vol. 5, essay 1, sec. 13, p. 279; essay 2, sec. 12, p. 314; and essay 3, sec. 7, p. 350.

13. Nietzsche, *Beyond Good and Evil*, in *KSA*, vol. 5, sec. 13, p. 27.

14. Ibid., 33.

15. For an example, see Wolfgang Schluchter, *The Rise of Western Rationalism: Max Weber's Developmental History*, trans. by Guenther Roth (Berkeley and Los Angeles: University of California Press, 1981). Some of the essays in Sam Whimster and Scott Lash, eds., *Max Weber, Rationality, and Modernity* (London: Allen & Unwin, 1987), provide a useful corrective.

16. Jeffrey Alexander points out, with a similar intention, that Weber's work shows a "dialectic of individuation and domination"; see "The Dialectic of Individuation and Domination: Weber's Rationalization Theory and Beyond," in Whimster and Lash, *Max Weber*, 185–206.

17. As Wolfgang Mommsen observes, "Weber demands that sociology has ultimately to relate all social processes to the active or passive individual and that any sociology that does not place the individual person as the essential point of reference in its analysis and interpretation is not fulfilling its task"; "Personal Conduct and Societal Change: Towards a Reconstruction of Max Weber's Concept of History," in Whimster and Lash, *Max Weber*, 39.

18. On the logic of rationality, see Friedrich Tenbruck, "The Problem of Thematic Unity in the Works of Max Weber," trans. M. S. Whimster, *British Journal of Sociology* 31 (1980): 316–51; Tenbruck, "Das Werk Max Webers: Methodologie und Sozialwissenschaften," *Kölner Zeitschrift für Soziologie und Sozialpsychologie* 38 (1936): 13–31. On developmental history, see Schluchter, *Rise of Western Rationalism*.

19. Karl Löwith, "Karl Marx und Max Weber," in *Gesammelte Abhandlungen* (Stuttgart: W. Kohlhammer Verlag, 1960), 1–67.

20. Weber, "Charismatic Domination and Its Transformation," in *Wirtschaft und Gesellschaft* [hereafter cited as *WG*], 5th ed., ed. Johannes Winckelmann (Tübingen: J.C.B. Mohr [Paul Siebeck], 1976), 687.

21. Weber, "The Protestant Ethic," in *Gesammelte Aufsätze zur Religionssoziologie* [hereafter cited as *GRS*], (Tübingen: J.C.B. Mohr [Paul Siebeck], 1920–23), 1:37, 204.

22. Mommsen, "Personal Conduct and Societal Change," 44.

23. Weber, "Fundamental Concepts of Sociology," *WG*, 28–29.

24. Foucault, "Technologies of the Self," in Martin, Gutman, and Hutton, *Technologies of the Self*, 17.

25. See Goldman, *Max Weber and Thomas Mann*, 18–51.

26. Foucault, *Power/Knowledge: Selected Interviews and Other Writings, 1972–1977*, ed. Colin Gordon; trans. Colin Gordon, Leo Marshall, John Mepham, and Kate Soper (New York: Pantheon Books, 1980), 133.

27. Weber, *Wirtschaftsgeschichte: Abriss der universalen Sozial- und Wirtschaftsgeschichte*, 2d ed., ed. S. Hellmann and M. Palyi (Munich and Leipzig: Duncker & Humblot, 1924), 314.

28. On this subject, see Goldman, *Max Weber and Thomas Mann*; and idem, "Images of the Other: Asia in Nineteenth-Century Western Thinking—Hegel, Marx, Weber," in *Asia in Western History and World History*, ed. Ainslee Embree and Carol Gluck (New York: East Asian Institute, Columbia University, forthcoming).

29. Wolfgang Mommsen speaks of how the "rationalization of the conduct of life" has often led, in the West, to a situation where "the individual or the group to which he belongs, accumulates a capacity for action whose force under certain conditions can have revolutionary consequences for the existing social system of which he is a part"; "Personal Conduct and Societal Change," 40.

30. According to Friedrich Tenbruck, "There cannot be the slightest doubt that *Science as a Vocation* is the authentic offspring of *The Protestant Ethic*, inasmuch as that essay shows us the genuine Puritan of *The Protestant Ethic*"; "Max Weber and the Sociology of Science: A Case Reopened," *Zeitschrift für Soziologie* 3 (1974): 318. See also Paul Honigsheim, *On Max Weber* (New York: Free Press, 1968), 114; and idem, "Max Weber: His Religious and Ethical Background and Development," *Church History* 18–19 (1949–50): esp. 235–37.

31. Weber, "Types of Domination," *WG*, 142. According to Luciano Cavalli, "charisma constitutes a 'calling' in a strong sense"; "Charismatic Domination, Totalitarian Dictatorship, and Plebiscitary Democracy in the Twentieth Century," in *Changing Conceptions of Leadership*, ed. Carl F. Graumann and Serge Moscovici (New York: Springer-Verlag, 1986), 61.

32. Thomas Metzger, *Escape from Predicament: Neo-Confucianism and China's Evolving Political Culture* (New York: Columbia University Press, 1977).

33. It would be valuable to ask whether Weber's historical analyses, and not only his prescriptions, were informed by a romance of individual power. Were the Puritans as individualistic in their social concerns as Weber says? What of the Puritan covenant, collective in its origin and orientation? Did the Hebrew prophets play the role they did only because of personal inspiration and strength vis-à-vis the corrupted community, or were their actions predicated on the existence and attention of that very religious community, bound by covenant, that was not created by a few individuals, aside from the crucial founding role of the patriarchs? In Weber's portrait, the prophets especially partake of the romantic archetype of heroes estranged from their time, struggling to return people to the revealed path, obliged by their role to do nothing but criticize and appeal to a deeper faith, cut off from associates and from any possibilities of political action apart from complaint.

34. On *Buddenbrooks*, see Goldman, *Max Weber and Thomas Mann*, 61–85.

35. On *Tonio Kröger*, see ibid., 85–105.

36. On *Death in Venice*, see ibid., 187–207.

37. On *Royal Highness*, see ibid., 175–82.

38. Mann, Preface to *Royal Highness*, trans. H. T. Lowe-Porter (1939; New York: Vintage Books, 1983), viii.

39. Mann, Letter of 25 July 1909 to Hugo von Hoffmansthal, in *Briefe*, vol. 1: *1889–1936*, ed. Erika Mann (1961; Frankfurt a. M.: Fischer Taschenbuch Verlag, 1979), 76.

40. On the nature and problems of allegory, see Angus Fletcher, *Allegory: The Theory of a Symbolic Mode* (New York: Columbia University Press, 1964); Northrop Frye, *Anatomy of Criticism: Four Essays* (Princeton: Princeton University Press, 1957); Maureen Quilligan, *The Language of Allegory* (Ithaca: Cornell University Press, 1979); Carolynn Van Dyke, *The Fiction of Truth* (Ithaca: Cornell University Press, 1985); Paul de Man, "The Rhetoric of Temporality," in *Blindness and Insight: Essays in the Rhetoric of Contemporary Criticism* (Minneapolis: University of Minnesota Press, 1983); and the essays by Murray Krieger, Samuel Levin, and J. Hillis Miller in Morton W. Bloomfield, ed., *Allegory, Myth, and Symbol*, Harvard English Studies, 9 (Cambridge, Mass.: Harvard University Press, 1981).

41. Northrop Frye, "Allegory," in *Princeton Encyclopedia of Poetry and Poetics*, enl. ed., ed. Alex Preminger (Princeton: Princeton University Press, 1974), 12.

CHAPTER 2

1. For the crisis of the sciences in academic circles, see Michael Ermarth, *Wilhelm Dilthey: The Critique of Historical Reason* (Chicago: University of Chicago Press, 1978), 79–90. See also Fritz Ringer, *The Decline of the German Mandarins, 1890–1933* (Cambridge, Mass.: Harvard University Press, 1969); and Erich Wittenberg, "Die Wissenschaftskrisis in Deutschland im Jahre 1919," *Theoria: A Swedish Journal of Philosophy and Psychology* 4, pt. 3 (1938): 235–64.

2. On education, see Konrad Jarausch, *Students, Society, and Politics in Imperial Germany: The Rise of Academic Illiberalism* (Princeton: Princeton University Press, 1982); idem, "Liberal Education as Illiberal Socialization: The Case of Students in Imperial Germany," *Journal of Modern History* 50 (1978): 609–30; idem, "The Social Transformation of the University: The Case of Prussia, 1865–1914," *Journal of Social History* 12 (1979): 609–36; and Charles E. McClelland, *State, Society, and University in Germany, 1700–1914* (Cambridge: Cambridge University Press, 1979). Frederic Lilge, *The Abuse of Learning: The Failure of the German University* (New York: Macmillan, 1948), is of value despite biases.

3. For a brief treatment of *Bildung*, see Goldman, *Max Weber and Thomas Mann*, 125–28. On the concept of *Bildung*, see Rudolf Vierhaus, "Bildung," in *Geschichtliche Grundbegriffe. Historisches Lexikon zur politisch-sozialen Sprache in Deutschland*, ed. Otto Brunner, Werner Conze, and Reinhart Koselleck, 5 vols. (Stuttgart: Ernst Klett Verlag, 1972–84), 1:508–51; Hans Weil, *Die Entstehung des deutschen Bildungsprinzips*, 2d ed. (Bonn: H. Bouvier Verlag, 1967); and Roy Pascal, "The Concept of 'Bildung' and the Division of Labor: Wilhelm von Humboldt, Fichte, Schiller, Goethe," in *Culture and the Division of Labor: Three Essays on Literary Culture in Germany*, University of Warwick Occasional Papers (Coventry: University of Warwick, 1974), 5–30. See also Karl Löwith, *From Hegel to Nietzsche*, trans. David E. Green (Garden City, N.Y.: Anchor Books, 1967), 286–303.

4. Herbert Schnädelbach, *Philosophie in Deutschland, 1831–1933* (Frankfurt a. M.: Suhrkamp Verlag, 1983), 35. For the concept of the *Bildungsbürgertum*, see Klaus Vondung, ed., *Das Wilhelminische Bildungsbürgertum* (Göttingen: Vandenhoeck & Ruprecht, 1976), esp. Vondung's "Zur Lage der Gebildeten in der Wilhelminischen Zeit," 20–33. Ernst Troeltsch, "The Ideas of Natural Law and Humanity in World Politics," in Otto Gierke, *Natural Law and the Theory of Society, 1500*

to 1800, trans. Ernest Barker (Cambridge: Cambridge University Press, 1934), 1:215, suggests that the "inwardness" of eighteenth- and nineteenth-century German theories derived from the idealism of a cultural elite destitute of a state.

5. Hans-Georg Gadamer, *Truth and Method* (New York: Seabury Press, 1975), 10. Heidegger treats the word as the early Humboldt did, as a translation of the Greek *paideia*. At the same time, he suggests that *Bildung* is not the "most complete" translation and that the concept was seriously misinterpreted in the later nineteenth century. See Heidegger, "Plato's Doctrine of Truth," in *Philosophy in the Twentieth Century*, ed. Henry Aiken and William Barrett (New York: Random House, 1962), 3:256: " 'Education' (*Bildung*) implies two things: it means first of all forming in the sense of developing and molding a character. This 'forming' however 'forms' (molds) at the same time through its preconceived adaptation to a standard aspect which is therefore called the prototype. Education (*Bildung*) is above all molding and giving direction by means of a form. The essence opposite to *paideia* is *apaideusia*, being uneducated (*Bildungslosigkeit*). In it there is neither the awakening of a development of a fundamental orientation nor the establishing of a standard prototype." This identification of *Bildung* with *paideia* is also in Hegel, on whom see Gadamer, *Truth and Method*, 10–19; and Judith Shklar, *Freedom and Independence: A Study of the Political Ideas of Hegel's "Phenomenology of Mind"* (Cambridge: Cambridge University Press, 1976), 43–46, 90–93. Also Vierhaus, "Bildung," 534–36.

6. Hans Rosenberg, *Bureaucracy, Aristocracy, and Autocracy: The Prussian Experience, 1660–1815* (Boston: Beacon Press, 1966), 182. See also Ringer, *Decline of the German Mandarins*, 86; and idem, "The German Academic Community, 1870–1920," *Internationales Archiv für Sozialgeschichte der deutschen Literatur* 3 (1978): 108–29.

7. On Humboldt, see Eduard Spranger, *Wilhelm von Humboldt und die Reform des Bildungswesens* (1910; Tübingen: Max Niemeyer Verlag, 1965); and idem, *Wilhelm von Humboldt und die Humanitätsidee*, 2d ed. (Berlin: Reuther & Reichard, 1928); Paul R. Sweet, *Wilhelm von Humboldt: A Biography*, 2 vols. (Columbus: Ohio State University Press, 1978); and David Sorkin, "Wilhelm von Humboldt: The Theory and Practice of Self-Formation (*Bildung*), 1791–1810," *Journal of the History of Ideas* 44 (1983): 55–73. Bruford, *German Tradition of Self-Cultivation*, has a good chapter on Humboldt. For critiques of Bruford, see R. Hinton Thomas, "The Uses of 'Bildung,' " *German Life and Letters*, n.s., 30 (1977): 177–86; and Ringer's review in *Central European History* 11 (1978): 107–13. See also the discussion of Humboldt in Lilge, *Abuse of Learning*, chap. 1; and in Vierhaus, "Bildung," 519–21, 536.

8. Fritz Stern, *The Failure of Illiberalism* (New York: Knopf, 1972), 7–8; see also Schnädelbach, *Philosophie in Deutschland*, 36.

9. Jarausch, "Liberal Education," 611, maintains that *Bildung* was even intended "to liberate man from the shackles of estate society." Vierhaus, "Bildung," 519, argues that there was a discrepancy between the classical-idealist-neohumanist conception of *Bildung* in the last third of the eighteenth century, on the one hand, and the bourgeois education for estate and calling as it was embodied in the utilitarian "state pedagogy" of enlightened absolutism, on the other. See also Jarausch, *Students, Society, and Politics*, 83. Stern, *Failure of Illiberalism*, 9, claims the reformers believed "in the perfectibility of the aesthetic or rational faculties of the individual, quite independently of political conditions."

10. Schnädelbach, *Philosophie in Deutschland*, 43; Jarausch, *Students, Society, and Politics*, 9. There is no exact equivalent for *Bildung* in other languages. According to Gadamer, the word originated in medieval mysticism, continued in Baroque mysticism, attained religious spiritualization in the work of Klopstock, and culminated in Herder's definition as "reaching up to humanity"; "between Kant and Hegel, the form that Herder had given to the concept was perfected." See *Truth and Method*, 10, 11.

According to Vierhaus, *Bildung*'s meaning and its "elevation over other concepts like 'education' [*Erziehung*] and 'training' [*Ausbildung*]" can be understood only in relation to the "governmental-social development of Germany." Vierhaus claims that the development of *Bildung* parallels the "qualitative distinction between 'culture' and 'civilization' in Germany." Ultimately, " 'Bildung' was understood mostly as the content and outcome of education." With Herder, *Bildung* came to mean the " 'living' effect of the learning and the activity of one who is forming himself [*des Sich-Bildenden*], and indeed not only individual persons, but whole peoples and humanity." *Bildung* as a goal of individual human beings was first used in relation to the coordinate concepts of "individuality" and "development" as they emerged in German idealism. See Vierhaus, "Bildung," 508–9, 511, 515. According to E. Lichtenstein, although the use of the word *Bildung* predates the eighteenth century, its later usage and meaning were dependent on several factors. "The secularization, humanization, and pedagogization of the *Bildung* concept in the eighteenth century is connected with the emancipation of the emotional in German Pietism and with the eminent influence of Shaftesbury on German spiritual life." The new "platonizing and aesthetic-humanistic meaning" of *Bildung* appeared first in the Shaftesbury translations of 1738, where "inner form" was rendered as *innere Bildung*. See E. Lichtenstein, "Bildung," in *Historisches Wörterbuch der Philosophie*, vol. 1, ed. Joachim Ritter (Basil: Schwabe & Co. Verlag, 1971), cols. 921–38; quoted material from 922–23.

11. Ringer, "German Academic Community," 110; idem, *Decline of the German Mandarins*, 86, 106. Ringer says *Bildung* expressed a desire

to affect the whole of the human being's nature through university training, to form the "soul" into an inner unity. Sweet, *Humboldt* 1:127, says Humboldt valued the Greeks because they "were more capable than others of achieving this harmonious development of the personality."

Hans Speier, "Zur Soziologie der bürgerlichen Intelligenz in Deutschland," in *Positionen der literarischen Intelligenz zwischen bürgerliche Reaktion und Imperialismus,* ed. Gert Mattenklott and Klaus R. Scherpe (Kronberg: Scriptor Verlag, 1973), 9–24, argues that German classicism was not rooted in society, but in an understanding of the social problem as an individual problem of *Bildung* and ethical improvement. Elias, *Civilizing Process,* 27, says that the German conception of *Kultur* reflects the position of the German intelligentsia "without a significant social hinterland." Peter Jelavich, "Art and Mammon in Wilhelmine Germany: The Case of Frank Wedekind," *Central European History* 12 (1979): 203–36, offers a succinct account of how the German classical tradition was appropriated, turned into an "affirmative culture," and defused by the German state. Classicism thus became divorced from life and was definitively defeated as a means toward collective politics and renewal by the later defeat of radical bourgeois "classicism" in 1848–49, which allowed the state's versions to become dominant.

12. Kant, quoted in Lichtenstein, "Bildung," col. 925, who says that with Kant the "concept of *Bildung* is connected for the first time in German idealism with the problem of subjectivity and of spiritual reality." This becomes the constitutive element and principle of the movement of the spirit in Fichte and Hegel, epitomized in Fichte's motto of "the I as 'a work of self.'"

See also Friedrich Meinecke, "Schiller und der Individualitätsgedanke," in *Werke* (Stuttgart: K. F. Koehler Verlag, 1965), 4:319. He says that Kant saw freedom, reason, and self-determination as aimed only toward a general and normative goal, universal in its import and application. Yet if one considers these views as applied to the individual, one can find the "secret of individuality" and the individual's "shaping law" even in Kant, although Meinecke maintains elsewhere that "Kant was inwardly far from the thought of the individual [*Individualitätsgedanke*]." See Meinecke, "Zur Entstehungsgeschichte des Historismus und des Schleiermacherschen Individualitätsgedankens," in *Werke* 4:342.

13. Goldman, *Max Weber and Thomas Mann,* 121–25.

14. Humboldt, quoted in Gadamer, *Truth and Method,* 11.

15. Gadamer, *Truth and Method,* 12. Gadamer, using a different text of Kant's in *Truth and Method,* 11, thus disagrees with Lichtenstein. He affirms that Kant "still does not use the word *Bildung*" in the sense and connection that Herder provided or in the sense of its later development. At an earlier stage, he says, "*Bildung* is intimately associated with the idea of culture and designates primarily the properly human way of de-

veloping one's natural talents and capacities." Kant "speaks of the 'culture' of a capacity (or of a 'natural talent') which as such is an act of freedom by the acting subject. Thus, among the duties to oneself he mentions not letting one's talents rust, without using the word *Bildung*." Thus, for Gadamer, though Kant does speak of "culture" or, better, the "cultivation" of a talent or capacity, this notion of culture is part of the obligation freedom imposes on the self, even though the self is cultivated according to its "natural" shape or capacity. It is Hegel, he says, who picks up the thread of Herder in analyzing *Sichbilden* in discussing Kantian duties toward the self. The issue for Gadamer, therefore, seems to be between "culture" as a duty in cultivating the self and "self-culture" or self-formation as a different approach to the *Bildung* of the self. It is Humboldt, for Gadamer, who treads a path between these two and distinguishes *Bildung* from *Kultur*.

16. Humboldt, quoted in Lichtenstein, "Bildung," col. 926; and in Vierhaus, "Bildung," 520. See also Sweet, *Humboldt* 1:88, 99, 111. Humboldt even defends war as something that can contribute to *Bildung*, because risking "everything for a high goal" is essential for *Bildung*. Stern, *Failure of Illiberalism*, 7, says that after the strengthening of the universities following the defeat of Napoleon, "the moral indispensability of education became an article of faith: the self-fulfillment of the individual required the humanistic cultivation of the mind."

17. Stern, *Failure of Illiberalism*, 9.

18. Lichtenstein, "Bildung," col. 924.

19. Humboldt, quoted in Schnädelbach, *Philosophie in Deutschland*, 42.

20. Humboldt, quoted in Vierhaus, "Bildung," 521, who observes: "The universal historical meaning of 'Bildung' could not be elevated higher." Also Jarausch, *Students, Society, and Politics*, 9. For changes in Humboldt's views, see Bruford, *German Tradition of Self-Cultivation*, 19, vii.

21. Humboldt, quoted in Sweet, *Humboldt* 1:84. See also Meinecke, *The Age of German Liberation, 1795-1815*, trans. and with intro. by Peter Paret (Berkeley and Los Angeles: University of California Press, 1977), 21. On the difference between the "being" of the noble and the "doing" of the bourgeois, see Manfred Riedel, "Bürger," in *Geschichtliche Grundbegriffe*, ed. Brunner, Conze, and Koselleck, 1:699–700.

22. Bruford, *German Tradition of Self-Cultivation*, 28.

23. See Pascal, " 'Bildung' and the Division of Labor," 5, 10–11, 12, 13. Pascal points out that for the figures of the *Sturm und Drang* period, the division of labor was a problem not for its social and political effects, which had been the concern of the Scottish Enlightenment, but for its effects on personal life and the fragmentation of the personality. The possible influence of Rousseau, so important for Kant and Goethe, must not be overlooked here either.

24. Humboldt, quoted in Bruford, *German Tradition of Self-Cultivation*, 24.

25. Humboldt, quoted in ibid., 19. For details on his withdrawal from the Prussian civil service and his "search for an intellectual vocation," see Sweet, *Humboldt* 1:83–150. Meinecke says, in "Schiller," *Werke* 4:310, that for Humboldt, "strength" (*Kraft*) was connected in life with "one-sidedness."

26. See Meinecke, *Age of German Liberation*, 55–56.

27. Humboldt, quoted in Bruford, *German Tradition of Self-Cultivation*, 123.

28. Jarausch, *Students, Society, and Politics*, 161.

29. H. Rosenberg, *Bureaucracy, Aristocracy, Autocracy*, 182, 184, 185, 186. See Ringer, *Decline of the German Mandarins*, 86, on how reflection on the classics produces qualities that rival those of the aristocrats.

30. Lichtenstein, "Bildung," col. 927; Jarausch, *Students, Society, and Politics*, 88. See also Stern, *Failure of Illiberalism*, 8.

31. H. Rosenberg, *Bureaucracy, Aristocracy, Autocracy*, 185, 188, 189, 191, 192, 187–88. See also Jarausch, *Students, Society, and Politics*, 82, 158, who says that even later in the nineteenth century, "both educated officials and free professionals were animated by a common ethos which, dominated by the neo-Kantian conception of duty, formed a cohesive life ideal focused on a shared notion of honorable service." See Meinecke, *Age of German Liberation*, 25, on Fichte's view of the state as working "in every way to accustom us to be machines, not independent beings." Yet with the new ideal, Meinecke observes (56), "the autonomous, creative individual entered state service because a promising sphere of activity was opened to it. . . . This new alliance also changed the state. The rigid, blind mechanism that had once so oppressed Humboldt unfolded into the policies of the new men who worked through the machinery. They personalized the impersonal element of the state."

Weber later distinguishes the patrimonial official with *Amtstreue*, loyalty to office based on purely personal submission to the ruler to whom the office belongs, from one with *Diensttreue*, personal commitment to impersonal tasks and purposes, in Weber, "Patrimonialism," *WG*, 597–98.

32. See also Meinecke, *Age of German Liberation*, 56.

33. Pascal, " 'Bildung' and the Division of Labor," 20, 23, 24. Pascal further observes (25) that in Goethe's novel class distinctions are the grounds *both* of the necessity of one-sidedness *and* of the fantasy of its overcoming, the "dream of all-sided and uncommitted 'Bildung.' " On Goethe, see also Goldman, *Max Weber and Thomas Mann*, 128–30.

On Schiller's contrasting notion of "the beautiful soul," which is essentially aristocratic, see *Über Anmut und Würde* (1793), in *Schillers*

286 / *Notes to Page 33*

Werke, Nationalausgabe, ed. Benno von Wiese (Weimar: Hermann Böhl-aus Nachfolger, 1962), vol. 20, pt. 1, p. 288. On Shaftesbury and Schiller, see Wilhelm Windelband, *A History of Philosophy*, rev. ed. (New York: Macmillan, 1901), 2:488–89, 508, 600–602. See also Pascal, " 'Bildung' and the Division of Labor," 21; and Meinecke, "Schiller," in *Werke* 4:313.

34. Kurt May, quoted in Bruford, *German Tradition of Self-Cultivation*, 56. Bruford points out (104) that Goethe, in the course of writing the two parts of *Wilhelm Meister*, "shifted the aim of 'Bildung' from the extension and elaboration of one's own mental life, the conversion of as much as possible of the world outside into inner experience and the moulding nearer to perfection of one's own personality . . . to work for the material and spiritual good of a specific group of one's fellow-men." Lichtenstein, "Bildung," col. 924, says that even in *Wilhelm Meister*, *Bildung* "meant essentially not spiritual *Bildung*, but rather the genesis of the persona, the elaboration of individuality into the ripe personality in an active environment."

35. Pascal, " 'Bildung' and the Division of Labor," 27. See also Vierhaus, "Bildung," 517, 518. Georg Simmel, *The Sociology of Georg Simmel*, trans. and ed. Kurt H. Wolff (New York: Free Press, 1950), 80, says of Goethe's *Wanderjahre* that specialization is not about the personality in itself but only about it for society: "The individualistic requirement of specificity does not make for the valuation of total personality within society, but for the personality's objective achievement for the benefit of society." He quotes Goethe: "Any man's task is to do *something* extraordinarily well, as no other man in his immediate environment can."

36. Schleiermacher is the most important figure in the tradition of *Bildung* after Humboldt, and perhaps even more influential. Bruford, *German Tradition of Self-Cultivation*, 26, speaks of Schleiermacher's *Reden über die Religion* as a "kind of gospel of 'Bildung' " and says (83) that the religious basis of Schleiermacher's thinking "keeps it, in spite of his preoccupation with self-culture, free from the self-centered narrowness even Spranger finds in Wilhelm von Humboldt." See also Simmel, *Sociology of Georg Simmel*, 80, 81.

According to Bruford (82–83), Schlegel was critical of Schleiermacher's preference "to form himself within rather than to 'form works.' " Schlegel looked to *Bildung* as "the antithesis of the utilitarian and the narrowly moral. . . . 'Do not squander your faith and love on the political world, but offer up your inmost being in the divine world of scholarship and art to swell the sacred fiery stream of eternal culture.' "

37. Fichte, despite his conviction of the need to concentrate on a single specialty, remained concerned with the human "drive toward identity, toward perfected coincidence with one's self," that is, toward the harmonious totality implied by *Bildung*. See Fichte, quoted in Pascal, " 'Bildung' and the Division of Labor," 13. On Fichte and the ideal of "humanity," see Meinecke, *Age of German Liberation*, 44, 45.

On Hegel and *Bildung*, see Gadamer, *Truth and Method*, 13–17, who says that, for Hegel, *Bildung* "requires the sacrifice of particularity for the sake of the universal." The nature of the individual given over to *Bildung* is "to constitute itself as a universal intellectual being. Whoever abandons himself to his particularity is ungebildet." Moreover, "practical *Bildung* is seen in one's filling one's profession [*Beruf*] wholly, in all its aspects. . . . To give oneself to the universality of a profession is at the same time 'to know how to limit oneself, i.e., to make one's profession wholly one's concern. Then it is no longer a limitation.' " See Shklar, *Freedom and Independence*, 43, 44, 45, and esp. 143, where she says, "The individual rises to universality and leaves his more natural self behind, by assimilating these 'givens' and absorbing them into his own personality."

38. Bruford, *German Tradition of Self-Cultivation*, 75. Bruford further points out (76): "New ideals of 'Bildung' were the natural concomitants" of the Romantics' "enlarged conceptions of human nature and destiny." But as he remarks: "The classical ideal of personality as an organic unity of fully developed, freely active human powers was taken over by the Romantics but extended by their fertile minds with little thought for observed reality."

39. On the Romantics, see Paul Kluckhohn, *Das Ideengut der deutschen Romantik*, 4th ed. (Tübingen: Max Niemeyer Verlag, 1961), 53, 56, 57, 58, 59, 61, 88; also idem, *Persönlichkeit und Gemeinschaft: Studien zur Staatsauffassung der deutschen Romantik* (Halle: Max Niemeyer Verlag, 1925), 2, 3, 4–5, 7, 9. Kluckhohn says that the Romantics hardly used the word "personality," but rather "individuality" or "characteristic." Moreover, he says, there were two decisive moments for the Romantic experience of "personality": the first was the new strong experience of individuality, known through Hamann, Herder, and Goethe, whose influence was felt most strongly in *Wilhelm Meisters Lehrjahre*, though the Romantics soon became dissatisfied with its "prosaic" approach; the second was Pietism, which emphasized the inner experience of God and the value of the individual soul.

Schleiermacher derives his conceptions of the worth of personality from religion, and links the development of the personality to an integration of natural impulses and inclinations that puts him in conflict with the rigoristic ethics of Kant. See Frederick Copleston, *A History of Philosophy*, vol. 7, pt. 1: *Modern Philosophy—Fichte to Hegel* (Garden City, N.Y.: Doubleday, 1965), chaps. 1, 4, 7, 8. For a different approach, focusing on the failure of Romanticism, see Judith Shklar, *After Utopia* (Princeton: Princeton University Press, 1957), chap. 2, "The Romantic Mind," esp. 37–53.

Simmel provides an interesting portrait of the struggle between the individual and society in the nineteenth century and the increasingly important role of "personality," in *Sociology of Georg Simmel*, 58–84, esp. 58–60, 62, 79, 84. He concludes (84) by saying: "I should prefer to believe . . . that the ideas of pure personality as such and of unique personality as such, are not the last words of individualism. I should like to think that the efforts of mankind will produce ever more numerous and varied forms for the human personality to affirm itself and to demonstrate the value of its existence."

40. Some of the differences line up this way: Schiller-Humboldt (self as organic totality) versus Goethe (self as fragment of the whole) versus Schleiermacher (self as moral will) versus Schlegel (aesthetic self-cultivation).

41. Ernest K. Bramsted, *Aristocracy and the Middle Classes in Germany: Social Types in German Literature, 1830–1900*, rev. ed. (Chicago: University of Chicago Press, 1964), 278.

42. Schnädelbach, *Philosophie in Deutschland*, 43. See also Hajo Holborn, "German Idealism in the Light of Social History," in *Germany and Europe* (Garden City, N.Y.: Doubleday, 1971), 1–32.

43. Ringer, Review of Bruford, 108. Stern, *Failure of Illiberalism*, 8–9, says the German exaltation of culture led to "the approximation of religion, more accurately of Protestantism, to culture and metaphysics, by stripping religion of the supernatural and the mysterious, of sin and redemption, reducing it to an ethical essence, to a universal core that was immune to higher biblical criticism."

44. Humboldt, quoted in Bruford, *German Tradition of Self-Cultivation*, 27. Meinecke, "Schiller," in *Werke* 4:311, says Humboldt later learned to experience religiously the divine *Urgrund* of life.

45. Ringer, Review of Bruford, 108, 109.

46. Ibid., 108.

47. Hinton Thomas, "Uses of 'Bildung,' " 177. Bruford, *German Tradition of Self-Cultivation*, 84–85, discusses the discovery of the "personality" of the state by the same figure who had carried "the ideal of the inward development of the personality to an unprecedented extreme, Schleiermacher."

48. The conservatives included the *völkisch* movement, and Treitschke, LaGarde, Lienhard, Langbehn, Chamberlain, and Krieck. For more on LaGarde and Langbehn, see Fritz Stern, *The Politics of Cultural Despair: A Study in the Rise of the Germanic Ideology* (Garden City, N.Y.: Doubleday Anchor, 1965). On Treitschke, see Jarausch, *Students, Society, and Politics*, 179, 209–12, and chap. 4.

49. Hinton Thomas, "Uses of 'Bildung,' " 185–86.

50. Ibid., 184, 185. Also Stern, *Failure of Illiberalism*, 15, who says that, after 1871, "*Bildung* became as much a conservative bulwark as *Besitz*, and both began to accept the refeudalization of German society."

51. Jarausch, *Students, Society, and Politics*, 133.

52. Ringer, "German Academic Community," 109.

53. Jarausch, *Students, Society, and Politics*, 33, 43, 70; idem, "Social Transformation of the University," 629.

54. Jarausch, *Students, Society, and Politics*, 50; idem, "Social Transformation of the University," 629–30.

55. Jarausch, "Liberal Education," 625, 628.

56. Ibid., 614, argues that the neohumanist conception of liberal education, *Bildung durch Wissenschaft*, could never accomplish its mission and left student socialization to the vagaries of life in the Second Empire, for it "was incomplete from its beginning, because it treated students as future scholars and did not take their noncognitive (i.e., emotional and social) needs sufficiently into account." Thus, reformers "failed to include the regeneration of student life in their ambitious plans."

57. Jarausch, *Students, Society, and Politics*, 103, 106, 146–48, 178, 189, 166, 186; idem, "Liberal Education," 615. See also Lilge, *Abuse of Learning*, chap. 3.

58. Schnädelbach, *Philosophie in Deutschland*, 43, 36.

59. Humboldt, quoted in ibid., 42, 43. However, he says, the state must not intervene in the university's enterprises; rather, it must trust in the conviction that if the university "reaches its own ultimate purpose, it also fulfills [the state's] purpose and indeed from a much higher standpoint."

60. Jarausch, *Students, Society, and Politics*, 9, 50–51, 76, 102–4, 107. Ringer, "German Academic Community," 110, points out that an important reason for the defense of *Wissenschaft* for its own sake was the desire to ward off the demands of the state for immediate practical learning and the simple training of officials. See also Schnädelbach, *Philosophie in Deutschland*, 36, 42–44, 49–50, 288n.96. As Schnädelbach observes, "in the age of Humboldt, Ranke, and Droysen," *Bildung durch Wissenschaft* ceased to convey what it originally meant, the study of classical philology and literature, and came to mean "*Bildung* through scientific history," including the history of different civilizations but particularly German.

61. Ernst Troeltsch, "Die Revolution in der Wissenschaft" (1921), in *Gesammelte Schriften* (Tübingen: J.C.B. Mohr [Paul Siebeck], 1925), 4:654.

62. Hofmannsthal, quoted in Ringer, *Decline of the German Mandarins*, 400. I have altered the quote slightly.

63. Stern, *Failure of Illiberalism*, 15; Jarausch, *Students, Society, and Politics*, 33, 43–45, 48–51, 81–82, 88–89, 102–4.

64. Troeltsch, "Revolution in der Wissenschaft," 653. See also Lukács's comments on the problem of specialization in the academic disciplines in *History and Class Consciousness*, trans. Rodney Livingstone (Cambridge, Mass.: MIT Press, 1971), 103–4.

65. Friedrich Paulsen, *Die deutsche Universitäten und das Universitätsstudium* (1902), quoted in Schnädelbach, *Philosophie in Deutschland*, 46. See also Georg Simmel, *The Philosophy of Money*, trans. Tom Bottomore and David Frisby (London: Routledge & Kegan Paul, 1978), 452–53.

66. Wolfgang Sauer, "Weimar Culture: Experiments in Modernism," *Social Research* 39 (1972): 263, 264.

67. Dilthey, in one of his last lectures from 1906, quoted in Ermarth, *Wilhelm Dilthey*, 80, 88. Dilthey, a principal analyst of *Weltanschauungen*, reveals the significance of the concept when he says: "The world-view is the more or less articulated and 'objectivated' form of the acquired coherence of personality which otherwise remains tacit and unreflective" (quoted in ibid., 325). Weber later follows this reasoning in "Science as a Vocation" when he advocates the creation of personality as the first and primary task, from which *Weltanschauungen* may then be derived.

68. Paulsen, quoted in Ermarth, *Wilhelm Dilthey*, 84. This quote is from before 1901.

69. Karl Joel, "Die Gefahr modernen Denkens" (1911–12), quoted in Ermarth, *Wilhelm Dilthey*, 89.

70. Ringer, *Decline of the German Mandarins*, 295–304. For more on this crisis, see H. Stuart Hughes, *Consciousness and Society: The Reorientation of European Social Thought, 1890–1930* (New York: Vintage Books, 1961), 33–66, 183–200, 229–48; Gerhard Masur, *Prophets of Yesterday: Studies in European Culture, 1890–1914* (New York: Harper & Row, 1961), 159–210; and Wittenberg, "Wissenschaftskrisis."

71. Simmel, "The Metropolis and Spiritual Life" (1902–3), in *Sociology of Georg Simmel*, 421.

72. Simmel, *Sociology of Georg Simmel*, 422. On Lukács's views of Simmel, see Michael Löwy, *Georg Lukács: From Romanticism to Bolshevism*, trans. Patrick Cammiller (London: New Left Books, 1979), 66–67; and the later work of Lukács, *The Destruction of Reason*, trans. Peter Palmer (Atlantic Highlands, N.J.: Humanities Press, 1980), 442–59.

Dilthey, too, drew on the concept of *objektiver Geist* after 1903, perhaps under the influence of Simmel, as Ermarth observes, shifting "the content of understanding from immediate experience," which had been his principal concern, to "culturally mediated experience," in which life was conceived as objective spirit. Dilthey says: "I understand by the concept of objective spirit the diverse forms in which the community among individuals objectifies itself in the sensible world. In objective spirit, the past is a constantly persisting present for us. Its province stretches from the style of life, the forms of intercourse, to the coherence of goals which society has posited, to morality, law, state, religion, art, science, and philosophy" (quoted in Ermarth, *Wilhelm Dilthey*, 277).

Thus, in Dilthey's use, "objective spirit" denotes the same thing Rickert and Weber denote with the concept "culture values." It means not just high culture, but practical values, techniques, and so on, all grounded in historical existence.

73. Simmel, *Sociology of Georg Simmel*, 59.

74. Ibid., 60.

75. Ibid., 61.

76. See Ringer, *Decline of the German Mandarins*, 263–64, 175, and, on the new orientations of the *Kulturwissenschaften* generally, 305–34; also Ringer, "German Academic Community," 126.

77. Simmel, *Sociology of Georg Simmel*, 59.

78. Martin Heidegger, *Prolegomena zu Geschichte des Zeitbegriffs*, vol. 20 of *Gesamtausgabe* (Frankfurt a. M.: Vittorio Klostermann, 1979), 3. The lecture of Weber's that Heidegger refers to is "Science as a Vocation." For Husserl's view, see *The Crisis of the European Sciences and Transcendental Phenomenology* (Evanston, Ill.: Northwestern University Press, 1970).

79. On the later developments of the crisis, see Stephen P. Turner and Regis A. Factor, *Max Weber and the Dispute over Reason and Value* (London: Routledge & Kegan Paul, 1984). Most of the central arguments in this discussion are included in part 2 of Peter Lassman and Irving Velody, eds., with Herminio Martins, *Max Weber's "Science as a Vocation"* (London: Unwin Hyman, 1989).

80. Erich Marcks and Eduard Spranger, quoted in Ringer, *Decline of the German Mandarins*, 256, 257. Other figures to whom Ringer refers for expressions of this crisis are Simmel, Theobald Ziegler, and Rudolf Eucken.

81. Ringer, *Decline of the German Mandarins*, 105, 283, 285, 336, 279. For more on the crisis of culture, work, and value among academics at the turn of the century, see ibid., 102–13, 253–304. Ringer maintains (267) that the theory of cultural decadence prominent in academic circles was a "projection of the intellectual's personal fears and doubts upon the rest of society" and that this "priestly caste" sought "primarily personal escape" from the psychic tensions of modern intellectual life. On school reform, see 269–82. Also idem, "German Academic Community," 123, 126–28.

82. Ringer, "German Academic Community," 126, 127. For a Marxist critique of science in this period, see Lukács, *History and Class Consciousness*, 103–4, 107, 109–10; and "The Antinomies of Bourgeois Thought" in the essay on reification in ibid.

83. Harnack, quoted in Ermarth, *Wilhelm Dilthey*, 84. Ermarth relies for much of his information about this crisis on Theobald Ziegler, *Die geistige Strömungen unserer Zeit* (1901).

84. Paulsen, *Deutsche Universitäten*, quoted in Schnädelbach, *Philosophie in Deutschland*, 45–46.

85. Alfred Vierkandt (1920), quoted in Ringer, *Decline of the German Mandarins*, 350.

86. Troeltsch, "Die Revolution in der Wissenschaft," 653–54.

87. Ibid., 669–70, 676.

88. Troeltsch, quoted in Ringer, *Decline of the German Mandarins*, 346, 345.

89. Ringer, *Decline of the German Mandarins*, 272.

90. Gadamer, *Truth and Method*, 57. Gadamer discusses the history and meaning of the word *Erlebnis* in ibid., 55–63. For more on *Erlebnis*, see Hermann Mau, "Die deutsche Jugendbewegung: Rückblick und Ausblick," *Zeitschrift für Religions- und Geistesgeschichte* 1–2 (1948–49): 135–49, esp. 135, 136, 137. For the obsessions of the Expressionists with life, youth, and feeling, see Walter Sokel, *The Writer in Extremis: Expressionism in Twentieth-Century Literature* (New York: McGraw-Hill, 1959), 86–96.

91. Wilhelm Windelband, "On the Mysticism of Our Time" (1910), quoted in Ermarth, *Wilhelm Dilthey*, 83–84. On the return to idealism, see Windelband, *Die Philosophie im deutschen Geistesleben des 19. Jahrhunderts*, 3d ed. (Tübingen: J.C.B. Mohr [Paul Siebeck], 1927), 96–120.

92. Jarausch, *Students, Society, and Politics*, 51–52.

93. Ibid., 331. See also 234–94 on the corporations.

94. Walter Laqueur, *Young Germany: A History of the German Youth Movement* (New York: Basic Books, 1962), 4, 5. For more on the youth movement, see George L. Mosse, *The Crisis of German Ideology: Intellectual Origins of the Third Reich* (New York: Grosset & Dunlap, 1964), 171–89; Robert Wohl, *The Generation of 1914* (Cambridge, Mass.: Harvard University Press, 1979), 42–48; Kurt Sontheimer, "Anti-Democratic Thought in the Weimar Republic," in Theodor Eschenburg et al., *The Path to Dictatorship, 1918–1933* (New York: Praeger, 1967), 38–40, 42–44; Jarausch, *Students, Society, and Politics*, 288–90; Thomas Nipperdey, "Jugend und Politik um 1900" and "Die deutschen Studentenschaft in den ersten Jahren der Weimarer Republik," in *Gesellschaft, Kultur, Theorie* (Göttingen: Vandenhoeck & Ruprecht, 1976), 338–59 and 390–416, respectively; Mau, "Deutsche Jugendbewegung," 135–49; and Jürgen Schwarz, *Studenten in der Weimarer Republik* (Berlin: Duncker & Humblot, 1971), 121–29, 147–52, 300–313, 381–89.

95. Troeltsch, quoted in Ringer, *Decline of the German Mandarins*, 346.

96. See Sokel, *Writer in Extremis*, 86–96, 102–4. See also Paul Honigsheim on the religious and mystical movements and the relation of the youth movement to economic ideas, in "Romantische und religiös-mystisch verankerte Wirtschaftsgesinnungen," in *Die Wirtschaftswissenschaft nach dem Kriege. Festgabe für Lujo Brentano zum 80. Geburtstag*, ed. M. J. Bonn and M. Palyi (Munich and Leipzig: Duncker & Humblot, 1925), 1:259–318.

97. Sauer, "Weimar Culture," 258, 265. As Arthur Mitzman says in *Sociology and Estrangement* (New York: Knopf, 1973), 31, "The years 1900–14 reveal a general decline of faith in the modernist option among the younger intellectuals and a channeling of formerly political energies into movements of apolitical aesthetics and philosophical speculation. These were the years of the youth movement, expressionism, Lebens-philosophie, and the George-Kreis."

98. On the attitude of academics, intellectuals, and students toward the outbreak of the war, see Jarausch, *Students, Society, and Politics*, 393–425; Klaus Schwabe, "Zur politischen Haltung der deutschen Professoren im ersten Weltkrieg," *Historische Zeitschrift* 193 (1961): 601–34; Klaus Schröter, "Chauvinism and Its Tradition: German Writers and the Outbreak of the First World War," *Germanic Review* 42 (1968): 120–35; and Ringer, *Decline of the German Mandarins*, 180–99.

CHAPTER 3

1. See Schnädelbach, *Philosophie in Deutschland*, 43, 44; Wolfgang Schluchter, *Rationalismus der Weltbeherrschung. Studien zu Max Weber* (Frankfurt a. M.: Suhrkamp Verlag, 1980), 62, 63.

2. Weber's practical interventions in university issues are collected in *Max Weber on Universities: The Power of the State and the Dignity of the Academic Calling in Imperial Germany*, trans. and ed. Edward Shils (Chicago: University of Chicago Press, 1973).

3. Weber's interest in education and the shaping of individuals by different social orders is strong throughout his work. The centrality of his concern with *Bildung* as an analytical problem is highly visible in the first version of his "Confucianism and Taoism," which appeared in 1915 in the *Archiv für Sozialwissenschaften und Sozialpolitik*; chapter 2 of that essay was entitled "The 'Spirit' of Confucian *Bildung* and the Economy." See Wolfgang Schluchter, *Rationalism, Religion, and Domination: A Weberian Perspective*, trans. Neil Solomon (Berkeley and Los Angeles: University of California Press, 1989), 87.

4. Weber, "Confucianism and Taoism," *GRS* 1:408; "Charismatic Domination," *WG*, 677.

5. Weber, "Bureaucratic Domination," *WG*, 578. According to Weber, education in different societies depended generally on whether military-knightly training or ecclesiastic instruction predominated. In the Middle Ages, clerical-rational and knightly education coexisted and cooperated. At the opposite pole of specialization, a type of " 'poetical' [*musische*] education" was cultivated in addition to military-gymnastic education among the knightly as a means of self-glorification and distinction. The feudal military and "poetical" education of the knight, Weber writes, is "opposed through its this-worldly orientation to charismatic magical

prophetic and heroic asceticism, through its warlike heroic ethos to literary 'Bildung,' through its playful and artistic formation to rational specialized schooling." This education, and later the genteel education of the Renaissance salon, appeared alongside, or supplemented, clerically centered education by books, priests, and monks. The Puritans, in contrast, and especially the Baptists, developed an "unbreakable power of resistance" from the "plebeian" and popular religious intellectualism they developed through diffusion of knowledge of the Bible. They opposed adjustment to the world, the self-perfection cultivated by Confucianism, and philosophical and literary education. See Weber, "Charismatic Domination," *WG*, 678; "Feudalism, Ständestaat, and Patrimonialism," *WG*, 639–40, 651; "Confucianism and Taoism," *GRS* 1:409–17, 524–25; "Sociology of Religion," *WG*, 312; also "Intermediate Reflection," *GRS* 1:564–65.

6. Weber, "Confucianism and Taoism," *GRS* 1:409.

7. Weber, "Bureaucratic Domination," *WG*, 578.

8. Weber, "Confucianism and Taoism," *GRS* 1:409–10; "Charismatic Domination," *WG*, 677.

9. Weber, "The Meaning of 'Value Freedom' in the Social and Economic Sciences," in *Gesammelte Aufsätze zur Wissenschaftslehre* [hereafter cited as *WL*], 5th ed., ed. Johannes Winckelmann (Tübingen: J.C.B. Mohr [Paul Siebeck], 1982), 491; "Science as a Vocation," *WL*, 602. See also Carlo Antoni, *From History to Sociology: The Transition in German Historical Thinking*, trans. Hayden White (Detroit: Wayne State University Press, 1959), 143, who quotes a similar remark of Weber's made in 1905.

10. On rationalization in Weber, see Jürgen Habermas, *Theory of Communicative Action*, vol. 1, trans. Thomas McCarthy (Boston: Beacon Press, 1984); Schluchter, *Rise of Western Rationalism*; Anthony T. Kronman, *Max Weber* (Stanford: Stanford University Press, 1983); G. H. Mueller, "The Notion of Rationality in the Work of Max Weber," *Archives européennes de sociologie* 20 (1979): 149–71; Stephen Kalberg, "Max Weber's Types of Rationality: Cornerstones for the Analysis of Rationalization Processes in History," *American Journal of Sociology* 85 (1980): 1145–79; Donald Levine, "Rationality and Freedom: Weber and Beyond," *Sociological Inquiry* 51 (1981): 5–25; Arnold Eisen, "The Meanings and Confusions of Weberian 'Rationality,' " *British Journal of Sociology* 29 (1978): 57–70.

11. This is brought out in the "Preliminary Remark," *GRS* 1:1–16. See also Benjamin Nelson, "Max Weber's 'Author's Introduction' (1920): A Master Clue to His Main Aims," *Sociological Inquiry* 44 (1974): 269–78.

12. The lecture was delivered November 7, 1917, in Munich, before the Bavarian branch of the Freistudentische Bund, a left-liberal student

group, in a student-organized series on "Intellectual Work as a Calling" (*Geistige Arbeit als Beruf*). For dating, see Schluchter, *Rationalismus der Weltbeherrschung*, 236–39n.2; Schluchter's dating is indebted to Martin Riesebrodt. See also Wolfgang J. Mommsen, *Max Weber und die deutsche Politik, 1890–1920*, 2d ed. (Tübingen: J.C.B. Mohr [Paul Siebeck], 1974), 289–90n.292, 345, 347.

13. Weber, "Basic Sociological Categories of the Economy," *WG*, 80.

14. Weber, "Science as a Vocation," *WL*, 599. For different approaches, see Wolfgang Schluchter, "Wertfreiheit und Verantwortungsethik," in *Rationalismus der Weltbeherrschung*, 41–74. Also Robert Eden, *Political Leadership and Nihilism: A Study of Weber and Nietzsche* (Gainesville: University Presses of Florida, 1983), esp. chaps. 4 and 5; and idem, "Bad Conscience for a Nietzschean Age: Weber's Calling for Science," *Review of Politics* 45 (1983): 366–92.

15. For the meaning of "cultural goods," see Heinrich Rickert, *Kulturwissenschaft und Geschichte*, 5th ed. (1926), translated as *Science and History*, trans. George Reisman (Princeton: Van Nostrand, 1962), 19, 22, 27, 88, 89. He says that "values always attach to cultural objects. Therefore, we shall call them *goods*, in order to distinguish them as *valuable entities* from the values as such. . . . Religion, church, law, the state, custom, science, language, literature, art, economy, and the technical means necessary for their preservation are . . . cultural objects or *goods* precisely in the sense that either the value attaching to them is acknowledged by all members of a community or its acknowledgement is *expected* of them." Weber generally uses the expression *Kulturgüter*, as, for example, in *WG*, 530. He also uses *Güterbesitz*, which means a "possession of goods" and implies an accepted, established area of "cultural values," i.e., things a culture values or to which it is oriented.

16. See Weber, "Intermediate Reflection," in *GRS* 1:536–73. See also Eduard Baumgarten, ed., *Max Weber: Werk und Person* (Tübingen: J.C.B. Mohr [Paul Siebeck], 1964), 473; Arthur Mitzman, *The Iron Cage: An Historical Interpretation of Max Weber* (New York: Knopf, 1970), 219; and Schluchter, *Rationalismus der Weltbeherrschung*, 209n.1, 213n.1.

17. Weber, "Economic Ethics of the World Religions," *GRS* 1: 265–66.

18. Weber, "Sociology of Religion," *WG*, 349.

19. Weber, "Intermediate Reflection," *GRS* 1:544.

20. Weber, "Intermediate Reflection," *GRS* 1:547, 544, 564, 569; "Sociology of Religion," *WG*, 307, 361–62; "Economic Ethics of the World Religions," *GRS* 1:254; "Market Relationships," *WG*, 382–83. The "Intermediate Reflection" is subtitled "Theory of the Stages and Directions of Religious Rejections of the World," yet, apart from its concern with religious rejections, Weber intended this work to be a "contribution to the typology and sociology of rationalism itself." See *GRS* 1:537. There

are three versions of this essay, the third of which is principally used here. On the dating of these versions, see Wolfgang Schluchter, "Die Paradoxie der Rationalisierung," in *Rationalismus der Weltbeherrschung*, 208–14n.1.

21. Weber, "Intermediate Reflection," *GRS* 1:541–42.

22. Ibid., 546.

23. Weber, "Sociology of Religion," *WG*, 361. It is put similarly in "Intermediate Reflection," *GRS* 1:546. For the consequences of this situation for law, see "The Economy and Social Norms," *WG*, 333.

24. Weber, "Intermediate Reflection," *GRS* 1:547. Also in "Sociology of Religion," *WG*, 361.

25. Weber, "Intermediate Reflection," *GRS* 1:546.

26. Weber, "Bureaucratic Domination," *WG*, 562.

27. Weber, "Intermediate Reflection," *GRS*, 1:544; also "Political and Hierocratic Domination," *WG*, 708–9.

28. Weber, "Political and Hierocratic Domination," *WG*, 708–10. For Marx on the relative "blamelessness" of the capitalist businessman and the domination of capital by its "own immanent laws," see *Capital*, trans. Ben Fowkes (New York: Vintage Books, 1977), 1:381.

29. Weber, "Sociology of Religion," *WG*, 353.

30. Weber, "Market Society," *WG*, 382–83. The term *Versachlichung*, translated here as objectification, can also be used to signify "impersonality," "objectivity," or even "reification."

31. Weber, "Bureaucratic Domination," *WG*, 562–63.

32. Weber, "Intermediate Reflection," *GRS* 1:564, 569; "Sociology of Religion," *WG*, 307; "Economic Ethics of the World Religions," *GRS* 1:254.

33. Weber, "Value Freedom," *WL*, 509.

34. Weber, "Science as a Vocation," *WL*, 599–600.

35. Ibid., 594. Weber, "Value Freedom," *WL*, 527, says he uses "'technique' in its widest sense" to mean "rational conduct [*Sichverhalten*] above all, in all spheres: also those of the political, social, educational, propagandistic manipulation and domination of human beings."

36. Weber, "Sociology of Religion," *WG*, 308. See also Friedrich Tenbruck, "'Science as a Vocation'—Revisited," in *Standorte im Zeitstrom. Festschrift für Arnold Gehlen zum 70. Geburtstag am 29. Januar 1974*, ed. Ernst Forsthoff and Reinhard Hörstel (Frankfurt a. M.: Atheneum Verlag, 1974), 357. Maurice Weyembergh, in *Le voluntarisme rationnel de Max Weber*, Mémoires de la Classe des Lettres, 2d ser., vol. 61, no. 1 (Brussels: Académie Royale de Belgique, 1972), 472, 473, 475–76, says Weber makes himself "the agent" of rationalization in an "engagement" on its behalf. Karl Löwith, "Max Weber und Karl Marx," 10, says Weber's question about the value of science is the same that Nietzsche posed to philosophy on the value of truth. But this is not true, for Nietzsche

reveals devotion to truth as one more asceticism, while Weber wants to defend science's search for truth, although on different grounds from those that scientists usually adopt.

37. Weber, "Science as a Vocation," *WL*, 599. See also Günter Abramowski, *Das Geschichtsbild Max Webers* (Stuttgart: Ernst Klett Verlag, 1966), 174, who says correctly that "the decision for science is consequently the untranscendable ground of its own existence and of its 'calling.' "

38. Weber, "The Objectivity of Social Scientific and Social Political Knowledge," *WL*, 213. See also Löwith, "Karl Marx und Max Weber," 10. On faith in science, see Weber, "Science as a Vocation," *WL*, 596–98; "Confucianism and Taoism," *GRS* 1:439; "The Protestant Ethic," *GRS* 1:141 and n. 5; and "Intermediate Reflection," *GRS* 1:564.

39. Weber, "Objectivity," *WL*, 149, 151.

40. Ibid., 154.

41. Ibid., 206.

42. Weber, "Science as a Vocation," *WL*, 588.

43. Weber, "The Protestant Ethic," *GRS* 1:203.

44. Weber, "Science as a Vocation," *WL*, 592, 588.

45. Ibid., 592. See also the comments of Theodor Mommsen in Jarausch, *Students, Society, and Politics*, 76, on the effect of *Großwissenschaft*, where "in comparison to this gigantic edifice the individual worker appears ever smaller." Lilge, *Abuse of Learning*, chap. 3, and esp. p. 74, says that Helmholtz, the nineteenth-century physicist, "asked devotion to a vaguely conceived 'cause,' usually described as progress. Its devotees were asked to throw their souls into the bargain and then hope for the best." This "wager" on progress and its significance for the worker in science was not new when Weber addressed it.

46. Weber, "Roscher and Knies and the Logical Problems of Historical Political Economy," *WL*, 33n.2.

47. Rickert, *Science and History*, 96; see also 19, 28, on the meaning of "culture" and "cultural goods." By culture we understand "the totality of real objects to which attach generally acknowledged *values* or complexes of meaning constituted by values and which are *fostered* with regard for these values." On the concept of culture, see Ringer, *Decline of the German Mandarins*, 88–90; also Weber, "Value Freedom," *WL*, 511; "Critical Studies in the Field of Social Scientific Logic," *WL*, 259, 261–62; "Political Communities," *WG*, 530. In "Objectivity," *WL*, 175, Weber says: "The concept of culture is a *value concept*. Empirical reality *is* for us 'culture,' because and insofar as we put it in relationship with value ideas." Wolfgang Mommsen, *The Age of Bureaucracy* (New York: Harper & Row, 1974), 4, says that "up to 1908, Weber used the concept of 'culture' rather than that of 'society.' "

48. Weber, "Science as a Vocation," *WL*, 594.

49. Weber, "Intermediate Reflection," *GRS* 1:569–70; and "Science as a Vocation," *WL*, 587.

50. Weber, "Science as a Vocation," *WL*, 594–95; "Intermediate Reflection," *GRS* 1:569–70. We know from Marianne Weber, *Max Weber: A Biography*, trans. and ed. Harry Zohn, intro. by Guenther Roth (New Brunswick, N.J.: Transaction Books, 1988), 466, that Weber was very influenced by Tolstoy and planned a book on him for some time; Tolstoy is also mentioned in several parts of Weber's religion essays and in *Economy and Society*. Tolstoy was very widely regarded in Europe at this time. For his influence in France after 1886, see Micheline Tison-Braun, *La crise de l'humanisme: le conflit de l'individu et de la société dans la littérature française moderne*, vol. 1: *1890–1914* (Paris: Librairie Nizet, 1958), 116–17. For his influence elsewhere in Europe, see Allan Janik and Stephen Toulmin, *Wittgenstein's Vienna* (New York: Simon & Schuster, 1975), 162ff., who single out Tolstoy's *My Confession, My Religion*, and *The Gospel in Brief*. Weber himself emphasized the late novels.

51. See Weber, "Intermedate Reflection," *GRS* 1:569–70.

52. Weber, "Science as a Vocation," *WL*, 598.

53. An intense argument sprang up around Weber's "Science as a Vocation." In 1923, Max Scheler called "Science as a Vocation" "the shocking document of a whole age—and this age is unfortunately our own"; "Weltanschauungslehre, Soziologie und Weltanschauungssetzung," in *Schriften zur Soziologie und Weltanschauungslehre* (Bonn: Francke Verlag, 1963), 15; see also 17. Erich von Kahler, *Der Beruf der Wissenschaft* (Berlin: Georg Bondi, 1920), attacked the idea that science had no role in creating *Weltanschauungen*. On behalf of "youth," he called for a "new founding" of science as the spiritual leader of humankind, a new connection between science and life, a new personal leadership for society, and a new "devotion to community" to escape the tragedy of intellectualism and the absurdity of university life through a transformation of spiritual life. This elicited a counterargument from Arthur Salz, a Heidelberg economist from the same Stefan George–centered intellectual circles as von Kahler, who argued that von Kahler's position would lead to either dilettantism or a return to religion. But although Salz defended science, he bitterly attacked the organization of scholarship in the universities, yet provided few new arguments. See Arthur Salz, *Für die Wissenschaft. Gegen die Gebildeten unter ihren Verächtern* (Munich: Dreimaskenverlag, 1921). See also Michael Winkler, *George-Kreis* (Stuttgart: J. B. Metzlersche Verlagsbuchhandlung, 1972), 75, 76. See the discussion of von Kahler and Salz in Troeltsch, "Revolution in der Wissenschaft," 668–73, 675, who remarks on "the symptomatic meaning" of these essays, which, in truth, have little substance. Troeltsch, too, disagrees with Weber. He speaks of "the somewhat frightening impression of the Weberian lecture" and of "Weber's skepticism and the

values of a powerfully affirming heroism which are also more impossible to me" (672, 673).

Ernst Robert Curtius, "Max Weber über Wissenschaft als Beruf," *Die Arbeitsgemeinschaft* 17 (1919): 197–203, speaks of Weber's position as a "sharply formulated subjectivism, which excludes agreement on a common, strictly understood foundation." Even though values cannot be proven, he argues, they can "be made evident," and although questions of value cannot be answered scientifically, they can perhaps be answered philosophically. Wittenberg, in "Die Wissenschaftskrisis in Deutschland im Jahre 1919," writes much later of the "deep inner tragedy of Max Weber," arguing that Weber's concept of science is bound up totally with Weber's time. "Max Weber, as the youth recognized, was the son of the Enlightenment, born too late." With Weber, "the age of rationalism goes into decline." He likens Weber's self-appointed task to that of the Puritans, to exclude the irrational and control the world through inner-worldly asceticism. But youth rightly felt, he said, that politics and science, science and *Weltanschauungen*, are closely related, not separated as they are for Weber.

For a rather idealized defense of Weber and a criticism of his critics, see Karl Löwith, "Die Entzauberung der Welt durch Wissenschaft," *Merkur* 18 (1964): 501–17. For a summary of the principal issues and partisans, see Ringer, *Decline of the German Mandarins*, 357–66, who notes that the future Nazi theorist Ernst Krieck also wrote a pamphlet against Weber's lecture in 1920, including in it a call for a common national religion. Ringer also discusses the contribution of the educational reformer Eduard Spranger. See also Turner and Factor, *Max Weber and the Dispute over Reason and Value*.

54. Franz Xaver Schwab, "Beruf und Jugend," *Die weissen Blätter* 4 (April–June 1917): 97–113. See also Schluchter, *Rationalismus der Weltbeherrschung*, 239n.3, who gets the author's name wrong. Sentiments similar to Schwab's were conveyed earlier by Friedrich Gundolf, a member of George's circle and close friend of Weber's, in Gundolf, "Wesen und Beziehung," *Jahrbuch für die geistige Bewegung* 2 (1911): 10–35. On this essay, see Troeltsch, *The Social Teaching of the Christian Churches*, vol. 2, trans. Olive Wyon (1931; Chicago: University of Chicago Press, 1981), 895n.344.

55. Weber, "Sociology of Religion," WG, 362. Weber was the most important participant in a series of discussions in May and September 1917 in the Lauenstein Castle, organized by the conservative publisher Eugen Diederichs. These *Tagungen* included one of the more important youth groups among its participants, the Freideutsche Jugend, oriented to the development of youth in accordance with its own desires and capabilities rather than in accordance with social purpose and priorities. Weber gave a lecture there entitled "The Life Spheres and the Person-

ality." For brief discussions of this meeting, see Max Weber, *Zur Politik im Weltkrieg. Schriften und Reden 1914–18*, ed. Wolfgang J. Mommsen, with Gangolf Hubinger, sec. 1, vol. 15 of *Max Weber Gesamtausgabe* (Tübingen: J.C.B. Mohr [Paul Siebeck], 1984), 701–7; Marianne Weber, *Max Weber*, 596–600; Baumgarten, *Max Weber*, 498–99; Theodor Heuss, *Erinnerungen, 1905–1933* (Tübingen: Rainer Wunderlich Verlag, 1963), 214–15; and Mommsen, *Max Weber und die deutsche Politik*, 50. See also Gary Stark, *Entrepreneurs of Ideology: Neoconservative Publishers in Germany, 1890–1933* (Chapel Hill: University of North Carolina Press, 1981), 136, 273nn.47, 48.

56. Weber, "Sociology of Religion," *WG*, 307; "Science as a Vocation," *WL*, 611; "Economic Ethics of the World Religions," *GRS* 1:251–52. See also Ermarth, *Wilhelm Dilthey*, 84; Mitzman, *Sociology and Estrangement*, 31.

57. Weber, "Science as a Vocation," *WL*, 591. Rickert maintained there could be no "philosophy of life," because experience was without order. See the discussion of Rickert's *Limits of the Formation of Concepts in Natural Science* in Ermarth, *Wilhelm Dilthey*, 191. Curtius, "Max Weber über Wissenschaft als Beruf," 202, defends the possibility, against Weber, that *Erleben* may be practical in certain areas. He wants to reopen "the critical and advancing position of today's youth against university *Wissenschaft*. . . . If today's youth advance 'personality' and 'experience,' there lies in such a position the deeply justified thought that the meaning of scientific existence must be anchored in an interpretation of the meaning of mankind."

58. Weber, "Science as a Vocation," *WL*, 598; "The Protestant Ethic," *GRS* 1:111–12n.1; "Sociology of Religion," *WG*, 314. But see also "Sociology of Religion," *WG*, 343, where Weber observes that intellectual strata of all periods have been skeptically inclined toward the possibility of finding "meaning" in the world! Also Löwith, "Entzauberung der Welt durch Wissenschaft," 501–17. Löwith mistakenly thinks that "Science as a Vocation" was delivered in 1919, after the war, and so refers to the "Religionsersatz" of the youth movement in the postwar period, though it was strongly evident both before and during the war. Weber refers to it as early as 1911–13, in "Sociology of Religion," *WG*, 307.

59. Weber, "Value Freedom," *WL*, 519; "Science as a Vocation," *WL*, 605, 612–13.

60. Weber calls the Sermon on the Mount and the idea "Resist not Evil" an ethic that bespeaks "lack of dignity" when seen from within the world, and he opposes it to the "manly dignity" of resisting evil and accepting the consequences; see "Science as a Vocation," *WL*, 604.

61. Ibid., 587. See also Tenbruck, " 'Science as a Vocation'—Revisited," 355, who says that for Weber, the search for scientific knowledge was clearly affected by the "quest for *inner* meaning," or at least by more

than material and technical interests. He argues in "Max Weber and the Sociology of Science," 320, that Weber claimed science was originally "not a purely cognitive venture, and the belief in the intrinsic value of rational knowledge was predicated on assumptions and expectations about its ulterior meanings"; see also 317.

62. Marianne Weber, *Max Weber*, 551–52.

63. The first edition is "Die Wirtschaftsethik der Weltreligionen. Zwischenbetrachtung: Stufen und Richtungen der religiösen Weltablehnung," in *Archiv für Sozialwissenschaft und Sozialpolitik* 41 (1915): 387–421. To see the crucial change, compare p. 398 of this essay with "Zwischenbetrachtung: Theorie der Stufen und Richtungen religiöser Weltablehnung," *GRS* 1:548. For dating, see Schluchter, *Rationalismus der Weltbeherrschung*, 208–214n.1, who fails to note this important difference between the two versions. The change is now recorded in passing in the apparatus to *Die Wirtschaftsethik der Weltreligionen. Konfuzianismus und Taoismus*, ed. Helwig Schmidt-Glintzer, with Petra Kolonko, sec. 1, vol. 19 of *Max Weber Gesamtausgabe* (Tübingen: J.C.B. Mohr [Paul Siebeck], 1989), 493.

64. Weber, "Intermediate Reflection," *GRS* 1:548–49.

65. Ibid., 548.

66. Weber, "Bureaucratic Domination," *WG*, 576.

67. Weber, "Sociology of Religion," *WG*, 362. See also 357, on how religious inner-worldly asceticism can use impersonal political power for rational ethical ends in the taming of the world.

68. Ibid., 361.

69. Weber, "Political and Hierocratic Domination," *WG*, 709, 710. Weber addressed the question of personal versus impersonal service in "Patriarchal and Patrimonial Domination," *WG*, 598. This was especially important given the existence of "cults" of personal service, to which friends of Weber's belonged, and given the widespread longings for personalization even apart from the cults. The most important example of this ideal was the circle around Stefan George. Although they differed a great deal, Weber and George were impressed with each other when they met, and Weber was affected by the seriousness "with which George personally faces his mission." But as Weber wrote in 1910, "in decisive points Stefan George and his pupils in the final analysis serve 'other gods' than I." As Marianne wrote of her husband, "Since he believed in the absolute value of intellectual and moral autonomy, he denied the necessity of new forms of *personal* dominion and *personal* service for him and his kind. He acknowledged service and absolute devotion to a *cause*, an ideal, but not to an earthly, finite human being and its limited aims, no matter how outstanding and venerable that person might be." See Marianne Weber, *Max Weber*, 457–62. See also Löwith, "Entzauberung der Welt durch Wissenschaft," 519; Sokel, *Writer in Extremis*, 157; Lilge,

Abuse of Learning, 121–25; Michael Winkler, *Stefan George* (Stuttgart: J. B. Metzlersche Verlagsbuchhandlung, 1970), 55–59; idem, *George-Kreis*, 58, 75–76, 89. See also Friedrich Wolters, *Stefan George und die Blätter für die Kunst* (Berlin: Georg Bondi, 1930), 380.

70. Weber, "Value Freedom," *WL*, 494. See also Rickert, *Limits of the Formation of Concepts in Natural Science* (1896), quoted in Georg G. Iggers, *The German Conception of History*, rev. ed. (Middletown, Conn.: Wesleyan University Press, 1983), 157.

71. Weber, "Sociology of Religion," *WG*, 332.

72. Weyembergh, *Voluntarisme rationnel de Max Weber*, 477, xxi.

73. Weber, "The Protestant Ethic," *GRS* 1:178.

74. Weber, "Science as a Vocation," *WL*, 589. The quote within the quote is from Carlyle.

75. During his severe depression, Weber felt freed from the burden of work he had borne previously. In a letter to his wife he wrote: "Such an illness has still its very good sides. . . . I could say with John Gabriel Borkman: 'An icy hand has let me go,' for my sickly condition expressed itself in the past years in a desperate clinging to scientific work as to a talisman, without my being able to say against what. That is quite clear to me now in thinking back, and I know that, sick or healthy, that will not be that way any more. The *need* to feel myself submerged under the work load is extinguished." See Marianne Weber, *Max Weber*, 249. Yet despite his words, Weber had not resolved the issue of work and its demands.

76. Frederic Jameson, "The Vanishing Mediator: Narrative Structure in Max Weber," *New German Critique* 1 (1974): 62, speaks of "Weber's concept of scientific research" as "that uncomfortable ascesis and renunciation which permits Value to come into being as an object of study."

77. Weber, "Science as a Vocation," *WL*, 591–92. The significance of personality is echoed by Rickert in *Science and History*, 110: "The nonrecurring individual can *never* be 'unessential' in a history of religion, the state, science, or art. Here, as everyone knows who does not want deliberately to close his mind to the historical facts for the sake of some theory, impulses to create new cultural goods almost always come from particular *personalities*." See also Stern, *Failure of Illiberalism*, 10, on the cult of the personality in idealism.

78. Weber, "Science as a Vocation," *WL*, 591–92. Schnädelbach, *Philosophie in Deutschland*, 43–44, says that in "Science as a Vocation" "the principle of personality, which was once the basis of *Bildung durch Wissenschaft*, is . . . replaced by the principle of 'objectivity' [*Sachlichkeit*]. . . . *Bildung* has become an ideology. . . . *Wissenschaft* . . . can *not educate* in the Humboldtian sense. . . . Despite all decisionistic elements, this ethos of 'Science as a Vocation' for Max Weber has a material-cultural philosophical foundation."

79. Weber, "Value Freedom," *WL*, 493–94; "Science as a Vocation," *WL*, 592. For different arguments about the centrality of *Persönlichkeit*, see Dieter Henrich, *Die Einheit Max Webers Wissenschaftslehre* (Tübingen: J.C.B. Mohr [Paul Siebeck], 1952), pt. 2; Schluchter, *Rationalismus der Weltbeherrschung*, 35, 47, 56, 247n.57; Edward Bryan Portis, *Max Weber and Political Commitment: Science, Politics, and Personality* (Philadelphia: Temple University Press, 1986); and Weyembergh, *Voluntarisme rationnel de Max Weber*, 478.

80. Weber, "Value Freedom," *WL*, 494. See also Ernst Troeltsch, *Christian Thought: Its History and Application* (London: University of London Press, 1923), 51: "Out of the flux and confusion of the life of the instincts, the unity and compactness of personality has first to be created and acquired. . . . No man is born a personality; everyone has first to make himself into a personality by obedience towards another instinct, which leads to unity and homogeneity." See also 71, 79, 80.

81. Weber, "Objectivity," *WL*, 152.

82. Weber, "Roscher and Knies," *WL*, 132; see also 46n.1.

83. Weber, "Antikritisches Schlußwort zum 'Geist des Kapitalismus,' " in Weber, *Die protestantische Ethik II—Kritiken und Antikritiken*, 2d ed., ed. Johannes Winckelmann (Hamburg: Siebenstern Taschenbuch Verlag, 1972), 319.

84. Ibid.

85. Weber, "Science as a Vocation," *WL*, 604.

86. Ibid., 605.

87. Weber, "Value Freedom," *WL*, 517.

88. Weber, "Science as a Vocation," *WL*, 603–4; "Value Freedom," *WL*, 505.

89. Weber, "Intermediate Reflection," *GRS* 1:565; "Science as a Vocation," *WL*, 603, 608, 604; "Value Freedom," *WL*, 507–8; "Zwischen zwei Gesetzen," in *Gesammelte Politische Schriften*, 3d ed., ed. Johannes Winckelmann [hereafter cited as *GPS*] (Tübingen: J.C.B. Mohr [Paul Siebeck], 1971), 145. The reference to Plato is to *Republic*, 617d–e: "A daimon will not select you, but you will choose a daimon."

Weber observes in "Sociology of Religion," *WG*, 252, that "increasing objective meaning and subjective reflection about the typical components and types of action lead to *objective* [*sachliche*] specialization" among the gods, that is, the imagined control by a specific god of a particular activity, or even of all activity, as in the case of a supreme god. No collective or individual action exists without its god. "Wherever an association or a social organization does not appear as a personal power base of a *single* holder of power, but rather as an 'association' [of persons], then it has need of its particular god." Thus the history of religions shows both the need for a god to be in charge of and watch over action and organization and the pointed need for such a god when a single leader or holder of power is not established. This may, by analogy, cast light on Weber's reasoning about the gods of the rationalized world, specialized and "sublimated through knowledge," needed and experienced even more strongly in the absence of a leader or prophet who controls and dominates action through his power.

90. Weber, "Value Freedom," *WL*, 507.

91. Weber, "Confucianism and Taoism," *GRS* 1:503.

92. See Walter Burkert, *Greek Religion: Archaic and Classical*, trans. John Raffan (Oxford: Basil Blackwell, 1985), 194–99. See also Martin P. Nilsson, *Greek Folk Religion*, with a foreword by Arthur Darby Nock (1940; Philadelphia: University of Pennsylvania Press, 1961); idem, *A History of Greek Religion*, 2d ed., trans. F. J. Fielden (New York: Norton, 1964); and W.K.C. Guthrie, *The Greeks and Their Gods* (Boston: Beacon Press, 1955).

93. Burkert, *Greek Religion*, 216.

94. Nietzsche, *Beyond Good and Evil*, in *KSA*, vol. 5, sec. 53, pp. 72–73.

95. Weber, "Objectivity," *WL*, 212, 154.

96. Weber, "Value Freedom," *WL*, 508; "Sociology of Religion," *WG*, 360–61; "Hinduism and Buddhism," *GRS* 2:142, 146, 200.

97. Weber, "Science as a Vocation," *WL*, 603.

98. Ibid., 608. See also "Objectivity," *WL*, 150–51; and "Value Freedom," *WL*, 508, 510–11.

99. Weber, "Value Freedom," *WL*, 493.

100. Weber, "Objectivity," *WL*, 150–51.

101. For the more neutral language, see Weber, "Value Freedom," *WL*, 508, 510–11; "Science as a Vocation," *WL*, 607.

102. Mommsen seems to recognize this in *Age of Bureaucracy*, 2: "Weber's belief in sociology as a rational discipline was embedded, as may be gathered from his famous public lecture 'Science as a Vocation,' in a very personal philosophy which had the dimension of a substantive ethic." But it is this point that Schluchter, *Rationalismus der Weltbeherrschung*, 44, misses when he says of Weber's lectures on vocation that the subject here is not "what must be done, rather he searches unmistakably to determine what may not be done." In fact, Weber is preaching that one hearken to a calling, which may not seem like much of a prescription, until one realizes what calling really means and implies. Weyembergh, *Voluntarisme rationnel de Max Weber*, 477, says: "If the occupation or profession are no longer the means of creating salvation, they constitute, nevertheless, the only form in which the individual can confer a meaning on his life."

103. Weber, "Science as a Vocation," *WL*, 609; "Intermediate Reflection," *GRS* 1:571. See "Ancient Judaism," *GRS* 3:220–21, where Weber says "in order for new conceptions of a religious kind to be possible,

the human being must not yet have unlearned to confront the happenings of the world with his own *questions.*" Only people who live far from the great culture centers are in a position to do so. "The capacity of *astonishment* over the course of the world is the presupposition of the possibility of questions about its meaning."

104. Weber, "Science as a Vocation," *WL,* 613.

105. Weber, "Bureaucratic Domination," *WG,* 553.

106. Compare the similar view of Honigsheim in *On Max Weber,* 132–33. Weyembergh, *Voluntarisme rationnel de Max Weber,* 483, says: "In the vision of the sociologist, neutrality and axiological discussion, the conflict of values, the necessity of 'calling,' were the consequences of the engagement for rationality postulated by scientific practice." Although the calling does serve as a means of "coping" with rationality, it does not derive from Weber's engagement for rationality, as Weyembergh believes.

107. Weber, "Objectivity," *WL,* 153; "Sociology of Religion," *WG,* 285, 314; "Value Freedom," *WL,* 515–16. Mommsen, *Age of Bureaucracy,* 7, calls this "individualist decisionism." See also Jürgen Habermas, *Toward a Rational Society,* trans. Jeremy J. Shapiro (Boston: Beacon Press, 1970), 62–80. Schluchter, *Rationalismus der Weltbeherrschung,* 70–71, claims to be writing a critique of this view of Weber. See also Löwith, "Karl Marx und Max Weber," 33. For a different view, see Maurice Natanson, "On Conceptual Nihilism," in Natanson, *Phenomenology, Role, and Reason: Essays on the Coherence and Deformation of Social Reality* (Springfield, Ill.: Charles C. Thomas, 1974), 336, 338.

108. Weber, "Value Freedom," *WL,* 517.

109. Weber, "Politics as a Vocation," *GPS,* 524–25, 552ff.; "Value Freedom," *WL,* 505, 508; "Intermediate Reflection," *GRS* 1:552–53. This issue is especially important for the political leader. Cf. Max Horkheimer, "Schopenhauer Today," in *The Critical Spirit: Essays in Honor of Herbert Marcuse,* ed. Kurt H. Wolff and Barrington Moore, Jr. (Boston: Beacon Press, 1967), 69; "A certain state of humanity, venerated as the true one, is an aim among others for which men may justifiably sacrifice themselves. But if it is hypostatized as the absolute aim, then, by definition, there is no authority, neither divine commandment, nor morality, nor even . . . the personal relation called friendship, which could control it."

110. Weber, "Intermediate Reflection," *GRS* 1:552–53; "Value Freedom," *WL,* 505; "Science as a Vocation," *WL,* 607. Schluchter disagrees in *Rationalismus der Weltbeherrschung,* 70–71, saying of Weber's science that it works "toward the expansion of an ethically responsible conviction." But although such an ethos can be decided for or *accepted* in Weber's logic, science cannot argue for it. It can only be a product of faith in one's cause or calling.

111. There were notable cases of discrimination and resistance in

academic life, among them Robert Michels and Georg Simmel. For a few other cases of academic and other judgments settled by standards of hostility toward socialists, Jews, and Catholics, see Weber, *Max Weber on Universities*, 4–23; and Ringer, *Decline of the German Mandarins*, 141–42.

CHAPTER 4

1. On academic reaction to the war, see Schwabe, "Zur politischen Haltung der deutschen Professoren im Ersten Weltkrieg," 601–34; and Ringer, *Decline of the German Mandarins*, 181, who quotes a pamphlet by professors proclaiming the "voluntary submission of all individuals and social groups to this army. . . . Our own ego with its personal interests was dissolved in the great historic being of the nation." On writers, see Schröter, "Chauvinism and its Tradition," 120–35.

2. T. J. Reed, *Thomas Mann: The Uses of Tradition* (Oxford: Clarendon Press, 1974), 200. On Mann's politics, see Kurt Sontheimer, *Thomas Mann und die Deutschen* (Frankfurt a. M.: Fischer Bücherei, 1965); and Hans Joachim Maître, *Thomas Mann: Aspekte der Kulturkritik in seiner Essayistik* (Bonn: H. Bouvier Co. Verlag, 1970).

3. On Heinrich as the "actual opponent" of the *Reflections*, see Klaus Schröter, *Thomas Mann in Selbstzeugnissen und Bilddokumenten* (Reinbeck bei Hamburg: Rowohlt, 1964), 82–83. See also André Banuls, *Thomas Mann und sein Bruder Heinrich* (Stuttgart: W. Kohlhammer Verlag, 1968).

4. Schröter, *Thomas Mann*, 85, however, maintains that in the foreword to the *Reflections* Mann took back most of his most extreme positions.

5. Some critics mistakenly maintain he overcame these attitudes by 1912. Reed, *Thomas Mann*, 200, however, has correctly remarked that while Aschenbach's abandonment of a critical attitude led to disaster in *Death in Venice*, Mann himself "joined in the far greater 'orgies of a complicated *naiveté* ' " in 1914.

6. He speaks there of having lived a long time in "brotherly nearness" to a naive French style of aggressive intellectuality whose "brotherly rage" far exceeded any "foreign hatred" aimed at him from abroad. See Mann, *Reflections of an Unpolitical Man*, in *Gesammelte Werke* [hereafter cited as *GW*], ed. Hans Bürgin (Frankfurt a. M.: S. Fischer Verlag, 1960, 1974), 12:151–52, 191, 64; see also 193–94. Hereafter references to the *Reflections* will be indicated in the text by page number in parentheses.

7. On culture versus civilization, see Ringer, *Decline of the German Mandarins*, 83–90; Elias, *Civilizing Process*, 3–34; Banuls, *Thomas Mann und sein Bruder Heinrich*, 61–76; Georg Michael Pflaum, "Geschichte des Wortes *Zivilization*" (Ph.D. diss., University of Munich, 1961).

8. Schröter, *Thomas Mann*, 86, maintains that Mann here takes up the ideas of Stefan George and his circle, which equated civilization with democracy, but that Mann, unlike them, "endeavored to clarify the antithesis 'culture/civilization' from its historical conditions." On the influences on Mann's wartime political writings, see Schröter, " 'Eideshelfer' Thomas Manns 1914/18," in *Literatur und Zeitgeschichte* (Mainz: Von Hase & Koehler Verlag, 1970), 47–65. See also Nigel Hamilton, *The Brothers Mann* (New Haven: Yale University Press, 1979), 161.

9. Mann, "Gedanken im Kriege," GW 13:528, 529.

10. Ibid., 529–30.

11. A. Williams has claimed that "Mann's central aim in his *Gedanken* was to demonstrate the identity and unity in the name of '*Kultur*' of Germany the land of the poet with Germany the land of the soldier"; see "Thomas Mann's Nationalist Phase: A Study of 'Friedrich und die grosse Koalition,' " *German Life and Letters* 22 (1969): 148.

12. Mann, "Gedanken im Kriege," GW 13:530.

13. Ibid. This is a distinction Mann will mock in *The Magic Mountain*.

14. Ibid., 533.

15. Schröter, *Thomas Mann*, 88–89, 87, maintains that in the Friedrich essay, published in 1915, Mann "reached the high point of his enthusiasm for the war." In letters and writings that followed, Mann weakened his adamant positions, even expressing in letters the wish for the democratization of Germany and the overcoming of Prussianization. Schröter argues that Burke, Sombart, Weber, and Treitschke were "the most important authorities for Thomas Mann's political convictions" at the outbreak of the war.

16. According to Reed, *Thomas Mann*, 188, this symbol "becomes increasingly a symbol not just for Germany but for Thomas Mann." Schröter, *Thomas Mann*, 69, points out that in his reference to his Friedrich material in the *Reflections*, Mann sees in the portrait of the lonely king "the *pure and free expression of his own nature.*"

17. Mann, *Friedrich and the Great Coalition*, in GW 10:134.

18. Ibid., 135, 133.

19. Mann even claims Kant's philosophy as a justification of German actions; see *Reflections*, in GW 12:174–75, 189–90; also "An die Redaktion des 'Svenska Dagbladet,' Stockholm," GW 13:549. Reed, *Thomas Mann*, 188–89, says this letter uses "ignorance to back up sophistry. No wonder the rationalist intellectuals . . . were appalled."

20. Fritz Kaufmann, *Thomas Mann: The World as Will and Representation* (1957; New York: Cooper Square Publishers, 1973), 14.

21. See his defense of himself in Mann, "Culture and Socialism," GW 12:639–49.

22. In fact, after the appearance of his first article on the war he wrote

to Richard Dehmel, already in the army, in December 1914: "I was heartily ashamed when I heard that you were marching, and finally it was this shame from which my small effort in the *Rundschau* arose—the need to place at least my head one time immediately in the service of the German task"; Mann, Letter of 14 December 1914 to Richard Dehmel, in *Briefe* 1:115.

23. Indeed, he wrote of the years spent composing the *Reflections*, "I am losing these years not very differently than if I had been drafted"; Mann, Letter of 25 March 1917, in *Briefe an Paul Amann, 1915–1952*, ed. Herbert Wegener (Lübeck: Verlag Max Schmidt-Römhild, 1959), 53.

24. Reed, *Thomas Mann*, 186, 202, links Mann to Fichte.

25. Mann, Letter of 3 August 1915, in *Briefe an Paul Amann*, 31.

26. Weber, "Parliament and Government in a Reconstructed Germany," *GPS*, 308, ridicules the purported contrast between "West European" and "German ideas of the state" as "frivolous talk" (*eitles Gerede*).

27. Weber, quoted in Marianne Weber, *Max Weber*, 581.

28. This is echoed in Mann, Letter of 25 November 1916, in *Briefe an Paul Amann*, 49.

29. Mann, Letter of 3 August 1915, in *Briefe an Paul Amann*, 30.

30. Mann, Letter of 25 November 1916, in *Briefe an Paul Amann*, 49.

31. On the ethical element in Nietzsche, Wagner, and Schopenhauer, see also Mann, *Reflections*, in *GW* 12:79, 146.

32. Reed, *Thomas Mann*, 181, says "the outsider had never been at ease outside."

33. According to Reed, *Thomas Mann*, 185, 195, 181, the official exclusion of modern artists from favor in Wilhelmine Germany fed the desire to be accepted, the urge to conform, and the belief that art and spirit were decadent and the "products of over-refinement and deficient vitality." For Heinrich, social integration had never seemed compatible with literary integrity, but Mann "suffered through his social detachment." Thus, although he had experimented with the rejection of psychology for moralism, of the world of the *bohème* for social acceptance, Mann turned in the *Reflections* to a "national" and political reevaluation of his earlier work, claiming that anyone could see in it his long-standing and firm support of Germany.

34. See Reed, *Thomas Mann*, 213.

35. Mann, quoted in Schröter, *Thomas Mann*, 84.

36. Heinrich argued in his *Zola* that Mann was obsessed with the possibility of acting "beyond all knowledge"; and Reed, *Thomas Mann*, 194–95, confirms that the longing for "reborn naivité" (*wiedergeborene Unbefangenheit*) was "an underlying impulse of Thomas Mann's early work."

37. Mann, Letter of 10 September 1915, in *Briefe an Paul Amann*, 32; *Reflections*, 573.

38. Jürgen Scharfschwerdt, *Thomas Mann und der deutsche Bildungsroman* (Stuttgart: W. Kohlhammer Verlag, 1967), 108, says that the most important contrast in the *Reflections* is actually between individualistic *Bildung* and social-political *Bildung*.

39. Mann, Rough draft of a letter of 21 January 1944 to C. B. Boutell, in *Briefe*, vol. 2: *1937–1947*, ed. Erika Mann (1963; Frankfurt a. M.: Fischer Taschenbuch Verlag, 1979), 352.

40. As Helmut Haug observes: "The *Reflections of an Unpolitical Man* cannot be grasped without this elementary supposition: Thomas Mann identifies himself with Germany"; *Erkenntnisekel: zum frühen Werk Thomas Manns* (Tübingen: Max Niemeyer Verlag, 1969), 148.

41. Mann, Letter of 25 November 1916 to Ernst Bertram, in *Thomas Mann an Ernst Bertram: Briefe aus den Jahren 1910–1955* (Pfullingen: Verlag Günther Neske, 1960), 43.

42. Mann, "Schopenhauer," *GW* 9:535.

43. Ibid., 534.

44. See Reed, *Thomas Mann*, 205.

45. See Mann, *Reflections*, in *GW* 12:370; also Mann, *Notizen*, ed. Hans Wysling (Heidelberg: Carl Winter Universitätsverlag, 1973), 54.

CHAPTER 5

1. At least one member of the Swedish Academy that awarded Mann the Nobel Prize in 1929 hated *The Magic Mountain* and found it "a nihilistic, decadent, and demoralizing book." See Peter de Mendelssohn, *Nachbemerkungen zu Thomas Mann*, vol. 1 (Frankfurt a. M.: Fischer Taschenbuch Verlag, 1982), 95.

2. Indeed, Kaufmann, *Thomas Mann*, 113, claims "the controversies of *The Magic Mountain* are really an artistic transcript of the polemical *Reflections*." See also Reed, *Thomas Mann*, 241.

3. Mann, Letter of 26 May 1926 to Ernst Fischer, in *Briefe* 1:256.

4. Alexander Nehamas, "Nietzsche and *The Magic Mountain*," *Philosophy and Literature* 5 (1981): 73–90, suggests that "Hans Castorp appears to be a character Nietzsche might have admired" because of his experimental attitude and his unwillingness to accept the meaning conventionally given to life.

5. On this subject, see Hans Eichner, "Thomas Mann und die deutsche Romantik," in *Das Nachleben der Romantik in der modernen deutschen Literatur*, ed. Wolfgang Paulsen (Heidelberg: Lothar Stiehm Verlag, 1969), 152–73.

6. See Mann, *Reflections*, in *GW* 12:54, 194. See also Mann, Letter of 25 November 1916, in *Briefe an Paul Amann*, 49.

7. Mann, *The Magic Mountain*, in *GW*, 3:49, 50. Hereafter all references to the novel will be indicated in the text by page numbers in parentheses.

8. Mann, quoted in Schröter, *Thomas Mann*, 99. Schröter remarks further that "the overall plan of Hans's path to *Bildung*, which was modeled after Thomas Mann's self-education, may have reminded him of the autobiographical world of his youthful work." De Mendelssohn, *Nachbemerkungen*, 108, maintains that *The Magic Mountain* "marks a new stretch of road in Thomas Mann's creations. Until *The Magic Mountain* the poet's view was directed inward and above all toward himself, the individual. With *The Magic Mountain* he turns outward and lays hold of European society."

9. Hans Wysling, "Probleme der *Zauberberg*-Interpretation," in *Thomas Mann Jahrbuch*, ed. Eckhard Heftrich and Hans Wysling (Frankfurt a. M.: Vittorio Klostermann, 1988), 1:24, notes that the lack of the answer to "Wozu?" is the way Nietzsche characterizes nihilism in the *Will to Power*.

10. Mann, *Tagebücher, 1918–1921*, ed. Peter de Mendelssohn (Frankfurt a. M.: S. Fischer Verlag, 1979), 261.

11. Kaufmann, *Thomas Mann*, 100–101, extrapolates too far from Hans's condition when he says that Hans stays on the mountain because "he is weary of the seemingly purposeful yet fundamentally meaningless life of his time, weary of its relativities, its unashamed finitude. . . . The depths of his soul cry out for certitude, for a firm foothold somewhere on absolute ground."

12. Mann, "On the German Republic," *GW* 11:851.

13. For an understanding of this term, see Mann, "Lübeck als geistige Lebensform," *GW* 11:376–98. For a brief discussion, see Goldman, *Max Weber and Thomas Mann*, 64–65.

14. Indeed, given the structure of the novel, Clawdia plays a purely symbolic role as a distanced object of desire in Hans's life. Roy Pascal, "*The Magic Mountain* and Adorno's Critique of the Traditional Novel," in *Culture and Society in the Weimar Republic*, ed. Keith Bullivant (Manchester: Manchester University Press/Rowman & Littlefield, 1977), 18, says of her that she "hardly emerges to any fuller or more individual personality, drifting in and out of the pages of the book according to the role she fulfills for the hero." He adds profoundly: "The whole structure of the novel obeys the same principle." For a very different view, see Albert S. Braverman and Larry Nachman, "Nature and the Moral Order in *The Magic Mountain*," *Germanic Review* 53 (1978): 1–12.

15. See Hermann J. Weigand, *The Magic Mountain: A Study of Thomas Mann's Novel "Der Zauberberg"* (1933; Chapel Hill: University of North Carolina Press, 1964), 39–58, on illness among the German Romantics.

16. Nietzsche, *Ecce Homo*, in *KSA* 6:272.

17. Ibid., 326.

18. Ibid., 325.

19. Erich Heller, *Thomas Mann: The Ironic German* (Cleveland: World Publishing Company, 1961), 199, says that Hans's "education and his illness are identical."

20. This parallel is indirectly noted by Heller, ibid., 199, when he remarks that Hermann Weigand is right "in saying of Hans Castorp's surrender to disease that 'it has the same symbolic significance as Faust's pact with the Devil.' "

21. Indeed, Kaufmann, *Thomas Mann*, 99, accepting the novel's own language, claims that the spiritual stimulant of disease takes hold of Hans and "ennobles him."

22. De Mendelssohn, *Nachbemerkungen*, 73–74, describes Mann's rediscovery of Novalis in 1920, through Georg Brandes's book on the German Romantics, as "one of the greatest enlightening and enlightened moments of the notes for *The Magic Mountain*." In Brandes Mann found discussions of Pascal's and Kierkegaard's interest in illness. But "Novalis goes much farther. Illness is for him the highest, the only true life: 'Life is an illness of the spirit. . . . Does not what is best begin everywhere with illness?' " De Mendelssohn remarks that this passage is underlined in Mann's copy of Brandes, and for good reason: "it contains the fundamental thesis of the book, to overcome which is Castorp's determination." Kaufmann, *Thomas Mann*, 100, quotes Novalis, *Fragments*, no. 987: "Illnesses, especially chronic ones, are years of apprenticeship in the art of life and in the formation of personality."

23. De Mendelssohn, *Nachbemerkungen*, 102, says, quoting Mann: "Joachim embodies unnoticed the 'soberly serving Prussian principle, a soberness in service that is raised beyond the purely military into the service of life.' Castorp on the contrary 'considers experimentation as the true service. He does not resist evil.' "

24. De Mendelssohn, *Nachbemerkungen*, 52, stresses more the effect of the mountain on Hans's relation to life than the consequences of his relation to life for his attraction to the mountain, when he remarks: "It is a kind of substitute for life [*Lebensersatz*] that completely estranges the young man in a relatively short time from real, active life."

25. Mann, *Betrachtungen*, in *GW* 12:421–26. See also Reed, *Thomas Mann*, 279n.7. Schröter, *Thomas Mann*, 89, claims that the expression "sympathy with death" contained, "beyond that antipolitical-political polemic, much of Thomas Mann's current life mood" and was an expression of his most personal feelings.

26. Mann, Letter of 9 September 1913 to Hans Hülsen, quoted in *Dichter über ihre Dichtungen*, vol. 14: *Thomas Mann*, ed. Hans Wysling and Marianne Fischer, part 1: *1889–1917* (Munich and Frankfurt: Ernst

Heimeran Verlag and S. Fischer Verlag, 1975), 451. As Mann says in 1926: "*Tonio Kröger* (a young man's work), *Death in Venice*, and *The Magic Mountain* are arch-romantic conceptions. Wagner was my strongest, most decisive artistic experience. In addition to this comes of course an element that links me to some extent to the new and today generally gives my production a possibility of being intellectual [*geistig*]: the experience of the self-overcoming of romanticism in Nietzsche." Mann, Letter of 26 May 1926 to Ernst Fischer, in *Briefe* 1:255–56. Heller, *Thomas Mann*, 198, 199, remarks that *Geist* and sickness "go together in the romantic tradition of German thought." Ultimately, *The Magic Mountain* "is also the *critique* of the romantic equation *la maladie c'est l'esprit.*"

27. Mann, Letter of 3 August 1915, in *Briefe an Paul Amann*, 29. See also de Mendelssohn, *Nachbemerkungen*, 53–63, on details of the writing of *The Magic Mountain*.

28. Indeed, the burden on Hans is not unlike the burden on Aschenbach. Each has two guilty secrets: the burdensomeness of his role and task in bourgeois society, and his passionate love for an object that his social position or background would brand as improper, if not illicit. In fact, from the start Clawdia is as remote from Hans as Tadzio is from Aschenbach in *Death in Venice*. Kaufmann, *Thomas Mann*, 109, observes: "For years Hans Castorp, the well-mannered North German youth, will be under her spell, just as the master-artist Gustav Aschenbach yields to the enchantment of the beautiful Polish boy Tadzio." Heller, *Thomas Mann*, 203, goes further: "Tadzio or Claudia—the nature of the passion is the same."

29. Weigand, *Magic Mountain*, 45–46.

30. De Mendelssohn, *Nachbemerkungen*, 100, says: "It is not only, as Thomas Mann himself has said, the 'attempt at a stock-taking of the European problematic after the turn of the century,' but rather more a world debate . . . as in a laboratory of *Weltanschauungen* every capacity of thought and idea is analyzed and expounded—'a pedagogical fool's paradise.' "

31. Kaufmann, *Thomas Mann*, 105, 106.

32. On the relationship of Lukács to Mann's portrait of Naphta, see Judith Marcus, "The Artist and His Philosopher: Reflections on the Relation Between Thomas Mann and Georg Lukács," in *Georg Lukács—Ersehnte Totalität*, ed. Gvozden Flego and Wolfdietrich Schmied-Kowarzik (vol. 1 of the Bloch-Lukács Symposium, Dubrovnik, 1985) (Bochum: Germinal Verlag, 1986), 45–59; and idem, *Georg Lukács and Thomas Mann: A Study in the Sociology of Literature* (Amherst: University of Massachusetts Press, 1987).

33. Heller, *Thomas Mann*, 200, maintains that Naphta "appears to be born for the highly diseased and highly intellectual career of the hitherto typical Thomas Mann hero."

34. Nietzsche, *Birth of Tragedy*, in *KSA* 1:155–56.

35. Ibid., 156. Schröter, *Thomas Mann*, 100 says: "Above the pedagogical conversations of conflict . . . Hans Castorp's—and so also Thomas Mann's—search takes place for a balance of the spheres of morality and of life, of spirit and of reality, until now experienced as contradictions."

36. Reed, *Thomas Mann*, 258, claims that Mann himself "learned long and painfully what he shows massively and at some aesthetic cost: that intellectual abstractions and involvements are to be taken with a pinch of salt."

37. As Mann says of himself in a letter of 5 February 1925 to Josef Ponten, in *Briefe* 1:232: "He is no Settembrini in his heart. But he wants to be free, reasonable, and good in his thoughts."

38. Reed, *Thomas Mann*, 252, 256, maintains that the episode in the snow shows Hans's realization that "the whole principle of antithetical argument is wrong . . . because antitheses are made by men and can be transcended and reconciled by men." That Hans forgets his lessons is no problem for Reed, who believes that "it is only in the finished *Zauberberg* that the long-held ideal of freedom from antitheses is realized, by the act of playing with them."

39. See Hermann Kurzke, *Auf der Suche nach der verlorenen Irrationalität. Thomas Mann und der Konservatismus* (Würzburg: Verlag Königshausen & Neumann, 1980), 176–77. There is great disagreement about Hans's episode in the snow. Reed, *Thomas Mann*, 263, says that the forgetfulness of the message in "Snow" allows Mann "to convey the message of the snow vision while still not turning Hans Castorp into a paragon of humanistic virtue, beyond the reach of eventual criticisms." Martin Swales, "The Story and the Hero: A Study of Thomas Mann's 'Der Zauberberg,' " *Deutsche Vierteljahrsschrift* 46 (1972): 359–76, affirms the great disparity between intellectual insight and action. Theodore Ziolkowski, *Dimensions of the Modern Novel* (Princeton: Princeton University Press, 1969), 88, believes Hans leaves the sanatorium "not a whit richer in belief." Pascal, "*Magic Mountain*," 1–23, responds to these critics and believes (7) "the failure to recognise the positive commitment in Hans Castorp's formula and final action [is] a serious . . . misinterpretation of the book."

40. Mann, "Fragment über das Religiöse" (1931), *GW* 11:423–24. There Mann also claims that the thought of his own death is his own most intimate thought: "It stands behind everything that I think and write, and the inclination to see all things in its light and sign is so natural to me that the sentence expressing the ultimate conclusion of my last novel . . . means a real overcoming." That is why de Mendelssohn, in *Nachbemerkungen*, 96, can claim that "*The Magic Mountain* has a marked autobiographical undercurrent." The novel tells "of his own

'overcoming of romanticism' [*Entromantisierung*], of the overcoming of his own song of songs of romanticism that the *Reflections* had been, of the self-overcoming that he is allowed to recognize (through his hero in the 'Snow' chapter)." Thus "in this sentence his own development was encapsulated."

41. Mann contradicts this in a letter of 5 February 1925 to Josef Ponten, *Briefe* 1:231–32, where he claims that Hans has forgotten the lessons because "on the whole he does not measure up personally to his heightened thoughts."

42. Mann, quoted in de Mendelssohn, *Nachbemerkungen*, 102.

43. Mann, Letter of 25 May 1926 to Ernst Fischer, in *Briefe* 1:255–56. On the autobiographical dimensions of this work, see Jens Rieckmann, *Der Zauberberg. Eine geistige Autobiographie Thomas Manns* (Stuttgart: Akademischer Verlag Hans-Dieter Heinz, 1977); and the essays by Saueressig and Reed in Heinz Saueressig, ed., *Besichtigung des Zauberbergs* (Biberich a. d. Riss: Wege & Gestalten, 1974).

44. Weigand, *Magic Mountain*, 20–21, disagrees, seeing Hans's development from the conversation with Clawdia in the "*Walpurgisnacht*" episode to the end of the novel as a sign of a new positive attitude toward life.

45. Hans Wikirchen, "Nietzsche-Imitatio: zu Thomas Manns politischem Denken in der Weimarer Republik," in *Thomas Mann Jahrbuch* 1:49, maintains that this reference to building empires on death is actually a reference to the *Bismarckreich*.

46. Mann seems to contradict this in a letter of 13 May 1939 to Agnes E. Meyer, in *Briefe* 2:91–92, where he says: "But purity, *Reinheit*, is not really what H. C. 'seeks.' Neither he nor I have ascetic inclinations." Yet the approach to life that seeks meaning in self-sacrifice for a higher principle is precisely ascetic.

47. Hermann Kurzke, *Thomas Mann: Epoche—Werk—Wirkung* (Munich: Verlag C. H. Beck, 1985), 207. See also Mann, "Vorspruch zu einer musikalischen Nietzsche-Feier," *GW* 10:180–84. Reed, *Thomas Mann*, 271, says, incredibly, that after the chapter on the "Lindenbaum," Hans Castorp is again a positive hero, learning the lessons of war before it breaks out.

48. Schröter, " 'Eideshelfer' Thomas Manns 1914/18," 61, suggests that the use of war here is a leftover from Mann's idealization of it in the *Reflections* and that it is shown as the "more powerful educator" than all the others on the mountain.

49. Kaufmann, *Thomas Mann*, 115, emphasizes this religious dimension even more. He says that, with the "Lindenbaum" on his lips, Hans dies "not only *with* it, but *for* it as well." This is his atonement, a "confession of sin" on the mountain.

50. See Mann, "Über die Lehre Spenglers," *GW* 10:172–80; and "On the German Republic," *GW* 11:841–42.

51. Mann, Entry of 17 April 1919, in *Tagebücher, 1918–1921*, 200–201.

52. Mann, "On the German Republic," *GW* 11:833–34.

53. Mann, "Lübeck as a Spiritual Way of Life," *GW* 11:396–97. Schröter, *Thomas Mann*, 102, says: "To grasp this 'idea' completely . . . is the goal of all the spiritual exercises to which the hero of *The Magic Mountain* is subjected."

54. Pascal, "*Magic Mountain*," 21, says: "We are not permitted to believe that the personal decision of Hans Castorp is of decisive importance or has symbolic representativeness for the generality."

55. Reed, *Thomas Mann*, 264, argues that there is a revaluation of illness: disease was originally a means to the dissolution of north German normality, then an allegorical means to express the values of the Romantic tradition against the Enlightenment. Finally it turned into a symbol of art itself elevated above the practical flatland. In *The Magic Mountain* Hans's humanistic investigations of life, he argues, come to "a wholeness of vision 'beyond antitheses,' " superseding "the 'Romantic' *Betrachtungen*." Mann, like his brother, now sees pre-1914 Europe as "aestheticist," which is the cause of its hopelessness.

56. Mann, quoted in de Mendelssohn, *Nachbemerkungen*, 104.

57. See Reed, *Thomas Mann*, 271.

58. Cf. Schröter, " 'Eideshelfer' Thomas Manns 1914/18," 62–63. Indeed, Hans Wikirchen, *Zeitgeschichte im Roman. Zu Thomas Manns "Zauberberg" und "Doktor Faustus,"* vol. 6 of *Thomas-Mann-Studien* (Bern: Francke Verlag, 1986), 196, says that *The Magic Mountain* "remained trapped in the aporetic exertions of conservative Romantic republicans like Meinecke and Troeltsch."

59. Reed, *Thomas Mann*, 273, 272, interprets this inability to return as a warning against the perils of a *Bildung* whose nonpolitical nature Mann defended in the *Reflections*. He claims that Hans "is left torpid on the Mountain as a warning against the sloth and quietism which *Bildung* in some circumstances may lead to. When he descends, it is not from any inner initiative." He further maintains that Mann's message is this: "At some stage in personal development, the open mind has to be closed, richness and many-sidedness are not the final aim. They may in some form be the ideal for art," but Hans is no artist. He even suggests that Mann, "who is an artist, is now uneasy about the old ideal of many-sidedness in its extreme form."

60. Despite the limitations of *Bildung* here, it is not the simple failure of *Bildung* as such that is at issue. Rather, the culture and society in which *Bildung* occurs and the materials that must therefore make it up are principally to blame. Only because he minimizes the substance of *Bildung* on the mountain can Reed, *Thomas Mann*, 249, maintain of Hans: "What we are to take seriously is the process of his *Bildung*, not

the material *Bildung* which is its medium." The novel is not just about a process, but about the specific issues that Mann imagines must be considered for *Bildung* to take place in our time.

61. De Mendelssohn, *Nachbemerkungen*, 68–69, notes that in the novel Mann "attempts for the first time a definition of the concept of *Humanität*," whose defender is the *Zivilisationsliterat* Settembrini. Indeed, Settembrini's view of *Humanität* linked to "the word," to literature, and to politics is drawn from an early notebook of Mann's and is "a very autobiographical section in which Thomas Mann's credo of the thirties and forties is forecast. As much as Hans Castorp's position as a child of the world between the prophets is in many respects [Mann's] own, so is it plain at the same time that Settembrini too bears not a few traces of his creator."

62. Mann, "On the German Republic," GW 11:809–52.

63. Ibid., 852.

64. As Schröter, *Thomas Mann*, 102, sees it, Mann defines art as "a humanistic discipline among the others." This, says Schröter, is new. "Nietzsche's early definition of art as the single 'metaphysical justification of life,' Schopenhauer's pessimistic aestheticism—both were still effective in the *Reflections*—are here given up; their philosophical antitheses: 'spirit/nature'—or 'critique/meaningfulness' . . . are equally overcome in the higher concept of *humanism*." After this, Mann's poetic creation "revolves around one and the same interest in man." He accomplishes this, Schröter maintains, in "Goethe and Tolstoy," contemporary with *The Magic Mountain*.

65. Reed, *Thomas Mann*, 248, 301, 303, 298–99, 304, claims that Mann drew on classical humanism as a countervailing tradition to Germanic obsessions with death and the past. *The Magic Mountain* is thus the work of a man who wants to put the materials of culture "where they belong: in the perspective of humane purposes." This "broader belief in a common humanity" was in the spirit of the Enlightenment. Indeed, Reed reveals his position by claiming further that "the right course in the Weimar situation lay nearer to Settembrini *tout pur* than to any synthesis such as Republicans hoped for and the chapter 'Schnee' enjoined." Still, to view *The Magic Mountain* as politically indecisive, though a common opinion, "is quite wrong." It is true that "in a sense the novel embodies political relations which had already failed. Yet its diagnosis remains accurate," for the novel "grasps the issues of its time correctly and arrives at a reasonable solution." Reed (273n.80) therefore qualifies his claim for the achievement of the novel ever so slightly, suggesting that Mann brings out "a positive and humane, if still apparently vague principle."

66. Hannah Arendt, *The Origins of Totalitarianism*, new ed. (New York: Harcourt Brace Jovanovich, 1968), 222–66.

67. See Hans Erich Bödeker, "Menschheit, Humanität, Humanismus," in *Geschichtliche Grundbegriffe* 3:1063–1128, esp. 1090–97. Also W. H. Bruford, *Culture and Society in Classical Weimar, 1775–1806* (Cambridge: Cambridge University Press, 1962), esp. 190–92, 231–36.

68. Mann, "Goethe and Tolstoy," *GW* 9:173.

CHAPTER 6

1. See Mommsen, *Max Weber und die deutsche Politik*; and David Beetham, *Max Weber and the Theory of Modern Politics* (Cambridge: Polity Press, 1985).

2. See Ludwig Dehio, *Germany and World Politics in the Twentieth Century*, trans. Dieter Pevsner (New York: Knopf, 1960).

3. See Walter Struve, *Elites Against Democracy: Leadership Ideals in Bourgeois Political Thought in Germany, 1890–1933* (Princeton: Princeton University Press, 1973); and Gustav Schmidt, *Deutscher Historismus und der Übergang zur parlamentarischen Demokratie. Untersuchungen zu den politischen Gedanken von Meinecke, Troeltsch, Max Weber*, Historische Studien, no. 389 (Lübeck and Hamburg: Matthiesen Verlag, 1964).

4. See Theodor Schieder, *The State and Society in Our Times*, trans. C.A.M. Sym (Edinburgh: Thomas Nelson, 1962); Charles S. Maier, *Recasting Bourgeois Europe* (Princeton: Princeton University Press, 1975); Paul Kennedy, *The Rise of the Anglo-German Antagonism, 1860–1914* (London: Allen & Unwin, 1980); Hermann Kantorowicz, *Der Geist der englischen Politik und das Gespenst der Einkreisung Deutschlands* (Berlin: Ernst Rowohlt Verlag, 1929); Charles E. McClelland, *The German Historians and England: A Study in Nineteenth-Century Views* (Cambridge: Cambridge University Press, 1971); and Arthur Rosenberg, *The Birth of the German Republic, 1871–1918*, trans. Ian F. D. Morrow (1931; New York: Russell & Russell, 1962).

5. Weber, "Non-legitimate Domination: Typology of the City," *WG*, 783.

6. See Herbert A. Deane, *The Political and Social Ideas of St. Augustine* (New York: Columbia University Press, 1963), 131, 300n.46; Ernest Barker, *From Alexander to Constantine* (Oxford: Oxford University Press, 1956), 236–38, 253–56, 303–8, 361–73, 477–79; and Lester K. Born, Introduction to *The Education of a Christian Prince*, by Desiderius Erasmus (1936; New York: Octagon Books, 1965), 44–130.

7. On the Renaissance literature of advice to princes, see Quentin Skinner, *The Foundations of Modern Political Thought*, vol. 1: *The Renaissance* (Cambridge: Cambridge University Press, 1978), 88–101, 118–38, 213–21. On the Renaissance and earlier, see Allan H. Gilbert, *Machiavelli's "Prince" and Its Forerunners* (Durham: University of North

Carolina Press, 1938); also Felix Gilbert, "The Humanist Concept of the Prince and *The Prince* of Machiavelli," in *History: Choice and Commitment* (Cambridge, Mass.: Harvard University Press, 1977), 91–114.

8. Sheldon Wolin, *Politics and Vision* (London: Allen & Unwin, 1961), 237.

9. Weber, "Capitalism and Rural Society in Germany," in *From Max Weber: Essays in Sociology*, ed. H. H. Gerth and C. Wright Mills (New York: Oxford University Press, 1946), 369. This is the English translation of a talk Weber delivered at the St. Louis World's Fair. Although it was written in German, no German text has ever been located. See also Weber, "The National State and Economic Policy," *GPS*, 20.

10. Weber, "The National State and Economic Policy," *GPS*, 19.

11. Weber, "Capitalism and Rural Society in Germany," *From Max Weber*, 373.

12. Weber, "The National State and Economic Policy," *GPS*, 19. For an argument that the landed elites nowhere gave up real power until World War I, see Arno Mayer, *The Persistence of the Old Regime: Europe to the Great War* (New York: Pantheon Books, 1981).

13. On the position of the Junkers, see Hans Rosenberg, "The Economic Impact of Imperial Germany," *Journal of Economic History* 3, supp. (December 1943): 101–7. See also Wolfgang Mommsen, "Domestic Factors in German Foreign Policy Before 1914," *Central European History* 6 (1973): 3–43.

14. Weber, "The National State and Economic Policy," *GPS*, 18, 22.

15. Ibid., 19–22. Weyembergh, *Voluntarisme rationnel de Max Weber*, 65, says of this address: "One can say that the 'Inaugural Address' constitutes the outcome of the first Weberian period, just as the lectures 'Politics as a Vocation' and 'Science as a Vocation' are the point of arrival of Weber's thought in his maturity."

16. Weber, "Economic Ethics of the World Religions," *GRS* 1:248.

17. Weber, "Sociology of Religion," *WG*, 298–99. See also "Political Communities," *WG*, 536.

18. Weber, "Parliament and Government in a Reconstructed Germany," *GPS*, 311, 318, 319, 320; and "The National State and Economic Policy," *GPS*, 20. See also Weber, Letter of 25 April 1887 to Hermann Baumgarten, in *Jugendbriefe* (Tübingen: J.C.B. Mohr [Paul Siebeck], 1936), 232. On the cult of personality, see Stern, *Failure of Illiberalism*, 10.

19. Weber, "Parliament and Government," *GPS*, 329–30.

20. Ibid., 335–36, 347.

21. Ibid., 352.

22. Ibid., 363, 379. See also Ringer, *Decline of the German Mandarins*, 149.

23. Weber, "The Protestant Ethic," *GRS* 1:204.

24. Weber, "Bureaucratic Domination," *WG*, 551, 569–70, 571; "Parliament and Government," *GPS*, 330.

25. Weber, "Parliament and Government," *GPS*, 332, 333.

26. Weber, "Bureaucratic Domination," *WG*, 571.

27. Weber, "Diskussionsreden auf der Tagung des Vereins für Sozialpolitik in Wien 1909," in *Gesammelte Aufsätze zur Soziologie und Sozialpolitik* [hereafter cited as *GSS*], 2d ed., ed. Marianne Weber (1924; Tübingen: J.C.B. Mohr [Paul Siebeck], 1988), 414. I am greatly indebted to Alan Milchman for pointing out to me the significance of the *Ordnungsmensch*.

28. Weber, "Bureaucratic Domination," *WG*, 560.

29. Meinecke, *Age of German Liberation*, 25.

30. See Bramsted, *Aristocracy and the Middle Classes in Germany*, 288–89.

31. Michel Foucault, *Discipline and Punish: The Birth of the Prison*, trans. Alan Sheridan (New York: Vintage Books, 1979), 189–91.

32. Weber, "Parliament and Government," *GPS*, 335.

33. Weber, "Bureaucratic Domination," *WG*, 570.

34. Ibid., 570.

35. Ibid., 553, 558.

36. Ibid., 553.

37. Weber, "Diskussionsreden auf der Tagung des Vereins für Sozialpolitik in Wien 1909," *GSS*, 414.

38. Weber, "Methodologische Einleitung für die Erhebungen des Vereins für Sozialpolitik über Auslese und Anpassung (Berufswahlen und Berufsschicksal) der Arbeiterschaft der geschlossenen Großindustrie," *GSS*, 60.

39. Weber, "The Types of Domination," *WG*, 154–55.

40. Cavalli, "Charismatic Domination, Totalitarian Dictatorship, and Plebiscitary Democracy," 61.

41. Weber, "Politics as a Vocation," *GPS*, 507, 508.

42. Weber, "Charismatic Domination and Its Transformation," *WG*, 654. As Weber observes, "The concept of 'charisma' ('gift of God') is taken from early Christian terminology. For the Christian hierocracy Rudolf Sohm's *Kirchenrecht* first clarified the matter, if not the terminology based on the concept"; "Types of Legitimate Domination," *WG*, 124. See also Rudolph Sohm, *Kirchenrecht*, sec. 8, vol. 1 of *Systematisches Handbuch der deutschen Rechtswissenschaft*, ed. Karl Binding (Leipzig: Duncker & Humblot, 1892), 1:26–27. On Sohm's importance, see Peter Haley, "Rudolph Sohm on Charisma," *Journal of Religion* 60 (1980): 185–97.

43. Weber, "Political and Hierocratic Domination," *WG*, 691.

44. Weber, "Bureaucratic Domination," *WG*, 552.

45. Weber, "Parliament and Government," *GPS*, 335.

46. Weber, "Bureaucratic Domination," *WG*, 129.

47. Weber, "Parliament and Government," *GPS*, 335, 334.

48. Weber, "Discipline and the Objectivation [*Versachlichung*] of the Forms of Domination," *WG*, 682.

49. Weber, "Bureaucratic Domination," *WG*, 552.

50. Weber, "Politics as a Vocation," *GPS*, 524; also "Parliament and Government," *GPS*, 351.

51. Weber, "Parliament and Government," *GPS*, 377–78.

52. Ibid., 347. These characterizations apply only to the "ideal types" of bureaucrat and politician, for, despite the principles reigning in theory, the conservative German bureaucracy concealed the reality of party partisanship behind a façade of neutrality. Thus, in practice the difference between official and politician is not always one of impartiality versus responsibility but often one of denial versus acceptance of responsibility.

53. Weber, "Types of Domination," *WG*, 129; "Bureaucratic Domination," *WG*, 553, 562–63.

54. Weber, "Intermediate Reflection," *GRS* 1:546–47.

55. Weber, "Sociology of Religion," *WG*, 361.

56. On the basic functions of the state, see Weber, "Political Communities," *WG*, 516.

57. See Weber, "Types of Domination," *WG*, 143, 147; and "Charismatic Domination," *WG*, 661, 669, 679.

58. Weber, "Politics as a Vocation," *GPS*, 545.

59. Ibid., 508, 513. The quote "trachtet nach seinem Werk" ("strives for his work") is from Nietzsche's *Thus Spoke Zarathustra*. Zarathustra says: "Was liegt am Glücke! antwortete er, ich trachte lange nicht mehr nach Glücke, ich trachte nach meinem Werke."

60. Weber, "Politics as a Vocation," *GPS*, 547, 546.

61. Ibid., 546.

62. Weber, "Wahlrecht und Demokratie in Deutschland," *GPS*, 285.

63. Weber, "Politics as a Vocation," *GPS*, 547–48.

64. Weber, "Value Freedom," *WL*, 494.

65. Ibid., 494.

66. On the language of *Eigengesetzlichkeit* in theology, see Friedrich Wilhelm Graf, "Max Weber und die protestantische Theologie seiner Zeit," *Zeitschrift für Religions- und Geistesgeschichte* 39 (1987): 122–47.

67. Weber, "Politics as a Vocation," *GPS*, 545.

68. Ibid., 545, 546.

69. Ibid., 546.

70. Ibid., 547.

71. Ibid., 525.

72. On Puritan personality, see Goldman, *Max Weber and Thomas Mann*, 142–68, esp. 165.

73. Weber, "Value Freedom," *WL*, 494.

74. Weber, "Bureaucratic Domination," *WG*, 554–55; "Charismatic Domination," *WG*, 655.

75. Weber, "Politics as a Vocation," *GPS*, 547.

76. Weber, "Sociology of Religion," *WG*, 361.

77. Weber, "Types of Domination," *WG*, 142.

78. Weber, quoted in Mommsen, *Max Weber und die deutsche Politik*, 100.

79. Weber, "The Protestant Ethic," *GRS* 1:98–99n.1, 154–55n.3. Weber even describes the Calvinist attitude as hostile to authority; see 97n.3.

80. Ibid., 167n.2. See also Troeltsch, *Social Teaching of the Christian Churches* 2:618, 619, 623–24.

81. Weber, "The Protestant Ethic," *GRS* 1:81.

82. Ibid., 145.

83. Weber, "Sociology of Religion," *WG*, 313.

84. Weber, "Charismatic Domination," *WG*, 675.

85. Marianne Weber, *Max Weber*, 580.

86. Weber, *Gesammelte Politische Schriften*, 1st ed. [hereafter cited as *GPS* (1st ed.)], ed. Marianne Weber (Munich: Dreimaskenverlag, 1921), 256.

87. Weber, "Types of Domination," *WG*, 174.

88. Weber, "The National State and Economic Policy," *GPS*, 23. See also Weber, "Die ländliche Arbeitsverfassung," in *Gesammelte Aufsätze zur Sozial- und Wirtschaftsgeschichte*, ed. Marianne Weber (Tübingen: J.C.B. Mohr [Paul Siebeck], 1924), 468; and Abraham Ascher, "Professors as Propagandists: The Politics of the Kathedersozialisten," *Journal of Central European Affairs* 23 (1963): 282–302.

89. Weber, quoted in Marianne Weber, *Max Weber*, 137, from the 5th Evangelisch-Sozialer Kongress, Frankfurt am Main, 1894. See also Weber, "The National State and Economic Policy," in *GPS*, 12–13.

90. See Mommsen, *Max Weber und die deutsche Politik*, 37–72; Mitzman, *Iron Cage*, 82, 83, 139; Antoni, *From History to Sociology*, 130; and Struve, *Elites Against Democracy*, 127.

91. On the *Vernunftrepublikaner*, see Peter Gay, *Weimar Culture: The Outsider as Insider* (New York: Harper & Row, 1968); and Ringer, *Decline of the German Mandarins*, 202–13. The quintessential expression of this viewpoint is Meinecke's. "One can . . . decide upon democracy today without feeling the slightest inclination toward the form of government. One places one's actual wants determined by disposition and ideals into the background in the process of it, and decides for what is rational, that is, for that which seems to be the most expedient for the whole." But Meinecke is wise enough to remark further: "This kind of thought and action is genuinely modern: however, any exaggerated ra-

tionalization of action reduces ideal values to a soulless substance." Meinecke, *Staat und Persönlichkeit* (1933), 159–60, quoted in Ilse Dronberger, *The Political Thought of Max Weber* (New York: Appleton-Century-Crofts, 1971), 183.

92. Weber, "Parliament and Government," *GPS*, 306, 309, 310. See also "Value Freedom," *WL*, 540, where Weber indirectly states that the form of state has no "intrinsic value" and is only "a technical means [*Hilfsmittel*] for the realization of completely other values."

93. Raymond Aron has claimed that Weber retained much from Treitschke; see "Max Weber and Power Politics," in *Max Weber and Sociology Today*, ed. Otto Stammer, trans. Kathleen Morris (New York: Harper & Row, 1971), 83–100. As a young man Weber expressed regard for "the great and passionate striving" of Treitschke "for ideal foundations," despite the biases and extravagances of his character and performance, biases that his audience seized upon and exalted; see Letter of 25 April 1887 to Hermann Baumgarten, in Baumgarten, *Max Weber: Werk und Person*, 54–55. But see also Mitzman, *Iron Cage*, 35–37, on Weber's ambivalence toward Treitschke.

94. See Ringer, *Decline of the German Mandarins*, 141, 181, and the quote from Alois Riehl (181) that with the first victory of the war, each person "lived for the whole and the whole lived in all of us. Our own ego with its personal interests was dissolved in the great historic being of the nation."

95. Weber, "The National State and Economic Policy," *GPS*, 18–19.

96. Ibid., 18.

97. Weber, "Sociology of Religion," *WG*, 361.

98. Weber, "Intermediate Reflection," *GRS* 1:547.

99. On the tradition of *Staatsräson*, see Friedrich Meinecke, *Machiavellism: The Doctrine of Raison d'État and Its Place in Modern History*, trans. Douglas Scott, intro. W. Stark (New York: Praeger, 1965).

100. Weber, "The National State and Economic Policy," *GPS*, 14–15.

101. On the collapse of Weimar, see Karl-Dietrich Bracher, *Die Auflösung der Weimarer Republik* (Stuttgart: Ring-Verlag, 1955); Franz Neumann, *Behemoth: The Structure and Practice of National Socialism, 1933–1944* (1942; New York: Harper Torchbooks, 1966).

102. Mitzman, *Iron Cage*, 167.

103. Leopold Ranke, "A Dialogue on Politics," trans. Theodore H. von Laue, in von Laue, *Leopold Ranke: The Formative Years* (Princeton: Princeton University Press, 1950), 167–68, 173.

104. Weber, Letter of 16 July 1917 to Ehrenberg, in *GPS* (1st ed.), 469–70.

105. Ranke, "Dialogue on Politics," 162, 178, 168–69.

106. Weber, "Value Freedom," *WL*, 539, 540.

107. Weber, "The Protestant Ethic," *GRS* 1:135n.1.

108. Mommsen, *Age of Bureaucracy*, 39, comments on the remarks found in the margin of the manuscript of "Political Communities" (*WG*, 530), which break off in midsentence while discussing the nation and its relation to culture: "He noted that the German victory in 1871 had not fostered the development of art and literature in the political centre of Germany. . . . Yet Weber did not follow this up by inquiring whether this might put his belief in the nation as an ultimate value into jeopardy."

109. Weber, "Parliament and Government," *GPS*, 309–10.

110. See Mommsen, *Max Weber und die deutsche Politik*, 407–41; idem, Introduction to Weber's *Zur Politik im Weltkrieg*, 1–14; and idem, Introduction to Weber's *Zur Neuordnung Deutschlands. Schriften und Reden 1918–1920*, sec. 1, vol. 16 of *Max Weber Gesamtausgabe* (Tübingen: J.C.B. Mohr [Paul Siebeck], 1988), 1–38.

111. Weber, "Parliament and Government," *GPS*, 401. See Wolfgang J. Mommsen, "Max Weber and Roberto Michels: An Asymmetrical Partnership," *Archives européennes de sociologie* 22 (1981): 114.

112. Weber, "Parliament and Government," *GPS*, 349.

113. Weber, "Types of Domination," *WG*, 157.

114. Weber, "Bureaucratic Domination," *WG*, 554–55.

115. Weber, "Types of Domination," *WG*, 156–57.

116. Weber, "Charismatic Domination," *WG*, 667.

117. Weber, "Parliament and Government," *GPS*, 403–4.

118. Weber, "Types of Domination," *WG*, 157. See also Mommsen, "Max Weber and Roberto Michels," 114–15.

119. Weber, "Parliament and Government," *GPS*, 404.

120. See ibid., 393.

121. Ibid., 388–89, 395, 393.

122. Weber, "Bureaucratic Domination," *WG*, 568.

123. Weber, "Parliament and Government," *GPS*, 339.

124. Ibid., 379, 395, 403, 401.

125. Ibid., 403.

126. Ibid., 392, 347.

127. Ibid., 340–41.

128. Ibid., 350.

129. Ibid., 353–54, 355, 365; and Weber, "Politics as a Vocation," *GPS*, 537.

130. Weber, "Parliament and Government," *GPS*, 364.

131. Ibid., 308.

132. Ibid., 365.

133. Ibid., 382.

134. On Weber and the crisis of liberalism, see Schieder, *State and Society in Our Times*, 44–45.

135. This is why Jeffrey Alexander calls Weber's political writings a "retreat from multidimensionality"; see *Theoretical Logic in Sociology*,

vol. 3: *The Classical Attempt at Theoretical Synthesis: Max Weber* (Berkeley and Los Angeles: University of California Press, 1983), 76–97.

136. Quoted in Ringer, *Decline of the German Mandarins*, 131.

137. Weber, "Politics as a Vocation," *GPS*, 508.

138. Weber, "Parliament and Government," *GPS*, 401.

139. Ibid., 394.

140. Weber, "Politics as a Vocation," *GPS*, 533.

141. Weber, "Types of Domination," *WG*, 156.

142. Ibid., 141.

143. Weber, "Politics as a Vocation," *GPS*, 544.

144. Weber, "The National State and Economic Policy," *GPS*, 24; "Parliament and Government," *GPS*, 351–69; "Politics as a Vocation," *GPS*, 537.

145. Weber, "Parliament and Government," *GPS*, 400–401.

146. Ibid., 403, 348.

147. Ibid., 356.

148. Ibid., 348.

149. Schmidt, *Deutscher Historismus und der Übergang zur parlamentarischen Demokratie*, 309.

150. Weber, "Politics as a Vocation," *GPS*, 544.

151. Weber, *Zur Neuordnung Deutschlands*.

152. Samuel P. Huntington, *Political Order in Changing Societies* (New Haven: Yale University Press, 1968), 137.

153. Mommsen also criticizes Weber's use of Gladstone; see *Max Weber und die deutsche Politik*, 450–51.

154. P. C. Griffiths, "The Caucus and the Liberal Party in 1886," *History* 61 (1976): 183.

155. For a general history of the period and Gladstone's ministries, see Richard Shannon, *The Crisis of Imperialism, 1865–1915* (St. Albans, Eng.: Paladin, 1976), esp. chap. 8. For a study of voting patterns and the meaning of the Home Rule crisis, see W. C. Lubenow, *Parliamentary Politics and the Home Rule Crisis: The British House of Commons in 1886* (Oxford: Clarendon Press, 1988).

156. Weber, "Politics as a Vocation," *GPS*, 544. Weber relied on M. Ostrogorski, *Democracy and the Organization of Political Parties*, 2 vols., trans. Frederick Clarke, pref. James Bryce (New York: Macmillan, 1902).

157. Weber, "Politics as a Vocation," *GPS*, 535–36.

158. Martin Pugh, *The Making of Modern British Politics, 1867–1939* (New York: St. Martin's Press, 1982), 35, 38; and Michael Barker, *Gladstone and Radicalism: The Reconstruction of Liberal Policy in Britain, 1885–94* (New York: Barnes & Noble, 1975), 75.

159. On Gladstone's life, there is the older biography by his associate John Morley, *The Life of William Ewart Gladstone* (1903; New York:

Greenwood Press, 1968). More recently there are Philip Magnus, *Gladstone: A Biography* (London: John Murray, 1954); J. L. Hammond and M.R.D. Foot, *Gladstone and Liberalism* (New York: Collier, 1966); Peter Stansky, *Gladstone: A Progress in Politics* (New York: Norton, 1979); and Richard Shannon, *Gladstone*, vol. 1: *1809–1865* (London: Methuen, 1984).

160. Harold Perkin, *The Origins of Modern English Society, 1780–1880* (London: Routledge & Kegan Paul, 1969), 378–80, 434–39, 453–54; Stansky, *Gladstone*, 157.

161. D. A. Hamer, "Gladstone: The Making of a Political Myth," *Victorian Studies* 22 (1978): 48, 41, 49, 47, 34.

162. J. L. Hammond, *Gladstone and the Irish Nation* (1938; Hamden, Conn.: Archon Books, 1964), 552–53.

163. Hamer, "Gladstone," 48–49, 46, 47 (Bagehot quote).

164. D. A. Hamer, *Liberal Politics in the Age of Gladstone and Rosebery: A Study in Leadership and Policy* (Oxford: Oxford University Press, 1972), 71, 68, 69 (Gladstone quote), 70.

165. T. A. Jenkins, *Gladstone, Whiggery, and the Liberal Party, 1874–1886* (Oxford: Clarendon Press, 1988), 24–31, 66n.61., 123–25, 181–82, 230–36. See also M. Barker, *Gladstone and Radicalism*, 2.

166. Lubenow, *Parliamentary Politics*, 257, maintains that Home Rule could not possibly have provided "an ideological basis for party unity."

167. Jenkins, *Gladstone, Whiggery, and the Liberal Party*, 247–48. On Gladstone's "conversion," see James Loughlin, *Gladstone, Home Rule, and the Ulster Question, 1882–93* (Atlantic Highlands, N.J.: Humanities Press International, 1987), 35–52.

168. Jenkins, *Gladstone, Whiggery, and the Liberal Party*, 242, 244; Shannon, *Crisis of Imperialism*, 189–90.

169. M. Barker, *Gladstone and Radicalism*, 17.

170. Hammond, *Gladstone and the Irish Nation*, 473–81; Hammond and Foot, *Gladstone and Liberalism*, 140–41; Ivor Bulmer-Thomas, *The Growth of the British Party System*, vol. 1: *1640–1923* (London: John Baker, 1965), 139.

171. H. J. Hanham, *Elections and Party Management: Politics in the Time of Disraeli and Gladstone*, 2d. ed. (Sussex: Harvester Press, 1978), xiii; Samuel H. Beer, *British Politics in the Collectivist Age* (New York: Vintage Books, 1969), 52–54, 255–56, 259. In the press, the Caucus was often and unfairly compared unfavorably to American machines like Tammany under control of a boss, though the Caucus had no spoils system. Conservatives and Whigs thought the Caucus was too democratic and likely to undermine their power; Labor leaders thought it was not democratic enough. See Henry Pelling, *America and the British Left: From Bright to Bevan* (London: Adam & Charles Black, 1956), 34, 38–40, 47.

172. On the origins of the NLF, see the work of one of its leaders, Robert Spence Watson, *The National Liberal Federation* (London: T. Fisher Unwin, 1907); also M. Ostrogorski, "The Introduction of the Caucus into England," *Political Science Quarterly* 8 (1893): 287–316; and, critical of Ostrogorski, Francis H. Herrick, "The Origins of the National Liberal Federation," *Journal of Modern History* 17 (1945): 116–29.

173. Hamer, *Liberal Politics*, 56; Jenkins, *Gladstone, Whiggery, and the Liberal Party*, 286.

174. Beer, *British Politics*, 258. On the workings of the Caucus, see Hanham, *Elections and Party Management*, chap. 7: "The Rise of the Caucus"; and M. Barker, *Gladstone and Radicalism*, chap. 4: "The Anatomy of Caucus Politics."

175. Jenkins, *Gladstone, Whiggery, and Liberal Politics*, 286, 288–89. Loughlin, *Gladstone, Home Rule, and the Ulster Question*, 50–52, reports a newspaper survey that suggested electors in the north of England and Scotland, in Leeds and Manchester, would support Home Rule as an act of faith in Gladstone—that he would not mislead them—"in opposition to their own sympathies and desires" (51). The part of the party that actually sits in Parliament is called the Parliamentary party.

176. Griffiths, "The Caucus and the Liberal Party," 191.

177. Hamer, *Liberal Politics*, 125–26; Griffiths, "The Caucus and the Liberal Party," 196, 197; M. Barker, *Gladstone and Radicalism*, 156.

178. Ostrogorski, "Introduction of the Caucus," 313–16.

179. Hugh Berrington, "Partisanship and Dissidence in the Nineteenth-Century House of Commons," *Parliamentary Affairs* 21 (1967–68): 338–74; Pugh, *Making of Modern British Politics*, 19, concurs. See also Gary Cox, "The Development of a Party-oriented Electorate in England, 1832–1918," *British Journal of Political Science* 16 (1986): 214.

180. Pugh, *Making of Modern British Politics*, 36–37; Loughlin, *Gladstone, Home Rule, and the Ulster Question*, 48–50.

181. Hanham, *Elections and Party Management*, 147–54; M. Barker, *Gladstone and Radicalism*, 110–11; Griffiths, "The Caucus and the Liberal Party," 195; Jenkins, *Gladstone, Whiggery, and the Liberal Party*, 285, 291. Despite the evidence of some class differences on the issue of support of Gladstone, Lubenow, *Parliamentary Politics*, 252, 255, 259, 319, 335, maintains that Liberal disagreement on Home Rule was ideological, not socially based, with Whigs on both sides of the issue.

182. Hammond, *Gladstone and the Irish Nation*, 489.

183. Hanham, *Elections and Party Management*, 200, 202, 204. Gladstone tried to give a lead to the country as a whole but did not limit the freedom of candidates to adjust his election proposals to the needs of their locality. Still, election manifestos were personal appeals from the leader, though leaders usually remained uncommitted to particular reform proposals.

184. Hamer, *Liberal Politics*, 126, 141–42; M. Barker, *Gladstone and Radicalism*, 47, 109; Griffiths, "The Caucus and the Liberal Party," 192.

185. Hanham, *Elections and Party Management*, 202.

186. Hammond, *Gladstone and the Irish Nation*, 478, 557–58; see also Stansky, *Gladstone*, 158; Hammond and Foot, *Gladstone and Liberalism*, 145.

187. See A. Lawrence Lowell, *The Government of England*, 2 vols., rev. ed. (New York: Macmillan, 1912), esp. 2:71–100.

188. Beer, *British Politics*, 256–58. Beer's table of coefficients of cohesion tells the story quite neatly. Ostrogorski concurs in this. See also Alan Beattie, *English Party Politics*, vol. 1: *1660–1906* (London: Weidenfeld & Nicolson, 1970), 140, 144.

189. Valerie Cromwell, "The Losing of the Initiative by the House of Commons," *Transactions of the Royal Historical Society* 18 (1968): 1–23. Cox, "Development of a Party-oriented Electorate," 187–216, concurs, maintaining that changes in electoral organization, limitations on and centralization of campaign finance, and the development of disciplined parties all postdate the procedural decline of private members.

190. Hanham, *Elections and Party Management*, 201, 203.

191. Lubenow, *Parliamentary Politics*, 118–19, 335.

192. Hanham, *Elections and Party Management*, 204, 209. On the organization of the parties, see ibid., chap. 16: "Central Party Organization"; and A. Aspinall, "English Party Organization in the Early Nineteenth Century," *English Historical Review* 41 (1926): 389–411.

193. Beattie, *English Party Politics*, 148.

194. Hamer, *Liberal Politics*, 141, 145.

195. Jenkins, *Gladstone, Whiggery, and the Liberal Party*, 292. Jenkins believes that from this there grew the conviction that the Liberals were always divided and that only Gladstone's great powers held them together.

196. M. Barker, *Gladstone and Radicalism*, 89, 96.

197. Weber, "Parliament and Government," *GPS*, 393, 394–95.

198. Martin Pugh, *Lloyd George* (London: Longman, 1988), 121.

199. Kenneth O. Morgan, "Lloyd George's Premiership: A Study in 'Prime Ministerial Government,'" *Historical Journal* 13 (1970): 131–32.

200. A.J.P. Taylor, *Politics in Wartime* (New York: Atheneum, 1965), 16, 33–37, 123–49. See also Michael Kinnear, *The Fall of Lloyd George: The Political Crisis of 1922* (Toronto: University of Toronto Press, 1973), 1–62.

201. Morgan, "Lloyd George's Premiership," 139.

202. Bulmer-Thomas, *Growth of the British Party System*, 237.

203. Kenneth O. Morgan, *Lloyd George*, intro. A.J.P. Taylor (London: Weidenfeld & Nicolson, 1974), 126.

204. Bulmer-Thomas, *Growth of the British Party System*, 241; also 246.

205. Martin Pugh, *Electoral Reform in War and Peace, 1906–18* (London: Routledge & Kegan Paul, 1978), 120–21.

206. Morgan, "Lloyd George's Premiership"; see also Trevor Wilson, *The Downfall of the Liberal Party, 1914–35* (Ithaca: Cornell University Press, 1966), 112–20, 144–49, 177–78, 385–87.

207. Pugh, *Lloyd George*, 130–31.

208. Morgan, *Lloyd George*, 136 (quote), 167–68. On the origins and breakup of the postwar coalition, see Kenneth O. Morgan, *Consensus and Disunity: The Lloyd George Coalition Government, 1918–1922* (Oxford: Clarendon Press, 1979), 1–25, 331–56.

209. Richard Neustadt, *Presidential Power: The Politics of Leadership* (New York: Wiley, 1962).

210. For a small part of the debate on this issue, see Arthur Rosenberg, *A History of the German Republic*, trans. Ian F. Morrow and L. Marie Sieveking (New York: Russell & Russell, 1965), 22–29; Reinhard Rürup, "Problems of the German Revolution, 1918–19," *Journal of Contemporary History* 3 (1968): 109–35; and Wolfgang J. Mommsen, "The German Revolution, 1918–1920: Political Revolution and Social Protest Movement," in *Social Change and Political Development in Weimar Germany*, ed. Richard Bessel and E. J. Feuchtwanger (London: Croom Helm, 1981), 21–54.

211. Quoted in Marianne Weber, *Max Weber*, 663–65.

212. Weber, "Politics as a Vocation," *GPS*, 559. Mommsen, "Max Weber and Roberto Michels," 103, even claims that Weber's attraction to "the prototype of a 'Gesinnungsethiker' " like Michels was due to the fact that "Weber himself had always been at heart a 'Gesinnungsethiker' also who, however, had never permitted himself to act and behave accordingly."

213. Weber, "Politics as a Vocation," *GPS*, 560.

214. Weber, "Confucianism and Taoism," *GRS* 1:521.

CHAPTER 7

1. See Schröter, " 'Eideshelfer' Thomas Manns," 61. Richard Winston has an unusual explanation of the origins of the novel in Mann's negative feelings for his brother; see *Thomas Mann: The Making of an Artist, 1875–1911* (New York: Knopf, 1981), 76–77.

2. Hans Rudolf Vaget, "Amazing Grace: Thomas Mann, Adorno, and the Faust Myth," in *Our Faust? Roots and Ramifications of a Modern German Myth*, ed. Reinhold Grimm and Jost Hermand (Madison: University of Wisconsin Press, 1987), 171.

3. Mann, *The Genesis of "Doctor Faustus": Novel of a Novel*, in *GW* 11:157.

4. Hubert Orlowski, *Prädestination des Dämonischen*, Seria *Filologia*

Germanska, no. 7 (Poznan: Adam Mickiewicz University, 1969), argues ingeniously that there is reason to doubt Zeitblom's reliability as narrator and that the novel should be understood as the reflection of the humanist part of the bourgeoisie allegorizing German decline in terms of predestination, thus falsifying history and excusing itself from responsibility.

5. Mann says he could not physically describe these two in the novel because they had "too much to conceal, namely, the secret of their identity [with one another]"; *Genesis of Doctor Faustus,* in GW 11:204.

6. Mann, "Notizenkonvolut zu *Doktor Faustus,*" quoted in Liselotte Voss, *Die Entstehung von Thomas Manns Roman "Doktor Faustus"* (Tübingen: Max Niemeyer Verlag, 1975), 79. Mann read Kierkegaard's *Either/Or* while writing the novel, whose section on Mozart's *Don Giovanni* speaks of music as "Christian art with negative prefix"; see de Mendelssohn, *Nachbemerkungen,* 160. See also Weber, "Intermediate Reflection," *GRS* 1:556, on music as the "most inward of the arts," which religion often considered as a competing power and a potential surrogate for religious experience.

7. For his earlier view of music, and of himself as essentially musical, see Mann, *Reflections,* in GW 12:319–20.

8. Cf. Reed, *Thomas Mann,* 368–69; and Maurice Colleville, "Nietzsche et le *Doktor Faustus* de Thomas Mann," *Études germaniques* 3 (1948): 343–54.

9. Mann, "Germany and the Germans," *GW* 11:1132.

10. Mann, "Notizenkonvolut," quoted in Voss, *Die Entstehung von "Doktor Faustus,"* 180.

11. Mann, Letter of 22 February 1949 to Wilhelm Buller, in *Briefe* 3:73. The note to this letter claims that Mann never actually said this, though Heinrich reports that, upon coming to the United States, Thomas said, "Where I am, is German culture"; see ibid., 504.

12. Mann, "Germany and the Germans," *GW* 11:1146.

13. Ibid., 1137. See also Antal Mádl, *Thomas Manns Humanismus* (Berlin: Rütten & Loening, 1980).

14. Quoted in Hans Wysling, "Zu Thomas Manns 'Maja'-Projekt," in Paul Scherrer and Hans Wysling, *Quellenkritische Studien zum Werk Thomas Manns,* vol. 1 of *Thomas-Mann-Studien* (Bern: Francke Verlag, 1967), 38.

15. Mann, "Notizenkonvolut," quoted in Voss, *Die Entstehung von "Doktor Faustus,"* 16–17.

16. Mann, *Genesis of Doctor Faustus,* in GW 11:172.

17. Cf. John Burt Foster, Jr., *Heirs to Dionysus: A Nietzschean Current in Literary Modernism* (Princeton: Princeton University Press, 1981), chap. 6: "Enter the Devil: Nietzsche's Presence in *Doctor Faustus*"; Eckhard Heftrich, "Ergänzende Betrachtung: Nietzsche als Hamlet der Zeitenwende," in *Über Thomas Mann,* vol. 1: *Zauberbergmusik* (Frankfurt

a. M.: Vittorio Klostermann, 1975), 281–316; idem, "Radikale Autobiographie und Allegorie der Epoche: *Doktor Faustus*," in *Über Thomas Mann*, vol. 2: *Vom Verfall zur Apokalypse* (Frankfurt a. M.: Vittorio Klostermann, 1982), 173–288; and Borge Kristiansen, "Thomas Mann und die Philosophie," in *Thomas-Mann-Handbuch*, ed. Helmut Koopman (Stuttgart: Alfred Kröner Verlag, 1990), 260–76.

18. Yet see William J. McGrath, *Dionysian Art and Populist Politics in Austria* (New Haven: Yale University Press, 1974), chap. 2: "Nietzsche as Educator," which deals with the infatuation of the bourgeoisie for the ideas of the early Nietzsche, especially *Birth of Tragedy*. On the relation of *Birth of Tragedy* to Nietzsche's view of a "bourgeois cultural-revolution," see Gert Mattenklott, "Nietzsches 'Geburt der Tragödie' als Konzept einer bürgerlichen Kulturrevolution," in Mattenklott and Scherpe, *Positionen der literarischen Intelligenz*, 103–20.

19. Mann, Letter of 26 July 1925 to Stefan Zweig, in *Briefe* 1:245; and "Lebensabriß," GW 11:136.

20. Mann, "Rede an der Sorbonne," GW 13:228.

21. Mann, *Doctor Faustus*, in GW 6:10. Hereafter all references to the novel will be indicated in the text by page numbers in parentheses.

22. See Hinton Thomas, "Uses of 'Bildung,' " 177–86. See further Bödeker, "Menschheit, Humanität, Humanismus," in Brunner, Conze, and Koselleck, *Geschichtliche Grundbegriffe* 3:1063–1128; and Bruford, *Culture and Society in Classical Weimar*, 1, 231–36.

23. See Mann, "Goethe and Tolstoy," GW 9:58–173; and "On the German Republic," GW 11:809–52.

24. On the Faust story, see William Rose, ed., *The History of the Damnable Life and Deserved Death of Doctor John Faustus, 1592* (London: George Routledge & Sons, n.d.), 1–2, 53. Also Frank Baron, *Doctor Faustus: From History to Legend* (Munich: Wilhelm Fink Verlag, 1978); and Margaret De Huszar Allen, *The Faust Legend: Popular Formula and Modern Novel* (New York: Peter Lang, 1985). The 1587 Faust text, with additions from later editions, can be found in Richard Benz, ed., *Historia von D. Johann Fausten* (Stuttgart: Reclam Universal Bibliothek, 1975).

25. Reed, *Thomas Mann*, 385–86, thinks Aschenbach the more appropriate comparison.

26. Mann, *Genesis of Doctor Faustus*, in GW 11:203–4. See *Doctor Faustus*, in GW 6:13. See also Conrad Rosenstein, "Vom Einsamkeitszauber und seiner Überwindung: eine Motivstudie zu Thomas Mann" (1972; Thomas Mann Archive, Zurich, mimeo).

27. On the similarities between Leverkühn and expressionist artists, see Sokel, *Writer in Extremis*, 78–82, 102–4, 114–18. See also Mann's attack on expressionists in *Reflections*, GW 12:564–65.

28. Burton Pike, "Thomas Mann and the Problematic Self," in *Publications of the English Goethe Society: Papers Read before the Society*,

1966–67, ed. Elizabeth M. Wilkinson, B. A. Rowley, and Ann C. Weaver (London: Maney, 1967), 125 says: "For these serious artists art amounts to a religious calling, and service to it demands in more than one sense their lives."

29. Mann, "Germany and the Germans," *GW* 11:1148.

30. Mann, "Notizenkonvolut," in Voss, *Die Entstehung von "Doktor Faustus,"* 179.

31. Mann, "Meine Zeit," *GW* 11:318. See also Kaufmann, *Thomas Mann*, 206. The great forerunner of this analysis of freedom is Dostoevsky's Grand Inquisitor.

32. See Chapter 2 above. Cf. Kurt Sontheimer, *Antidemokratisches Denken in der Weimarer Republik* (1962; Munich: Deutscher Taschenbuch Verlag, 1978).

33. Mann, *Reflections*, in *GW* 12:515–17. On the political form of the problem, see Leonard Krieger, *The German Idea of Freedom* (Boston: Beacon Press, 1957).

34. Russell Berman describes Mann's "modernist project" as "the analysis of the objective construction of contemporary individuality" in the context of the failure of laissez-faire individualism; see *The Rise of the Modern German Novel* (Cambridge, Mass.: Harvard University Press, 1986), 263–64. Sauer, "Weimar Culture," 268, says that "Wilhelmian society had been an anarchy, externally controlled by militarism and concealed by the shining cover of a nationalist emperorship and imperialist pseudosuccesses. The Weimar republic ... was a system of balanced power, an open-anarchy internally controlled by ad-hoc compromises in the fashion of diplomatic alliances. Not much seems to have changed, then, except that the democratic constitution prevented concealment and falsification of the situation."

35. Wassily Kandinsky, *Concerning the Spiritual in Art*, trans. and intro. M.T.H. Sadler (New York: Dover, 1977), 14.

36. Weber, "Intermediate Reflection," *GRS* 1:555. See also "Sociology of Religion," *WG*, 365–66.

37. On the avant-garde, see Peter Bürger, *The Theory of the Avant Garde*, trans. Michael Shaw, intro. Jochen Schulte-Sasse (Minneapolis: University of Minnesota Press, 1984); Michael Hamburger, *Contraries: Studies in German Literature* (New York: Dutton, 1970), 263–90; Victor H. Meisel, ed., *Voices of German Expressionism* (Englewood Cliffs, N.J.: Prentice-Hall, 1970); Roy Pascal, *From Naturalism to Expressionism: German Literature and Society, 1880–1918* (New York: Basic Books, 1973); Charles Russell, *Poets, Prophets, and Revolutionaries: The Literary Avant-Garde from Rimbaud to Postmodernism* (New York: Oxford University Press, 1985); and Edmund Wilson, *Axel's Castle: A Study in the Imaginative Literature of 1870–1930* (New York: Scribner, 1931).

38. Mann, *Reflections*, in *GW* 12:496.

39. Weber, "Intermediate Reflection," GRS 1:570.

40. Paul Klee, On Modern Art, trans. Paul Findlay, intro. Herbert Read (1948; London: Faber & Faber, 1967), 55. Cf. Georg Lukács, The Theory of the Novel (Cambridge, Mass.: MIT Press, 1971), 29–39.

41. This view is also Tolstoy's; see What Is to Be Done? in Novels and Other Works (New York: Scribner, 1913), 18:232. See also Ulrich Simon, "The Theological Challenge of 'Doctor Faustus,'" Church Quarterly Review 151 (1950): 547–53.

42. Cf. Sauer, "Weimar Culture," 258.

43. This is a view whose real origin is Schoenberg, through Adorno. See Theodor W. Adorno, Philosophy of Modern Music, trans. Anne G. Mitchell and Wesley V. Blomster (New York: Continuum, 1985), 41–42, who quotes Schoenberg. See also Janik and Toulmin, Wittgenstein's Vienna, 111. On Adorno's influence on Mann, see Hansjörg Dörr, "Thomas Mann und Adorno: ein Beitrag zur Entstehung des 'Doktor Faustus,'" in Thomas Manns "Doktor Faustus" und die Wirkung, ed. Rudolf Wolff (Bonn: Bouvier Verlag Herbert Grundmann, 1983), pt. 2, 48–91; Jan Maegaard, "Zu Th. W. Adornos Rolle in Mann/Schoenberg-Streit," in Gedenkschrift für Thomas Mann, 1875–1975, ed. Rolf Wiecker (Copenhagen: Verlag Text & Kontext, 1975), 215–22; Jan Albrecht, "Leverkühn oder die Musik als Schicksal," Deutsche Vierteljahresschrift für Literaturwissenschaft und Geistesgeschichte 45 (1971): 375–88; Rosemarie Puschmann, Magisches Quadrat und Melancholie in Thomas Manns "Doktor Faustus." Von der musikalischen Struktur zum semantischen Beziehungsnetz (Bielefeld: AMPAL Verlag, 1983), 24–70; and Wikirchen, Zeitgeschichte im Roman, 170–84.

44. Mann, Genesis of "Doctor Faustus," in GW 11:187.

45. Weber, "Critical Studies in the Area of the Logic of the Cultural Sciences," WL, 226–27.

46. Mann, Letter of 1 March 1945 to Bruno Walter, in Briefe 2:416.

47. See André von Gronicka, "Thomas Mann's Doktor Faustus: Prolegomena to an Interpretation," Germanic Review 23 (1948): 212.

48. Mann, work notes for Doctor Faustus, quoted in Reed, Thomas Mann, 374.

49. Anton Webern, The Path to the New Music, ed. Willi Reich (Bryn Mawr, Penn.: Theodore Presser, 1963), 54–55. For Schoenberg's own reflections, see Arnold Schoenberg, Style and Idea: Selected Writings of Arnold Schoenberg, ed. Leonard Stein, trans. Leo Black (Berkeley and Los Angeles: University of California Press, 1984). On Schoenberg, see Carl Dahlhaus, Schoenberg and the New Music, trans. Derek Puffett and Alfred Clayton (Cambridge: Cambridge University Press, 1987); and Charles Rosen, Arnold Schoenberg (New York: Viking, 1975). On Schoenberg, Berg, and Webern, see The New Grove: Second Viennese School (New York: Norton, 1983).

50. See Mann, "Dostoevsky—in Moderation," introduction to *The Short Novels of Dostoevsky* (New York: Dial Press, 1945), xiv, xv. Mann speaks there of "the great invalids" who are "crucified victims, sacrificed to humanity and its advancements, to the broadening of its feeling and knowledge."

51. On this, see H. S. Gilliam, "Mann's Other Holy Sinner: Adrian Leverkühn as Faust and Christ," *Germanic Review* 52 (1977): 122–47.

52. Mann, "Lübeck as a Spiritual Way of Life," GW 11:398; "Nietzsche's Philosophy in the Light of Our Experience," GW 9:680. Also *Reflections*, in GW 12:146.

53. This claim is rejected by Hildegarde Drexl Hannum, "Self-Sacrifice in *Doktor Faustus*: Thomas Mann's Contribution to the Faust Legend," *Modern Language Quarterly* 35 (1974): 289–301.

54. See Nietzsche, *The Will to Power*, ed. Walter Kaufmann, trans. Walter Kaufmann and R. J. Hollingdale (New York: Vintage Books, 1968), no. 721, p. 384. Also see Mann's note, in Voss, *Die Entstehung von "Doktor Faustus,"* 40.

55. Reed, *Thomas Mann*, 386, describes this as "Nietzschean vitalism." De Mendelssohn, *Nachbemerkungen*, 121, refers to it as "Enthemmung um jeden Preis."

56. Mann, *Royal Highness*, in GW 2:177–78.

57. Cf. Jean Finck, *Thomas Mann und die Psychoanalyse* (Paris: Belles Lettres, 1973), 323, 337.

58. Mann, "Dostoevsky," viii–ix, xv. See also "Germany and the Germans," GW 11:1144–45.

59. Hans Mayer, *Thomas Mann* (Frankfurt a. M.: Suhrkamp Verlag, 1980), 290–91. See also Kaufmann, *Thomas Mann*, 6–7, who discusses the changing religious scene of Mann's works.

60. Berman, *Rise of the Modern German Novel*, 263, says Mann thematizes the crisis of individuality and the search for an alternative community, the "renewed collective," throughout his work, and that *Doctor Faustus* reveals the goal of Mann's modernist project to be the achievement of a "new objectivity in a revitalized culture."

61. Simon, "Theological Challenge of 'Doctor Faustus,' " 54.

62. For examples of this view, see Käte Hamburger, "Anachronistische Symbolik: Fragen an Thomas Manns Faustus-Roman," in Wolff, *Thomas Manns "Doktor Faustus" und die Wirkung*, pt. 1, 124–50; and Kurzke, *Thomas Mann*, 275–80.

63. Foster, *Heirs to Dionysus*, 366, notes that in Mann's hands, Nietzsche's "mythic self-dramatization that envisions the end of Christianity has become a reassertion of Christianity's power to enforce some sense of absolute values." Wikirchen, *Zeitgeschichte im Roman*, 184–95, argues that the religious dimension of the novel was strongly influenced by Mann's reading of Kierkegaard and Walter Benjamin, mediated

by Adorno. See also Martin Müller, "Walter Benjamin und Thomas Manns *Doktor Faustus*," *Archiv für das Studium der neueren Sprachen und Literaturen* 210 (1973): 327–30.

64. Mann, Letter of 5 February 1948 to Kuno Fiedler, in *Blätter der Thomas Mann Gesellschaft* (Zurich), no. 11 (1971): 19. On the religious dimensions of the work, see Herbert Lehnert, *Thomas Mann—Fiktion, Mythos, Religion* (Stuttgart: W. Kohlhammer Verlag, 1965), 195–204.

65. Weber, "Science as a Vocation," *WL*, 604.

66. Cf. Edward W. Said, *Beginnings: Intention and Method* (Baltimore: Johns Hopkins University Press, 1975), 182–88.

67. Mann, "Lübeck as a Spiritual Way of Life," *GW* 11:398.

68. See Mann, *Genesis of Doctor Faustus*, in *GW* 11:272.

69. Nietzsche, *Thus Spoke Zarathustra*, "Zarathustra's Prologue," sec. 3, in *KSA* 4:15.

70. For an insightful and provocative critique of Mann's ending and the problems it creates, set within a comprehensive interpretation of the significance of Faust stories, see Harry Redner, *In the Beginning Was the Deed: Reflections on the Passage of Faust* (Berkeley and Los Angeles: University of California Press, 1982), 223–24, 232, 238–40, 247–48.

71. Mann, "Nietzsche's Philosophy," *GW* 9:695.

72. Mann, Letter of 5 February 1948 to Kuno Fiedler, in *Blätter der Thomas-Mann-Gesellschaft*, no. 11 (1971): 19.

73. Mann, "Nietzsche's Philosophy," *GW* 9:710.

74. Nietzsche, *Beyond Good and Evil*, no. 53, in *KSA* 5:72–73.

75. Simon, "Theological Challenge of 'Doctor Faustus,'" 548. Indeed, Schröter, *Thomas Mann*, 136, claims that during the years he was writing *The Magic Mountain* Mann said that he could easily have become a theologian! See also Mann, *Genesis of Doctor Faustus*, in *GW* 11:723: "A difficult work of art, like battle, trouble at sea, or danger to life, brings God nearest, in that it engenders a religious mood in the soul, a pious upward look for blessing, help, grace."

76. Foster, *Heirs to Dionysus*, 390, says that the works Mann has Leverkühn write "show that Mann has broken with Nietzsche's criticism of Christian art."

77. Mann, Letter of 17 December 1946 to Agnes Meyer, quoted in de Mendelssohn, *Nachbemerkungen*, 184–85, and in *Thomas Mann*, ed. Hans Wysling and Marianne Fischer, part 3: *1944–1955*, vol. 14 of *Dichter über ihre Dichtungen* (Munich and Frankfurt a. M.: Ernst Heimeran Verlag and S. Fischer Verlag, 1981), 80. See also Mann, Letter of 1 January 1947 to Karl Kerenyi, in *Mythology and Humanism: The Correspondence of Thomas Mann and Karl Kerenyi*, trans. Alexander Gelley (Ithaca: Cornell University Press, 1975), 151, for an almost identical expression.

78. Theodor W. Adorno, "Zu einem Porträt Thomas Manns," in

Noten zur Literatur, vol. 3 (Frankfurt: Suhrkamp Verlag, 1965), 27. See also Kurzke, *Thomas Mann,* 275. J. P. Stern, *History and Allegory in Thomas Mann's "Doktor Faustus"* (London: H. K. Lewis for University College, 1975), 11, says: "The theology of *Doktor Faustus,* which Thomas Mann takes from his peculiar reading of Martin Luther, is the theology of *fortiter peccari,* of salvation through a superabundance of sins."

79. On the struggle between Adorno and Mann over the ending, and the importance of Mann's reading of Kierkegaard and of Adorno's book on him, see Vaget, "Amazing Grace," 168–89; and idem, "Thomas Mann und James Joyce: Zur Frage des Modernismus im *Doktor Faustus,*" in *Thomas Mann Jahrbuch* 2:121–50. Vaget believes that this ending shows that Mann is closer to Goethe's version of Faust than normally thought, since Mann preserves the possibility of redemption, which the sixteenth-century Faust does not. On Mann's relation to Christianity, see Werner Frizen, "Thomas Mann und das Christentum," in Koopman, *Thomas-Mann-Handbuch,* 307–26, esp. 320–22; and Lehnert, *Thomas Mann,* 253–54n.95.

80. Mann, "Germany and the Germans," *GW* 11:1131.

81. Cf. Reed, *Thomas Mann,* 366. See also Gunter Reiss, *"Allegorisierung" und moderne Erzählkunst. Eine Studie zum Werk Thomas Manns* (Munich: Wilhelm Fink, 1970). Stern, *History and Allegory in "Doktor Faustus,"* 10, speaks of the book as "a 'total' novel of interconnections and allegorical correspondences," yet goes on to say (13) that the relation between the hero and Germany "is not one of determinism or of consistent on-going allegory, but of an illuminating and sustaining symbolism."

82. Reed, *Thomas Mann,* 396, maintains, to the contrary, that the bedrock of *Doctor Faustus* is not the Faust myth, but the theory of the Dionysiac.

83. Mann, "Germany and the Germans," *GW* 11:1145, 1146, 1141.

84. Ibid., 1131.

85. On the symbolic value of the war, see Roland N. Stromberg, *Redemption By War: The Intellectuals and 1914* (Lawrence: Regents Press of Kansas, 1982).

86. Reed, *Thomas Mann,* 377; and Stern, *History and Allegory in "Doktor Faustus,"* 12. Yet Reed still considers the novel to be essentially an allegory, and Adorno concurs: "The novel is no longer naturalistic-psychological and more allegorical than symbolical"; see de Mendelssohn, *Nachbemerkungen,* 191.

87. Mann, "Germany and the Germans," *GW* 11:1144. Jeffrey Herf, *Reactionary Modernism: Technology, Culture, and Politics in Weimar and the Third Reich* (New York: Cambridge University Press, 1984), calls this Germany's "reactionary modernism."

88. Mann, "Germany and the Germans," *GW* 11:1131.

89. Cf. E. M. Butler, *The Fortunes of Faust* (Cambridge: Cambridge University Press, 1952), 336: "An artist's fate is something much too individual to symbolize a nation's destiny. The attempt to do so here would result in laying the blame for the tragedy Germany brought about and suffered at the door of her musical gifts. . . . Ruthless political ambitions are in a different category from the *hubris* of genius."

90. Mann, "Nietzsche's Philosophy," *GW* 9:695, 696, 702, 697.

91. Mann, Letter of 5 May 1926 to Ernst Fischer, in *Briefe* 1: 255-56.

92. Mann, "Nietzsche's Philosophy," *GW* 9:706, 707-8, 701, 703, 710. Ehrhard Bahr believes Mann overcame these terms through Adorno; see " 'Identität des Nichtidentischen': zur Dialektik der Kunst in Thomas Manns *Doktor Faustus* und Theodor W. Adornos *Ästhetischer Theorie*," in *Thomas Mann Jahrbuch* 2:102-20.

93. Mann, Letter of 3 May 1948 to Oscar Schmitt-Halin, in *Briefe* 3:31.

94. For a different view, see Kristiansen, "Thomas Mann und die Philosophie," in Koopman, *Thomas-Mann-Handbuch*, 271-76. Hermann Kurzke believes that for Mann, "Nietzsche is not a forerunner of fascism," but that Nietzsche's "philosophy and his ethics are rejected from the standpoint of a Christian humanism, which Mann had won from the experiences of the Weimar Republic and of the Third Reich"; see Kurzke's notes on Mann's Nietzsche essay in Mann, *Essays*, vol. 3: *Musik und Philosophie*, ed. Hermann Kurzke (Frankfurt a. M.: Fischer Taschenbuch Verlag, 1978), 295.

95. Stern, *History and Allegory in "Doktor Faustus,"* 17, believes that Mann "comes to identify belief in the saving power of strenuousness with Christian salvation," but he believes this is an existential, not a religious truth, and that it therefore transcends the Christian theme, "that salvation and freedom beyond determination can only come at the issue of the kind of existential effort and strenuousness that he has here depicted. It is . . . the belief and mode of thought of a whole epoch. Rilke, George, Hofmannsthal and Gottfried Benn have all expressed it. Even Bertolt Brecht voices it." He therefore sees Mann's confusion as the product of a mind "both critical and in need of a traditional framework." Yet he acknowledges (19): "This idea of a salvation of man through his supreme effort was open to horrifying abuse."

96. Mann, *Tagebücher, 1918-1921*, 208. Mann reaffirms his claim of Nietzsche as a prophet of the synthesis of "the third *Reich* . . . of humanity" in "Germany and Democracy," *GW* 13:580.

CONCLUSION

1. For discussions of these themes, see Carl Schorske, *Fin-de-Siècle Vienna: Politics and Culture* (New York: Knopf, 1980); Wolfdietrich

Rasch, *Zur deutschen Literatur seit der Jahrhundertwende. Gesammelte Aufsätze* (Stuttgart: J. B. Metzlersche Verlagsbuchhandlung, 1967); Sokel, *Writer in Extremis*; and M. Hamburger, *Contraries*.

2. George Herbert Mead, *Mind, Self, and Society: From the Standpoint of a Social Behaviorist*, ed. with intro. by Charles W. Morris (1934; Chicago: University of Chicago Press, 1962), 140, 144, 154–55, 164, 175, 179.

3. Nietzsche, *The Case of Wagner*, in *KSA* 6:52–53.

4. Theodor Adorno, *Minima Moralia: Reflections from Damaged Life*, trans. E.F.N. Jephcott (London: Verso, 1978), 97.

5. Nietzsche, *On the Genealogy of Morals*, in *KSA*, vol. 5, essay three, sec. 9, p. 356, and sec. 24, p. 400.

6. Ibid., sec. 28, p. 411.

7. Ibid., sec. 1, p. 339.

8. Nietzsche, *Beyond Good and Evil*, in *KSA*, vol. 5, sec. 2, p. 16.

9. Ibid., sec. 260, p. 209.

10. Ibid., sec. 287, p. 233.

11. On the Nietzschean traditions, see Bruno Hillebrand, ed., *Nietzsche und die deutsche Literatur*, 2 vols. (Munich: Deutsche Taschenbuch Verlag; Tübingen: Max Niemeyer Verlag, 1978); Hubert Cancik, "Der Nietzsche-Kult in Weimar," *Nietzsche-Studien* 16 (1987): 405–29; Peter Heller, "Concerning the Nietzsche Cult and Literary Cults Generally," in *Nietzsche: Literature and Values*, ed. Volker Dürr, Reinhold Grimm, and Kathy Harms (Madison: University of Wisconsin Press, 1988), 199–218; R. Hinton Thomas, "Nietzsche in Weimar Germany—and the Case of Ludwig Klages," in *The Weimar Dilemma: Intellectuals in the Weimar Republic*, ed. Anthony Phelan (Manchester: Manchester University Press, 1985), 71–91; Jürgen Krause, *"Märtyrer" und "Prophet." Studien zum Nietzsche-Kult in der bildenden Kunst der Jahrhundertwende* (Berlin: Walter de Gruyter, 1984); Richard Frank Krummel, *Nietzsche und der deutsche Geist*, 2 vols. (Berlin: Walter de Gruyter, 1974–83); H. F. Peters, *Zarathustra's Sister: The Case of Elisabeth and Friedrich Nietzsche* (New York: Markus Wiener, 1977); Peter Pütz, *Friedrich Nietzsche*, 2d ed. (Stuttgart: Metzler, 1975); Heinz Raschel, *Das Nietzsche-Bild im George-Kreis* (Berlin: Walter de Gruyter, 1983); Kurt Lenk, "Das tragische Bewußtsein in der deutschen Soziologie," *Kölner Zeitschrift für Soziologie und Sozialpsychologie* 16 (1964): 257–87; Hubert Treiber, "Gruppenbilder mit einer Dame," *Forum*, January/February 1988, 40–54; idem, "Im Westen Nichts Neues: Menschwerdung durch Askese; Sehnsucht nach Askese bei Weber und Nietzsche," in *Religionswissenschaft und Kulturkritik*, ed. Hans G. Kippenberg and Brigitte Luchesi (Marburg: Diagonal-Verlag, 1991); and idem, "Nietzsche's 'Kloster für freiere Geister': Nietzsche und Weber als Erzieher," in *Die Religion von Oberschichten. Religion—Profession—Intellektualismus*, ed. Peter Antes and Donate Pahnke (Marburg: Diagonal-Verlag, 1989).

12. For the influence of Nietzsche in these respects, see Margot Fleischer, "Das Spektrum der Nietzsche-Rezeption im geistigen Leben seit der Jahrhundertwende," *Nietzsche-Studien* 20 (1991): 1–47; Klaus Lichtblau, "Das 'Pathos der Distanz': Präliminarien zur Nietzsche-Rezeption bei Georg Simmel," in *Georg Simmel und die Moderne*, ed. Heinz-Jürgen Dahme and Ottheim Rammstedt (Frankfurt a. M.: Suhrkamp Verlag, 1984), 231–81; Wilhelm Hennis, *Max Weber: Essays in Reconstruction*, trans. Keith Tribe (London: Allen & Unwin, 1988); and Horst Baier, "Die Gesellschaft—ein langer Schatten des toten Gottes: Friedrich Nietzsche und die Entstehung der Soziologie aus dem Geist der Décadence," *Nietzsche Studien* 10/11 (1981/1982): 6–33.

13. On the importance of agency and power in *The Protestant Ethic*, see Goldman, *Max Weber and Thomas Mann*, 34–35.

14. For analyses of such projects, see Albert Camus, *The Rebel*, trans. Anthony Bower (New York: Vintage Books, 1956); Eugene Lunn, *Prophet of Community: The Romantic Socialism of Gustav Landauer* (Berkeley and Los Angeles: University of California Press, 1973); Mary Gluck, *Georg Lukács and His Generation, 1900–1918* (Cambridge, Mass.: Harvard University Press, 1985); Dagmar Barnouw, *Weimar Intellectuals and the Threat of Modernity* (Bloomington: Indiana University Press, 1988); and Bernard Yack, *The Longing for Total Revolution: Philosophic Sources of Social Discontent from Rousseau to Marx and Nietzsche* (Princeton: Princeton University Press, 1986).

15. See Adorno, *Minima Moralia*, 247: "The only philosophy which can be responsibly practised in face of despair is the attempt to contemplate all things as they would present themselves from the standpoint of redemption [*Erlösung*]. Knowledge has no light but that shed on the world by redemption: all else is reconstruction, mere technique. Perspectives must be fashioned that displace and estrange the world, reveal it to be, with its rifts and crevices, as indigent and distorted as it will appear one day in the messianic light."

16. Martin Green, *Mountain of Truth: The Counterculture Begins—Ascona 1900–1920* (Hanover, N.H.: University Press of New England, 1986).

17. This is the general argument of Ringer's *Decline of the German Mandarins*.

18. Mitzman, *Iron Cage*, 291, 296. On the affair, see also Martin Green, *The von Richthofen Sisters: The Triumphant and the Tragic Modes of Love* (New York: Basic Books, 1974).

19. Mann, "*Joseph and His Brothers*: A Lecture," GW 11:666–67.

20. R. J. Hollingdale, *Thomas Mann; A Critical Study* (Lewisburg, Penn.: Bucknell University Press, 1971), 116–17. See also Willy R. Berger, *Die mythologischen Motive in Thomas Manns Roman "Joseph und seine Brüder"* (Cologne: Böhlau Verlag, 1971).

21. Kaufmann, *Thomas Mann*, 168.

22. Mann, *"Joseph and His Brothers*: A Lecture," *GW* 11:668–69.

23. Ibid., 658.

24. See Seth Taylor, *Left-Wing Nietzscheans: The Politics of German Expressionism, 1910–1920* (Berlin: Walter de Gruyter, 1990); and R. Hinton Thomas, *Nietzsche in German Politics and Society, 1890–1918* (LaSalle, Ill.: Open Court, 1983).

Bibliography

WORKS OF MAX WEBER

From Max Weber: Essays in Sociology. Edited and translated by H. H. Gerth and C. Wright Mills. New York: Oxford University Press, 1946.

Gesammelte Aufsätze zur Religionssoziologie [GRS]. 3 vols. Tübingen: J.C.B. Mohr [Paul Siebeck], 1920-23.

Gesammelte Aufsätze zur Sozial- und Wirtschaftsgeschichte. Edited by Marianne Weber. Tübingen: J.C.B. Mohr [Paul Siebeck], 1924.

Gesammelte Aufsätze zur Soziologie und Sozialpolitik [GSS]. 2d ed. Edited by Marianne Weber. 1924; Tübingen: J.C.B. Mohr [Paul Siebeck], 1988.

Gesammelte Aufsätze zur Wissenschaftslehre [WL]. 5th ed. Edited by Johannes Winckelmann. Tübingen: J.C.B. Mohr [Paul Siebeck], 1982.

Gesammelte Politische Schriften [GPS (1st ed.)]. 1st ed. Edited by Marianne Weber. Munich: Dreimaskenverlag, 1921.

Gesammelte Politische Schriften [GPS]. 3d ed. Edited by Johannes Winckelmann. Tübingen: J.C.B. Mohr [Paul Siebeck], 1971.

Jugendbriefe. Tübingen: J.C.B. Mohr [Paul Siebeck], 1936.

Max Weber on Universities: The Power of the State and the Dignity of the Academic Calling in Imperial Germany. Translated and edited by Edward Shils. Chicago: University of Chicago Press, 1973.

Die protestantische Ethik II—Kritiken und Antikritiken. 2d ed. Edited by Johannes Winckelmann. Hamburg: Siebenstern Taschenbuch Verlag, 1972.

Die Wirtschaftsethik der Weltreligionen. Konfuzianismus und Taoismus. Edited by Helwig Schmidt-Glintzer, with Petra Kolonko. Sec. 1, vol. 19 of *Max Weber Gesamtausgabe.* Tübingen: J.C.B. Mohr [Paul Siebeck], 1989.

"Die Wirtschaftsethik der Weltreligionen. Zwischenbetrachtung: Stufen und Richtungen der religiösen Weltablehnung." *Archiv für Sozialwissenschaft und Sozialpolitik* 41 (1915): 387-421.

Wirtschaftsgeschichte: Abriss der universalen Sozial- und Wirtschaftsgeschichte. 2d ed. Edited by S. Hellman and M. Palyi. Munich and Leipzig: Duncker & Humblot, 1924.

Wirtschaft und Gesellschaft [WG]. 5th ed. Edited by Johannes Winckelmann. Tübingen: J.C.B. Mohr [Paul Siebeck], 1976.

Zur Neuordnung Deutschlands. Schriften und Reden 1918-1920. Edited by Wolfgang J. Mommsen, with Wolfgang Schwentker. Sec. 1, vol. 16 of *Max Weber Gesamtausgabe.* Tübingen: J.C.B. Mohr [Paul Siebeck], 1988.

Zur Politik im Weltkrieg. Schriften und Reden 1914-1918. Edited by Wolfgang J. Mommsen, with Gangolf Hubinger. Sec. 1, vol. 15 of *Max Weber Gesamtausgabe.* Tübingen: J.C.B. Mohr [Paul Siebeck], 1984.

WORKS OF THOMAS MANN

Blätter der Thomas Mann Gesellschaft (Zurich), no. 11 (1971).
Briefe. Vol. 1: *1889–1936*; vol. 2: *1937–1947*; vol. 3: *1948–1955.* Edited by Erika Mann. Frankfurt am Main: S. Fischer Verlag, 1961–65. Reprint Frankfurt am Main: Fischer Taschenbuch Verlag, 1979.
Briefe an Paul Amann, 1915–1952. Edited by Herbert Wegener. Lübeck: Verlag Max Schmidt-Römhild, 1959.
"Dostoevsky—in Moderation." Introduction to *The Short Novels of Dostoevsky.* New York: Dial Press, 1945.
Essays. Vol. 3: *Musik und Philosophie.* Edited by Hermann Kurzke. Frankfurt am Main: Fischer Taschenbuch Verlag, 1978.
Gesammelte Werke [GW]. 13 vols. Edited by Hans Bürgin. Frankfurt am Main: S. Fischer Verlag, 1960, 1974.
Mythology and Humanism: The Correspondence of Thomas Mann and Karl Kerenyi. Translated by Alexander Gelley. Ithaca: Cornell University Press, 1975.
Notizen. Edited by Hans Wysling. Heidelberg: Carl Winter Universitätsverlag, 1973.
Royal Highness. Translated by H. T. Lowe-Porter. 1939; New York: Vintage Books, 1983.
Tagebücher, 1918–1921. Edited by Peter de Mendelssohn. Frankfurt am Main: S. Fischer Verlag, 1979.
Thomas Mann. Edited by Hans Wysling and Marianne Fischer. Vol. 14 of *Dichter über ihre Dichtungen.* Part 1: *1889–1917*; Part 3: *1944–1955.* Munich and Frankfurt am Main: Ernst Heimeran Verlag and S. Fischer Verlag, 1975, 1981.
Thomas Mann an Ernst Bertram: Briefe aus den Jahren 1910–1955. Pfullingen: Verlag Günther Neske, 1960.

OTHER WORKS

Abramowski, Günther. *Das Geschichtsbild Max Webers.* Stuttgart: Ernst Klett Verlag, 1966.
Adorno, Theodor W. *Minima Moralia: Reflections from Damaged Life.* Translated by E.F.N. Jephcott. London: Verso, 1978.
———. *Noten zur Literatur.* Vol. 3. Frankfurt: Suhrkamp Verlag, 1965.
———. *Philosophy of Modern Music.* Translated by Anne G. Mitchell and Wesley V. Blomster. New York: Continuum, 1985.
Albrecht, Jan. "Leverkühn oder die Musik als Schicksal." *Deutsche Vierteljahresschrift für Literaturwissenschaft und Geistesgeschichte* 45 (1971): 375–88.
Alexander, Jeffrey, "The Dialectic of Individuation and Domination: Weber's Rationalization Theory and Beyond." In *Max Weber, Rationality, and Modernity,* edited by Sam Whimster and Scott Lash. London: Allen & Unwin, 1987.
———. *Theoretical Logic in Sociology.* Vol. 3: *The Classical Attempt at Theoretical Synthesis: Max Weber.* Berkeley and Los Angeles: University of California Press, 1983.

Allen, Margaret De Huszar. *The Faust Legend: Popular Formula and Modern Novel.* New York: Peter Lang, 1985.

Antoni, Carlo. *From History to Sociology: The Transition in German Historical Thinking.* Translated by Hayden White. Detroit: Wayne State University Press, 1959.

Arendt, Hannah. *The Origins of Totalitarianism.* New ed. New York: Harcourt Brace Jovanovich, 1968.

Aron, Raymond. "Max Weber and Power Politics." In *Max Weber and Sociology Today,* edited by Otto Stammer, translated by Kathleen Morris. New York: Harper & Row, 1971.

Ascher, Abraham. "Professors as Propagandists: The Politics of the Kathedersozialisten." *Journal of Central European Affairs* 23 (1963): 282–302.

Aspinall, A. "English Party Organization in the Early Nineteenth Century." *English Historical Review* 41 (1926): 389–411.

Bahr, Ehrhard. " 'Identität des Nichtidentischen': zur Dialektik der Kunst in Thomas Manns *Doktor Faustus* und Theodor W. Adornos *Ästhetischer Theorie.*" In *Thomas Mann Jahrbuch,* vol. 2, edited by Eckhard Heftrich and Hans Wysling. Frankfurt am Main: Vittorio Klostermann, 1989.

Baier, Horst. "Die Gesellschaft—ein langer Schatten des Toten Gottes: Friedrich Nietzsche und die Entstehung der Soziologie aus dem Geist der Décadence." *Nietzsche Studien* 10/11 (1981/1982): 6–33.

Banuls, André. *Thomas Mann und sein Bruder Heinrich.* Stuttgart: W. Kohlhammer Verlag, 1968.

Barker, Ernest. *From Alexander to Constantine.* Oxford: Oxford University Press, 1956.

Barker, Michael. *Gladstone and Radicalism: The Reconstruction of Liberal Policy in Britain, 1885–94.* New York: Barnes & Noble, 1975.

Barnouw, Dagmar. *Weimar Intellectuals and the Threat of Modernity.* Bloomington: Indiana University Press, 1988.

Baron, Frank. *Doctor Faustus: From History to Legend.* Munich: Wilhelm Fink Verlag, 1978.

Baumgarten, Eduard, ed. *Max Weber: Werk und Person* Tübingen: J.C.B. Mohr [Paul Siebeck], 1964.

Beattie, Alan. *English Party Politics.* Vol. 1: *1660–1906.* London: Weidenfeld & Nicolson, 1970.

Beetham, David. *Max Weber and the Theory of Modern Politics.* Cambridge: Polity Press, 1985.

Beer, Samuel H. *British Politics in the Collectivist Age.* New York: Vintage Books, 1969.

Benz, Richard, ed. *Historia von D. Johann Fausten.* Stuttgart: Reclam Universal Bibliothek, 1975.

Berman, Russell. *The Rise of the Modern German Novel.* Cambridge, Mass.: Harvard University Press, 1986.

Bernauer, James, and David Rasmussen, eds. *The Final Foucault.* Cambridge, Mass.: MIT Press, 1988.

Berger, Willy R. *Die mythologischen Motive in Thomas Manns Roman "Joseph und seine Brüder."* Cologne: Böhlau Verlag, 1971.

Berrington, Hugh. "Partisanship and Dissidence in the Nineteenth-Century House of Commons." *Parliamentary Affairs* 21 (1967–68): 338–74.

Bloomfield, Morton W., ed. *Allegory, Myth, and Symbol.* Harvard English Studies, 9. Cambridge, Mass.: Harvard University Press, 1981.

Bödeker, Hans Erich. "Menschheit, Humanität, Humanismus." In *Geschichtliche Grundbegriffe. Historisches Lexikon zur politisch-sozialen Sprache in Deutschland*, edited by Otto Brunner, Werner Conze, and Reinhart Koselleck, vol. 3. Stuttgart: Ernst Klett Verlag, 1982.

Born, Lester K. Introduction to *The Education of a Christian Prince*, by Desiderius Erasmus. 1936; New York: Octagon Books, 1965.

Bracher, Karl-Dietrich. *Die Auflösung der Weimarer Republik.* Stuttgart: Ring-Verlag, 1955.

Bramsted, Ernest K. *Aristocracy and the Middle Classes in Germany: Social Types in German Literature, 1830-1900.* Rev. ed. Chicago: University of Chicago Press, 1964.

Braverman, Albert S., and Larry Nachman. "Nature and the Moral Order in *The Magic Mountain.*" *Germanic Review* 53 (1978): 1-12.

Bruford, W. H. *Culture and Society in Classical Weimar, 1775-1806.* Cambridge: Cambridge University Press, 1962.

———. *The German Tradition of Self-Cultivation: "Bildung" from Humboldt to Thomas Mann.* Cambridge: Cambridge University Press, 1975.

Brunner, Otto, Werner Conze, and Reinhart Koselleck, eds. *Geschichtliche Grundbegriffe: Historisches Lexikon zur politisch-sozialen Sprache in Deutschland*, 5 vols. Stuttgart: Ernst Klett Verlag, 1972-84.

Bulmer-Thomas, Ivor. *The Growth of the British Party System.* Vol. 1: *1640-1923.* London: John Baker, 1965.

Bürger, Peter. *The Theory of the Avant-Garde.* Translated by Michael Shaw, with an introduction by Jochen Schulte-Sasse. Minneapolis: University of Minnesota Press, 1984.

Burkert, Walter. *Greek Religion: Archaic and Classical.* Translated by John Raffan. Oxford: Basil Blackwell, 1985.

Butler, E. M. *The Fortunes of Faust.* Cambridge: Cambridge University Press, 1952.

Camus, Albert. *The Rebel.* Translated by Anthony Bower. New York: Vintage Books, 1956.

Cancik, Hubert. "Der Nietzsche-Kult in Weimar." *Nietzsche-Studien* 16 (1987): 405-29.

Carrithers, Michael, Steven Collins, and Steven Lukes, eds. *The Category of the Person: Anthropology, Philosophy, History.* Cambridge: Cambridge University Press, 1985.

Cavalli, Luciano. "Charismatic Domination, Totalitarian Dictatorship, and Plebiscitary Democracy in the Twentieth Century." In *Changing Conceptions of Leadership*, edited by Carl F. Graumann and Serge Moscovici. New York: Springer-Verlag, 1986.

Colleville, Maurice. "Nietzsche et le *Doktor Faustus* de Thomas Mann." *Études germaniques* 3 (1948): 343-54.

Copleston, Frederick. *A History of Philosophy.* Vol. 7, pt. 1: *Modern Philosophy—Fichte to Hegel.* Garden City, N.Y.: Doubleday, 1965.

Cox, Gary. "The Development of a Party-oriented Electorate in England, 1832-1918." *British Journal of Political Science* 16 (1986): 187-216.

Cromwell, Valerie. "The Losing of the Initiative by the House of Commons." *Transactions of the Royal Historical Society* 18 (1968): 1–23.

Curtius, Ernst Robert. "Max Weber über Wissenschaft als Beruf." *Die Arbeitsgemeinschaft* 17 (1919): 197–203.

Dahlhaus, Carl. *Schoenberg and the New Music.* Translated by Derek Puffett and Alfred Clayton. Cambridge: Cambridge University Press, 1987.

Deane, Herbert A. *The Political and Social Ideas of St. Augustine.* New York: Columbia University Press, 1963.

Dehio, Ludwig. *Germany and World Politics in the Twentieth Century.* Translated by Dieter Pevsner. New York: Knopf, 1960.

de Man, Paul. "The Rhetoric of Temporality." In *Blindness and Insight: Essays in the Rhetoric of Contemporary Criticism.* Minneapolis: University of Minnesota Press, 1983.

Dörr, Hansjörg. "Thomas Mann und Adorno: ein Beitrag zur Entstehung des 'Doktor Faustus.' " In *Thomas Manns "Doktor Faustus" und die Wirkung,* ed. Rudolf Wolff, pt. 2. Bonn: Bouvier Verlag Herbert Grundmann, 1983.

Dreyfus, Hubert, and Paul Rabinow. *Michel Foucault: Beyond Structuralism and Hermeneutics.* 2d. ed. Chicago: University of Chicago Press, 1983.

Dronberger, Ilse. *The Political Thought of Max Weber.* New York: Appleton-Century-Crofts, 1971.

Eden, Robert. "Bad Conscience for a Nietzschean Age: Weber's Calling for Science." *Review of Politics* 45 (1983): 366–92.

———. *Political Leadership and Nihilism: A Study of Weber and Nietzsche.* Gainesville: University Presses of Florida, 1983.

Eichner, Hans. "Thomas Mann und die deutsche Romantik." In *Das Nachleben der Romantik in der modernen deutschen Literatur,* edited by Wolfgang Paulsen. Heidelberg: Lothar Stiehm Verlag, 1969.

Eisen, Arnold. "The Meanings and Confusions of Weberian 'Rationality.' " *British Journal of Sociology* 29 (1978): 57–70.

Elias, Norbert. *The Civilizing Process: The Development of Manners.* Translated by Edmund Jephcott. New York: Urizen Books, 1978.

Ermarth, Michael. *Wilhelm Dilthey: The Critique of Historical Reason.* Chicago: University of Chicago Press, 1978.

Finck, Jean. *Thomas Mann und die Psychoanalyse.* Paris: Belles Lettres, 1973.

Fleischer, Margot. "Das Spektrum der Nietzsche-Rezeption im geistigen Leben seit der Jahrhundertwende." *Nietzsche-Studien* 20 (1991): 1–47.

Fletcher, Angus. *Allegory: The Theory of a Symbolic Mode.* New York: Columbia University Press, 1964.

Foster, John Burt, Jr. *Heirs to Dionysus: A Nietzschean Current in Literary Modernism.* Princeton: Princeton University Press, 1981.

Foucault, Michel. *Discipline and Punish: The Birth of the Prison.* Translated by Alan Sheridan. New York: Vintage Books, 1979.

———. *Politics, Philosophy, Culture: Interviews and Other Writings, 1977–1984.* Edited with an introduction by Lawrence D. Kritzman; translated by Alan Sheridan et al. New York: Routledge, 1988.

———. *Power/Knowledge: Selected Interviews and Other Writings, 1972–1977.* Edited by Colin Gordon; translated by Colin Gordon, Leo Marshall, John Mepham, and Kate Soper. New York: Pantheon Books, 1980.

————. "Technologies of the Self." In *Technologies of the Self: A Seminar with Michel Foucault*, edited by Luther H. Martin, Huck Gutman, and Patrick H. Hutton. Amherst: University of Massachusetts Press, 1988.

Frizen, Werner. "Thomas Mann und das Christentum." In *Thomas-Mann-Handbuch*, edited by Helmut Koopman. Stuttgart: Alfred Kröner Verlag, 1990.

Frye, Northrop. "Allegory." In *Princeton Encyclopedia of Poetry and Poetics*, enlarged ed., edited by Alex Preminger. Princeton: Princeton University Press, 1974.

————. *Anatomy of Criticism: Four Essays*. Princeton: Princeton University Press, 1957.

Gadamer, Hans-Georg. *Truth and Method*. New York: Seabury Press, 1975.

Gay, Peter. *Weimar Culture: The Outsider as Insider*. New York: Harper & Row, 1968.

Gilbert, Allan H. *Machiavelli's "Prince" and Its Forerunners*. Durham: University of North Carolina Press, 1938.

Gilbert, Felix. "The Humanist Concept of the Prince and *The Prince* of Machiavelli." In *History: Choice and Commitment*. Cambridge, Mass.: Harvard University Press, 1977.

Gilliam, H. S. "Mann's Other Holy Sinner: Adrian Leverkühn as Faust and Christ." *Germanic Review* 52 (1977): 122–47.

Gluck, Mary. *Georg Lukács and His Generation, 1900–1918*. Cambridge, Mass.: Harvard University Press, 1985.

Goldman, Harvey. "Images of the Other: Asia in Nineteenth-Century Western Thinking—Hegel, Marx, Weber." In *Asia in Western History and World History*, edited by Ainslee Embree and Carol Gluck. New York: East Asian Institute, Columbia University, forthcoming.

————. *Max Weber and Thomas Mann: Calling and the Shaping of the Self*. Berkeley and Los Angeles: University of California Press, 1988.

————. "The Problem of the Person in Weberian Social Theory." In *Critical Issues in Social Theory*, edited by Murray Milgate and Cheryl Welch. London: Academic Press.

Graf, Friedrich Wilhelm. "Max Weber und die protestantische Theologie seiner Zeit." *Zeitschrift für Religions- und Geistesgeschichte* 39 (1987): 122–47.

Green, Martin. *Mountain of Truth: The Counterculture Begins—Ascona 1900–1920*. Hanover, N.H.: University Press of New England, 1986.

————. *The von Richthofen Sisters: The Triumphant and the Tragic Modes of Love*. New York: Basic Books, 1974.

Greenblatt, Stephen. *Renaissance Self-Fashioning: From More to Shakespeare*. Chicago: University of Chicago Press, 1980.

Griffiths, P. C. "The Caucus and the Liberal Party in 1886." *History* 61 (1976): 183–97.

Gronicka, André von. "Thomas Mann's *Doktor Faustus*: Prolegomena to an Interpretation." *Germanic Review* 23 (1948): 206–18.

Gundolf, Friedrich. "Wesen und Beziehung." *Jahrbuch für die geistige Bewegung* 2 (1911): 10–35.

Guthrie, W.K.C. *The Greeks and Their Gods*. Boston: Beacon Press, 1955.

Habermas, Jürgen. *Theory of Communicative Action*. Vol. 1. Translated by Thomas McCarthy. Boston: Beacon Press, 1984.

———. *Toward a Rational Society*. Translated by Jeremy J. Shapiro. Boston: Beacon Press, 1970.

Haley, Peter. "Rudolph Sohm on Charisma." *Journal of Religion* 60 (1980): 185–97.

Hamburger, Käte. "Anachronistische Symbolik: Fragen an Thomas Manns Faustus-Roman." In *Thomas Manns "Doktor Faustus" und die Wirkung*, edited by Rudolf Wolff, pt. 1. Bonn: Bouvier Verlag Herbert Grundmann, 1983.

Hamburger, Michael. *Contraries: Studies in German Literature*. New York: Dutton, 1970.

Hamer, D. I. "Gladstone: The Making of a Political Myth," *Victorian Studies* 22 (1978): 29–50.

———. *Liberal Politics in the Age of Gladstone and Rosebery: A Study in Leadership and Policy*. Oxford: Oxford University Press, 1972.

Hamilton, Nigel. *The Brothers Mann*. New Haven: Yale University Press, 1979.

Hammond, J. L. *Gladstone and the Irish Nation*. 1938; Hamden, Conn.: Archon Books, 1964.

Hammond, J. L., and M.R.D. Foot. *Gladstone and Liberalism*. New York: Collier, 1966.

Hanham, H. J. *Elections and Party Management: Politics in the Time of Disraeli and Gladstone*. 2d ed. Sussex: Harvester Press, 1978.

Hannum, Hildegarde Drexl. "Self-Sacrifice in *Doktor Faustus*: Thomas Mann's Contribution to the Faust Legend." *Modern Language Quarterly* 35 (1974): 289–301.

Haug, Helmut. *Erkenntnisekel: zum frühen Werk Thomas Manns*. Tübingen: Max Niemeyer Verlag, 1969.

Heftrich, Eckhard. "Ergänzende Betrachtung: Nietzsche als Hamlet der Zeitenwende." In *Über Thomas Mann*, vol. 1: *Zauberbergmusik*. Frankfurt am Main: Vittorio Klostermann, 1975.

———. "Radikale Autobiographie und Allegorie der Epoche: *Doktor Faustus*." In *Über Thomas Mann*, vol. 2: *Vom Verfall zur Apokalypse*. Frankfurt am Main: Vittorio Klostermann, 1982.

Heidegger, Martin. "Plato's Doctrine of Truth." In *Philosophy in the Twentieth Century*, ed. Henry Aiken and William Barrett, vol. 3. New York: Random House, 1962.

———. *Prolegomena zu Geschichte des Zeitbegriffs*. Vol. 20 of *Gesamtausgabe*. Frankfurt am Main: Vittorio Klostermann, 1979.

Heller, Erich. *Thomas Mann: The Ironic German*. Cleveland: World Publishing Company, 1961.

Heller, Peter. "Concerning the Nietzsche Cult and Literary Cults Generally." In *Nietzsche: Literature and Values*, edited by Volker Dürr, Reinhold Grimm, and Kathy Harms. Madison: University of Wisconsin Press, 1988.

Heller, Thomas C., Morton Sosna, and David Wellbury, eds. *Reconstructing Individualism: Autonomy, Individuality, and the Self in Western Thought*. Stanford: Stanford University Press, 1986.

Hennis, Wilhelm. *Max Weber: Essays in Reconstruction*. Translated by Keith Tribe. London: Allen & Unwin, 1988.

Henrich, Dieter. *Die Einheit Max Webers Wissenschaftslehre*. Tübingen: J.C.B. Mohr [Paul Siebeck], 1952.

Herf, Jeffrey. *Reactionary Modernism: Technology, Culture, and Politics in Weimar and the Third Reich.* New York: Cambridge University Press, 1984.

Herrick, Francis H. "The Origins of the National Liberal Federation." *Journal of Modern History* 17 (1945): 116–29.

Heuss, Theodor. *Erinnerungen, 1905–1933.* Tübingen: Rainer Wunderlich Verlag, 1963.

Hillebrand, Bruno, ed. *Nietzsche und die deutsche Literatur.* 2 vol. Munich: Deutsche Taschenbuch Verlag; Tübingen: Max Niemeyer Verlag, 1978.

Hinton Thomas, R. *Nietzsche in German Politics and Society, 1890–1918.* LaSalle, Ill.: Open Court, 1983.

————. "Nietzsche in Weimar Germany—and the Case of Ludwig Klages." In *The Weimar Dilemma: Intellectuals in the Weimar Republic,* edited by Anthony Phelan. Manchester: Manchester University Press, 1985.

————. "The Uses of 'Bildung.'" *German Life and Letters,* n.s., 30 (1977): 177–86.

Holborn, Hajo. "German Idealism in the Light of Social History." In *Germany and Europe.* Garden City, N.Y.: Doubleday, 1971.

Hollingdale, R. J. *Thomas Mann: A Critical Study.* Lewisburg, Penn.: Bucknell University Press, 1971.

Honigsheim, Paul. "Max Weber: His Religious and Ethical Background and Development." *Church History* 18–19 (1949–50): 219–39.

————. *On Max Weber.* New York: Free Press, 1968.

————. "Romantische und religiös-mystisch verankerte Wirtschaftsgesinnungen." In *Die Wirtschaftswissenschaft nach dem Kriege. Festgabe für Lujo Brentano zum 80. Geburtstag,* edited by M. J. Bonn and M. Palyi. Munich and Leipzig: Duncker & Humblot, 1925.

Horkheimer, Max. "Schopenhauer Today." In *The Critical Spirit: Essays in Honor of Herbert Marcuse,* edited by Kurt H. Wolff and Barrington Moore, Jr. Boston: Beacon Press, 1967.

Hughes, H. Stuart. *Consciousness and Society: The Reorientation of European Social Thought, 1890–1930.* New York: Vintage Books, 1961.

Huntington, Samuel P. *Political Order in Changing Societies.* New Haven: Yale University Press, 1968.

Husserl, Edmund. *The Crisis of the European Sciences and Transcendental Phenomenology.* Evanston, Ill.: Northwestern University Press, 1970.

Iggers, Georg G. *The German Conception of History.* Rev. ed. Middletown, Conn.: Wesleyan University Press, 1983.

Jameson, Frederic. "The Vanishing Mediator: Narrative Structure in Max Weber." *New German Critique* 1 (1974): 52–89.

Janik, Allan, and Stephen Toulmin. *Wittgenstein's Vienna.* New York: Simon & Schuster, 1975.

Jarausch, Konrad. *Students, Society, and Politics in Imperial Germany: The Rise of Academic Illiberalism.* Princeton: Princeton University Press, 1982.

————. "Liberal Education as Illiberal Socialization: The Case of Students in Imperial Germany." *Journal of Modern History* 50 (1978): 609–30.

————. "The Social Transformation of the University: The Case of Prussia, 1865–1914." *Journal of Social History* 12 (1979): 609–36.

Jelavich, Peter. "Art and Mammon in Wilhelmine Germany: The Case of Frank Wedekind." *Central European History* 12 (1979): 203–36.

Jenkins, T. A. *Gladstone, Whiggery, and the Liberal Party, 1874–1886*. Oxford: Clarendon Press, 1988.

Kahler, Erich von. *Der Beruf der Wissenschaft*. Berlin: Georg Bondi, 1920.

Kalberg, Stephen. "Max Weber's Types of Rationality: Cornerstones for the Analysis of Rationalization Processes in History." *American Journal of Sociology* 85 (1980): 1145–79.

Kandinsky, Wassily. *Concerning the Spiritual in Art*. Translated and with introduction by M.T.H. Sadler. New York: Dover, 1977.

Kantorowicz, Hermann. *Der Geist der englischen Politik und das Gespenst der Einkreisung Deutschlands*. Berlin: Ernst Rowohlt Verlag, 1929.

Kaufmann, Fritz. *Thomas Mann: The World as Will and Representation*. 1957; New York: Cooper Square Publishers, 1973.

Kennedy, Paul. *The Rise of the Anglo-German Antagonism, 1860–1914*. London: Allen & Unwin, 1980.

Kinnear, Michael. *The Fall of Lloyd George: The Political Crisis of 1922*. Toronto: University of Toronto Press, 1973.

Klee, Paul. *On Modern Art*. Translated by Paul Findlay, with an introduction by Herbert Read. 1948; London: Faber & Faber, 1967.

Kluckhohn, Paul. *Das Ideengut der deutschen Romantik*. 4th ed. Tübingen: Max Niemeyer Verlag, 1961.

———. *Persönlichkeit und Gemeinschaft: Studien zur Staatsauffassung der deutschen Romantik*. Halle: Max Niemeyer Verlag, 1925.

Kocka, Jürgen, ed. *Bürger und Bürgerlichkeit im 19. Jahrhundert*. Göttingen: Vandenhoeck & Ruprecht, 1987.

Koopman, Helmut, ed. *Thomas-Mann-Handbuch*. Stuttgart: Alfred Kröner Verlag, 1990.

Krause, Jürgen. *"Märtyrer" und "Prophet." Studien zum Nietzsche-Kult in der bildenden Kunst der Jahrhundertwende*. Berlin: Walter de Gruyter, 1984.

Krieger, Leonard. *The German Idea of Freedom*. Boston: Beacon Press, 1957.

Kristiansen, Borge. "Thomas Mann und die Philosophie." In *Thomas-Mann-Handbuch*, edited by Helmut Koopman. Stuttgart: Alfred Kröner Verlag, 1990.

Kronman, Anthony T. *Max Weber*. Stanford: Stanford University Press, 1983.

Krummel, Richard Frank. *Nietzsche und der deutsche Geist*. 2 vols. Berlin: Walter de Gruyter, 1974–83.

Kurzke, Hermann. *Auf der Suche nach der verlorenen Irrationalität. Thomas Mann und der Konservatismus*. Würzburg: Verlag Königshausen & Neumann, 1980.

———. *Thomas Mann. Epoche—Werk—Wirkung*. Munich: Verlag C. H. Beck, 1985.

Laqueur, Walter. *Young Germany: A History of the German Youth Movement*. New York: Basic Books, 1962.

Lassman, Peter, and Irving Velody, eds., with Herminio Martins. *Max Weber's "Science as a Vocation."* London: Unwin Hyman, 1989.

Lawrence, D. H. *Studies in Classic American Literature*. 1924; London: Mercury Books, 1965.

Lehnert, Herbert. *Thomas Mann—Fiktion, Mythos, Religion*. Stuttgart: W. Kohlhammer Verlag, 1965.

Lenk, Kurt. "Das tragische Bewußtsein in der deutschen Soziologie." *Kölner Zeitschrift für Soziologie und Sozialpsychologie* 16 (1964): 257–87.

Levine, Donald. "Rationality and Freedom: Weber and Beyond." *Sociological Inquiry* 51 (1981): 5–25.

Lichtblau, Klaus. "Das 'Pathos der Distanz': Präliminarien zur Nietzsche-Rezeption bei Georg Simmel." In *Georg Simmel und die Moderne*, edited by Heinz-Jürgen Dahme and Ottheim Rammstedt. Frankfurt am Main: Suhrkamp Verlag, 1984.

Lichtenstein, E. "Bildung." In *Historisches Wörterbuch der Philosophie*, vol. 1, edited by Joachim Ritter. Basel: Schwabe & Co. Verlag, 1971.

Lilge, Frederic. *The Abuse of Learning: The Failure of the German University.* New York: Macmillan, 1948.

Loughlin, James. *Gladstone, Home Rule, and the Ulster Question, 1882–93.* Atlantic Highlands, N.J.: Humanities Press International, 1987.

Lowell, A. Lawrence. *The Government of England.* 2 vols. Rev. ed. New York: Macmillan, 1912.

Löwith, Karl. "Die Entzauberung der Welt durch Wissenschaft." *Merkur* 18 (1964): 501–17.

———. *From Hegel to Nietzsche.* Translated by David E. Green. Garden City, N.Y.: Anchor Books, 1967.

———. "Karl Marx und Max Weber." In Karl Löwith, *Gesammelte Abhandlungen.* Stuttgart: W. Kohlhammer Verlag, 1960.

Löwy, Michael. *Georg Lukács: From Romanticism to Bolshevism.* Translated by Patrick Cammiller. London: New Left Books, 1979.

Lubenow, W. C. *Parliamentary Politics and the Home Rule Crisis: The British House of Commons in 1886.* Oxford: Clarendon Press, 1988.

Lukács, Georg. *The Destruction of Reason.* Translated by Peter Palmer. Atlantic Highlands, N.J.: Humanities Press, 1980.

———. *History and Class Consciousness.* Translated by Rodney Livingstone. Cambridge, Mass.: MIT Press, 1971.

———. *The Theory of the Novel.* Cambridge, Mass.: The MIT Press, 1971.

Lunn, Eugene. *Prophet of Community: The Romantic Socialism of Gustav Landauer.* Berkeley and Los Angeles: University of California Press, 1973.

McClelland, Charles E. *The German Historians and England: A Study in Nineteenth-Century Views.* Cambridge: Cambridge University Press, 1971.

———. *State, Society, and University in Germany, 1700–1914.* Cambridge: Cambridge University Press, 1979.

McGrath, William J. *Dionysian Art and Populist Politics in Austria.* New Haven: Yale University Press, 1974.

Mádl, Antal. *Thomas Manns Humanismus.* Berlin: Rütten & Loening, 1980.

Maegaard, Jan. "Zu Th. W. Adornos Rolle in Mann/Schoenberg-Streit." In *Gedenkschrift für Thomas Mann, 1875–1975*, edited by Rolf Wiecker. Copenhagen: Verlag Text & Kontext, 1975.

Magnus, Philip. *Gladstone: A Biography.* London: John Murray, 1954.

Maier, Charles S. *Recasting Bourgeois Europe.* Princeton: Princeton University Press, 1975.

Maître, Hans Joachim. *Thomas Mann: Aspekte der Kulturkritik in seiner Essayistik.* Bonn: H. Bouvier Verlag, 1970.

Marcus, Judith. "The Artist and His Philosopher: Reflections on the Relation Between Thomas Mann and Georg Lukács." In *Georg Lukács—Ersehnte Totalität*, edited by Gvozden Flego and Wolfdietrich Schmied-Kowarzik (vol. 1 of the Bloch-Lukács Symposium, Dubrovnik, 1985). Bochum: Germinal Verlag, 1986.

———. *Georg Lukács and Thomas Mann: A Study in the Sociology of Literature*. Amherst: University of Massachusetts Press, 1987.

Martin, Luther H., Huck Gutman, and Patrick H. Hutton, eds. *Technologies of the Self: A Seminar with Michel Foucault*. Amherst: University of Massachusetts Press, 1988.

Marx, Karl. *Capital*. Vol. 1. Translated by Ben Fowkes. New York: Vintage Books, 1977.

Masur, Gerhard. *Prophets of Yesterday: Studies in European Culture, 1890–1914*. New York: Harper & Row, 1961.

Mattenklott, Gert. "Nietzsches 'Geburt der Tragödie' als Konzept einer bürgerlichen Kulturrevolution." In *Positionen der literarischen Intelligenz zwischen bürgerliche Reaktion und Imperialismus*, edited by Gert Mattenklott and Klaus R. Scherpe. Kronberg: Scriptor Verlag, 1973.

Mattenklott, Gert, and Klaus R. Scherpe, eds. *Positionen der literarischen Intelligenz zwischen bürgerliche Reaktion und Imperialismus*. Kronberg: Scriptor Verlag, 1973.

Mau, Hermann. "Die deutsche Jugendbewegung: Rückblick und Ausblick." *Zeitschrift für Religions- und Geistesgeschichte* 1–2 (1948–49): 135–49.

Mayer, Arno. *The Persistence of the Old Regime: Europe to the Great War*. New York: Pantheon Books, 1981.

Mayer, Hans. *Thomas Mann*. Frankfurt am Main: Suhrkamp Verlag, 1980.

Mead, George Herbert. *Mind, Self, and Society: From the Standpoint of a Social Behaviorist*. Edited with introduction by Charles W. Morris. 1934; Chicago: University of Chicago Press, 1962.

Meinecke, Friedrich. *The Age of German Liberation, 1795–1815*. Translated and with an introduction by Peter Paret. Berkeley and Los Angeles: University of California Press, 1977.

———. *Machiavellism: The Doctrine of Raison d'État and Its Place in Modern History*. Translated by Douglas Scott, with an introduction by W. Stark. New York: Praeger, 1965.

———. "Schiller und der Individualitätsgedanke." In *Werke*, vol. 4. Stuttgart: K. F. Koehler Verlag, 1965.

Meisel, Victor H., ed. *Voices of German Expressionism*. Englewood Cliffs, N.J.: Prentice-Hall, 1970.

Mendelssohn, Peter de. *Nachbemerkungen zu Thomas Mann*. Vol. 1. Frankfurt am Main: Fischer Taschenbuch Verlag, 1982.

Metzger, Thomas. *Escape from Predicament: Neo-Confucianism and China's Evolving Political Culture*. New York: Columbia University Press, 1977.

Milgate, Murray, and Cheryl Welch, eds. *Critical Issues in Social Theory*. London: Academic Press, 1989.

Mitzman, Arthur. *The Iron Cage: An Historical Interpretation of Max Weber*. New York: Knopf, 1970.

———. *Sociology and Estrangement*. New York: Knopf, 1973.

Mommsen, Wolfgang J. *The Age of Bureaucracy.* New York: Harper & Row, 1974.

———. "Domestic Factors in German Foreign Policy Before 1914." *Central European History* 6 (1973): 3–43.

———. "The German Revolution, 1918–1920: Political Revolution and Social Protest Movement." In *Social Change and Political Development in Weimar Germany,* edited by Richard Bessel and E. J. Feuchtwanger. London: Croom Helm, 1981.

———. "Max Weber and Roberto Michels: An Asymmetrical Partnership." *Archives européennes de sociologie* 22 (1981): 100–116.

———. *Max Weber und die deutsche Politik, 1890–1920.* 2d ed. Tübingen: J.C.B. Mohr [Paul Siebeck], 1974.

———. "Personal Conduct and Societal Change: Towards a Reconstruction of Max Weber's Concept of History." In *Max Weber, Rationality, and Modernity,* edited by Sam Whimster and Scott Lash. London: Allen & Unwin, 1987.

Morgan, Kenneth O. *Consensus and Disunity: The Lloyd George Coalition Government, 1918–1922.* Oxford: Clarendon Press, 1979.

———. *Lloyd George.* Introduction by A.J.P. Taylor. London: Weidenfeld & Nicolson, 1974.

———. "Lloyd George's Premiership: A Study in 'Prime Ministerial Government.'" *Historical Journal* 13 (1970): 130–57.

Morley, John. *The Life of William Ewart Gladstone.* 1903; New York: Greenwood Press, 1968.

Mosse, George L. *The Crisis of German Ideology: Intellectual Origins of the Third Reich.* New York: Grosset & Dunlap, 1964.

Mueller, G. H. "The Notion of Rationality in the Work of Max Weber." *Archives européennes de sociologie* 20 (1979): 149–71.

Müller, Martin, "Walter Benjamin und Thomas Manns *Doktor Faustus.*" *Archiv für das Studium der neueren Sprachen und Literaturen* 210 (1973): 327–30.

Natanson, Maurice. *Phenomenology, Role, and Reason: Essays on the Coherence and Deformation of Social Reality.* Springfield, Ill.: Charles C. Thomas, 1974.

Nehamas, Alexander. "Nietzsche and *The Magic Mountain.*" *Philosophy and Literature* 5 (1981): 73–90.

Nelson, Benjamin. "Max Weber's 'Author's Introduction' (1920): A Master Clue to His Main Aims." *Sociological Inquiry* 44 (1974): 269–78.

Neumann, Franz. *Behemoth: The Structure and Practice of National Socialism, 1933–1944.* 1942; New York: Harper Torchbooks, 1966.

Neustadt, Richard. *Presidential Power: The Politics of Leadership.* New York: Wiley, 1962.

The New Grove: Second Viennese School. New York: Norton, 1983.

Nietzsche, Friedrich. *Kritische Studienausgabe* [*KSA*]. Edited by Giorgio Colli and Mazzino Montinari. Munich: Deutscher Taschenbuch Verlag; Berlin: Walter de Gruyter, 1988.

———. *The Will to Power.* Edited by Walter Kaufmann; translated by Walter Kaufmann and R. J. Hollingdale. New York: Vintage Books, 1968.

Nilsson, Martin P. *Greek Folk Religion.* Foreword by Arthur Darby Nock. 1940; Philadelphia: University of Pennsylvania Press, 1961.

————. *A History of Greek Religion.* 2d ed. Translated by F. J. Fielden. New York: Norton, 1964.

Nipperdey, Thomas. *Gesellschaft, Kultur, Theorie.* Göttingen: Vandenhoeck & Ruprecht, 1976.

Nordau, Max. *Degeneration.* Translated from the 2d German ed. London: William Heineman, 1898.

Orlowski, Hubert. *Prädestination des Dämonischen.* Seria *Filologia Germanska,* no. 7. Poznan: Adam Mickiewicz University, 1969.

Ostrogorski, M. *Democracy and the Organization of Political Parties.* 2 vols. Translated by Frederick Clarke, with a preface by James Bryce. New York: Macmillan, 1902.

————. "The Introduction of the Caucus into England." *Political Science Quarterly* 8 (1893): 287–316.

Pascal, Roy. "The Concept of 'Bildung' and the Division of Labor: Wilhelm von Humboldt, Fichte, Schiller, Goethe." In *Culture and the Division of Labor: Three Essays on Literary Culture in Germany.* University of Warwick Occasional Papers. Coventry: University of Warwick, 1974.

————. *From Naturalism to Expressionism: German Literature and Society, 1880–1918.* New York: Basic Books, 1973.

————. "*The Magic Mountain* and Adorno's Critique of the Traditional Novel." In *Culture and Society in the Weimar Republic,* edited by Keith Bullivant. Manchester: Manchester University Press/Rowman & Littlefield, 1977.

Pelling, Henry. *America and the British Left: From Bright to Bevan.* London: Adam & Charles Black, 1956.

Perkin, Harold. *The Origins of Modern English Society, 1780–1880.* London: Routledge & Kegan Paul, 1969.

Peters, H. F. *Zarathustra's Sister: The Case of Elisabeth and Friedrich Nietzsche.* New York: Markus Wiener, 1977.

Pflaum, Georg Michael. "Geschichte des Wortes *Zivilization.*" Ph.D. diss., University of Munich, 1961.

Pierrot, Jean. *The Decadent Imagination, 1880–1900.* Translated by Derek Coltman. Chicago: University of Chicago Press, 1981.

Pike, Burton. "Thomas Mann and the Problematic Self." In *Publications of the English Goethe Society: Papers Read Before the Society, 1966–67.* Edited by Elizabeth M. Wilkinson, B. A. Rowley, and Ann C. Weaver. London: Maney, 1967.

Portis, Edward Bryan. *Max Weber and Political Commitment: Science, Politics, and Personality.* Philadelphia: Temple University Press, 1986.

Pugh, Martin. *Electoral Reform in War and Peace, 1906–18.* London: Routledge & Kegan Paul, 1978.

————. *Lloyd George.* London: Longman, 1988.

————. *The Making of Modern British Politics, 1867–1939.* New York: St. Martin's Press, 1982.

Puschmann, Rosemarie. *Magisches Quadrat und Melancholie in Thomas Manns "Doktor Faustus." Von der musikalischen Struktur zum semantischen Beziehungsnetz* Bielefeld: AMPAL Verlag, 1983.

Pütz, Peter. *Friedrich Nietzsche.* 2d ed. Stuttgart: Metzler, 1975.

Quilligan, Maureen. *The Language of Allegory.* Ithaca: Cornell University Press, 1979.

Ranke, Leopold. "A Dialogue on Politics," translated by Theodore H. von Laue. In von Laue, *Leopold Ranke: The Formative Years*. Princeton: Princeton University Press, 1950.

Rasch, Wolfdietrich. *Zur deutschen Literatur seit der Jahrhundertwende. Gesammelte Aufsätze*. Stuttgart: J. B. Metzlersche Verlagsbuchhandlung, 1967.

Raschel, Heinz. *Das Nietzsche-Bild im George-Kreis*. Berlin: Walter de Gruyter, 1983.

Redner, Harry. *In the Beginning Was the Deed: Reflections on the Passage of Faust*. Berkeley and Los Angeles: University of California Press, 1982.

Reed, T. J. *Thomas Mann: The Uses of Tradition*. Oxford: Clarendon Press, 1974.

"Reflections on the Self." Special issue of *Social Research* 54, no. 1 (1987).

Reiss, Gunter. *"Allegorisierung" und moderne Erzählkunst. Eine Studie zum Werk Thomas Manns*. Munich: Wilhelm Fink, 1970.

Rickert, Heinrich. *Science and History*. Translated by George Reisman. Princeton: Van Nostrand, 1962.

Rieckmann, Jens. *Der Zauberberg. Eine geistige Autobiographie Thomas Manns*. Stuttgart: Akademischer Verlag Hans-Dieter Heinz, 1977.

Riedel, Manfred. "Bürger." In *Geschichtliche Grundbegriffe. Historisches Lexikon zur politisch-sozialen Sprache in Deutschland*, edited by Otto Brunner, Werner Conze, and Reinhart Koselleck, vol. 1. Stuttgart: Ernst Klett Verlag, 1972.

Ringer, Fritz. *The Decline of the German Mandarins, 1890–1933*. Cambridge, Mass.: Harvard University Press, 1969.

———. "The German Academic Community, 1870–1920." *Internationales Archiv für Sozialgeschichte der deutschen Literatur* 3 (1978): 108–29.

———. Review of *The German Tradition of Self-Cultivation: "Bildung" from Humboldt to Thomas Mann*, by W. H. Bruford. *Central European History* 11 (1978): 107–13.

Rose, William, ed. *The History of the Damnable Life and Deserved Death of Doctor John Faustus, 1592*. London: George Routledge & Sons, n.d.

Rosen, Charles. *Arnold Schoenberg*. New York: Viking, 1975.

Rosenberg, Arthur. *The Birth of the German Republic, 1871–1918*. Translated by Ian F. D. Morrow. 1931; New York: Russell & Russell, 1962.

———. *A History of the German Republic*. Translated by Ian F. D. Morrow and L. Marie Sieveking. New York: Russell & Russell, 1965.

Rosenberg, Hans. *Bureaucracy, Aristocracy, and Autocracy: The Prussian Experience, 1660–1815*. Boston: Beacon Press, 1966.

———. "The Economic Impact of Imperial Germany." *Journal of Economic History* 3, supp. (December 1943): 101–7.

Rosenblum, Nancy, and Sherry Turkle. "Political Philosophy's Psychologized Self: 'Speaking Prose Without Knowing It.'" In *Critical Issues in Social Theory*, edited by Murray Milgate and Cheryl Welch. London: Academic Press.

Rosenstein, Conrad. "Vom Einsamkeitszauber und seiner Überwindung: eine Motivstudie zu Thomas Mann." 1972. Thomas Mann Archive, Zurich. Mimeo.

Rürup, Reinhard. "Problems of the German Revolution, 1918–19." *Journal of Contemporary History* 3 (1968): 109–35.

Russell, Charles. *Poets, Prophets, and Revolutionaries: The Literary Avant-Garde from Rimbaud to Postmodernism*. New York: Oxford University Press, 1985.

Said, Edward W. *Beginnings: Intention and Method*. Baltimore: Johns Hopkins University Press, 1975.

Salz, Arthur. *Für die Wissenschaft. Gegen die Gebildeten unter ihren Verächtern*. Munich: Dreimaskenverlag, 1921.

Sauer, Wolfgang. "Weimar Culture: Experiments in Modernism." *Social Research* 39 (1972): 254–84.

Sauereßig, Heinz, ed. *Besichtigung des Zauberbergs*. Biberich an der Riss: Wege & Gestalten, 1974.

Scharfschwerdt, Jürgen. *Thomas Mann und der deutsche Bildungsroman*. Stuttgart: W. Kohlhammer Verlag, 1967.

Scheler, Max. *Schriften zur Soziologie und Weltanschauungslehre*. Bonn: Francke Verlag, 1963.

Schieder, Theodor. *The State and Society in Our Times*. Translated by C.A.M. Sym. Edinburgh: Thomas Nelson, 1962.

Schiller, Friedrich. *Über Anmut und Würde*. In *Schillers Werke*, Nationalausgabe, edited by Benno von Wiese, vol. 20. Weimar: Hermann Böhlaus Nachfolger, 1962.

Schluchter, Wolfgang. *Rationalism, Religion, and Domination: A Weberian Perspective*. Translated by Neil Solomon. Berkeley and Los Angeles: University of California Press, 1989.

———. *Rationalismus der Weltbeherrschung. Studien zu Max Weber*. Frankfurt am Main: Suhrkamp Verlag, 1980.

———. *The Rise of Western Rationalism: Max Weber's Developmental History*. Translated and with an introduction by Guenther Roth. Berkeley and Los Angeles: University of California Press, 1981.

Schmidt, Gustav. *Deutscher Historismus und der Übergang zur parlamentarischen Demokratie. Untersuchungen zu den politischen Gedanken von Meinecke, Troeltsch, Max Weber*. Historische Studien, no. 389. Lübeck and Hamburg: Matthiesen Verlag, 1964.

Schnädelbach, Herbert. *Philosophie in Deutschland, 1831–1933*. Frankfurt am Main: Suhrkamp Verlag, 1983.

Schoenberg, Arnold. *Style and Idea: Selected Writings of Arnold Schoenberg*. Edited by Leonard Stein, translated by Leo Black. Berkeley and Los Angeles: University of California Press, 1984.

Schorske, Carl. *Fin-de-Siècle Vienna: Politics and Culture*. New York: Knopf, 1980.

Schröter, Klaus. "Chauvinism and Its Tradition: German Writers and the Outbreak of the First World War." *Germanic Review* 42 (1968): 120–35.

———. "'Eideshelfer' Thomas Manns 1914/18." In *Literatur und Zeitgeschichte*. Mainz: Von Hase & Koehler Verlag, 1970.

———. *Thomas Mann in Selbstzeugnissen und Bilddokumenten*. Reinbeck bei Hamburg: Rowohlt, 1964.

Schwab, Franz Xaver. "Beruf und Jugend." *Die weissen Blätter* 4 (April–June 1917): 97–113.

Schwabe, Klaus. "Zur politischen Haltung der deutschen Professoren im ersten Weltkrieg." *Historische Zeitschrift* 193 (1961): 601–34.

Schwarz, Jürgen. *Studenten in der Weimarer Republik*. Berlin: Duncker & Humblot, 1971.

Shannon, Richard. *The Crisis of Imperialism, 1865–1915.* St. Albans, Eng.: Paladin, 1976.

———. *Gladstone.* Vol. 1: *1809–1865.* London: Methuen, 1984.

Shklar, Judith. *After Utopia.* Princeton: Princeton University Press, 1957.

———. *Freedom and Independence: A Study of the Political Ideas of Hegel's "Phenomenology of Mind."* Cambridge: Cambridge University Press, 1976.

Simmel, Georg. *The Philosophy of Money.* Translated by Tom Bottomore and David Frisby. London: Routledge & Kegan Paul, 1978.

———. *The Sociology of Georg Simmel.* Translated and edited by Kurt H. Wolff. New York: Free Press, 1950.

Simon, Ulrich. "The Theological Challenge of 'Doctor Faustus.' " *Church Quarterly Review* 151 (1950): 547–53.

Skinner, Quentin. *The Foundations of Modern Political Thought.* Vol. 1: *The Renaissance.* Cambridge: Cambridge University Press, 1978.

Sohm, Rudolph. *Kirchenrecht.* Sec. 8, vol. 1 of *Systematisches Handbuch der deutschen Rechtswissenschaft,* edited by Karl Binding. Leipzig: Duncker & Humblot, 1892.

Sokel, Walter. *The Writer in Extremis: Expressionism in Twentieth-Century Literature.* New York: McGraw-Hill, 1959.

Sontheimer, Kurt. "Anti-Democratic Thought in the Weimar Republic." In Theodor Eschenburg et al., *The Path to Dictatorship, 1918–1933,* translated by John Conway, with an introduction by Fritz Stern. Garden City, N.Y.: Anchor Books, 1966.

———. *Antidemokratisches Denken in der Weimarer Republik.* 1962; Munich: Deutscher Taschenbuch Verlag, 1978.

———. *Thomas Mann und die Deutschen.* Frankfurt am Main: Fischer Bücherei, 1965.

Sorkin, David. "Wilhelm von Humboldt: The Theory and Practice of Self-Formation (*Bildung*), 1791–1810." *Journal of the History of Ideas* 44 (1983): 55–73.

Speier, Hans. "Zur Soziologie der bürgerlichen Intelligenz in Deutschland." In *Positionen der literarischen Intelligenz zwischen bürgerliche Reaktion und Imperialismus,* edited by Gert Mattenklott and Klaus R. Scherpe. Kronberg: Scriptor Verlag, 1973.

Spranger, Eduard. *Wilhelm von Humboldt und die Humanitätsidee.* 2d ed. Berlin: Reuther & Reichard, 1928.

———. *Wilhelm von Humboldt und die Reform des Bildungswesens.* 1910; Tübingen: Max Niemeyer, 1965.

Stansky, Peter. *Gladstone: A Progress in Politics.* New York: Norton, 1979.

Stark, Gary. *Entrepreneurs of Ideology: Neoconservative Publishers in Germany, 1890–1933.* Chapel Hill: University of North Carolina Press, 1981.

Stern, Fritz. *The Failure of Illiberalism.* New York: Knopf, 1972.

———. *The Politics of Cultural Despair: A Study in the Rise of the Germanic Ideology.* Garden City, N.Y.: Doubleday Anchor, 1965.

Stern, J. P. *History and Allegory in Thomas Mann's "Doktor Faustus."* London: H. K. Lewis for University College, 1975.

Stromberg, Roland N. *Redemption By War: The Intellectuals and 1914.* Lawrence: Regents Press of Kansas, 1982.

Struve, Walter. *Elites Against Democracy: Leadership Ideals in Bourgeois Political Thought in Germany, 1890–1933.* Princeton: Princeton University Press, 1973.

Swales, Martin. "The Story and the Hero: A Study of Thomas Mann's 'Der Zauberberg.' " *Deutsche Vierteljahrsschrift* 46 (1972): 359–76.

Sweet, Paul R. *Wilhelm von Humboldt: A Biography.* 2 vols. Columbus: Ohio State University Press, 1978.

Taylor, A.J.P. *Politics in Wartime.* New York: Atheneum, 1965.

Taylor, Charles. *Sources of the Self.* Cambridge, Mass.: Harvard University Press, 1989.

Taylor, Seth. *Left-Wing Nietzscheans: The Politics of German Expressionism, 1910–1920.* Berlin: Walter de Gruyter, 1990.

Tenbruck, Friedrich. "Max Weber and the Sociology of Science: A Case Reopened." *Zeitschrift für Soziologie* 3 (1974): 312–20.

———. "The Problem of Thematic Unity in the Works of Max Weber." Translated by M. S. Whimster. *British Journal of Sociology* 31 (1980): 316–51.

———. " 'Science as a Vocation'—Revisited." In *Standorte im Zeitstrom. Festschrift für Arnold Gehlen zum 70. Geburtstag am 29. Januar 1974,* edited by Ernst Forsthoff and Reinhard Hörstel. Frankfurt am Main: Atheneum Verlag, 1974.

———. "Das Werk Max Webers: Methodologie und Sozialwissenschaften." *Kölner Zeitschrift für Soziologie und Sozialpsychologie* 38 (1936): 13–31.

Tison-Braun, Micheline. *La crise de l'humanisme: le conflit de l'individu et de la société dans la littérature française moderne.* Vol. 1: *1890–1914.* Paris: Librairie Nizet, 1958.

Tolstoy, Leo. *What Is to Be Done?* In *Novels and Other Works,* vol. 13. New York: Scribner, 1913.

Treiber, Hubert. "Gruppenbilder mit einer Dame." *Forum,* January/February 1988, 40–54.

———. "Im Westen Nichts Neues: Menschwerdung durch Askese; Sehnsucht nach Askese bei Weber und Nietzsche." In *Religionswissenschaft und Kulturkritik,* edited by Hans G. Kippenberg and Brigitte Luchesi. Marburg: Diagonal-Verlag, 1991.

———. "Nietzsche's 'Kloster für freiere Geister': Nietzsche und Weber als Erzieher." In *Die Religion von Oberschichten. Religion—Profession—Intellektualismus.* Marburg: Diagonal-Verlag, 1989.

Troeltsch, Ernst. *Christian Thought: Its History and Application.* London: University of London Press, 1923.

———. *Gesammelte Schriften.* 4 vols. Tübingen: J.C.B. Mohr [Paul Siebeck], 1925.

———. "The Ideas of Natural Law and Humanity in World Politics." In Otto Gierke, *Natural Law and the Theory of Society, 1500 to 1800,* vol. 1. Translated by Ernest Barker. Cambridge: Cambridge University Press, 1934.

———. "Die Revolution in der Wissenschaft." In *Gesammelte Schriften* 4: 653–77.

———. *The Social Teaching of the Christian Churches.* Vol. 2. Translated by Olive Wyon. 1931; Chicago: University of Chicago Press, 1981.

Turner, Stephen P., and Regis A. Factor. *Max Weber and the Dispute over Reason and Value.* London: Routledge & Kegan Paul, 1984.

Vaget, Hans Rudolf. "Amazing Grace: Thomas Mann, Adorno, and the Faust Myth." In *Our Faust? Roots and Ramifications of a Modern German Myth*, edited by Reinhold Grimm and Jost Hermand. Madison: University of Wisconsin Press, 1987.

———. "Thomas Mann und James Joyce: Zur Frage des Modernismus im *Doktor Faustus.*" In *Thomas Mann Jahrbuch*, vol. 2, edited by Eckhard Heftrich and Hans Wysling. Frankfurt am Main: Vittorio Klostermann, 1989.

Van Dyke, Carolynn. *The Fiction of Truth*. Ithaca: Cornell University Press, 1985.

Vierhaus, Rudolf. "Bildung." In *Geschichtliche Grundbegriffe. Historisches Lexikon zur politisch-sozialen Sprache in Deutschland*, edited by Otto Brunner, Werner Conze, and Reinhart Koselleck, vol. 1. Stuttgart: Ernst Klett Verlag, 1972.

Vondung, Klaus, ed. *Das Wilhelminische Bildungsbürgertum*. Göttingen: Vandenhoeck & Ruprecht, 1976.

Voss, Liselotte. *Die Entstehung von Thomas Manns Roman "Doktor Faustus."* Tübingen: Max Niemeyer Verlag, 1975.

Watson, Robert Spence. *The National Liberal Federation*. London: T. Fisher Unwin, 1907.

Weber, Marianne. *Max Weber: A Biography*. Translated and edited by Harry Zohn, with a new introduction by Guenther Roth. New Brunswick, N.J.: Transaction Books, 1988.

Webern, Anton. *The Path to the New Music*. Edited by Willi Reich. Bryn Mawr, Penn.: Theodore Presser, 1963.

Weigand, Hermann J. *The Magic Mountain: A Study of Thomas Mann's Novel "Der Zauberberg."* 1933; Chapel Hill: University of North Carolina Press, 1964.

Weil, Hans. *Die Entstehung des deutschen Bildungsprinzips*. 2d ed. Bonn: H. Bouvier Verlag, 1967.

Weyembergh, Maurice. *Le voluntarisme rationnel de Max Weber*, Mémoires de la Classe des Lettres, 2d ser., vol. 61, no. 1. Brussels: Académie Royale de Belgique, 1972.

Whimster, Sam, and Scott Lash, eds. *Max Weber, Rationality, and Modernity*. London: Allen & Unwin, 1987.

Williams, A. "Thomas Mann's Nationalist Phase: A Study of 'Friedrich und die grosse Koalition.'" *German Life and Letters* 22 (1969): 147–55.

Wilson, Edmund. *Axel's Castle: A Study in the Imaginative Literature of 1870–1930*. New York: Scribner, 1931.

Wilson, Trevor. *The Downfall of the Liberal Party, 1914–35*. Ithaca: Cornell University Press, 1966.

Windelband, Wilhelm. *A History of Philosophy*. Rev. ed. Vol. 2. New York: Macmillan, 1901.

———. *Die Philosophie im deutschen Geistesleben des 19. Jahrhunderts*. 3d ed. Tübingen: J.C.B. Mohr [Paul Siebeck], 1927.

Winkler, Michael. *George-Kreis*. Stuttgart: J. B. Metzlersche Verlagsbuchhandlung, 1972.

———. *Stefan George*. Stuttgart: J. B. Metzlersche Verlagsbuchhandlung, 1970.

Winston, Richard. *Thomas Mann: The Making of an Artist, 1875–1911*. New York: Knopf, 1981.

Wikirchen, Hans. "Nietzsche-Imitatio: zu Thomas Manns politischem Denken in der Weimarer Republik." In *Thomas Mann Jahrbuch*, edited by Eckhard Heftrich and Hans Wysling, vol. 1. Frankfurt am Main: Vittorio Klostermann, 1988.

———. *Zeitgeschichte im Roman. Zu Thomas Manns "Zauberberg" und "Doktor Faustus."* Vol. 6 of *Thomas-Mann-Studien.* Bern: Francke Verlag, 1986.

Wittenberg, Erich. "Die Wissenschaftskrisis in Deutschland im Jahre 1919." *Theoria: A Swedish Journal of Philosophy and Psychology* 4, pt. 3 (1938): 235–64.

Wohl, Robert. *The Generation of 1914.* Cambridge, Mass.: Harvard University Press, 1979.

Wolin, Sheldon. *Politics and Vision.* London: Allen & Unwin, 1961.

Wolff, Rudolf, ed. *Thomas Manns "Doktor Faustus" und die Wirkung.* 2 pts. Bonn: Bouvier Verlag Herbert Grundmann, 1983.

Wolters, Friedrich. *Stefan George und die Blätter für die Kunst.* Berlin: Georg Bondi, 1930.

Wysling, Hans. "Probleme der *Zauberberg*-Interpretation." In *Thomas Mann Jahrbuch*, edited by Eckhard Heftrich and Hans Wysling, vol. 1. Frankfurt am Main: Vittorio Klostermann, 1988.

———. "Zu Thomas Manns 'Maja'-Projekt." In Paul Scherrer and Hans Wysling, *Quellenkritische Studien zum Werk Thomas Manns.* Vol. 1 of *Thomas-Mann-Studien.* Bern: Francke Verlag, 1967.

Yack, Bernard. *The Longing for Total Revolution: Philosophic Sources of Social Discontent from Rousseau to Marx and Nietzsche.* Princeton: Princeton University Press, 1986.

Ziolkowski, Theodore. *Dimensions of the Modern Novel.* Princeton: Princeton University Press, 1969.

Index

Abramowski, Günter, on calling and science, 297n.37

Action: political, dependent on redemption, 180; and service of cause, 68; strength of, 179

Adorno, Theodor, 226; on absolute, 263; on allegory in *Doctor Faustus*, 335n.86; and ending of *Doctor Faustus*, 255; and redemption, 270, 338n.15

Aestheticism, 107, 109; and aesthetics versus ethics, 258; in art and politics, 258

Alcibiades, 162

Alexander, Jeffrey, 227n.16, 323–24n.135

Allegory, 22, 23, 226; in *Doctor Faustus*, 231, 256, 257, 335n.86; in *The Magic Mountain*, 124, 147; and realism, 23, 146; and symbol, 23

Aquinas, Saint Thomas, 162

Arendt, Hannah, 157

Aristocracy: and "being," 167; decline of, as ruling class, 164; as leaders, 165; as nonascetic, 167

Aron, Raymond, 322n.93

Art, 110–13, 232–34; autonomy of, 236; avant-garde, 236, 237; bourgeoisification of, 236; crisis of, 236–41; as critique of life, 111; demonic, 89; exhaustion of, 231; stands in middle, 117; pact with, 242; relation to politics of, 258, 336n.89; salvation of, 240; and service,

233, 237; and truth, 238; as vampire, 233; and *Volk*, 21, 238; and war, 89–90, 111; according to Weber, 236

Artist, 110–13, 232–34, 239; and ascetic ideal, 248; and calling, 19; and critique of self, 110; and strength, 18, 20; avant-garde, 247; avant-garde and fascism, 230; pact with art of, and devil's pact, 228, 245–46

—and need for relation to greater whole, 19; and need to be representative, 231; and relation to bourgeoisie, 18, 19; and relation to bourgeoisie of expressionist artist, 233; and relation to community, 226; and representative of nation, 228; and identification with Germany, 20

—identity of, 20; as aristocrat, 20; as conscience of humankind, 112; as humankind's "suffering leader," 113; as powerless, 240; as soldier, 20, 89, 90

Asceticism, 7, 81, 261–73; active, and the nation, 184; and calling, 68; and collectivity, 184; and meaning, 69; as source of strength, 183

Aschenbach, Gustav, 19; and *Durchhalten*, 240

Asquith, Herbert, 217

Augustine, Saint, xii, 162

Autonomy, 166

commitment to concept of German nation, 92; and criticism of Germany, 102; and defense of Germany, 87, 89; and defense of self and German identity, 93; and desire to serve nation, 92, 307–308n.22, 308n.23, 311n.23; and Faust and Germany, 227, 256; and freedom and terror, 235; and himself as representative of Germany, 118; and himself as true German, 93, 101; and his identification with Germany, 2, 228; and his interpretation of German waywardness, 230; and his symbolic relation to Germany, 99, 107, 118, 119, 228; and identification of self and nation, 89; and mystification of Germany, 119; and similarity of his views to Weber's, 232; and World War I, 87

—narrative issues in work of: and allegory, 22; and allegory in *The Magic Mountain*, 146–47; and Hans Castorp's lessons, 314n.41; and problem endings, 23, 124–25; and narratives of redemption, 260; and problems of novelistic form, 22; and textual strategies, 6

—Nietzsche in work of: and Christianity, 243, 266; and devilish artist, 253; and disease, 246; and Germany, 227; and humanity, 252, 336n.96; and influence of Nietzsche on him, 312n.26; and politics, 258, 259; and purpose in *Doctor Faustus*, 259; and revolt against reason, 254; and will to power, 9; and Weber, 99. *See also* Nietzsche

—personal views of: and bourgeoisie, 5, 100, 267; and brother Heinrich, 87, 88, 306n.6; as defender of Settembrini, 137, 155; on himself as representative of nineteenth century, 94, 99; on his asceticism, 314n.46; on his own death, 313n.40; on his own demonic side, 228; on his romanticism, 311–12n.26

—religious issues in work of: and Christianity and humanism, 260; and Christian solution to meaning, 254; and Christian views of service, 247; and invalids and sacrifice, 333n.50; and Protestantism, 5; and religious feeling in difficult works of art, 334n.75; and theology in *Joseph and His Brothers*, 272

—self in work of: and alternative practices of the self, 270; and ascetic calling as key to empowerment, 262; and death, 2; and decadence, 91; and defense of humanity, 5, 231; and higher ideals, 229, 267; and humanity in *The Magic Mountain*, 146, 153; and identity, 88, 119; and individualist solutions, 265; and life, 49; and modern type of hero, 103, 105; and power, 19, 88, 246; and progress, 102; and project of redemption, 265; and self as tool of higher power, 91; and service, 90; and turn to humanism, 266

—Works: "At the Prophet's," 135; "Culture and Socialism," 140; *Diaries*, 123; and exhaustion, 21; *Friedrich the Great*

Parties (*continued*)
200, 201; political, in Germany, 195
Pascal, Roy, 32; on division of labor, 284n.23; on Goethe, 285n.33; on *The Magic Mountain*, 310n.14, 313n.39, 315n.54
Passion: for bureaucratization, 172; lack of, in German politics, 181; and political calling, 181; and politician, 176
Paulsen, Friedrich, 41; and science, 40; and *Weltanschauungen*, 46
Peace: social conflict in, 189; and struggle, 84
Pericles, 162
Perkin, Harold, on British capitalist class, 206
Person, xi, 10; noble type of, 265; as symbol, 122. *See also* Personhood
Personality: and *Bildung*, 35; and bureaucracy, 199; and calling, 72, 73, 182; and Christianity, 78; and conflict, 114; creation of, 182, 223; cultivated, 52; degeneration of, 36; exhaustion of, 270; and Hegel, 287n.38; and humanity, 36; and ideals in politics, 198; versus individual, 113; and Kant, 3, 28; Occidental, 6, 13, 16; Rickert on, 302n.77; and Romantics, 287–88n.39; roots of, 7; separated from ideal of Humanity, 35; and service, 72, 84; and specialization, 72; of state, 288n.47; strength of, 179, 181; and submission, 73; and *Volk*, 35; and youth, 65, 300n.57; in Weber, xi, 72, 114
Personhood, democratic foundation of, 200; grounded in service, 224; political, 193. *See also* Person
Pessimism, 262
Pfitzner, Hans, 119; and sympathy with death, 133
Pietism, 184, 282n.10; and personality, 287n.39; and the state, 185
Pike, Burton, on calling, 331n.28
Plato, xii, 163; and leaders, 162
Platonism, 162
Politician, 174–84; versus bureaucrats, 176; called, but without a calling, 201; with a calling, 175, 221; with a calling, and masses, 200; with a calling, need for, 195; and demands from others, 222; and followers, 200, 202; like Puritan, 180; need for, 169; and responsibility, 222; and service of others, 183; and shaping of self in parliament, 202; strength of, 179; as tool, 179, 182; Weber's, as prisoner of asceticism, 221
Politics: and American political machine, 201; as calling, 184; as calling, limits of, 201; defended by Settembrini, 139; as essence of West, 95; and middle ground, 117; and rationalization, 199; and reason of state, 57, 58; sins in, 182; and social order, 198; as struggle, 196; and technique, 197; technique of, 198
Polytheism, 74, 79; among Greeks, 76; as metaphysics, 11
Power, xi, 8; and asceticism, 15; definition of, 13; and destiny of West, 15; and devil, 232, 244; dionysian flights of, 230;

Compositor: Impressions
Printer: Edwards Brothers, Inc.
Binder: Edwards Brothers, Inc.
Text: 10/13 Sabon
Display: Sabon